Software Internationalization and Localization

An Introduction

Emmanuel Uren
Robert Howard
and
Tiziana Perinotti

VAN NOSTRAND REINHOLD
New York

©1993 by Emmanuel Uren, Robert Howard, and Tiziana Perinotti

Library of Congress Catalog Card Number 93-3316

ISBN 0-442-01498-8

I(T)P   Van Nostrand Reinhold is an International Thomson Publishing company.
        ITP logo is a trademark under license.

Van Nostrand Reinhold
115 Fifth Avenue
New York, NY 10003

International Thomson Publishing
Berkshire House, 168–173
High Holborn, London WC1V 7AA
England

Thomas Nelson Australia
102 Dodds Street
South Melbourne 3205
Victoria, Australia

Nelson Canada
1120 Birchmount Road
Scarborough, Ontario
M1K 5G4, Canada

International Thomson Publishing GmbH
Königswinterer Str. 518
5300 Bonn 3
Germany

International Thomson Publishing Asia
38 Kim Tian Rd., #0105
Kim Tian Plaza
Singapore 0316

International Thomson Publishing Japan
Kyowa Building, 3F
2-2-1 Hirakawacho
Chiyada-Ku, Tokyo 102
Japan

Printed in the United States of America

16   15   14   13   12   11   10   9   8   7   6   5   4   3   2   1

Library of Congress Cataloging in Publication Data
Uren, Emmanuel, 1935–
      Software internationalization and localization: An introduction
   by Emmanuel Uren, Robert Howard & Tiziana Perinotti.
         p.   cm.
      Includes bibliographical references and index.
      ISBN 0-442-01498-8
      1. Computer software.   2. Electronic data processing
   documentation.   I. Howard, Robert, 1952– .   II. Perinotti, Tiziana,
   1960– .   III. Title.
   QA76.754.U84   1993
   005.1'2—dc20   93-3316
                                                  CIP

Trademarks

Apple, Hypercard, and Macintosh are registered trademarks of Apple Computer Corporation.

Canon is a registered trademark of Canon USA.

Clipper is a trademark of Computer Associates.

CompuServe is a trademark of H&R Block, Inc.

dBASE, QuattroPro, and Paradox are registered trademarks of Borland International, Inc.

DR-DOS is a trademark of Digital Research Corporation.

Epson, FX80, and FX100 are trademarks of Epson America Inc.

Foxpro is a trademark of Microsoft Corporation.

Hewlett-Packard, Image, and New Wave are registered trademarks of Hewlett-Packard Company.

IBM, PC/AT, and PC-DOS are registered trademarks of International Business Machines Corporation.

IBM PC/XT is a trademark of International Business Machines Corporation.

Lotus and Lotus 1-2-3 are registered trademarks of Lotus Corporation.

Motif is a registered trademark of Open Software Foundation.

MS-DOS, MSWord, Windows, and XENIX are registered trademarks of Microsoft Corporation.

Nomad is a trademark of Must Software International.

Open Look is a trademark of Sun Microsystems Inc.

PDP-7 is a trademark of Digital Equipment Corporation.

PostScript is a trademark of Adobe Systems Inc.

Red Ryder is a registered trademark of Red Ryder Enterprises Inc.

Quiz and Quick are registered trademarks of Cognos.

SAS is a trademark of The SAS Institute, Cary, North Carolina.

UNIX is a trademark of Unix System Laboratories, Inc.

Disclaimer

The world of computers is a fast-changing one, so fast that many professionals believe that it is impossible to buy a computer that is not obsolete by the time it is available in stores. Someone somewhere will have a faster, more powerful machine or variation in the development and marketing pipeline. This thinking extends to software products, although occasionally one product will be "king" for perhaps a couple of years before a competing product with more and better features becomes available.

There has been, and there continues to be, a lot of excellent technical work in the field of Internationalizing and Localizing software. Much of this work is described in excellent technical manuals produced by various software manufacturers. Apart from our own experience in producing Localized versions of software, we have had recourse to many of these manuals in writing this book. Some of the manuals may have been replaced by later editions describing later versions of tools or techniques. We have tried to use the latest information available consistent with the task of actually writing the book.

Since we have no control over what the software manufacturers produce, we must introduce the caveat that there may be some technical inaccuracies.

In any case, if you are going to Internationalize, then we urge you to familiarize yourself with the details of your computing environment manufacturer's products.

Credits

Reprinted from John G. Nelson, "Japanese Double Byte Character Processing," *Windows/DOS Developer's Journal* 3, no. 1. Copyright © 1992 R&D Publications.
Figure 6–1.Cursor Movement
Figure 6–2. Search Substring 'Eat' Produces Illegal Find

Reprinted by permission from IBM, *Disk Operating System, Keyboard and Code Pages. Version 5.00,* First Edition March 1991, pages 18 through 25.
Figure 3–2. DOS Code Pages: 437—U.S. English and 850—Multilingual (Latin 1)
Figure I–1. DOS Code Pages: 437—U.S. English and 850—Multilingual (Latin 1)
Figure I–2. DOS Code Pages: 852—Slavic (Latin 1) and 860—Portugal
Figure I–3. DOS Code Pages: 863—Canadian-French and 865—Nordic

Reprinted by permission from IBM System/370 Reference Summary, GX20-1850-3, Sections 9 through 12.
Figure 3–4. IBM EBCDIC Character Set

Reprinted by permission by Lexmark International Inc. from IBM *Disk Operating System, Keyboard and Code Pages, Version 5.00,* First Edition March 1991, pages 5 and 15.
Figure E–1. U.S. and Foreign Keyboards 101 and 102.

Table 2 of ISO-8859-1 to ISO-8859-9 is reproduced with the permission of the International Organization for Standardization (ISO). The complete standards are available in the United States from the ISO member body, ANSI, 11 West 42nd Street, 13th Floor, New York, NY 10036 or from the ISO Central Secretariat, Case postale 56, CH-1211, Geneva, Switzerland.

Figure 7–1. ISO Character Sets: ISO-8859/1—Latin 1 and ISO-8859/5—Latin/Cyrillic
Figure J–1. ISO Character Sets: ISO-8859/1—Latin 1 and ISO-8859/2—Latin 2
Figure J–2. ISO Character Sets: ISO-8859/3—Latin 3 and ISO-8859/2—Latin 4
Figure J–3. ISO Character Sets: ISO-8859/5—Latin/Cyrillic and ISO-8859/6—Latin/Arabic
Figure J–4. ISO Character Sets: ISO-8859/7—Latin/Greek and ISO-8859/8—Latin/Hebrew
Figure J–5. ISO Character Sets: ISO-8859/9—Latin 5

Foreword

There is no choice. Personal computers and telecommunications have stitched the world together. Creating world-ready software is an imperative, not an option. The software market is global, and to compete you must design software for worldwide customers.

Five to ten years ago the United States dominated the market for technology.

Today it is still the biggest market, but it is no longer dominant. Europe, Japan, and even the emerging markets in Asia and Eastern Europe are setting the pace in many technologies. To support their businesses they are demanding the best and the most modern software products.

In addition, the world is fast becoming a community of technological peers.

The days are gone when customers outside the United States would use products in English, or the previous version of a product because the new version had not been translated. Now, multinational companies making consumer goods in Poland or computer chips in Thailand demand software that supports all of their employees. Customers demand that quality standards be the same in Asia, Eastern Europe, the United States, Europe, and Japan.

To survive and prosper software companies must design and build global products. Designing software for the U.S. market and then retrofitting it to European, Japanese, or Asian standards is no longer practical or economical. The process is too slow, too error-prone, and too expensive. Designs *must* be global in both concept and detail.

Software Internationalization and Localization covers both of those goals. It provides a survey of design problems and backs that up with a wealth of details about specific international standards and local exceptions. It will be equally valuable to marketers, product managers, and developers. In the past, development companies had to build their own compendia of standards and experience. The authors now provide a ready-made guide. They offer the beginner a head start and the experienced practitioner a review list.

The market is demanding excellent international products and will reward those companies that can satisfy the demand. Those who read *Software Internationalization and Localization* will be well prepared to take advantage of the global software market opportunities.

Kevin Cavanaugh
Director, International Product Management
Lotus Development Corporation
Cambridge, Massachusetts, U.S.A.

Preface

The genesis for this book was an attempt to answer a translator's question of "what do these computer companies mean when they talk about Internationalization and Localization of software?" After we completed the first draft of the book, we realized that our audience was not only translators: anybody who designs, builds, markets, and sells any software product outside his or her own country has to confront and resolve the issues that we present.

Computer software applications and operating systems for both business and personal computers are proliferating at a high rate. A substantial number of these programs are written in the United States and many of the manufacturers are then marketing their products outside the United States.

In the early days, software was delivered in one language only: English and U.S. English at that. If someone spoke a different language that person had to accept the program as written and figure out how to use it. Most computer users were highly educated professionals who had considerable exposure to English during their education and who had experience in working with programs written in English. Both their computer experience and knowledge of English were of use in making programs work.[1]

As computers, especially personal computers, became more and more common, the typical users were no longer professional computer programmers, software engineers, or hardware engineers. Software manufacturers realized that making

---

[1] In the world of computers, "early days" are usually only a year or so in the past. Any computer popular ten years ago is now an amusing curiosity, while a machine in general use twenty years ago is now fit only for a museum and the derisive laughter of the current crop of computer wizards.

useful products for people who were not computer professionals could attract a large market. The first problem was to make American programs attractive to the average American; the task was to make software that performs complex functions easy to use by people unfamiliar with technical ideas. To this end, documentation and on-line help were both improved, along with the software itself. While experienced professionals had become adept in detecting bugs and working around them, the new users expected, indeed demanded, that the software they bought operate exactly as described in the manuals. Benign acceptance of anomalies in the operation of software could no longer be tolerated.

Along with making software more reliable and easier to use (what we now call "user friendly"), the marketing of software to people who didn't speak English became attractive. While many foreign users tolerated software in English, the new mass markets could not be expected to do so. For a software product to have wide market acceptance in a non-English-speaking environment, it was essential to convert the software so that users saw a product in their own language and firmly based in their own culture. To manufacturers, the incremental cost involved in producing software in several languages appeared small relative to the potential markets. Many companies have invested in such conversion and the interest in, and demand for, software packages overseas has indeed mushroomed.[2]

What is entailed in converting a product from American English to another language or in building a multilingual product? At first glance it appeared that all that was necessary was to translate the manual into the new language. A moment's thought showed that this was not enough; what was to be done with the many messages that appear in the course of using a program? All the menus and dialog boxes need to be translated as well.

Other problems also arise, some due to the nature of software and some because of engineering constraints on the equipment. Many of these turn out to be of no small complexity, as you will discover when you read this book.

As a result of people becoming aware of the number and the complexity of the problems involved in converting a software package from one language to another, a particular aspect of software engineering, called *Localization,* came into being. Localization is the formal process that makes a program written for one language freely usable by people who speak a different language. This means adapting, translating, and adding international features to U.S.-based programs.

In considering the problems that arise just in translating a program (operating system or application) from, say, U.S. English to French, a new question appears: If there are specific problems in going from U.S. English to French, are there similar problems in going from U.S. English to German, to Dutch, to British English, to Portuguese, to Italian, to Spanish, and so on? If so, are there some more general

---

[2]The fact that American computerized bulletin boards now provide interfaces in other languages is just one testament to this worldwide use of computers. The June 1992 issue of *CompuServe* magazine announces a German interface and a Borland User Forum in German, and January 1993 saw the introduction of a German Toshiba Forum. *GO FLEFO* directs you to a foreign language forum with a computer subsection. For many U.S. software companies, as much as half their revenues stems from overseas. And, of course, many European companies only operate in Europe.

steps that can be taken that will prepare a program for conversion to a second or further new language without having to go back to square one each time? It turned out, on examination, that there are indeed steps that can be taken that make Localization to one language a single case of a more general process.

The process by which Localization is generalized is called *Internationalization*. Using the techniques of Internationalization it is possible to establish a general structure that *enables* a program written in one language to be converted to any of several other languages without having to duplicate every step in each case, although, of course, translation of individual words and phrases into the target language is also needed. Of course, since there are so many languages and so many varieties, Internationalization (at least at present) does not claim to be a procedure that will convert *any* language to *any other* language with a minimum of difficulty. This book focuses on the issues of Internationalization and Localization involved in converting U.S. software products into the Western European languages with an overview of more complex languages.

You can contact the authors on CompuServe at 76020,155, directly by mail at 83 Seward Street, San Francisco, CA 94114, USA, or by phone at 001-(415) 552-9085. We encourage you to do so for any reason whatsoever, but particularly if you have found errors, if you think that something is missing, or if you want to hire us at exorbitant rates.

Acknowledgments

We could not have written this book without the moral and material support that Ted Lewis and Simon Blattner provided. Ted, a friend and colleague for 30 years, is a fourth author who helped us through writing blocks, edited, and provided constructive critiques at the appropriate times and even lent us word processors. Simon, a squash partner for many years, allowed us use of his office machinery, a step that greatly reduced the demands on our limited budgets.

Also, Bill Champ, Jim Davis, Jim Finke, Bill Hall, Ernst Hofmann, Cem Kaner, Anthony Letts, James Lindauer, Joseph McConnell, Will Mitchell, Martha Newton, Athan Pasadis, Clark Parsons, Randy Redenius, Merle Tenney, Angela Thorbeck, and Erik Wendelboe all provided useful information and insights at critical times.

Last, but not least, there are many excellent manuals available, produced by corporations without naming the people who wrote them. Many thanks to these anonymous authors.

We thank all of them. Needless to say, any mistakes and errors are ours alone.

Contents

FOREWORD vii

PREFACE ix

1 INTRODUCTION 1

1.1   What Is So Special About Translating Software and Its Documentation?   1
1.2   Points of View   4
1.3   Internationalization and Localization   5
1.4   Organization of This Book   6

PART 1   ISSUES   9

2 ISSUES IN SOFTWARE INTERNATIONALIZATION AND LOCALIZATION   11

2.1   Introduction   11
2.2   Engineering Issues   12
           2.2.1   Character Handling (and Non-American Characters)   12
           2.2.2   Subsystems and the Character Set   13
           2.2.3   Importing and Exporting All the Character Set   13
           2.2.4   Sorting   14
           2.2.5   Search and Replace   16
           2.2.6   Case Conversion   16
           2.2.7   Word Boundaries   17
           2.2.8   Character Boundaries   17
           2.2.9   Hyphenation/Syllabification   18

2.2.10 Expansion of Text   18
2.2.11 Dialog Boxes and Menu Names Also Need Space to Grow   19
2.2.12 Meaningful Values for Accelerators   20
2.2.13 Numbered and Unnumbered Messages   20
2.2.14 Are Strings Made Up of Substrings Meaningful or Correct in Other Languages?   21
2.2.15 Non-American Spell Checkers   21
2.2.16 Parsing Input   22
2.2.17 The Significance of Special Characters   22
2.2.18 Keyboards and Entry of Non-Keyboard Characters   23
2.2.19 Tracking   24
2.2.20 Kerning   24
2.2.21 Diacritical Marks, the Height of Characters, and Leading   24
2.2.22 Printers and Character Sets   24
2.2.23 Address Formats   25
2.2.24 Translation of Filenames   26
2.2.25 Numeric Formats, Separators, Negatives, and Decimal Tabs   26
2.2.26 Arithmetic Operations, Including Rounding   27
2.2.27 Monetary Symbols and Currency   28
2.2.28 Dates and Times   28
2.2.29 Time Zones   30
2.2.30 Measurement Scales   30
2.2.31 Page Sizes   30
2.2.32 Colors   31
2.2.33 Cultural Considerations   31
2.2.34 Translation of Clip Art   32
2.2.35 Translation of Icons   32
2.2.36 Recognition of Translated Clip Art, Icons, and Files   33
2.2.37 Memory   33
2.2.38 Non-U.S. Manufacturers and Non-American Hardware   34
2.2.39 Mice   34
2.2.40 Setup and Installation Procedures   34
2.3. Translation Issues   34
2.3.1 Translation   35
2.3.2 Components to Translate   36
2.3.3 Special Cases—Tutorials, Examples, and Software/Hardware Interaction   37

PART 2   INTERNATIONALIZATION AND LOCALIZATION FOR WESTERN EUROPEAN LANGUAGES ON THE IBM PC   39

3   GENERAL TOPICS   41

3.1 Introduction   41
3.2 Character Sets   41
3.2.1 WordPerfect 5.1   42
3.2.2 DOS   43

      3.2.3   Windows 3.0/3.1   44

      3.2.4   BCD, BCDIC, and EBCDIC   47

      3.2.5   Unicode   47

      3.2.6   Character Set to Character Set   47

3.3   International Considerations   50

      3.3.1   WordPerfect 5.1   50

      3.3.2   DOS   51

      3.3.3   Windows 3.x   56

3.4   Reference Material   58

4   SPECIFIC TOPICS   60

4.1   Introduction   60

4.2   Design Issues   60

      4.2.1   Compile-Time, Link-Time, or Run-Time?   60

      4.2.2   Software Product Design   61

      4.2.3   Scheduling   64

      4.2.4   Character Set to Character Set   65

      4.2.5   Tools   65

4.3   Engineering Issues from Chapter 2   66

      4.3.1   Character Handling (and Non-American Characters)   67

      4.3.2   Subsystems and the Character Set   67

      4.3.3   Importing and Exporting All the Character Set   68

      4.3.4   Sorting   68

      4.3.5   Search and Replace   68

      4.3.6   Case Conversion   69

      4.3.7   Word Boundaries   69

      4.3.8   Character Boundaries   69

      4.3.9   Hyphenation/Syllabification   69

      4.3.10 Expansion of Text   70

      4.3.11 Dialog Boxes and Menu Names Also Need Space to Grow   70

      4.3.12 Accelerators   70

      4.3.13 Numbered and Unnumbered Messages   70

      4.3.14 Are Strings Made Up of Substrings Meaningful or Correct
             in Other Languages?   71

      4.3.15 Spell Checking   71

      4.3.16 Parsing Input   71

      4.3.17 The Significance of Special Characters   71

      4.3.18 Keyboards and Entry of Non-Keyboard Characters   71

      4.3.19 Tracking   72

      4.3.20 Kerning   72

      4.3.21 Diacritical Marks, the Height of Characters, and Leading   72

      4.3.22 Printers and Character Sets   73

      4.3.23 Address Formats   73

      4.3.24 Translation of Filenames   73

      4.3.25 Numeric Formats, Separators, Negatives, and Decimal Tabs   74

      4.3.26 Arithmetic Operations, Including Rounding   75

        4.3.27   Monetary Symbols and Currency   75
        4.3.28   Dates and Times   75
        4.3.29   Time Zones   76
        4.3.30   Measurement Scales   77
        4.3.31   Page Sizes   77
        4.3.32   Colors   77
        4.3.33   Cultural Considerations   77
        4.3.34   Translation of Clip Art   77
        4.3.35   Translation of Icons   77
        4.3.36   Recognition of Translated Clip Art, Icons, and Filenames   77
        4.3.37   Memory   78
        4.3.38   Non-U.S. Manufacturers and Non-American Hardware   78
        4.3.39   Mice   78
        4.3.40   Setup and Installation Procedures   79
4.4   Translation Issues   79
        4.4.1   Introduction   79
        4.4.2   Software   80
        4.4.3   Documentation   80
        4.4.4   Automated Translation, Machine Translation (MT), or Computer-Assisted Translation (CAT)   84
4.5   Validation and Quality Assurance   87
        4.5.1   Has Everything to Be Translated Been Identified?   88
        4.5.2   Some Obvious Errors to Look for First   88
        4.5.3   Testing   89
        4.5.4   Translating Back into American English   90
        4.5.5   Beta and Other Types of Testing   91

PART 3   OTHER COMPUTERS AND OTHER LANGUAGES   93

5 OTHER COMPUTERS 95

5.1   Introduction   95
5.2   The UNIX World   96
        5.2.1   History of UNIX   97
        5.2.2   Technical Aspects—Issues Supported   99
        5.2.3   Technical Aspects—Issues Not Supported   104
5.3   UNIX Reference Material   104
5.4   The Macintosh World   105
        5.4.1   History of Apple and Macintosh   105
        5.4.2   Technical Aspects—Issues Supported   106
        5.4.3   Technical Aspects—Issues Not Supported   114
5.5   Macintosh Reference Material   114

6 OTHER LANGUAGES 116

6.1   Introduction   116
6.2   The PC World   118
        6.2.1   Introduction   118

6.2.2   Routines   123
6.2.3   Windows 3.0/3.1   123
6.2.4   Character Sets   124
6.3   The UNIX World   124
6.3.1   Introduction   124
6.3.2   Character Sets   124
6.3.3   Routines   125
6.4   The Macintosh World   126
6.4.1   Introduction   126
6.4.2   Character Representation   127
6.4.3   Text Direction   128
6.4.4   Routines   128
6.4.5   Text Manipulation   129

7   STANDARDS AND STANDARDS ORGANIZATIONS   131

7.1   Introduction   131
7.2   Organizations   134
7.3   Issues from Chapter 2   135
7.3.1   Non-American Characters   136
7.3.2   What Standards Handle and Do Not Handle   140
7.4   Localization Industry Standards Association (LISA)   143
7.5   Guidelines   143
7.6   ISO 9000 and ISO 9660   144

PART 4   BUSINESS ASPECTS   145

8   LOGISTICS, ROLES, AND RESPONSIBILITIES   147

8.1   Introduction   147
8.2   Time   148
8.3   Organization   148
8.4   Availability of Resources   149
8.5   Accuracy   149
8.6   Geography   149
8.6.1   Model 1: All Work Done in the United States   151
8.6.2   Model 2: Development and Internationalization in the United States
and Localization and Manufacture in the Target Country   151
8.6.3   Model 3: Development in Both the United States and the Target Locale,
and Localization and Manufacture in the Target Locale   152
8.7   Business Relationships   152
8.7.1   Distribution Channels   153
8.7.2   Contract Negotiation   154
8.7.3   Relationship with Your Distributors   154
8.7.4   Marketing Issues   155
8.7.5   Ownership of the Localized Product—
Intellectual Property Laws   156
8.7.6   Gray Marketing and Piracy   156

8.8   Logistics   157
      8.8.1   Some Actual Cases   157
      8.8.2   International Technical Support   157
      8.8.3   Maintenance and Repairs of Anomalies   158
8.9   Roles and Responsibilities   158
      8.9.1   The Localizer   159
      8.9.2   The Translator   159
8.10 Qualifications of a Localizing Agency   159
8.11 Standards in Europe and in America   160
8.12 Reference Material   161

9   COST CONSIDERATIONS   162

9.1   Introduction   162
9.2   Costs to Build International Products   163
      9.2.1   Development Costs   163
      9.2.2   Translation Costs   164
      9.2.3   Internationalization and Localization of an Already
              Existing Product   165
      9.2.4   Internationalization and Localization of a New Product   165
      9.2.5   Marketing Costs and Revenue   165
      9.2.6   Manufacturing Costs   166
9.3   Customs Duties and Taxes   166
9.4   Import and Export Regulations   167
9.5   Repatriation of Funds   168
9.6   Freight Costs   168

10   GOING THE OTHER WAY: EUROPE TO AMERICA   170

10.1 Introduction   170
10.2 Market   171
      10.2.1   IBM PC   171
      10.2.2   Macintosh   172
10.3 Import Regulations   172
10.4 Customs and Excise   172
10.5 Other Costs   173
10.6 Distributors   173
10.7 Localizers   173
10.8 Technical Support   173
10.9 Maintenance   174
10.10 Ownership   174
10.11 Competition   174
10.12 Accounting Practices   174

APPENDIX A   PAPER SIZES   177

A.1   American   177
A.2   European ISO-JISA Series   177
A.3   Japanese JISA Series   179

APPENDIX B UNIX 180

B.1 Introduction   180
B.2 Character Sets   181
B.3 Preparation   183
    B.3.1 Routines   183
    B.3.2 Data   185
    B.3.3 Directories and Files   189
B.4 Operation   189
    B.4.1 Development   189
    B.4.2 Error Checking   191
    B.4.3. Interaction with C   191

APPENDIX C MACINTOSH   192

C.1 Introduction   192
C.2 Character Sets   192
C.3 Preparation   193
    C.3.1 Routines   193
    C.3.2 Localization Tools   195
C.4 Operation   196
    C.4.1 Development   196
    C.4.2 Use   196

APPENDIX D THE BASIC CONCEPTS OF COMPUTERS: SOFTWARE   197

D.1 Introduction   197
D.2 Bits, Nibbles, Bytes, and Words   200
D.3 Programs and Data   200
D.4 Files and File Directories   202
D.5 Codes   203
D.6 Types of Software   205
    D.6.1 Firmware   205
    D.6.2 Operating Systems   206
    D.6.3 Graphic User Interfaces and Other Operating Environments   207
    D.6.4 Applications   208
    D.6.5 Programming Languages   208
    D.6.6 Miscellaneous: Macros and 4GLs   210
D.7 Software Production Process   211
    D.7.1 International Sales and Marketing   212
    D.7.2 Development and Software Quality Assurance   212
    D.7.3 Documentation   212
    D.7.4 Maintenance   213
    D.7.5 Technical Support   213

APPENDIX E THE BASIC CONCEPTS OF COMPUTERS: HARDWARE   214

E.1 Introduction   214
E.2 Hardware Components   215
    E.2.1 Keyboards   215

E.2.2   Monitors and Video Adapter Cards   217
E.2.3   System Unit   219
E.2.4   Printers   224
E.2.5   Mouse   226
E.3   Fonts   226
E.3.1   Native Fonts   226
E.3.2   Scalable Fonts   227
E.3.3   Downloadable Fonts   227
E.4   Modes   227
E.4.1   Graphics Mode   227
E.4.2   Character Mode   227
E.5   Drivers   228
E.5.1   Printer Drivers   228
E.5.2   Mouse Drivers   229
E.5.3   Miscellaneous Drivers   229
E.6   Ports   229
E.7   Other Peripherals   229
E.7.1   Tapes   229
E.7.2   CD ROMs   230
E.7.3   Scanners   230
E.8   Non-American Hardware   230
E.8.1   Amstrad   231
E.8.2   Olivetti   231
E.8.3   Japanese Computers   231
E.9   Non-American Versions of Hardware Available in the United States   231
E.9.1   Printers   231
E.9.2   Monochrome Display Adapters   231

APPENDIX F   ALPHABETIC LIST OF LOCALIZERS WITH EXPERIENCE IN WESTERN EUROPEAN LANGUAGES   232

APPENDIX G   NAMES AND ADDRESSES OF STANDARDS ORGANIZATIONS   235

APPENDIX H   WORDPERFECT 5.1 CHARACTER SETS   238

APPENDIX I   DOS CODE PAGES   243

APPENDIX J   ISO CHARACTER SETS   247

APPENDIX K   MACINTOSH CHARACTER SETS   253

APPENDIX L   HP-UX CHARACTER SETS   264

APPENDIX M   DOS NATIONAL LANGUAGE SUPPORT SYSTEM FUNCTIONS   271

GLOSSARY   274

BIBLIOGRAPHY   286

INDEX   291

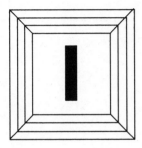

Introduction

1.1. WHAT IS SO SPECIAL ABOUT TRANSLATING SOFTWARE AND ITS DOCUMENTATION?

What is so special about software is that it is *active*. It behaves, operates, runs, and executes. It is dynamic. It processes characters, text, numbers, pictures, and sounds. It *acts* on data so as to record them, store them, retrieve them, transform them, manipulate them, move them, display them, and print them. Those mechanisms that the software uses to process data also have to be "translated" or converted when you translate software, so that they can handle the data in conformity with a different set of rules.

By contrast, a letter or a book or documentation does not do anything; it is *passive*. If you are asked to translate a letter or a book or documentation, you begin with something passive and you end with something passive. It is always the object of an action. It is static and inert.

When you "translate" software, the translated software becomes an ongoing mechanism in the target language just as the original software is a mechanism in its source language. *Its* work is never completed—certainly not when the translator has finished. The translated software will be used to process input, and it must be explicitly programmed to handle every eventuality that can come up in processing such input according to the rules of the new language.

For example, in translating a letter, you might have alphabetized one short list of names. In translating software, the translated software must know how to alphabetize any and all lists of names. Figure 1–1 portrays this process schematically.

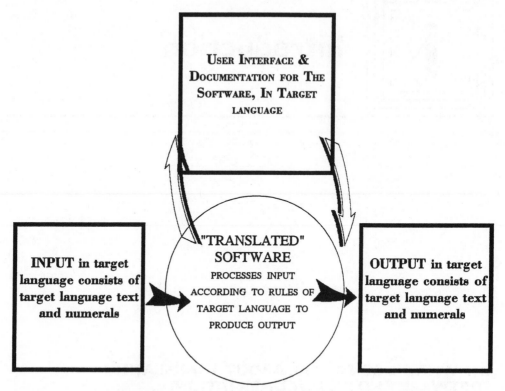

Figure I–I.   What Is So Special About Translating Software and Its Documentation?

A software product contains both an active part and a passive part. The conversion of the active software so that it functions correctly under the new rules is a task that requires the skills not only of a translator but also of a software engineer.

The goal of this book is to describe the technical issues involved in converting an American software product into a form that is consistent with a different culture. A major part of the process is the translation of the documentation and the many messages that can appear on the computer screen or the printer, but that is by no means sufficient to do the job. The other modifications that the software translator must make derive from the limitations imposed by the very nature of computer hardware and the ways in which that hardware and the accompanying software interact to handle information.

Thus, the ability to translate U.S. English into one or more European languages is insufficient for the purpose of Localizing a U.S. software product, and even less sufficient if Internationalization is the goal. In a translated *Localized* software product there must be functional equivalence between the original and its translated counterpart. Software and *hardware* engineering skills are required to translate and Localize as well. In this book we will focus on these software and hardware engineering aspects; we will also discuss administrative, logistical, and business issues that you will meet in practice.

The United States has played such a dominant role in the development of hardware and software that many non-American users have a familiarity with American English that enables them to use American computers and software. Many American computer terms are used by non-Americans without translation. But such use imposes a burden on the non-American user, particularly one whose command of English is limited.

A properly Localized software package allows users to concentrate on exploiting the power of the software without having their attention distracted by the need to accommodate to the requirements of a language other than their own, or to tolerate imprecise or ambiguous features that result from inadequate attention to cultural and linguistic differences.

The first issue to solve when translating software is handling characters used in other languages that are not part of American English. Figure 1–2 portrays output from an American program and the equivalent output from its Localized French version. Note that the French version contains some alphabetic characters that you will not normally see in English; somehow they have been put into the computer, stored, and displayed on the computer screen, and it must also be possible to print them.

Does the French version make any sense to you? Do you understand it at all or just a little bit? When you are observing it and wondering what to do with the information that it displays, you are putting yourself in the same shoes as a non-English speaker contemplating the American version. See how much simpler it is and how much more comfortable you are in dealing with the version in your native language.

A few years ago, an American computer could not have displayed or manipulated the extra French characters. Modifying software and hardware to do these simple-appearing operations is part of the Localization and Internationalization process. In addition, attention must be given to *menus* (the way in which a software program offers choices to the users), the so-called *quick-keys* (keyboard shortcuts for making menu choices), and the lengths of *input data fields* (the amount of space that the software program has allocated to receive input). The translated documentation, the instructions for installing and operating the software, must still correspond exactly with the functions actually performed by the software.

Other features in different languages that cannot be preserved through the medium of translation alone are sorting or collating in the correct order, performing arithmetical operations on numbers with different formats, and hyphenating correctly, to name just a few. Since the software must operate on a computer, features of this type must be made explicit.[1]

---

[1]In practice, however, it is not very unusual to see hybrids in which translated software contains elements from the original or source language. In these cases, although the computer output is in the translated language, input could be a mixture of American (the source) and the target language. As a rule, such a mélange is to be seen in the non-American version of an operating system. For the **copy** command, the input command might still be the American word "copy" while all output messages pertaining to its use are in the target language. Presumably the rationale for this kind of behavior is that it is too complicated and expensive to completely Localize the operating system, but that some translation is better than none. Some early and primitive Localizations allowed users to use their own language only in answering **Yes/No?**

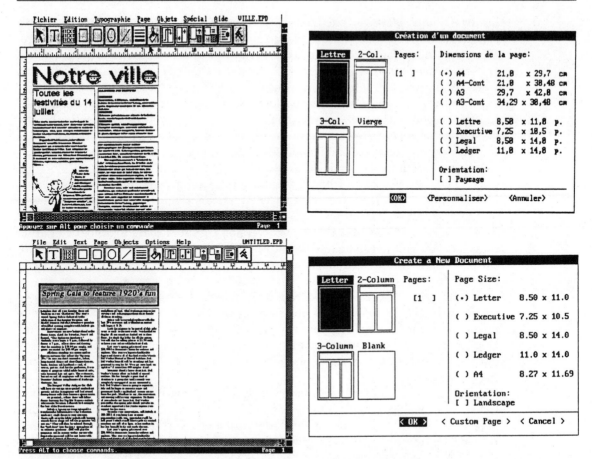

Figure 1–2. Express Publisher French Version 2.03 (above) and Express Publisher U.S. Version 2.03 (below)

The software must be changed to handle such types of differences in other languages. Making these changes in the software constitutes the additional work required for Localization, beyond straightforward language translation. A Localizer working on Localization or Internationalization has to understand the software and hardware limitations as well as the structural differences between the original language and the languages into which the software is to be Localized. For example, the French version in Figure 1–2 is not completely Localized. Can you see why?[2]

1.2. POINTS OF VIEW

In this book we will discuss Localization mostly in the context of the IBM PC as the basic computer. This machine is quite complex and among its variations con-

---

[2]The French ruler shown is in English units of inches, not in centimeters. In practice, Express Publisher uses inches, centimeters, and points.

tains nearly all the features to be found in the computer world. We discuss it as it operates for WordPerfect 5.1, DOS, and Windows 3.x (3.0 and 3.1). In addition to its use as a stand-alone computer, under different operating systems it can serve as a multi-user and multitasking machine. In Chapters 5 and 6 we mention other computing environments and natural languages that are more complex from the point of view of Localization. Of all the varieties of DOS, we tend to use Microsoft's DOS rather than other manufacturers' versions. For UNIX, we rely on Hewlett-Packard's HP-UX.

We direct most of our discussion toward applications such as spreadsheets, word processors, or desktop publishing programs that are designed for use by the public at large, not exclusively by specialists.

Western Europe is our main geographical area of focus as a target, so we will discuss primarily translations from American English into other Western languages.[3,4] In Chapter 10, we present an overview of the United States for European manufacturers looking to Localize for the U.S. market.

1.3. INTERNATIONALIZATION AND LOCALIZATION

It is possible to Localize a software product without Internationalizing it first. That is, a piece of existing software can be translated into another language without the preparation that constitutes the Internationalization process. This process, sometimes called *retrofitting,* is inefficient in the event that Localization into more than one language is required or contemplated. It would be inefficient because each Localization would have to start from scratch, whereas Internationalization would *enable* the software so that each Localization becomes little more than a translating task.

In the past, single-language Localization was the usual procedure. A distributor in Europe who wanted to market a U.S. product would undertake to translate or Localize that product specifically for his or her market. The distributor would work with the complete and original source code for the software and modify all the strings, sort procedures, and so on for the single language in which he or she was interested. To Localize this product for yet another culture and language would require a repetition of every one of the steps taken in the first Localization.

The purpose of Internationalization is to *enable* a software product, that is, to provide the features so that Localizers may conveniently and easily choose the appropriate form of the feature for their particular language. Under this approach, the U.S. software developer usually produces an *International English*

---

[3]We are distinguishing between different varieties of English. If you believe that American English is the same as other varieties of English, then read the sports pages and the business pages from newspapers written in another variety of English. You may not understand them.

[4]There are 864 million people in the world who speak Mandarin, 443 English, 352 Hindi, 341 Spanish, 293 Russian, 197 Arabic, 184 Bengali, 142 Malay-Indonesian, 125 Japanese, 121 French, and 118 German, according to the *1991 World Almanac.* Clearly, factors other than the number of people speaking a language influence its importance and status.

version of the product first, that is, a version in which all the text is in English and whose software program component contains all the logic required for the target languages as well as for the American English. Then, producing a *French* or *Spanish* version from the *International English* version is a matter of translating text files and setting parameters for *French* or *Spanish* in the software program, a component of the software product that remains unchanged. Thus, the International English version of the software is also the version of the program *Localized* for English.

Some people define Internationalization to be the process of preparing software so that it can handle several languages during actual execution.[5] To use the software in a French context, all that is required is to set the French switch, for Spanish, set the Spanish switch, and so on. On the Macintosh, you can switch from one language to another through the medium of the Script Manager. More is involved than merely producing translated messages; the cultural differences and nuances that we discuss in Chapter 2 must also be included. Indeed, both UNIX and the Macintosh provide more support, as we discuss in Chapter 5. In fact, they and Windows aim to produce "world-ready" software where multiple users can work in different natural languages at the same time.

Some software does not lend itself immediately to the processes of Internationalization and Localization that we discuss here. These include accounting systems that incorporate the accounting standards of the country of origin. A U.S. accounting application that computes depreciation would be inappropriate in other countries because different procedures and time periods almost certainly apply. Another country's accounting standards for FIFO or LIFO inventory control is a question for the accounting analyst and program specifier rather than the software engineers and translators. Other professional areas that come to mind include medicine, insurance, and law. Obviously, any application that follows legal or regulatory requirements of one country will be inappropriate to any other, no matter how well the Localization is executed.

1.4. ORGANIZATION OF THIS BOOK

This is an introductory technical work oriented toward people who are curious about what—apart from translation—needs to be done in order to transform software programs into forms suitable for use in other cultures.

Part 1 consists of Chapter 2, which analyzes Localization issues from a user perspective.

Part 2 consists of Chapters 3 and 4, which describe how to approach the Localization issues for Western European languages on the IBM PC. Chapter 3 describes some general fundamental topics, while Chapter 4 discusses specific topics.

Part 3 consists of Chapters 5, 6, and 7. Chapter 5 discusses what has been done in computer environments other than that of the IBM PC, Chapter 6 out-

---

[5]Others use the term *Globalization* to distinguish severally Localized software from singly Localized and Internationalized software.

lines the issues raised in other languages and outlines some approaches to resolving these issues, and Chapter 7 outlines the role of computing standards.

Part 4 consists of Chapters 8, 9, and 10. Chapter 8 discusses some of the organizational and logistical considerations involved in Internationalization and Localization, Chapter 9 describes some business aspects, and Chapter 10 discusses some general issues involved in introducing software from Europe to America.

There are many appendixes. Appendix A lists various standard paper sizes, Appendixes B and C provide brief overviews about the UNIX and Macintosh computing environments, while Appendixes D and E provide basic information about computer software and hardware. Although we are concerned with software, it is not possible to tackle this subject without discussing hardware, and so we have an appendix on hardware. If you know nothing about computer hardware or software, then these two appendixes will provide an introduction; if you know hardware and software, ignore them.

Appendix F contains a list of larger Localizing agencies specializing in European translations, Appendix G contains a list of names and addresses of standards organizations, and Appendixes H through L contain copies of computer character sets for WordPerfect®, DOS, ISO, Macintosh, and Hewlett-Packard's HP-UX. Appendix M lists DOS National Language Support System Functions (Interrupts).

PART I
Issues

2 Issues in Software Internationalization and Localization

2.1. INTRODUCTION

Internationalization of software is *enabling* software—so that it may be converted fairly easily and smoothly to operate in more than one human culture or locale.[1] Internationalization requires planning for and arranging software so that all the peculiarities and idiosyncrasies in how cultures manage their languages—features that the individual Localization processes employ—can be handled efficiently and simply. Internationalization may be thought of as the general case of all the individual Localization cases.

For example, if you are writing software that is concerned only with the U.S. market and that handles only American English, then the sorting process is straightforward. In American English, it has been customary to sort characters according to some numerical equivalent of the character encoding. But, as we discuss in Section 2.2.4, this would not be satisfactory in handling German, French, or Spanish. It is not even satisfactory in English, since it places all lowercase characters after all uppercase characters.

Therefore, to Internationalize software, or to adapt software so that it will handle French and Spanish and German as well as American English, the sorting process must be written to handle all the individual Localized cases. The German sort will not actually be invoked until the German environment is used; but the capability to accommodate this sort is made available during the Internationalization process.

---

[1] In the computer world a locale is a combination of language, region, and code or character set.

There are many issues for the software developer to consider. In this chapter, we discuss the most common ones. Some may appear obvious, yet obvious or not, they must be addressed.

We are deliberately ignoring some issues that pertain more to software specification and design. The basic operations of a desktop publishing program, spreadsheet program, word processor program, or operating system are similar across nationalities. This is not true of all applications, however, particularly those designed for use by professionals. For instance, it is almost certain that an accounting program will need substantial redesign before it meets the accounting standards of another country, because of variations in inventory and tax laws.

We discuss next some issues that a simple translation of software doesn't handle, but that the software itself must take care of.[2] Mostly, these issues come down to handling *extended* characters (those characters to be found in other languages that don't exist in American English) and to handling the many structural rules that have been taken for granted in American software but turn out to be handled differently in other languages.

2.2. ENGINEERING ISSUES

2.2.1. Character Handling (and Non-American Characters)

The most fundamental issue in preparing software that will handle non-American languages is ensuring that the computer hardware and software can handle the appropriate characters. Non-American languages contain characters that are not to be found in English of any variety. These non-American characters, also known as extended characters, include accented vowels like *é, è, ê;* characters like the French *ç,* the Spanish *ñ,* the Portuguese *ã,* and the Scandinavian *å,* the German *ß* and *ü,* and diphthongs like *œ,* and so on.[3]

If your product cannot handle these characters, particularly if it cannot be made to handle those characters used in the language of your goal, and if there is

---

[2]There is at least one software company that does not consider any translation at all to be necessary in internationalizing their software and doesn't do any. This company sells its software in countries where many people are familiar with some variety of English, as in Hong Kong, Malaysia, Singapore, and the Philippines. The company in question only modifies its accounting packages so that individual modules conform to the specific country's accounting standards and it then markets the product, still in U.S. English, in those countries. The basic U.S. product is Internationalized in that it can handle different number and currency formats, and thus this company considers the product with Malaysian accounting principles incorporated to be Localized for Malaysia, and so on. In this book, we assume some language translation to be part of the normal process.

[3]Pedantically, academically, and strictly speaking, one can indeed argue that the most precise English does include these characters, resulting from the fact that nearly every variety of English contains words imported from other languages. When the imported word contains an extended character, such as the ç in façade or the à in vis-à-vis, or the æ in encylopædia, there is clearly the question of what to do with the strange characters. Obviously, in everyday use, the practice is to replace them with the closest "normal" characters or pairs of characters from the English alphabet. In the absence of an undisputed authority that can rule on such matters, we will stick with our statement that such extended characters are not part of the English language.

no way in which it can be made to handle them, then you cannot Localize or Internationalize your product. In Greek, the letter *sigma* has a different form when at the end of a word than elsewhere. The product must handle such a variation if Greek is the target language.

2.2.2. Subsystems and the Character Set

Software systems sometimes consist of subsystems that to a certain extent are independent of the main system. This independence can lead to a lack of information about the system and the subsystem or, more precisely, it can lead to a lack of coordination. Therefore, it is possible that the subsystem changes the environment, including the character set, because its developer didn't know that it shouldn't.

An example of a subsystem developed by a third-party developer would be a spell checker invoked by a word processor. It is rare that a word processor developer also develops spell checkers or dictionaries; it is far more common that the word processor developer buys the spell checker from specialized manufacturers and bundles it with the word processor. We have seen instances where the imported spell checker's ability to process non-American characters did not correlate with the word processor's method. Since the two are developed independently, it is quite possible that there are some underlying incompatibilities that must be straightened out.

This kind of situation could lead to the system assuming it is operating with a particular character set, operating and manipulating on that assumption, and yet, by invoking the subsystem, also invoking situations where the character set is changed so that on return to the main system the wrong character set is in use.

Further examples include the use of some DOS *TSR*s. These *T*erminate and *S*tay *R*esident programs, almost certainly purchased from a different manufacturer, may not have been Internationalized themselves. Their assumptions about the character sets have been made completely independently of the software under development.

Another example is the operating system. It is quite possible that you name a file within your product before you save it, and that your name includes lowercase extended characters. When you return to the operating system, your filename may be changed because the operating system doesn't distinguish between uppercase and lowercase. The operating system may have (mis-)converted the name because of this.

Last and not least is the effect of the **cut, copy, paste, move,** and **duplicate** commands. Do the extended characters survive the effects of these operations?

2.2.3. Importing and Exporting All the Character Set

This issue pertains to older software that may have been written before manufacturers devoted much attention to Internationalization and under the assumption that no one is interested in the expanded character sets that contain the extended characters required for non-American versions.

Some characters, traditionally called *low ASCII* because their numerical equivalents are less than 32 (see Chapter 3), have traditionally been reserved for use by computer system developers. They include printer controls such as *line feed* and *carriage return*. A similar situation exists with other types of character sets. Some people prefer to use the term *control character range*. If part of the system ignores these parts of the character set, or worse, if the system strips them out of the data stream, then clearly you cannot correctly perform the operations that depend on these parts of the character set .

Most software these days is delivered in a compressed or compacted form in order to save floppy disk space. Data compressors and decompressors must be able to handle the entire character set.

2.2.4. Sorting

Considering how to sort a set of characters identifies problems where you may not suspect there are any. In everyday life in the United States, we are presented with different ways of sorting, and it is unclear if one is more correct than another. If you look up words in a dictionary, you will probably find that upper-case and lowercase are indistinguishable as far as their place in the order goes. The phone book is another matter; you would not be surprised to find the prefix *Mc* mixed up with the prefix *Mac*. This clearly becomes more complicated than you would expect if you are trying to program a sort routine. Which one should you use and why? And just how do you express a functional equivalence between *Mac* and *Mc* without destroying the natural order of *a, b,* and *c?* How would you know where to look up *St* and *Street* and *Saint?* Is *-t* equivalent to *-aint* or *-treet?*

In computing, the trend has been to sort, character by character, in order of the equivalent numerical value of the character code (we explain this more in Chapter 3). This would place the *Mc*'s after the *Ma*'s and *Mb*'s and the *St*'s a long way after the *Saint*'s. That is not always acceptable. There are hints that things become more complicated when a second character has to be considered at the same time.

In non-American languages, with double characters that sort as one combined character, it does indeed become far more complicated, as the following examples illustrate.

In German, *β* is one character, but it is treated in dictionaries as a double character. It must, wherever it is to be found in a word, be treated as equivalent to *ss.* That is to say that this single character must be treated as a double character if sorting results are to look authentic. And German speakers are accustomed to treating *ue, ae,* and *oe* as equivalent to *ü, ä,* and *ö,* respectively. These three latter characters must sort in the same order as the unaccented vowels.

In French, accented vowels are treated like unaccented vowels from the point of view of their sorting order. Then within each vowel set, the order is no accent, acute accent, grave accent, circumflex accent, and umlaut. (To be 100 percent correct, this order should be evaluated from right to left within the strings or words that are being compared, but we have not heard of any computer procedure that takes this last step.) For example, the following French words should sort as listed:

a	aménager
à	aménité
abbaye	amène
âme	ânier
améliorer	anis
amen	

In Spanish, *ch,* a double character, is treated as a separate single character and is ordered after *c* and before *d.* In the middle of a word, it comes after the dual characters *cz* and before the single character *d.* For example, the following Spanish words should sort as listed:

caracola	chácara
carácter	chacarero
caracterizar	danza
cizalia	ductil
cizaña	ducho
clamar	dudo
curador	

Also in Spanish, *ll,* a double character, is treated as a separate single character and is ordered after *l* and before *m.* In the middle of a word, it comes after the dual characters *lz* and before the single character *m.* For example:

cabalmente	linón
caballa	linotipia
lindo	lunar
línea	llama
linero	lleno
lino	macabro

Ñ is a separate letter after *N* and before *O.* For example:

nutrir	ñapa
ñame	ñudo
ñandu	oasis
ñaño	

and

cantina	caña

These rules cannot be implemented using traditional computer methods unless the computer software is specifically enabled to do so. Further, while the order of the French accented vowels such as *ê* is the same as that of the unaccented vowel, this is not true for the pair *ñ* and *n* in Spanish.

Sometimes a character is unimportant. For example, the dash is often ignored so that *re-locate* and *relocate* sort to the same place.

Note, too, that some European languages such as Danish have letters after *z* so that you cannot assume that the range ending in *z* includes all letters. In Lithuanian, *y* sorts with *i*.[4]

Traditional American sorting methods on a computer do not handle all these cases or the many more that exist.[5] Traditional American ways have been to sort by order of the numerical equivalent of the single character. We discuss this more fully in Chapter 3.

2.2.5. Search and Replace

In addition to its basic function, to find and/or replace a string of text, the Search and Replace function must be able to find and replace hyphenated words in the target language. As indicated in Section 2.2.9, some words in German change when they are hyphenated.

As mentioned in Section 2.2.6, certain accented vowel characters used in Parisian French change in the transition from lower- to uppercase. Will the Search (and Replace) function, set to find the accented vowel, work in these situations? Will the Replace function be appropriately case-sensitive?

In many languages, publishers often use ligatures; you might think of ligatures as a special case of kerning. In English, the letters *f* and *i* are often combined to make one special character because the combination looks better when printed than the separate letters that would be subject to general tracking rules. But often, in an American version of Search or Replace, there is no way to pack the two characters *f* and *i* into one character in the search expression.

Other common ligatures are *ct, st, ff,* and *qu.*

2.2.6. Case Conversion

Lowercase to uppercase conversion and vice versa in American English has traditionally been handled quite simply by adding or subtracting a constant to or from the numerical code for the character. This constant is 32 in the traditional American English character set (see Chapter 3), and it simply changes the code for the character. With Internationalized software you should not assume a difference of 32 between character code points for the case of a letter.

With extended characters, such a simple operation is impossible to define as there is no constant difference like 32 between the numerical equivalents for upper- and lowercase representations of characters (see Chapter 3). Furthermore, the definition of uppercase and lowercase characters can become quite ambiguous in many languages, assuming that such a feature exists at all.

---

[4] Peter Gulutzan, "How to Compare Characters with European Collating Sequences," *Windows / DOS Developer's Journal* 3, no. 1 (January 1992) shows the collating order for 25 languages, Albanian through Welsh.

[5] The programming language COBOL (see Section D.6.5) does provide the programmer with some options in sorting one character at a time. The order in which the **SORT** verb collates can be specified as *ASCII, EBCDIC,* or as per the contents of a file *ALPHABETNAME* in the *Special Names* paragraph of the *Configuration* section of the *Environment Division.* The programmer defines the file Alphabetname. We define the terms ASCII and EBCDIC later in Chapter 3.

For example, in Parisian French, all accented vowels lose their accents in the transition from lowercase to uppercase. Thus *é, è, ê,* and *e* all have the same uppercase character of *E.* Conversely, the transition from uppercase *E* to lowercase can have four possible outcomes, any one of which could be correct depending on context. In Canadian French, the characters retain their accents in uppercase.

Older Swiss Germans were taught that *UE* took the place of what would be uppercase *ü,* but that is no longer common practice. In Italian, the rules for accents are applied less rigorously.[6]

We discussed ligatures in Section 2.2.5. It would be unusual, to say the least, to find an algorithm that permitted the change of case for such an event; in American English, we are aware only of *QU* being used as an uppercase ligature. See Section 2.2.2 as well. It is entirely possible that other subsystems linked to the product make assumptions about case.

2.2.7. Word Boundaries

A word in text consists of a string of characters between delimiters. It has been common practice in the United States. to use blanks or spaces and/or the unused portion of a character set as delimiters. (We discuss this further in Chapter 3; higher ASCII characters are those that were not used in the United States.) This latter practice does not work when you are dealing with text where it is quite legitimate to have extended characters. Non-American English characters should be recognized, not taken for delimiters.

Further, while the usual delimiter is a blank, in some languages a blank is also an acceptable character as part of a numeral—a thousands separator. The software developer must provide for this possibility, and some manufacturers provide two blanks to take care of this. One blank is the standard word delimiter and the other is a nonbreaking space specifically used as a thousands separator. Both print or display on the monitor as a space.

2.2.8. Character Boundaries

For Western languages where the system works only in character mode with fixed width characters, the issue of character boundaries is a hardware issue that we explain in Section E.4.2. If the system uses graphic mode and generates its fonts from software, however, then the character boundaries must be tracked by the software.

For cursive scripts like Arabic, Farsi, and Urdu, there is a marked difference in the widths of the letters, and proportional spacing is required for printing. Descenders may be much greater in these languages than in others. Some of the characters simply require more space than Roman characters.

---

[6]There are no supreme arbiters in Italian or (many) other languages that serve the same function as l'Académie française serves for the French language. In German, the *Duden* dictionary serves as the arbiter.

2.2.9. Hyphenation/Syllabification

Each language has its own rules about hyphenation or syllabification. It is unlikely that any of these rules are the same as they are for U.S. English. For example, in German, a syllable begins with a consonant if one is present and in general, syllables are divided before single consonants and between double consonants:

se-hen   die Men-schen   der Win-ter

Consonant combinations such as *ch, st,* and *sch* are never separated; they are considered one sound.

A single vowel, although it can constitute a syllable, is never separated:

die Ader   eben   der Eber   aber   oder

Diphthongs are treated as single vowels.

There are two curiosities; some of the characters in some words change when the words are hyphenated at the end of a line. For example, the *ck* in noncompound words such as *drucken, hacken, beglücken,* and die *jacken* becomes *k-k.*[7] Hence we get *druk-ken, hak-ken, beglük-ken,* and *jak-ken* when they are hyphenated at the end of a line. (Compound words are hyphenated at the junction of the component words, as in *zweck-mässig.*)

The character *ß* also changes after long vowels and diphthongs; in noncompound words it is expanded and treated as *ss* would be in the same situation. Thus, die *Straße* and *dreißig* become *Stras-se* and *dreis-sig.* Similarly, die *Grüße* and die *Füße* become *Grüs-se* and *Füs-se.* The question here is will a Search (and Replace) for *drucken* or *Straße* successfully find *druk-ken* or *Stras-se* as well?

In Spanish, *ll, ch,* and *rr* are treated as single consonants that cannot be hyphenated. Most consonants when combined with *l* or *r* cannot be hyphenated, and paired consonants are divided in the middle. If there are more than two consonants, then the last one forms a new syllable with the vowels that follow it.

In French, hyphenation is quite common; at the end of a line you split double consonants or syllables. Hyphenation is also used after a personal pronoun before *même,* as in *eux-mêmes,* before personal pronouns in expressions like *Aime-t-il?,* after imperatives such as *allez-vous-en* unless there follows an infinitive, between *ce* or *là* and a joint word, as in *celui-ci,* or *là-haut,* and finally, in numbers less than one hundred, as in *dix-huit* (unless they contain *et,* as in *vingt et un*).

If your hyphenator does not allow for these nuances, then it doesn't work properly as a hyphenator for the language with which you are dealing.

2.2.10. Expansion of Text

It is expected that translated text will require more characters than the original American English text. Many suggest that equivalent text can be as much as 200

---

[7]Also *backen, bezwecken, der Buckel, die Böcke, der Dackel, der Deckel, decken, die Deckung, ducken, drücken, die Hecken, der Feinschmecker, lecken, lecker, die Mücke, der Pickel, die Röcke, der Rücken, rucken, scheckig, die Schickeria, schmecken, der Schrecken, steken, der Sockel, die Socken, strecken, stricken, wecken,* and *zwicken.*

percent longer, depending on the length of the original. An example of this expansion of text is the translation *Start laufwerk* for *Startup*.

Some of the extra characters may very well include *spaces*; for example, *Update* translates into *Mettre à jour* in French. The introduction of spaces or blanks could well lead to other problems—see Sections 2.2.16 on Parsing Input and 2.2.7 on Word Boundaries.

2.2.11. Dialog Boxes and Menu Names Also Need Space to Grow

Dialog boxes provide a way for the user to interact with the software. Like anything else that appears on the screen, they have a certain size. If translated text takes more space, will the dialog box grow to accommodate it or will it truncate it? What happens if less space is needed?

Menus are another way for the user to interact with the software running on a computer. They allow the user to make a choice. There are many kinds of menus, some quite simple and some more complex. The simplest is called a *prompt*. In this type, for example, an IBM PC computer might display

C:>

on the video screen. The cursor is shown blinking to the right and indicates where the typed command will be displayed on the screen. The user would then type in a *command* such as **dir,** which would instruct the computer to list all the files on the *C* disk.

In another kind of menu, the computer software displays a list of functions on the video screen with an appended number, such as:

1)Install New Program

2)Update Old Program

3)Quit

The user selects one of the three choices by typing **1, 2,** or **3**.

The most common kind of menu these days consists of a row of functions displayed on the top of the screen, such as:

File   Edit   Format   Font   Document   Utilities   Window

The user chooses one of these by moving the cursor with a mouse to the physical location of the function's title and clicking the mouse button.

In the latter two cases, the software's response to the user's choice is often to present another menu, called a *submenu*, from which the user makes further choices. The submenu *scrolls* down or it *pops up*.

As an example, clicking on the **File** menu may produce a list of the following on the screen:

New

Open

Close

Save

Save as

Again, the user may choose by moving the mouse cursor to the location of choice and clicking or double clicking the mouse button.

Can all the translated menus fit on a screen and can individual menus fit on a screen, given the expected growth in length of menu item names?

2.2.12. Meaningful Values for Accelerators

For many applications, the functions in menus and submenus can also be accessed from the keyboard by using an accelerator combination that is essentially an abbreviation for the menu item. For example, the combination *Alt-O* is often used to *Open* a file, an action that is normally to be found on the *File* menu. This wouldn't make the same intuitive sense in Spanish since few Spanish-speaking office workers would think that *O* is an abbreviation for *Abrir*.[8]

The accelerator is often identified by an underline on the menu line and usually relates to the initial letter of the function. There is no reason why the initial letters should be unique, even in the original (Save and Save As), and no reason why the initial letters should be unique in the translated version. Thus, in many programs, the underline can appear anywhere, not just under the initial character.

2.2.13. Numbered and Unnumbered Messages

Software communicates with the user by writing a *message* on the screen or other output device. The message consists of a string of characters constituting text that the user can read and understand. It can appear as a *prompt* or as a part of a *dialog box* or as part of a menu. The message should be pertinent and clear in meaning to the user. In most cases existing messages are clear and pertinent, in some cases they are not. They should be appropriate for the state of the software at the time that the message is issued.

For a number of reasons, a translated message can be the same as another translated message: the originals may be the same (not very smart programming on the part of the developers); the originals may just be very similar, although not exactly the same; one of the originals may be ambiguous in meaning, and so on. This leads to the surprising conclusion that accurate translation alone is not sufficient to identify a message or its origins.

When it comes to chasing down a program error (they exist in all software, even when released to the public), it can be difficult to describe the symptoms accurately. Output messages are part of the symptoms describing the anomalous event. If more than one situation can invoke the same message, then ambiguity creeps into the description of the problem. Sometimes, it is necessary to make

---

[8]On the Macintosh personal computer, however, it is customary to preserve certain traditional commands for popular or common functions and not to Localize them. *Save, Copy, Paste, Cut,* and *Open* are usually left as *Command S, Command C, Command V, Command X* and *Command O.*

inquiries of engineering staff in the United States even though the bug may have arisen in Luxembourg. The U.S. staff may be familiar with the English version but have difficulty relating the English message to the non-American message.

The Technical Support department of a software manufacturer will continue to receive inquiries for some time after all the programmers, Localizers, project managers, and translators have packed their bags and moved on to other projects. If the inquiry is sophisticated enough, it is possible that only someone associated with the original program will be able to develop an appropriate response, and it is unlikely that this person will know the translated message. Consequently, for coordination reasons alone, there is considerable motivation to identify messages uniquely with numbers.

The sheer volume of messages can compound the issue. If you have thousands of messages in the software package to convert, keeping track of them without some unique identifier such as a number is difficult. You need to be certain that you have the correct message when verifying the translation and when verifying computer operation. Unfortunately, many standards proscribe such additional identification.

2.2.14. Are Strings Made Up of Substrings Meaningful or Correct in Other Languages?

A string is a sequence of characters that the computer software can handle as a unit. For example, displayed messages are stored as strings within the computer software. Messages are sometimes assembled from substrings. Sometimes, programmers have added or concatenated the letter *s* to portray the plural. Of course, this doesn't always work in American English (what's the plural of child and sheep?) and there is even less reason for it to work in other languages. Using strings made up of substrings to express the plural is just not a general enough procedure. On the other hand, other languages can contain adjectives whose spelling depends on the gender of the noun that they are modifying. For example, many Spanish adjectives end in *o* when masculine and in *a* when feminine.

Nouns and adjectives have different orders in different languages. For example, *red house* is *maison rouge, casa roja,* and *casa rossa* in French, Spanish, and Italian, respectively, since the adjective comes after the noun in those languages. Parts of the verb in German are located at the end of a sentence.

In some cases, it is necessary to add special characters at the beginning of a Spanish sentence or phrase where there is no equivalent in English. Spanish exclamations and questions start with ¡ and ¿, respectively. Note that ¿ actually comes at the beginning of the question, not necessarily at the beginning of the sentence, as in *Pero, ¿como es posible?*

The same issue arises for *embedded parameters* in strings. Will the string make grammatical sense in another language?

2.2.15. Non-American Spell Checkers

In the event that the software application provides a spellchecking capability, it is necessary to verify that the appropriate spell checking module works with the software. This can mean as little as ensuring that you can invoke the correct speller and that all its functions work, as well as verifying that it is an adequate package. Spell checkers or dictionaries often are provided by third-party vendors. These vendors may differ from language to language; one vendor may not make all the dictionaries that you want, or one vendor's dictionaries may be superior or cheaper in some languages and less attractive in others. For example, it is possible that a spell checker has a problem with the second-person singular of the future tense of Spanish "*ar*" verbs.

Spell checkers must also handle the distortions of words that occur under hyphenation, as discussed in Section 2.2.9, or any changes that occur when there is a change of case, such as those discussed in Section 2.2.6.

In some more complex languages, the glyph representing a character can have different forms depending on its position in the word. In Greek, the glyph for *sigma* differs according to its location in the word; at the end it is like *s* and in the middle of a word it is like σ. Thus, a spellchecker should recognize its different forms.

2.2.16. Parsing Input

If your software obtains information from analyzing input data, or parsing, then you may have trouble both Internationalizing and Localizing those segments of the software that perform the parsing function. Unless the input information is organized or coded according to some standards that do not change from locale to locale, you may have to reprogram those parts of the software that perform the parsing functions, or you may have to limit the manner in which the user enters the data.

In the most obvious case, the parsing software may expect to find some limited variation of English. Will it work with French or with extended characters of any type? Different sentence structures in other languages may require changing the location and/or order of variables mixed with static text in messages. For example, the command **Update variable** translates into French as ***Mettre à jour variable,*** but the parsing program expects the value for the variable after the first space! In this case it would find *à*, not the name of the variable.[9] In Japanese, they do not use spaces at all to delimit words.

2.2.17. The Significance of Special Characters

Programming in American English for American users in relative isolation has allowed some conventions to develop that do not translate easily to the rest of the world. Perhaps the most pervasive (and far from unreasonable) is the habit of using blanks as delimiters between words or tokens.

Other special characters have developed some significance. The apostrophe is

---

[9]There is an apochryphal story in the computer industry of an International program that worked successfully everywhere until it was tried in Ecuador. When it came time to input the name of Ecuador's capital city, *Quito,* the program would *quit,* or cease operation. The converse could be true, too. The Spanish *con exito* means successfully, not *leave the program.*

sometimes used as a delimiter in strings to the extent that its use in other situations is prohibited. The prohibition in such languages as French and Italian would be constrictive. There are many occurrences in French and Italian where the terminal vowel in the French and Italian article is replaced by an apostrophe because the following noun has an initial vowel.

In Spanish, exclamations and questions traditionally start with ¡ and ¿. In Greek, the question mark looks like an American English semicolon (;), and the semicolon looks like a superscripted period (.). In traditional French, quotation marks are « and », but we have seen many manuals that use American English quotation marks. Further, in French, there is a space between the last word of a sentence and a concluding exclamation or question mark.

Americans use a variety of abbreviations for numbers or numerals. Most common are # and N^o. The first of these, a special character, is not recognized even in England. The second is used in Argentina, Belgium, Bulgaria, France, Israel, Italy, Portugal, and the United Kingdom. And @ means *at* in the United States, but in the United Kingdom it means *each*. It is not likely to mean that anywhere else. At least one book, *Fowler's Modern English Usage,* has been written using & in every place where the rest of us would use *and*. The traditional abbreviations for ordinals are 1st, 2nd, 3rd, and 4th, although nowadays they are commonly written 1st, 2nd, and 3rd. In Spanish and Portuguese the ordinals are abbreviated 1°, 2°, 3° or 1^a, 2^a, 3^a, depending on the gender of the subject.

The French abbreviation for "Compagnie" is "Cie," following a common practice of using the superscript mode for part of the abbreviation. It may be necessary to use different versions of the trademark and copyright symbols for different languages. Percent may be expressed as *pct*, not %, in Belgium. Sometimes there is a space between the number and the percent symbol, sometimes not.

And last, but certainly not least, in the software world, many special characters have special significance as *wild cards*. In DOS, a question mark (?) is used to indicate that a character can have any value, and an asterisk (*) means that a *field* (a succession of characters) can have any value during an operation. Further, a period (.) can mean any filename, including its extension. These meanings have become traditional in the American software industry. In footnotes and headers in many applications, you can invoke the date or time or such text attributes as bold, italic, or underlining by inserting such special codes as *&d, &t, &b,* and so on.

2.2.18. Keyboards and Entry of Non-Keyboard Characters

The computer is made up of various physical devices such as a keyboard, a mouse, and a printer, among others. The keyboard is the traditional and currently the most common way of entering text into a document on the computer. But sometimes, you want to enter certain characters and it doesn't appear to be possible. Suppose you have an IBM PC with an American keyboard and you want to enter an extended character such as Ç. There is no obvious way to do it.[10]

---

[10]We discuss the ways to enter such characters in Section 4.3.18.

Keyboards can come from different manufacturers and suppliers. It is entirely possible that even after a successful Internationalization and Localization process here in the United States on a "typical" French computer, your software will not be completely Localized for the average user in France because some part of the computer has come from a different manufacturer and is not Localized for France. So it is possible that your keyboard will work while those in the target locale will not. You may need to verify other manufacturers' keyboards. Messages and documentation relating to the keyboards may not have been Localized.

2.2.19. Tracking

Tracking defines the horizontal spacing between all characters. Again, you must be careful that non-American characters are recognized in the algorithms that take care of the spacing.

2.2.20. Kerning

Kerning describes the horizontal spacing between specific pairs of characters. It is a specific case of the general case of *tracking*. Conventional wisdom holds that the pair of characters *f i* just looks better if its particular spacing is less than that for other pairs. Other pairs have the same property—*Ye, Yo,* and *Wi,* for example. You must be able to specify how pairs of non-American characters including the extended characters are to be spaced.

If your software needs explicit commands (different than those for tracking or spacing) to accomplish this, then you will need to be explicit about all the characters involved.

2.2.21. Diacritical Marks, the Height of Characters, and Leading

U.S. English characters may print well and display well on the computer monitor. Printing extended characters, those with accents, and particularly those in uppercase may provide the first indication that leading is inadequate. (Leading— pronounced "ledding"—is a printer's term for the vertical spacing between lines.) The ascender of the letter may be too high or the descender too low, although this latter is unlikely since there are U.S. English characters with large descenders such as *y* and *g*.

2.2.22. Printers and Character Sets

It is possible that the printer will not work while all the other parts of the hardware do. You need to verify that non-American characters can be produced. The printer may not have non-American character sets, or you may not be able to load it with appropriate character sets. We discuss this more fully in Sections E.2.4, E.3, and E.5.1 of the Appendix.

There can be a slight mismatch between the computer and the printer. In the event that a printer cannot print a character, what do you do? At the very least it seems that you can print a "place holder," a character that indicates that something should be there, rather than throw the nonprinting character away. After all, you may use another machine and printer on which the character will print.

2.2.23. Address Formats

The format of a simple address in the United States is as follows (where we use the slash mark to distinguish between fields):

Salutation/Name
Number/Street Name/Type of Street/Apt #
City/State Abbreviation/ZIP Code

The ZIP Code can be five numbers, or five numbers/hyphen/four numbers.

However, if you have ever had occasion to work with many U.S. addresses, you will already know that this simple case is far from the only format used. Often, you must also provide for the addressee's title and name of company, and perhaps some further identification for a branch or division or department. Then, additional organizational mail addresses such as "Mail Stop number" are sometimes encountered.

In the United Kingdom you find:

Salutation/Name/Letters denoting degrees, honors, and memberships
House Name
Number/Street Name/Type of Street
Region of City
City
Country/Postal Code[11]

The postal code has a format different from the American code, and comes after the country. It has various formats, up to seven characters and numbers including a space, such as OX2 6LD and PL5 4LZ, or it could be as short as S2.

It is a decreasing tradition to use commas as separators (particularly between the Number and the Street Name fields) and at the end of lines.

In many continental European countries, the postal code is to be found ahead of the city name:

Salutation/Name
Street Name/Number
Region of City
Postal Code/City

The postal code includes an abbreviation for the name of the country, such as B for Belgium, F for France, D for Germany, E for Spain, I for Italy, and NL for the Netherlands. There may be a further code after the name of the city. In con-

---

[11]Many people, particularly residents of the country sending domestic mail, put the postal code after the city.

trast to the U.S. and U.K. addresses, the house number comes after the street name, except in Luxembourg.

2.2.24. Translation of Filenames

Many files (collections of data or programs stored on the computer) have mnemonic names such as *README*. There is a *viewer* associated with them. As with clip art and icons, translation of filenames may be necessary and the software must still function. There are rules as to how files can be named in most environments and operating systems. Under DOS, even non-American versions, a filename consists of one or two parts—a filename (always necessary) and an optional extension separated by a period. The filename can be up to 8 characters long and the extension up to three. There are no spaces allowed in the eleven characters, and you cannot use * ? / . ; [ ] + = + \ < >. You should examine the interaction between an application that names files and its environment to verify the behavior of extended characters. In particular, make sure that the operating environment does not change any of the characters independent of the application.

2.2.25. Numeric Formats, Separators, Negatives, and Decimal Tabs[12]

In the United States, numbers contain a decimal point and use a comma as a thousands separator. In other countries, there is a decimal *comma* and a *period* or a *blank* or an *apostrophe* as a thousands separator. France doesn't always require an explicit thousands separator for numbers less than 10,000. One country—Portugal—uses *$* as a decimal separator in its currency.[13]

The software must be able to recognize numbers in these different formats. The use of a blank as a thousands separator is particularly troublesome since it is used, almost invariably, as a word delimiter.[14] As a word delimiter, its role is to signify the beginning or end of a word. As such, it is possibly the most frequently occurring character in a body of text!

Americans use many different ways to express the (algebraic) sign of a number. Not every piece of American software will recognize or use all ways. Some are peculiar to specific professions such as accounting, and in such cases software for users from other professions would not recognize them. Nevertheless,

---

[12]There are four kinds of tabs available in today's word processors; left, right, center, and decimal. The left tab, the one that was on typewriters, helps you align columns by the left edge. The right tab helps you align columns by the right edge, the center tab helps align by the center of the block of text, and the decimal tab helps align by the decimal separator.

[13]According to *Software Development for International Markets: A Technical Reference*, APDA Draft, by Apple Computer, Inc. Norway also uses its currency symbol *kr* as a decimal separator in formatted monetary amounts.

[14]To confuse the issue even further, some Asians, we are told, cluster numbers to the left of the decimal point in groups of four, not three! They have separators for each group of four!

they exist, and depending on the specific application need to be addressed or converted into the notation used by the profession in the other culture.

A negative number may be denoted by:

a leading hyphen
a trailing hyphen
enclosing the number in parentheses

Financial numbers can also contain a trailing *CR* (for *credit*) or a leading hyphen that can come before the currency symbol (the normal case) or after it (Panama).

A lot of software programs that manipulate text—word processors and desktop publishers, for example—provide for different forms of tabulation (tabs). One of the versions is a decimal tab, that is, a tab that aligns numbers in columns around the decimal separator.

Will the decimal tab work with commas rather than points? Will it work with the Portuguese *$*? Will the right tab work with trailing *CR* or with parentheses? These are all issues that must be addressed.

2.2.26. Arithmetic Operations, Including Rounding

Some countries have their own traditions about rounding numbers. Americans use the following rule:

<= 4   drop the digit
>= 5   add one to the previous digit and drop the digit

For example, rounding 123.46 gives 123.5, and rounding 123.44 gives 123.4.

Other locales may have different rules. For example, Argentines have the following rule for the third decimal digit, call it x:

$x < 3$ change the last digit x to 0 or drop it
$x < 8$ and > 2 change the last digit x to 5
$x > 8$ add one to the second digit and the last digit x is 0 or it is dropped

For example, rounding 123.452 gives 123.45, rounding 123.456 gives 123.455, and 123.459 gives 123.46. Contrary to American practice, there is a time when the last digit is not dropped or converted to zero.

For money, the Swiss round as follows (where A, B, and C are digits):

$AB.(C-1)76$ through $AB.C25$ rounds to $AB.C0$
$AB.C26$ through $AB.C75$ rounds to $AB.C5$

For example, rounding 12.48 gives 12.50, rounding 12.523 gives 12.50, 12.533 gives 12.55, and rounding 12.567 gives 12.55. Again, contrary to American practice, there is a time when the last digit is not dropped or converted to zero.[15]

---

[15]See IBM, *National Language Information and Design Guide—Volume 2. National Language Support Reference Manual.*

2.2.27. Monetary Symbols and Currency

Here are some schematic examples of how an amount of currency is expressed.

Location	Symbols
U.S.	$1,234.56
Norway[16]	kr1.234,56
Switzerland[17]	sFr 1 234,56
Germany[18]	1.234,56 DM
Portugal	123$45ESC

Many countries require more places on both sides of the decimal point than used in the United States.

A negative currency value may be denoted by:

a leading hyphen
a trailing hyphen
enclosing the number in parentheses

Financial numbers can also contain a trailing *CR* (for *credit*) or a leading hyphen that can come before or after the currency symbol.

2.2.28. Dates and Times

There are many different calendars in use throughout the world, some based on the relative movements of the moon and some on the relative movements of the sun:

Gregorian
Era name (from founding of the republic, or linked to the Emperor)
Buddhist
Islamic (there are two Islamic calendars)
Hebrew

Some countries use more than one, and the user must specify which one is being used.

Within the Gregorian calendar, we have the following (using the slash mark as a field separator again):

---

[16]But see footnote 13. If that were true, this would be written as 1.234kr56. Our source for these formats is Volume 2 of IBM's *National Language Information and Design Guide*.

[17]In correspondence with the International Organization for Standardization in Geneva, (French-speaking) Switzerland, the ISO used the International standard *CHF* rather than *sFr*. They also used the date format of *yy.mm.dd*. See Section 2.2.28 and Chapter 7. Under such standards, Danes in Denmark would use 100kr while the International standard would be 100DKK.

[18]In Germany, there are different ways of expressing a price that has an exact number of (deutsche) marks, that is, a price with zero pfennigs. A German can write any one of the three following:
251,00 DM,   251,^{00}DM,   or 251,—DM

Formats: yy/mm/dd

                yyddd

                yyyy/mm/dd

                dd/mm/yy

                mm/dd/yy

where   *mm* is a decimal number representing the month
dd and *ddd* are decimal numbers representing the day in the month and in the year, respectively
yy is a decimal number representing the last two digits of the year
yyyy is the year

Implicit in this format are certain questions. Are two characters adequate to express the year, or should there be four? Remember we are soon to be entering a new century. Should leading zeroes or spaces be allowed for the days and months?

Some examples of dates from different countries are:

3/10/90	U.S.
10/3/90	U.K.
10.3.90	German
10.3.90	French
10-3-90	French
10/3/90	Italian
1990/3/10	Japanese
2/3/10	Japanese (relating to the year of the current emperor's reign)[19]

Note the variations in the separators between fields.

The month of September 1752 had only 20 days in British possessions.
Lunar calendars are far more complex

Times have a variety of formats too:

3:20 P.M.	U.S.
15h20:00.000	South African
15,20,00	Swiss
15.20.00.000	Finnish[20]

Note that there are 12-hour clocks and 24-hour clocks. Again, note the varieties in the separators between fields. Separators include:

:

h

---

[19]See IBM, *National Language Information and Design Guide—Volume 2. National Language Support Reference Manual.* This source also indicates some alternative formats that are available in many countries.

[20]See IBM, *National Language Information and Design Guide—Volume 2. National Language Support Reference Manual.*

,

.

2.2.29. Time Zones

On some computer systems, particularly those using the UNIX operating system, the operating system keeps track of the time zone in which the system is operated. This refers to the number of hours ahead of or behind Greenwich Mean Time (GMT). For example, Paris is one hour ahead of Greenwich while San Francisco in the Pacific Time Zone is eight hours behind (–8 GMT). Note that the term GMT is gradually being replaced by UCT, Universal Coordinated Time.

2.2.30. Measurement Scales

A lot of software uses internal units to keep track of measurements. A common internal measurement scheme in many computer applications is to use the *twip*. A *twip* is a twentieth of a point. In the Macintosh, one one-hundred-and-twentieth of an inch is used as the basic measuring unit. This can cause some rounding problems when a metric measurement is converted to twips internally and then reconverted for display.

The rest of the world (outside the United States and some English-speaking countries that use the Imperial system) uses the metric system, which is defined in terms of a subdivision of the longitude through Greenwich (=40,000 kilometers). Its biggest advantage is that each division is related to the next by a factor of ten. The American user employs inches and fractions of an inch: halves, quarters, eighths, sixteenths, thirty-seconds, and even sixty-fourths, only occasionally tenths.

Some countries that have changed from one system to another may still use both the old and the new system.

For computer purposes, we are interested mostly in centimeters and millimeters. One inch equals 2.54 centimeters or 25.4 millimeters.

Publishers have traditionally used points as a unit of measurement, defined at 72 to the inch.[21] Picas are twelve points; there are six to the inch. In addition, some European publishers use different scales; in France, many use the *Didot* point, which is approximately equal to 1.04 American points.

2.2.31. Page Sizes

Americans use one set of paper sizes, the rest of the world uses others. Appendix A contains a more complete list. The following sections show some of the more common proper sizes.[22]

---

[21]Actually, there are 72.2700072 points to an inch, but in the computer world they are "defined" at 72 to the inch. This makes a twip 1/1440 of an inch.

[22]From Appendix B of *Software Development for International Markets: A Technical Reference*, APDA Draft, by Apple Computer, Inc. Also in IBM, *National Language Information and Design Guide—Volume 2. National Language Support Reference Manual*.

2.2.31.1. United States

	Inches	Millimeters
A3	11 × 17	279 × 432 (ledger)
A4	8.5 × 11	216 × 279 (letter)
International Fanfold	210 mm × 12 inches	
Computer Paper	14 × 11	336 × 279
U.S. Legal	8.5 × 14	216 × 336 (legal)

2.2.31.2. ISO Series

The biggest size of paper is A0, with an area of one square meter and with sides that are in the ratio of one to the square root of two. Smaller sizes are derived by dividing the next larger format into two equal pieces.

	Inches	Millimeters
A3	11.7 × 16.5	297 × 420
A3 continuous	13.5 × 12	342.9 × 304.8
A4	8.25 × 11.66	210 × 297
A4 continuous	8.25 × 12	210 × 304.8

You must be able to handle these and the other paper sizes.

2.2.32. Colors

Colors have traditional meanings in the West and presumably in other cultures. Black is a color associated with death and funerals in the West, while for the Chinese, white is the color associated with funerals and red with marriages. On the other hand, white is associated with purity in the West. Thus colors of screens and icons can have cultural implications that are not immediately obvious.

In the West, orange and yellow are considered warm, green and blue are cool and calm, and red is hot.

There are some standards for colors, but we don't know how widespread they are. You would expect most cultures to recognize the colors of the ubiquitous traffic light, thereby giving red (stop), amber (caution), and green (go) the same meanings worldwide, but dont't take this for granted.

2.2.33. Cultural Considerations

Culture can be one of the limiting factors in the Localization process. Other factors include linguistic and dialect considerations, type of Localization (complete or partial Localization, when for instance, only the documentation is translated), and source code (the overall product design and how it is "enabled"). Culture is defined as the collective mental programming of the people in an environment, something that an individual learns while growing up with parents in a community or society.

People with different mental programming can perceive the same object in different ways. What is obvious for an American might not be obvious at all for a person of different nationality. Problems occurring in Localization projects can arise from misunderstandings due to different mental programming. For example, "as soon as possible" means "immediately" in the United States, but "when convenient" in another country. When cooperating with companies located in different countries, it is important to be aware of these differences. For example, "left hand" is offensive in some cultures. Use "on the left" or "left side" instead. Be wary of how you depict men and women together and how they are dressed (in particular, that the women are dressed discreetly), and be sure that gestures are not offensive.

Some symbols like the swastika, hammer and sickle, rising sun, crosses, stars, and so on represent political or religious forces that others find objectionable.

If you intend to Localize for an Islamic country, and particularly one of the Islamic fundamentalist countries, you might note that these people appear to take offense at things that are quite innocuous in the West. Depictions of bikini-clad women, alcoholic drinks like wine and champagne, the bottoms of feet, and probably even pigs and pork may offend the consumer in some of these countries. In addition, their asterisk is five-pointed. Be wary if your software product is going to Iran, Pakistan, Algeria, Afghanistan, and so on. Some gestures such as nodding the head or waving one's hand can have totally different meanings in different parts of the world.

If you supply clip media, you should note that sounds, particularly emergency sounds, can differ from country to country. The sounds of vehicle engines, ambulances, police cars, fire engines, telephones, and air-raid warnings vary and so do their computer representations. Similarly, photographic clip images of street scenes may seem out of place if not chosen carefully.

2.2.34. Translation of Clip Art

A piece of clip art is a computer-usable picture that can be manipulated—resized, rotated—and inserted in a newsletter or other publication that the user is producing with the software product.

Clip art is often obtained from a third party, that is, from a supplier. A set of clip art can contain culturally dependent messages such as *Happy Birthday* or *Touchdown* that presumably should be translated. In order to perform the translation on the clip art, it may be necessary to use some software tool from the supplier. The software must still function with the revised clip art. Also the art itself may be considered a cultural oddity if shipped with your product to the target market. Imagine buying a product in the United States supplied with clip art that contained many variations of the Australian flag. How would you feel? (This is based on an actual situation one of us encountered when a manufacturer was assessing clip art to ship with its product.)

Also, there is always the possibility that the clip art contains abbreviations in American English such as *wedcake,* or slang such as *bubbly.*

Normally, the Localizer or translator will need a software tool in order to make changes.

2.2.35. Translation of Icons

An icon is a symbol displayed on the computer screen that indicates the presence of a computer file of data or a computer program. It has a name associated with it that is usually displayed, too. Normally you can activate or invoke an application by clicking the mouse on its icon or on the icon of a document associated with the application.

Icons' names are often mnemonic (and perhaps their shapes have meaning, too). As with clip art, it is possible that embedded text will need to be translated and that the software manufacturer may have to supply a tool for editing the icon. The software must still function with the revised icon. Embedded text may consist of an initial that represents a function, such as **W** for *Write,* or the initial letter of the name of the program, such as **W** for *Word.* If you are converting to French, **W** for *Write* may become **E** for *Ecrivez.* (Or should we write *Écrivez?*)

Normally, the Localizer or translator will need a software tool in order to make such changes.

2.2.36. Recognition of Translated Clip Art, Icons, and Files

The meaning of special pictures, drawings, and symbols may not be easily recognized by other cultures. Will someone—an end user such as a secretary in another culture—recognize any "intuitive" or "user-friendly" features such as a mailbox or wastepaper basket once they have been converted?

Cultural differences may cause different interpretations around the world; for example, chopsticks in a rice bowl represent the Cantonese symbol of death.

2.2.37. Memory

Memory is the part of the computer where software and data can be stored, usually temporarily, and where data processing takes place physically. This memory is particularly distinguished by the speeds at which software and data stored there can be accessed under computer control. This memory is also limited in "volume," that is to say, it can hold only so much software and programs. It has to hold all the pertinent parts that allow software to run.

The amount of memory available to run software is important; if you don't have enough, you can't run the software, unless someone reconfigures the machine or rewrites some software. As to whether you can get enough, the situation has been alleviated greatly by the availability of Extended Memory and Expanded Memory (see Section E.2.3.2).

More and more software products are graphically based; they have graphical interfaces with which the users interact, and they often provide for colors. As a result, they require substantially more memory to operate in than software written for use in character mode.

Even when a machine is in stand-alone mode—when it's not connected to any other machine—there is competition for the use of memory. You can't count on having all the memory available for use by your product. The operating system uses some of it, and there is a group of useful tools—TSRs like notepads and calculators—that use memory. Once you invoke them, they stay available for use in memory, until you take the concrete steps to unload them from memory. If you are accustomed to using such tools, you must make allowances for them.

From the point of view of Internationalization and Localization, you must be aware that Localized versions of operating systems may take different amounts of memory than the U.S. versions. There may also be different versions of the TSRs that take different amounts of memory.

If your machine has multiple users or is used for multitasking (one user running many tasks), then again there is competition for use of the memory. If your machine is on a network, then there is further competition for use of memory. The software for connecting to the network needs some of the memory for operation.

2.2.38. Non-U.S. Manufacturers and Non-American Hardware

If you are preparing software that will run in non-American locations, you need to know the specifications of the equipment and the environment in which it will operate. Preferably, you would even have examples in hand for testing purposes. While it is an easy task to find questions to ask (e.g., What are the specifications of such non-American hardware as a Video Card?), it isn't always easy to get an answer in which you also have confidence. Finding the people who can give a definitive and authoritative answer—even knowing that they exist—is difficult.

Even if the manufacturer is a subsidiary of a U.S. manufacturer, it is likely that extremely few people in the United States will know enough about the details of the non-American operation to answer such questions. Clearly, nothing beats development and testing on actual samples of the target hardware and environments.

2.2.39. Mice

It is possible that some mice will not work in other countries, either because the mouse driver has not been modified to work in a non-American environment or because the messages and documentation have not been Localized.

2.2.40. Setup and Installation Procedures

Since file sizes of the Localized software will be different than those in the base software, it is to be expected that the software's arrangement on disk will be different. Accordingly, the installation procedure and setup programs must be modified to ensure that they prompt for the correct disk at the appropriate time. It is possible that some Localized versions will need more disks than the U.S. versions.

Further, the programs involved in installation and setup may have to be Internationalized and Localized themselves. Any file compression and decompression routines must be checked to ensure that they do not inhibit these functions in the presence of extended characters.

2.3. TRANSLATION ISSUES

The first point that we want to make about translation is that it is still mostly a manual process. While what we are discussing involves translation of computer software and its accompanying documentation, you cannot expect much computer software assistance in the actual translation—yet.

Second, it's not enough to specify language alone; you must specify the region or territory, too. Written French in Canada differs slightly from that in France, and Spanish in Spain, Central America, Northern South America, and Southern South America is all somewhat different. Certain characters are necessary for French Canada—mainly the uppercase accented vowels. These can be used in France, but their use is unusual and is certainly unnecessary.

Computer is *ordenador* in Spain, *computador* in Mexico and Puerto Rico, and changes gender to *computadora* in the rest of Latin America. In Spain, Argentina, Uruguay, and to some extent Chile, the formal plural *you* is translated by *vosotros* with the second-person plural of the verb, while elsewhere it is *Ustedes (Vds, Uds)* with the third-person plural. In Spain you *bebe* a drink while in Latin America you use the verb *tomar*. There are other variations, some undoubtedly derived from the many different indigenous Indian languages of Latin America.

2.3.1. Translation

Many similar, but not identical, strings of text end up by being translated into the same non-American string. Some nuances can be lost. As one simple example, the German *ich gehe* is the only present tense for the verb *gehen,* to go. There are, of course, three present tenses in English, namely, *I go, I am going,* and *I do go.*[23] There is another simple example in French; **cancel** and **undo** are two commands that are both normally translated as **annulez,** even though the first means *discontinue the present command* and the second means *reverse the effects of a previous command.*[24]

It often happens that the target language does not have an adequate vocabulary containing specific translations of technical words. In fact, it may be commonly accepted practice to use the English words directly. This appears to be particularly true of such acronyms as ROM (Read Only Memory), EDI (Electronic Data Interchange), and WORM (Write once, read many). This practice could stem from the fact that there is probably a hard core of computer professionals in the locale who have had to familiarize themselves with some technical English purely in order to remain current with developments in the computer hardware and software fields. While the prospective market has broadened to include noncomputer professionals and perhaps nonprofessionals in general, nevertheless, the tradition of accepting some of the more esoteric computer terms still exists. Still, the translator has to decide whether to use the English word without translation or the translation.

---

[23]The converse is true at times; for example, you can translate *hit* into Spanish using *chocar, golpear, acertar,* and many other verbs. In other words, there are more nuances in Spanish than in English.

[24]We think these should be translated as **annulez** and **défaites** (from *défaire*), respectively, and that is indeed what IBM says in its *IBM Systems Application Architecture; Common User Access; Advanced Interface Design Reference.* However we know of at least three extremely popular American programs whose translation for both is indeed **annulez.** The native speaker Localizer in France whom we know, who has Localized over 100 American products, insists that "everyone" uses **annulez** in both cases. This demonstrates the benefits of developing a *glossary* of terms as one of the initial steps.

As an example, if we take the software documentation produced in the United States in general, we can list a number of areas with which non-American readers consistently have difficulty.[25] These are the areas of major concern:

Convoluted sentences	Humor
Non-sentences	Regionalisms
Noun strings	Terms with no cultural equivalent
Punctuated words	Informality or flippancy
Slang	Idioms
Jargon	Homonyms and second-cousin words
Synonyms	Acronyms

2.3.2. Components to Translate

2.3.2.1. Software

The software to translate usually consists of strings of text in menus, dialog boxes, alert boxes, messages, and help files.

2.3.2.2. Documentation

Documentation consists of several components:

Manuals and documentation supplements
Quick reference cards
README files
Messages in on-line Help
Boxes
Slipcovers
Registration cards
Labels for the disks containing the software product
Warranties or license agreements
Promotional flyers

Often the material to be translated is marketing material on the slipcover, and often there is technical information, normally about the machine configuration and environment in which the software works. Registration cards can contain information about how to obtain technical support. Any cards designed for mailing that are preprinted according to specific Post Office regulations and/or that contain free mailing franking must be converted.

Warranties, of course, are legal documents; they need to be reviewed by a lawyer conversant with legal matters in the target locale.

---

[25]We would not translate American English into British English, by the way, without having a native speaker verify the result of the translation. There are too many words with different meanings, like *biscuit, boot, braces, bum, chips, crisps, duck, English major, six, 15/4/85, home, ring, rise, call, football coach, lift, NB, PTO, public school, redundant, silly square leg, stone, football,* and *flat*. There are instances of what is all right in one language being vulgar or archaic in the other, such as *bum* or *knock up*. Some mean the opposite, such as *bomb*. Some are *spelt* differently, like *centre, colour, Internationalisation, judgement, Localisation, metre, programme,* and *speciality*.

Manuals describe how to install the software and how to operate it. Most modern packages also have an on-line Help feature that allows the user to find out how to do something without leaving the computer to look it up in a book. README files are computer files that contain information for the user that was prepared too late for inclusion in the manual or the on-line Help.

Documentation and the software can overlap in a number of ways. Manuals often include pictures of menus and input and output in general, and often they contain a section about errors that lists all the error messages. So, just as with the original base manuals, there needs to be extensive coordination between the Localized software and the Localized documentation. You must at times wait until the software is ready before proceeding with the production of the manual.

Clearly, sections of the manual that display photographs or other real images of the screen cannot be produced until the software is in an advanced enough state to produce the figure. The figures, diagrams, pictures, and messages in the manual must match those in the released version of the product. It can be very hard to keep track of all the messages when there is a large number of them. Verifying that the correct one is appearing can be quite difficult sometimes and quite easy at others. Normally, the manual contains a list of the messages, but again the question of whether this is the correct message arises. As mentioned earlier, life would be much easier if one were allowed to number those messages, even though many standards do not allow for this and quite explicitly prohibit it. Numbering is so useful that at times during translation it is worth numbering just to keep track of the messages and then deleting the numbers at the end of Localization development.

As in the base English case, it is necessary to verify that the specific operating instructions for the computer software do indeed make sense.

License agreements and copyright messages need to be modified for non-American markets. This involves more than translation, as a lawyer familiar with the locale's laws needs to review these documents as well.

Copyright messages, which are usually listed in the first pages of users' manuals, may have to be Localized as well. Depending on the customs of the non-American country under consideration, these copyright messages will be translated, modified, or left in the original language.

2.3.3. Special Cases—Tutorials, Examples, and Software/Hardware Interaction

In some cases, more than an accurate translation of the original American English is required. This is particularly true of such introductory material as tutorials and of such instances as templates and examples. By their very nature, these might contain many references to American culture; a sample newsletter may contain stories about political events in San Francisco. In such cases, it behooves the Localizer to create similar but more familiar events in Madrid or Berlin.

If the software under consideration interacts closely with certain kinds of hardware, such as telephones, then it is highly likely that the engineering content of the software will be substantially different because the telephones in the target locales are different. Obviously, in such a case more than an accurate translation is required.

PART 2
Internationalization and Localization for Western European Languages on the IBM PC

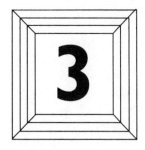

3 General Topics

3.1. INTRODUCTION

In this part we begin to describe how the computer processes data, information or text. There is more basic material on how the computer software and hardware handles information in Appendixes D and E. If you already know about bits and bytes, then ignore them. We shall concentrate first, in this chapter, on character sets and some International issues; this is continued in the next chapter, in which we are more specific about the issues of Chapter 2.

3.2. CHARACTER SETS

One of the most important features required for Localization is the computer's or the operating system's ability to represent characters, particularly those that occur in the non-American languages and that do not appear in American English.

Different systems and different computers approach this issue differently in the detail, but they all appear to use the same basic ideas. They all provide the user or the software developer a choice of character sets or code sets.[1]

One way or another, the user chooses a character set. The character set may be provided by the computer manufacturer and selected by the medium of the oper-

---

[1]Each character has both a numerical value and a character representation, depending on how you want to use it. The traditional sorting method in U.S. programs was to sort by numerical value, but as we have seen, this is no longer adequate.

ating system. The character set should contain all the characters and their glyph representations that are needed.

With the exception of WordPerfect character sets, it is customary to display character sets in the form of a 16-by-16 matrix or table. The columns are in increasing order from left to right. Each character is assigned a location within the table. This location or address is its numerical equivalent or codepoint. Addresses start at 000 in the upper left cell and increase along each vertical column in groups of 16 to the largest address of 255 in the lower right cell.

The addresses are often stated in hexadecimal, too; for example, the first two columns, on the left, cover the range 000 to 01F. (These particular addresses have often been reserved for characters that control printers, in the sense that one character may instruct the printer to start a new line and another may instruct the "carriage" to "return" as if in a typewriter.) When you see a range of addresses stated in numbers that include an "H," those addresses are in hexadecimal format. An example is 20H through 7FH; this range omits the first two columns of characters (addresses 000 through 01FH) and pertains to the next six.

A 7-bit code covers the first eight columns, the range 000 through 127 or 000 through 07F. An 8-bit code uses all 16 columns, 000 through 255 or 000 through 0FF.

3.2.1. WordPerfect 5.1[2]

While WordPerfect 5.1 runs in a DOS environment, it manages character sets in its own way. Presumably this is because at the time that WordPerfect was under development, DOS had not initiated its own International character sets and a method of switching them, so it was inadequate for the tasks and goals that the developers had in mind. Also WordPerfect continues to be ahead of DOS; it contains over 1,500 characters and, depending on your printer, you can print some, or all, of these characters.

If your printer cannot print graphics, then it must have a font that contains the character you want to print.

According to the WordPerfect Developers' Guide, there are 13 character sets available to users (within the sets, individual characters are numbered starting with count 000):

---

[2]Our rationale for mentioning WordPerfect 5.1 is that it is a very popular word processor with extensive capabilities for foreign languages. Many people use it without bothering with DOS or Windows. There is another word processor available that handles even more languages; it is Multi-Lingual Scholar, by Gamma Productions Inc. of Santa Monica, CA. According to Birrell Walsh in *Micro Times,* 17 February 1992, Multi-Lingual Scholar handles right-to-left languages and presently available are such languages as Bengali, Burmese, Devangari, Gujarati, Nepali, Pushtu, and so on. From third-party vendors you can get Amharic, Syriac, Aramaic, Phoenician, and even Ugaritic. Because you can design fonts with a packaged utility called Font Scholar, sophisticated users make new languages available. Version 4 has spell checkers for the more common languages, snaking and multiple columns. In our point of view, this word processor seems to be designed for the academic world and not the commercial world. Accordingly, while the descriptions are impressive, we won't say anything more about it. *Multilingual Computing Magazine and Buyer's Guide,* Vol. IV, issue 1, contains descriptions of other exotic word processors.

Set	Name and Number of Characters (starting at 000)
0	ASCII (to 126)[3]
1	Multinational 1 (to 233)
2	Multinational 2 (to 27)
3	Box Drawing (to 87)
4	Typographic Symbols (to 84)
5	Iconic Symbols (to 34)
6	Mathematic/Scientific (to 234)
7	Mathematic/Scientific Extension (to 228)
8	Greek (to 226)
9	Hebrew (to 43)
10	Cyrillic (to 147)
11	Hiragana and Katakana (to 184)
12	user-defined—made up of user-chosen characters from the others

You can insert any one of these characters in a document with the ***Compose*** command. Press ***Compose,*** type the character set number, comma, then the number of the character within the set.

You cannot export these characters directly to DOS, even though that is the operating system. DOS itself (see Section 3.2.2) will recognize only 256 characters, although the active code page specifies what character appears for what code. Figure 3–1 shows the Multinational and Cyrillic sets (1 and 10). Appendix H shows all 13. The sets are in the form of tables of various sizes; the addresses increase by row and are in decimal format.

3.2.2. DOS[4]

International character sets were introduced to DOS with the advent of DOS 3.0. There was a substantial advance with version 3.3.

As of DOS 5.0, six character sets are available. They are called code pages:

437	U.S. English
850	Multilingual (Latin 1) Introduced in DOS 3.0
852	Slavic (Latin 2) Introduced in DOS 5.0
860	Portugal Introduced in DOS 3.3
863	Canadian-French Introduced in DOS 3.3
865	Nordic Introduced in DOS 3.3

Figure 3–2 shows pages 437 and 850, and Appendix I shows all six.

One, code page 437, comes with the hardware in the United States. You must *prepare* your configuration for each of the others by invoking *National Language*

---

[3]While the reference material in the WordPerfect Developers' Guide clearly shows 126, this might be 127.

[4]There are different manufacturers of DOS: Microsoft produces MS-DOS, Digital Research produces DR DOS, and IBM produces PC-DOS. MS-DOS has six code pages.

0	1	2	3	4	5	6	7	8	9	0	1	2	3	4	5	6	7	8	9	0	1	2	3	4	5	6	7	8	9
`	.	~	^	_	/	´	¨	˝	ʼ	ʻ	,	.	·	·	ˮ		ˇ	˘	_	˜	ß	ĳ	ŋ	Á	á	Â	â		
Ä	ä	À	à	Å	å	Æ	æ	Ç	ç	É	é	Ê	ê	Ë	ë	È	è	Í	í	Î	î	Ï	ï	Ì	ì	Ñ	ñ	Ó	ó
Ô	ô	Ö	ö	Ò	ò	Ú	ú	Û	û	Ü	ü	Ù	ù	Ÿ	ÿ	Ã	ã	Đ	đ	Ø	ø	Õ	õ	Ý	ý	Ð	ð	Þ	þ
Ă	ă	Ā	ā	Ą	ą	Ć	ć	Č	č	Ĉ	ĉ	Ċ	ċ	Ď	ď	Ě	ě	Ė	ė	Ē	ē	Ę	ę	Ǵ	ǵ	Ğ	ğ	Ǧ	ǧ
Ģ	ģ	Ĝ	ĝ	Ġ	ġ	Ĥ	ĥ	Ħ	ħ	İ	ı	Ī	ī	Į	į	Ĩ	ĩ	Ĳ	ĳ	Ĵ	ĵ	Ķ	ķ	Ĺ	ĺ	Ľ	ľ	Ļ	ļ
Ŀ	ŀ	Ł	ł	Ń	ń	Ň	ň	Ŋ	ŋ	Ő	ő	Ō	ō	Œ	œ	Ŕ	ŕ	Ř	ř	Ŗ	ŗ	Ś	ś	Š	š	Ş	ş		
Ŝ	ŝ	Ť	ť	Ţ	ţ	Ŧ	ŧ	Ŭ	ŭ	Ů	ů	Ű	ű	Ū	ū	Ų	ų	Ů	ů	Ũ	ũ	Ŵ	ŵ	Ŷ	ŷ	Ź	ź	Ž	ž
Ŋ	ŋ	Đ	đ	Ļ	ļ	Ī	ī	Ñ	ñ	Ŕ	ŕ	Š	š	Ŧ	ŧ	Ě	ě	Ŷ	ŷ	Ỳ	ỳ	Ɗ	ɗ	Ơ	ơ	Ư	ư		
0	1	2	3	4	5	6	7	8	9	0	1	2	3	4	5	6	7	8	9	0	1	2	3	4	5	6	7	8	9

0	1	2	3	4	5	6	7	8	9	0	1	2	3	4	5	6	7	8	9	0	1	2	3	4	5	6	7	8	9
А	а	Б	б	В	в	Г	г	Д	д	Е	е	Ё	ё	Ж	ж	З	з	И	и	Й	й	К	к	Л	л	М	м	Н	н
О	о	П	п	Р	р	С	с	Т	т	У	у	Ф	ф	Х	х	Ц	ц	Ч	ч	Ш	ш	Щ	щ	Ъ	ъ	Ы	ы	Ь	ь
Э	э	Ю	ю	Я	я	Ґ	ґ	Ђ	ђ	Ѓ	ѓ	Є	є	Ѕ	ѕ	І	і	Ї	ї	Ј	ј	Љ	љ	Њ	њ	Ћ	ћ	Ќ	ќ
Ў	ў	Џ	џ	Ѣ	ѣ	Ѳ	ѳ	Ѵ	ѵ	Ҳ	ҳ	Ӡ	ӡ	Ш̩	ш̩	Ҥ	ҥ	А̄	а̄	Á	á	Е́	е́	Й̄	й̄	О́	о́	Ý	ý
Ы́	ы́	Э́	э́	Ю́	ю́	Я́	я́	А̀	а̀	Ѐ	ѐ	Ё̀	ё̀	Й̀	й̀	О̀	о̀	У̀	у̀	Ы̀	ы̀	Э̀	э̀	Ю̀	ю̀	Я̀	я̀	´	`
0	1	2	3	4	5	6	7	8	9	0	1	2	3	4	5	6	7	8	9	0	1	2	3	4	5	6	7	8	9

Figure 3–1. WordPerfect 5.1 Character Sets: (1) Multinational 1 (above) and (10) Cyrillic (below)

Support (NLS). From DOS 3.3 on, applications had access to DOS functions for switching code pages.

All code pages contain 256 characters and the first 128 of all are identical.[5] In these lower 128, you will see that the difference in numerical value between uppercase letters and their lowercase counterparts is 32. It is possible in this limited range to convert from upper- to lowercase and vice versa by adding or subtracting the value 32, treating the character code as a number for that purpose. This has been known to be done but is not recommended. It is better to use a lookup table of some form.

3.2.3. Windows 3.0/3.1[6]

Windows 3.0/3.1 runs on top of DOS, but does not use the DOS character sets. It refers to them as OEM. ANSI is the name of the character set used internally by

---

[5] Volume 2 of IBM's *National Language Information and Design Guide. National Language Support Reference Manual* lists 34 code pages in the IBM world, including the ones shown here. We don't know where they are all used.

[6] Windows 3.0 is available in Localized form for Chinese, Danish, Dutch, Finnish, French, German, Hanguel, Italian, Japanese, Norwegian, Portuguese, Spanish, and Swedish. Microsoft Corporation has also scheduled Arabic, Czech, Hebrew, Hungarian, Russian, Thai, Bahasa Malaysian, Bahasa Indonesian, and Polish with the advent of Windows 3.1.

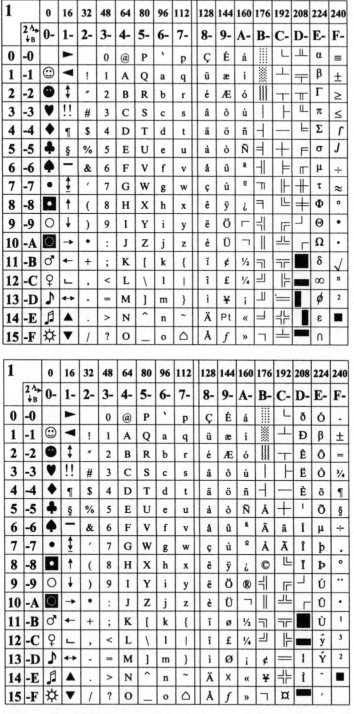

Figure 3–2. DOS Code Pages: 437—U.S. English (above) and 850—Multilingual (Latin 1) (below)

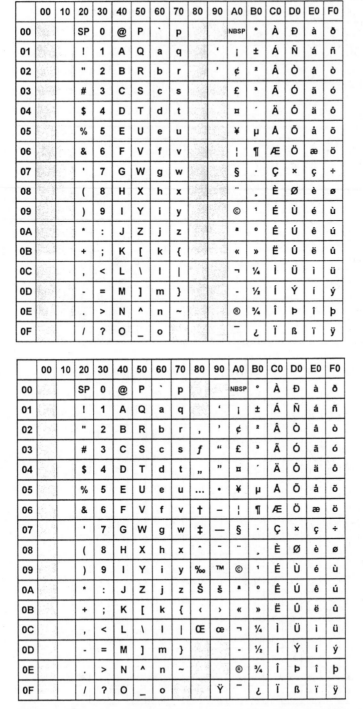

Figure 3–3. Windows 3.0 (above) and 3.1 (below) ANSI Character Sets. ANSI Character Sets © 1985–1992 Microsoft Corporation. Reprinted with permission.

Windows. When Windows is first installed, the Windows Setup program looks at the DOS-installed character set and then installs the correct ANSI-OEM translation tables and Windows OEM fonts for use in the Windows DOS box. There is an ANSI version for Windows 3.0 and a similar one for Windows 3.1. Figure 3–3 shows the Windows 3.0/3.1 ANSI character sets.

While the authors of Windows call their character set ANSI, strictly speaking it is a superset of the ANSI standard. Nevertheless, we will call it ANSI, as does everyone we know who works with Windows.

3.2.4. BCD, BCDIC, and EBCDIC

IBM developed these codes. They are mostly of historical interest for our purposes in this book, but we include them for the sake of completeness.

BCD—Binary Coded Decimal is a 4-bit (nibble) representation of numerals for *0* through *9*. Ten of the sixteen possible codes are used. Numeral *1* is encoded as "0001" and *9* as "1001" (which of course also happens to be the binary equivalent number). A byte usually encompasses two of these codes. It is extremely accurate for accounting arithmetic.

BCDIC—Binary Coded Decimal Interchange Code was used by IBM in the past on its early mainframes, and the character set consisted of uppercase letters, numerals, punctuation and some graphic symbols.

EBCDIC—Extended Binary Coded Decimal Interchange Code was designed for use with the IBM-360/370. It was the exclusive code in use on the 370. Competitive machines also used it to reduce compatibility problems. It is an 8-bit code and similar in concept to 8-bit ASCII, but with a different collating (sorting) sequence. Figure 3–4 shows this character set.

(There is a sports car to be seen on freeways in Northern California with the personalized license plate *ASCII 27,* meaning *"Escape"* in EBCDIC!)

3.2.5. Unicode

In Unicode, all characters are 16 bits wide. With 16 bits, it is possible to encode 65,536 different characters, and Unicode contains all characters that are used in text interchange. It uses 34,000 places for most of the characters needed in all writing systems, another 6,500 are reserved, leaving another 25,000 for expansion. At present, the major source of information about Unicode is the Unicode Consortium's *The Unicode Standard,* published by Addison-Wesley, 1991.

This book doesn't have room to portray all 34,000 characters. Suffice to say that many software manufacturers in many platforms see implementing this standard as a goal. We have more to say about it and ISO 10646, with which it has merged, in Chapter 7.

3.2.6. Character Set to Character Set

The introduction of these character sets (and there are more in UNIX and on the Macintosh) raises another issue that some software applications must address. What happens when you take a file constructed in one environment to another

CODE TRANSLATION TABLE ⑨

Dec.	Hex	Instruction (RR)	BCDIC	EBCDIC(1)	ASCII	7-Track Tape BCDIC(2)	Card Code EBCDIC	Binary
0	00			NUL	NUL		12-0-1-8-9	0000 0000
1	01			SOH	SOH		12-1-9	0000 0001
2	02			STX	STX		12-2-9	0000 0010
3	03			ETX	ETX		12-3-9	0000 0011
4	04	S PM		PF	EOT		12-4-9	0000 0100
5	05	BALR		HT	ENQ		12-5-9	0000 0101
6	06	BCTR		LC	ACK		12-6-9	0000 0110
7	07	BCR		DEL	BEL		12-7-9	0000 0111
8	08	SSK		GE	BS		12-8-9	0000 1000
9	09	ISK		RLF	HT		12-1-8-9	0000 1001
10	0A	SVC		SMM	LF		12-2-8-9	0000 1010
11	0B			VT	VT		12-3-8-9	0000 1011
12	0C			FF	FF		12-4-8-9	0000 1100
13	0D			CR	CR		12-5-8-9	0000 1101
14	0E	MVCL		SO	SO		12-6-8-9	0000 1110
15	0F	CLCL		SI	SI		12-7-8-9	0000 1111
16	10	LPR		DLE	DLE		12-11-1-8-9	0001 0000
17	11	LNR		DC1	DC1		11-1-9	0001 0001
18	12	LTR		DC2	DC2		11-2-9	0001 0010
19	13	LCR		TM	DC3		11-3-9	0001 0011
20	14	NR		RES	DC4		11-4-9	0001 0100
21	15	CLR		NL	NAK		11-5-9	0001 0101
22	16	OR		BS	SYN		11-6-9	0001 0110
23	17	XR		IL	ETB		11-7-9	0001 0111
24	18	LR		CAN	CAN		11-8-9	0001 1000
25	19	CR		EM	EM		11-1-8-9	0001 1001
26	1A	AR		CC	SUB		11-2-8-9	0001 1010
27	1B	SR		CU1	ESC		11-3-8-9	0001 1011
28	1C	MR		IFS	FS		11-4-8-9	0001 1100
29	1D	DR		IGS	GS		11-5-8-9	0001 1101
30	1E	ALR		IRS	RS		11-6-8-9	0001 1110
31	1F	SLR		IUS	US		11-7-8-9	0001 1111
32	20	LPDR		DS	SP		11-0-1-8-9	0010 0000
33	21	LNDR		SOS	! !		0-1-9	0010 0001
34	22	LTDR		FS	"		0-2-9	0010 0010
35	23	LCDR			#		0-3-9	0010 0011
36	24	HDR		BYP	$		0-4-9	0010 0100
37	25	LRDR		LF	%		0-5-9	0010 0101
38	26	MXR		ETB	&		0-6-9	0010 0110
39	27	MXDR		ESC	'		0-7-9	0010 0111
40	28	LDR			(		0-8-9	0010 1000
41	29	CDR			)		0-1-8-9	0010 1001
42	2A	ADR		SM	*		0-2-8-9	0010 1010
43	2B	SDR		CU2	+		0-3-8-9	0010 1011
44	2C	MDR			,		0-4-8-9	0010 1100
45	2D	DDR		ENQ	-		0-5-8-9	0010 1101
46	2E	AWR		ACK	.		0-6-8-9	0010 1110
47	2F	SWR		BEL	/		0-7-8-9	0010 1111
48	30	LPER			0		12-11-0-1-8-9	0011 0000
49	31	LNER			1		1-9	0011 0001
50	32	LTER		SYN	2		2-9	0011 0010
51	33	LCER			3		3-9	0011 0011
52	34	HER		PN	4		4-9	0011 0100
53	35	LRER		RS	5		5-9	0011 0101
54	36	AXR		UC	6		6-9	0011 0110
55	37	SXR		EOT	7		7-9	0011 0111
56	38	LER			8		8-9	0011 1000
57	39	CER			9		1-8-9	0011 1001
58	3A	AER			:		2-8-9	0011 1010
59	3B	SER		CU3	;		3-8-9	0011 1011
60	3C	MER		DC4	<		4-8-9	0011 1100
61	3D	DER		NAK	=		5-8-9	0011 1101
62	3E	AUR			>		6-8-9	0011 1110
63	3F	SUR		SUB	?		7-8-9	0011 1111

CODE TRANSLATION TABLE (Contd) ⑩

Dec.	Hex	Instruction (RX)	BCDIC	EBCDIC(1)	EBCDIC(1)	ASCII	7-Track Tape BCDIC(2)	Card Code EBCDIC	Binary
64	40	STH		Sp	Sp	@	(3)	no punches	0100 0000
65	41	LA				A		12-0-1-9	0100 0001
66	42	STC				B		12-0-2-9	0100 0010
67	43	IC				C		12-0-3-9	0100 0011
68	44	EX				D		12-0-4-9	0100 0100
69	45	BAL				E		12-0-5-9	0100 0101
70	46	BCT				F		12-0-6-9	0100 0110
71	47	BC				G		12-0-7-9	0100 0111
72	48	LH				H		12-0-8-9	0100 1000
73	49	CH				I		12-1-8	0100 1001
74	4A	AH		¢	¢	J		12-2-8	0100 1010
75	4B	SH	.	.	.	K	B A 8 2 1	12-3-8	0100 1011
76	4C	MH	⌑)	<	<	L		12-4-8	0100 1100
77	4D		[	(	(	M		12-5-8	0100 1101
78	4E	CVD	<	+	+	N	B A 8 4 2	12-6-8	0100 1110
79	4F	CVB	≠	|	|	O	B A 8 4 2 1	12-7-8	0100 1111
80	50	ST	& +	&	&	P	B A	12	0101 0000
81	51					Q		12-11-1-9	0101 0001
82	52					R		12-11-2-9	0101 0010
83	53					S		12-11-3-9	0101 0011
84	54	N				T		12-11-4-9	0101 0100
85	55	CL				U		12-11-5-9	0101 0101
86	56	O				V		12-11-6-9	0101 0110
87	57	X				W		12-11-7-9	0101 0111
88	58	L				X		12-11-8-9	0101 1000
89	59	C				Y		11-1-8	0101 1001
90	5A	A		!	!	Z		11-2-8	0101 1010
91	5B	S	$	$	$	[	B 8 2 1	11-3-8	0101 1011
92	5C	M	•	*	*	\	B 8 4	11-4-8	0101 1100
93	5D	D	]	)	)	]	B 8 4 1	11-5-8	0101 1101
94	5E	AL	;	¬	¬	^	B 8 4 2	11-6-8	0101 1110
95	5F	SL	Δ	¬	¬	_	B 8 4 2 1	11-7-8	0101 1111
96	60	STD	-	-	-	`	B	11	0110 0000
97	61		/	/	/	a	A 1	0-1	0110 0001
98	62					b		11-0-2-9	0110 0010
99	63					c		11-0-3-9	0110 0011
100	64					d		11-0-4-9	0110 0100
101	65					e		11-0-5-9	0110 0101
102	66					f		11-0-6-9	0110 0110
103	67	MXD				g		11-0-7-9	0110 0111
104	68	LD				h		11-0-8-9	0110 1000
105	69	CD				i		0-1-8	0110 1001
106	6A	AD		¦	¦	j		12-11	0110 1010
107	6B	SD	,	,	,	k	A 8 2 1	0-3-8	0110 1011
108	6C	MD	% (	%	%	l	A 8 4	0-4-8	0110 1100
109	6D	DD	γ	_	_	m	A 8 4 1	0-5-8	0110 1101
110	6E	AW	\	>	>	n	A 8 4 2	0-6-8	0110 1110
111	6F	SW	⚹	?	?	o	A 8 4 2 1	0-7-8	0110 1111
112	70	STE				p		12-11-0	0111 0000
113	71					q		12-11-0-1-9	0111 0001
114	72					r		12-11-0-2-9	0111 0010
115	73					s		12-11-0-3-9	0111 0011
116	74					t		12-11-0-4-9	0111 0100
117	75					u		12-11-0-5-9	0111 0101
118	76					v		12-11-0-6-9	0111 0110
119	77					w		12-11-0-7-9	0111 0111
120	78	LE				x		12-11-0-8-9	0111 1000
121	79	CE		`	`	y		1-8	0111 1001
122	7A	AE	⌀	:	:	z	A	2-8	0111 1010
123	7B	SE	# •	#	#	{	8 2 1	3-8	0111 1011
124	7C	ME	@ '	@	@	|	8 4	4-8	0111 1100
125	7D	DE	:	'	'	}	8 4 1	5-8	0111 1101
126	7E	AU	>	=	=	~	8 4 2	6-8	0111 1110
127	7F	SU	√	"	"	DEL	8 4 2 1	7-8	0111 1111

1. Two columns of EBCDIC graphics are shown. The first gives IBM standard U.S. bit pattern assignments. The second shows the T-11 and TN text printing chains (120 graphics).
2. Add C (check bit) for odd or even parity as needed, except as noted.
3. For even parity use CA.

TWO-CHARACTER BSC DATA LINK CONTROLS

Function	EBCDIC	ASCII
ACK-0	DLE,X'70'	DLE,0
ACK-1	DLE,X'61'	DLE,1
WACK	DLE,X'6B'	DLE, ;
RVI	DLE,X'7C'	DLE,<

Figure 3–4. IBM EBCDIC Character Set

CODE TRANSLATION TABLE (Contd) ⑪

Dec.	Hex	Instruction and Format	Graphics and Controls BCDIC EBCDIC(1) ASCII			7-Track Tape BCDIC(2)	Card Code EBCDIC	Binary
128	80	SSM -S					12-0-1-8	1000 0000
129	81			a	a		12-0-1	1000 0001
130	82	LPSW -S		b	b		12-0-2	1000 0010
131	83	Diagnose		c	c		12-0-3	1000 0011
132	84	WRD		d	d		12-0-4	1000 0100
133	85	RDD ⎱SI		e	e		12-0-5	1000 0101
134	86	BXH		f	f		12-0-6	1000 0110
135	87	BXLE		g	g		12-0-7	1000 0111
136	88	SRL		h	h		12-0-8	1000 1000
137	89	SLL		i	i		12-0-9	1000 1001
138	8A	SRA					12-0-2-8	1000 1010
139	8B	SLA ⎱RS		{			12-0-3-8	1000 1011
140	8C	SRDL		≤			12-0-4-8	1000 1100
141	8D	SLDL		(			12-0-5-8	1000 1101
142	8E	SRDA		+			12-0-6-8	1000 1110
143	8F	SLDA		+			12-0-7-8	1000 1111
144	90	STM					12-11	1001 0000
145	91	TM		j	j		12-11-1	1001 0001
146	92	MVI ⎱SI		k	k		12-11-2	1001 0010
147	93	TS -S		l	l		12-11-3	1001 0011
148	94	NI		m	m		12-11-4	1001 0100
149	95	CLI		n	n		12-11-5	1001 0101
150	96	OI ⎱SI		o	o		12-11-6	1001 0110
151	97	XI		p	p		12-11-7	1001 0111
152	98	LM -RS		q	q		12-11-8	1001 1000
153	99			r	r		12-11-9	1001 1001
154	9A						12-11-2-8	1001 1010
155	9B			}			12-11-3-8	1001 1011
156	9C	SIO, SIOF		□			12-11-4-8	1001 1100
157	9D	TIO, CLRIO ⎱S		)			12-11-5-8	1001 1101
158	9E	HIO, HDV		±			12-11-6-8	1001 1110
159	9F	TCH		■			12-11-7-8	1001 1111
160	A0			⁻			11-0-1-8	1010 0000
161	A1			~	°		11-0-1	1010 0001
162	A2			s	s		11-0-2	1010 0010
163	A3			t	t		11-0-3	1010 0011
164	A4			u	u		11-0-4	1010 0100
165	A5			v	v		11-0-5	1010 0101
166	A6			w	w		11-0-6	1010 0110
167	A7			x	x		11-0-7	1010 0111
168	A8			y	y		11-0-8	1010 1000
169	A9			z	z		11-0-9	1010 1001
170	AA						11-0-2-8	1010 1010
171	AB			∟			11-0-3-8	1010 1011
172	AC	STNSM		┌			11-0-4-8	1010 1100
173	AD	STOSM ⎱SI		[			11-0-5-8	1010 1101
174	AE	SIGP -RS		≥			11-0-6-8	1010 1110
175	AF	MC -SI		●			11-0-7-8	1010 1111
176	B0			0			12-11-0-1-8	1011 0000
177	B1	LRA -RX		1			12-11-0-1	1011 0001
178	B2	See below		2			12-11-0-2	1011 0010
179	B3			3			12-11-0-3	1011 0011
180	B4			4			12-11-0-4	1011 0100
181	B5			5			12-11-0-5	1011 0101
182	B6	STCTL ⎱RS		6			12-11-0-6	1011 0110
183	B7	LCTL		7			12-11-0-7	1011 0111
184	B8			8			12-11-0-8	1011 1000
185	B9			9			12-11-0-9	1011 1001
186	BA	CS ⎱RS					12-11-0-2-8	1011 1010
187	BB	CDS		⌐			12-11-0-3-8	1011 1011
188	BC			¬			12-11-0-4-8	1011 1100
189	BD	CLM		]			12-11-0-5-8	1011 1101
190	BE	STCM ⎱RS		≠			12-11-0-6-8	1011 1110
191	BF	ICM		—			12-11-0-7-8	1011 1111

Op code (S format)

B202 - STIDP	B207 - STCKC	B20D - PTLB
B203 - STIDC	B208 - SPT	B210 - SPX
B204 - SCK	B209 - STPT	B211 - STPX
B205 - STCK	B20A - SPKA	B212 - STAP
B206 - SCKC	B20B - IPK	B213 - RRB

CODE TRANSLATION TABLE (Contd) ⑫

Dec.	Hex	Instruction (SS)	Graphics and Controls BCDIC EBCDIC(1) ASCII			7-Track Tape BCDIC(2)	Card Code EBCDIC	Binary
192	C0		?	{		B A 8 2	12-0	1100 0000
193	C1		A	A	A	B A 1	12-1	1100 0001
194	C2		B	B	B	B A 2	12-2	1100 0010
195	C3		C	C	C	B A 21	12-3	1100 0011
196	C4		D	D	D	B A 4	12-4	1100 0100
197	C5		E	E	E	B A 4 1	12-5	1100 0101
198	C6		F	F	F	B A 42	12-6	1100 0110
199	C7		G	G	G	B A 421	12-7	1100 0111
200	C8		H	H	H	B A 8	12-8	1100 1000
201	C9		I	I	I	B A 8 1	12-9	1100 1001
202	CA						12-0-2-8-9	1100 1010
203	CB						12-0-3-8-9	1100 1011
204	CC			ʃ			12-0-4-8-9	1100 1100
205	CD						12-0-5-8-9	1100 1101
206	CE			ɥ			12-0-6-8-9	1100 1110
207	CF						12-0-7-8-9	1100 1111
208	D0		!	}		B 8 2	11-0	1101 0000
209	D1	MVN	J	J	J	B 1	11-1	1101 0001
210	D2	MVC	K	K	K	B 2	11-2	1101 0010
211	D3	MVZ	L	L	L	B 21	11-3	1101 0011
212	D4	NC	M	M	M	B 4	11-4	1101 0100
213	D5	CLC	N	N	N	B 4 1	11-5	1101 0101
214	D6	OC	O	O	O	B 42	11-6	1101 0110
215	D7	XC	P	P	P	B 421	11-7	1101 0111
216	D8		Q	Q	Q	B 8	11-8	1101 1000
217	D9		R	R	R	B 8 1	11-9	1101 1001
218	DA						12-11-2-8-9	1101 1010
219	DB						12-11-3-8-9	1101 1011
220	DC	TR					12-11-4-8-9	1101 1100
221	DD	TRT					12-11-5-8-9	1101 1101
222	DE	ED					12-11-6-8-9	1101 1110
223	DF	EDMK					12-11-7-8-9	1101 1111
224	E0		‡	\		A 8 2	0-2-8	1110 0000
225	E1						11-0-1-9	1110 0001
226	E2		S	S	S	A 2	0-2	1110 0010
227	E3		T	T	T	A 21	0-3	1110 0011
228	E4		U	U	U	A 4	0-4	1110 0100
229	E5		V	V	V	A 4 1	0-5	1110 0101
230	E6		W	W	W	A 42	0-6	1110 0110
231	E7		X	X	X	A 421	0-7	1110 0111
232	E8		Y	Y	Y	A 8	0-8	1110 1000
233	E9		Z	Z	Z	A 8 1	0-9	1110 1001
234	EA						11-0-2-8-9	1110 1010
235	EB						11-0-3-8-9	1110 1011
236	EC			⌐			11-0-4-8-9	1110 1100
237	ED						11-0-5-8-9	1110 1101
238	EE						11-0-6-8-9	1110 1110
239	EF						11-0-7-8-9	1110 1111
240	F0	SRP	0	0	0	8 2	0	1111 0000
241	F1	MVO	1	1	1	1	1	1111 0001
242	F2	PACK	2	2	2	2	2	1111 0010
243	F3	UNPK	3	3	3	21	3	1111 0011
244	F4		4	4	4	4	4	1111 0100
245	F5		5	5	5	4 1	5	1111 0101
246	F6		6	6	6	42	6	1111 0110
247	F7		7	7	7	421	7	1111 0111
248	F8	ZAP	8	8	8	8	8	1111 1000
249	F9	CP	9	9	9	8 1	9	1111 1001
250	FA	AP					12-11-0-2-8-9	1111 1010
251	FB	SP					12-11-0-3-8-9	1111 1011
252	FC	MP					12-11-0-4-8-9	1111 1100
253	FD	DP					12-11-0-5-8-9	1111 1101
254	FE						12-11-0-6-8-9	1111 1110
255	FF			EO			12-11-0-7-8-9	1111 1111

ANSI-DEFINED PRINTER CONTROL CHARACTERS (A in RECFM field of DCB)	
Code	Action before printing record
blank	Space 1 line
0	Space 2 lines
-	Space 3 lines
+	Suppress space
1	Skip to line 1 on new page

Figure 3–4. (Continued)

environment? What happens is predictable, but not necessarily desired. To illustrate just using examples within DOS, suppose you have entered the character α in code page 437.

Its numerical equivalent is *224* (starting counting at zero). In the other code pages, 224 is the numerical equivalent of the following characters:

Code page	Character
850	Ó
852	Ó
860	α
863	α
865	α

In other words, even in the DOS family, there are two different characters for the one numerical equivalent. Going outside the DOS family, with the same numerical equivalent, to ANSI, we get à.

What this means is that if your application *imports* files from another application or another environment, you may have to *translate* or *map* the characters in one way or another. The same goes for *exporting*.

When you are importing a file from WordPerfect, an application that has over 1,500 characters, into DOS, an environment that has only 256 characters, then you have to make a choice on how to *map* the WordPerfect character set into DOS code pages as the basis for your translation. One thing you can do to start with is to follow the procedure that the WordPerfect program itself does when it exports a file into another more limited format.

This same issue arises when you communicate with another computer. In the old days, for PC to mainframe, this was a well recognized (7-bit) ASCII to EBCDIC conversion and vice versa. Its scope has been considerably enlarged because there are now so many character sets. But there are many tools now as well. It is trivial to exchange documents from the IBM PC in DOS format with Macintosh formats using Apple's *Apple File Exchange*.

3.3. INTERNATIONAL CONSIDERATIONS

3.3.1. WordPerfect 5.1

We present WordPerfect as an example of how a word processor application has been Internationalized. In WordPerfect 5.1 you can insert any one of the characters from the character sets described in Section 3.2.1 into a document with the **Compose** command. (As we described, just press **Compose,** type the character set number, comma, then the number of the character within the set.) It provides support for users in another locale who want to use a word processor.

WordPerfect supplies Language Modules that allow you to write multilingual documents. Each language module contains a spell checker, thesaurus, and hyphenation and keyboard files for a specific language. This means that you can change languages on the fly. Modules are available in DOS and in Windows, on the Macintosh, VAX, Data General, and UNIX. Languages include Afrikaans, Arabic, Catalan, Danish, Dutch, three varieties of English, Finnish, Canadian French, French, Galician, German, Swiss German, Greek, Hebrew, Icelandic, Italian, Norwegian, Brazilian and Portuguese Portuguese, Russian, Spanish, and Swedish. Input for Arabic and Hebrew can be right to left.

Of course, in all cases, you need to verify that your peripherals—printers in particular—can handle all the individual characters.

3.3.2. DOS

You choose date, time, currency formats, and sort order with the country command in the CONFIG.SYS file. You choose character sets either with the **CHCP** command or the mode select command. However, you must prepare for varying code pages with the **mode** command in the AUTOEXEC.BAT file. One code page (usually 437) is in the ROM/BIOS and the others must be *prepared*.

To prepare your computer, you make certain additions to your AUTOEXEC.BAT and CONFIG.SYS *files:*

Add to **autoexec.bat**

nlsfunc c:\dos\country.sys

mode console code page prepare=({list of code pages to be prepared}) {path of CPI file}

For example,

mode con cp prepare=((850 852 860 863 865)c:\dos\ega.cpi[7])

Keyb{country}, {code page}, {path of KEYBOARD.SYS}

Select a code page *either* with the **mode** DOS command:

mode con cp sel={code page number}

For example,

mode con cp sel=850

or with the **chcp** DOS command:

chcp {code page number}

For example,

chcp 850

For LCD, use graftabl {code page number} if you have problems displaying

---

[7]**ega.cpi** also handles **vga.** Certain abbreviations such as *con* for *console, cp* for *code page,* and *sel* for *select* are allowed. The examples also assume that all the programs are in the directory *c:\dos.*

extended characters. For example,

graftabl 850

Choose a keyboard layout with the ***keyb*** command. For example:

keyb sp, 437, c:\dos\keyboard.sys

This chooses a Spanish keyboard from code page 437. Under this arrangement, you can change back to an American keyboard on the fly using ***ctrl-alt-F1*** and back to Spanish with ***ctrl-alt-F2.***

An IBM parallel printer (4201, 4208, and 5202) on port LPT# can also be prepared using the ***mode*** command:

mode LPT# code page=({list of code pages to be prepared}) {path of CPI file}

Add to ***CONFIG.SYS***

For LCD

country={country code}, {related code page},{path of COUNTRY.SYS file}

device={path of DISPLAY.SYS} CON:=(LCD)

For EGA/VGA

country={country code}, {related code page},{path of COUNTRY.SYS file}

Device={path of DISPLAY.SYS} CON:=({Video Type},,nn)

where   Video Type=EGA (It also supports VGA)
         nn=number of additional (to 437) code pages to reserve space for

TABLE 3–1   Countries and Languages—Recommended Code Pages

Country or Language	Country Code	Recommended and Valid Code Pages	Keyb Code
Australia	061	437, 850	us (or default blank)
Belgium	032	850, 437	be
Canada (French	002	863, 850	cf
Denmark	045	850, 865	dk
Finland	358	850, 437	su
France	033	850, 437	fr
Germany	049	850, 437	gr
Italy	039	850, 437	it
Latin America	003	850, 437	la
Netherlands	031	850, 437	nl
Norway	047	850, 865	no
Portugal	351	850, 860	po
Spain	034	850, 437	sp
Switzerland	041	850, 437	sf,
United Kingdom	044	437, 850	uk
United States	001	437, 850	us (or default blank)

Country code controls the date and time formats for DOS. Table 3–1 shows the recommended code pages and keyb codes for countries using Western European languages.

You select a code page from the prepared set at any time, once the computer has been booted with the CONFIG.SYS statements and AUTOEXEC.BAT file using either:

Mode CON cp select=*cp* (for the specific device CON)

or the *chcp* command (for all devices):

chcp *cp*

For LCD, use graftabl *cp*

Country code also implies a sorting order; see Table 3–2 for the results of sorting the words of Section 2.2.4 according to different country codes and code pages in MS-DOS 5.0.[8] This version of DOS does not address all issues. In the Spanish sort *ll*, for example, is in the wrong order, coming at the same location as it would in English, and the same is true for *ch*. The German sort seems appropriate for *β* and *ü*. The French sorts separate some of the uppercase accented vowels from their lowercase and unaccented counterparts, which is not correct.

In DOS, the COUNTRY.SYS command identifies the date, time, collating sequence, capitalization, folding format, currency symbol, and decimal separator for a particular country.[9] For instance, if you want to set the date and time format for Belgium using the 032 country code, you need to set the code page of the desired country information to 850, and set the name of the file containing country information, COUNTRY.SYS .

So, the COUNTRY.SYS command identifies:

the currency symbol (five-character ASCII string);
the currency format code (one byte) where:

- bit 0   0=symbol precedes value and 1=symbol follows value
- bit 1   0=no space between symbol and value and 1=one space between symbol and value
- bit 2   0=symbol and decimal separate and 1=symbol replaces decimal separator

DOS provides a series of *INT 21H* function calls to support these features. Also know as *interrupts,* they are procedures for low-level features. They are listed in Appendix M.

---

[8]The italicized words contain characters that are not available in the specific code page. In French French, German, and Italian, DOS sorted in the same order. All the other cases are distinctive. The difference between Canadian French and French French centers on the treatment of uppercase accented vowels.

[9]*Folding* means that uppercase and lowercase characters are sorted the same. Conversely, in *nonfolding* format, they are not sorted in the same order.

TABLE 3–2   Results of Sorting, by Country Code and Code Page, in MS-DOS 5.0

USA 001/437	CAN FR 002/863	FR FR 033/850	GERMAN 049/850	ITALIAN 039/850	SPANISH 034/850
a	a	a	a	a	a
A	A	À	À	À	À
à	à	A	A	A	A
abbaye	abbaye	à	à	à	à
ABBAYE	ABBAYE	abbaye	abbaye	abbaye	abbaye
âme	âme	ABBAYE	ABBAYE	ABBAYE	ABBAYE
AME	AME	âme	âme	âme	âme
améliorer	améliorer	ÂME	ÂME	ÂME	ÂME
AMÉLIORER	AMÉLIORER	AME	AME	AME	AME
AMELIORER	AMELIORER	améliorer	améliorer	améliorer	améliorer
amen	amen	AMÉLIORER	AMÉLIORER	AMÉLIORER	AMÉLIORER
AMEN	AMEN	AMELIORER	AMELIORER	AMELIORER	AMELIORER
aménager	aménager	amen	amen	amen	amen
AMÉNAGER	AMÉNAGER	AMEN	AMEN	AMEN	AMEN
AMENAGER	AMENAGER	aménager	aménager	aménager	aménager
amène	amène	AMÉNAGER	AMÉNAGER	AMÉNAGER	AMÉNAGER
AMENE	AMENE	AMENAGER	AMENAGER	AMENAGER	AMENAGER
aménité	aménité	amène	amène	amène	amène
AMÉNITÉ	AMÉNITÉ	*AMÈNE*	*AMÈNE*	*AMÈNE*	*AMÈNE*
AMENITE	AMENITE	AMENE	AMENE	AMENE	AMENE
AMÈNE	AMÈNE	aménité	aménité	aménité	aménité
ânier	ánier	AMÉNITÉ	AMÉNITÉ	AMÉNITÉ	AMÉNITÉ
ANIER	ANIER	AMENITE	AMENITE	AMENITE	AMENITE
anis	anis	ânier	ânier	ânier	ânier
ANIS	ANIS	ÂNIER	ÂNIER	ÂNIER	ANIER
außen	aussehen	ANIER	ANIER	ANIER	ÂNIER
Außendienst	aussein	anis	anis	anis	anis
außer	aussenden	ANIS	ANIS	ANIS	ANIS
äußer	aussetzen	außen	außen	außen	aussehen
aussehen	außen	Außendienst	Außendienst	Außendienst	aussein
aussein	Außendienst	außer	außer	außer	aussenden
aussenden	außer	äußer	äußer	äußer	aussetzen
aussetzen	*äußer*	aussehen	aussehen	aussehen	außen
Buße	busen	aussein	aussein	aussein	Außendienst
busen	Büste	aussenden	aussenden	aussenden	außer
büßen	Butter	aussetzen	aussetzen	aussetzen	äußer
Büste	Butzen	Buße	Buße	Buße	busen
Butter	Buße	busen	busen	busen	Büste
Butzen	büßen	büßen	büßen	büßen	Buße
caballa	caballa	Büste	Büste	Büste	büßen
cabalmente	cabalmente	Butter	Butter	Butter	Butter
caña	cantina	Butzen	Butzen	Butzen	Butzen
cantina	caracola	caballa	caballa	caballa	caballa
caracola	caracterizar	cabalmente	cabalmente	cabalmente	cabalmente
carácter	*carácter*	caña	caña	caña	cantina
caracterizar	*caña*	cantina	cantina	cantina	caña
chácara	chacarero	caracola	caracola	caracola	caracola
chacarero	*chácara*	carácter	carácter	carácter	carácter
cizalia	cizalia	caracterizar	caracterizar	caracterizar	caracterizar

TABLE 3–2 (Continued)

USA 001/437	CAN FR 002/863	FR FR 033/850	GERMAN 049/850	ITALIAN 039/850	SPANISH 034/850
cizaña	*cizaña*	chácara	chácara	chácara	chácara
clamar	clamar	chacarero	chacarero	chacarero	chacarero
curador	curador	cizalia	cizalia	cizalia	cizalia
danza	danza	cizaña	cizaña	cizaña	cizaña
ducho	ducho	clamar	clamar	clamar	clamar
ductil	ductil	curador	curador	curador	curador
dudo	dudo	danza	danza	danza	danza
Gruß	gruselig	ducho	ducho	ducho	ducho
gruselig	gruseln	ductil	ductil	ductil	ductil
gruseln	Gruß	dudo	dudo	dudo	dudo
grüßen	grüßen	Gruß	Gruß	Gruß	gruselig
gucken	gucken	gruselig	gruselig	gruselig	gruseln
gültig	gültig	gruseln	gruseln	gruseln	Gruß
Gunst	Gunst	grüßen	grüßen	grüßen	grüßen
günstig	günstig	gucken	gucken	gucken	gucken
Gurke	Gurke	gültig	gültig	gültig	gültig
Gurte	Gurte	Gunst	Gunst	Gunst	Gunst
Guß	Gut	günstig	günstig	günstig	günstig
Gut	Güte	Gurke	Gurke	Gurke	Gurke
Güte	Guß	Gurte	Gurte	Gurte	Gurte
Haß	Haspe	Guß	Guß	Guß	Guß
häßlich	Hassen	Gut	Gut	Gut	Gut
Haspe	Hast	Güte	Güte	Güte	Güte
Hassen	*hätschein*	Haß	Haß	Haß	Haspe
Hast	Haß	häßlich	häßlich	häßlich	Hassen
hätschein	*häßlich*	Haspe	Haspe	Haspe	Hast
lindo	lindo	Hassen	Hassen	Hassen	Haß
línea	linero	Hast	Hast	Hast	häßlich
linero	lino	hätschein	hätschein	hätschein	hätschein
lino	linón	lindo	lindo	lindo	lindo
linón	linotipia	línea	línea	línea	línea
linotipia	llama	linero	linero	linero	linero
llama	lleno	lino	lino	lino	lino
lleno	lunar	linón	linón	linón	linón
lunar	*línea*	linotipia	linotipia	linotipia	linotipia
macabro	macabro	llama	llama	llama	llama
ñame	nutrir	lleno	lleno	lleno	lleno
ñandu	oasis	lunar	lunar	lunar	lunar
ñaño	re-locate	macabro	macabro	macabro	macabro
ñapa	relocate	ñame	ñame	ñame	nutrir
ñudo	*ñame*	ñandu	ñandu	ñandu	ñame
nutrir	*ñandu*	ñaño	ñaño	ñaño	ñandu
oasis	*ñapa*	ñapa	ñapa	ñapa	ñaño
re-locate	*ñaño*	ñudo	ñudo	ñudo	ñapa
relocate	*ñudo*	nutrir	nutrir	nutrir	ñudo
ÂME	ÂME	oasis	oasis	oasis	oasis
ÂNIER	ÂNIER	re-locate	re-locate	re-locate	re-locate
À	À	relocate	relocate	relocate	relocate

3.3.3. Windows 3.x

As we discussed in Section 3.2.3, Windows uses an ANSI character set.

In Windows 3.x, International information is stored in the WIN.INI file and can be accessed by the application using a *GetProfileString* function or *Get-ProfileInt* function. The user can access the International settings from the International Control Panel and change the language. Applications can also monitor the WM_WININICHANGE message to verify there is no change. Charles Petzold's *Programming Windows* and Microsoft's *Windows Software Development Kit* contain more detailed information. William S Hall's article in the Nov.–Dec. 1991 issue of *Microsoft Systems Journal,* "Adapting Your Program for Worldwide Use with Windows Internationalization Support," is becoming a classic.

Figure 3–5 shows the Windows 3.0/3.1 Control Panel International Dialog Box. Effectively, it reduces the tasks of Localization to choosing date and time formats, numeric and currency formats (with thousands separators, decimal radix characters, and currency symbols chosen in sub-dialog boxes), keyboard layouts, and countries.

Windows stores the country settings in the [Intl] section of the WIN.INI file. These settings can be modified by the user via the Control Panel or by the application via the *WriteProfileString* function. Applications can access the current country settings through the *GetProfileInt* and *GetProfileString* functions. Applications should read the country settings at startup and monitor the WM_WININICHANGE message to update the settings when they are changed.

WIN.INI contains:

iCountry	A country code based on telephone country codes, except that Canada=2
sCountry	A String defining the country name.
sLanguage	National language selected by the user. These are three-character codes such as "dan," "eng," "fra," "frc," and so on.

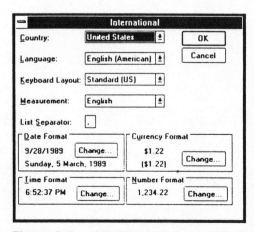

Figure 3–5. Windows 3.0/3.1 Control Panel International Dialog Box. International Dialog Box © 1985–1992 Microsoft Corporation. Reprinted with permission.

sList	List separator, which is used to separate elements in a list and is different from the decimal separator.
iMeasure	Measurement system. 0=metric and 1=English.
iTime	Time format. 0=12-hour clock and 1=24-hour clock.
sTime	Time separator—the separator between hours, minutes, and seconds.
s1159	The trailing string (such as "am," or "a.m.") that some places use with times before noon.
s2359	The trailing string (such as "pm," or "p.m.") that some places use with times after noon.
iTLZero	Indicates whether times use a leading zero or not. 0=no leading zero and 1=leading zero.
iDate	Windows 2.x code for the date format. Recommended that you use sDate. 0=mm/dd/yy, 1=dd/mm/yy, 2=yy/mm/dd.
sDate	Date separator for Windows 2.x. Use sShortDate instead.
sShortDate	Defines a picture of the date.
sLongDate	Like sShortDate with the addition of strings defining names of days of the week, months, etc.
sCurrency	Definition of the currency symbol.
iCurrency	Definition of the currency format.
iCurrDigits	Defines the number of digits used for the fractional part of a currency amount
iNegcurr	Defines the negative currency format.
sThousand	The symbol used to separate thousands.
sDecimal	Character used to separate the integer part of a number from the fractional part.
iDigits	Value defining the number of decimal digits that should be used in a number.
iLzero	Defines whether a decimal value between 1.00 and –1.00 should contain a leading zero.

In addition, Windows 3.x has a number of language-sensitive functions:

AnsiLower	*IsCharAlphaNumeric*	*AnsiNext*
AnsiLowerBuff	*IsCharLower*	*AnsiPrev*
AnsiUpper	*IsCharUpper*	
AnsiUpperBuff	*lstrcmp*	
IsCharAlpha	*lstrcmpi*	

The functions *lstrcmp* and *lstrcmpi* take the place of the C functions *strcmp* and *strcmpi* and allow applications to compare and/or sort strings based on the natural language selected by the user. The comparison done is based on a primary and a secondary value for each character. When the application compares two strings, the primary value takes precedence over the secondary value. The secondary value is ignored unless a comparison based on primary values shows the strings as equivalent. The function *lstrcmpi* ignores the effect of case in determining secondary value.

When the application compares strings of different lengths, the length takes precedence over secondary values. In other words, the shorter string will always precede the longer string as long as the primary values in the shorter string equal the primary values of the equivalent characters in the longer string.

Depending on the language module installed, some characters will be treated differently. For example, in German, the β character is expanded figuratively to *ss* and in the Spanish module, *ch* is treated as a single character between *c* and *d*.[10]

AnsiLower, AnsiLowerBuff, AnsiUpper and ***AnsiUpperBuff*** are case conversion functions that again depend on the language module installed. As indicated in Section 2.2.6, different languages need to treat case conversion differently, so you should use these functions rather than the C case conversion function which does not take into account characters with values of more than 128.

IsCharAlpha, IsCharAlphaNumeric, IsCharLower, and ***IsCharUpper*** are functions that classify characters and are also language dependent.

Other functions include ***AnsitoOEM*** and ***OEMtoAnsi*** for transferring data to and from DOS. Unfortunately, there is no one-to-one mapping between the two, so that applying these functions will not always give the same result.

In dealing with filenames, use ANSI for all filenames and use the functions ***_lcreat, _lopen*** and ***Openfile*** to deal with DOS and the OEM character set.

For the keyboard, use the ***VtKeyScan*** function to translate an ANSI character into a virtual-key code plus a shift state. Depending on the keyboard layout chosen by the user, the locations of the VK_OEM keys change. Also use this function when one application sends text to another using simulated keyboard input. ***ToAscii*** is the opposite of ***VtKeyScan. GetkeynameText*** delivers the name of a key in the language of the keyboard layout. ***GetKbCodePage*** will return the number of the DOS or OEM code page that was running at the time that Windows was installed.

You can enter OEM characters not found on your keyboard using ***Alt*** and the numeric keypad. For ANSI characters, use an initial ***0*** before the three-digit code.

See also 6.2.3.

3.4. REFERENCE MATERIAL

Each language has its own peculiarities. For more general information, we recommend the following.

Apple Computer, Inc., *Inside Macintosh, Volume VI*. Reading, MA: Addison-Wesley Publishing Company.

Apple Computer, Inc., *Guide to Macintosh Software Localization*. Reading, MA: Addison-Wesley Publishing Company, 1992.

Apple Computer, Inc., *Software Development for International Markets: A Technical Reference*. APDA Draft. Cupertino, CA: Apple Computer, Inc., 1988. A7G0016.

---

[10]We verified this independently by entering index cards into the Localized American, French, Spanish, Italian, and German versions of the Windows accessory *CardFile*. In each case, the appropriate sorting occurred.

Apple Computer, Inc., *Worldwide Software Development Overview*. Apple Computer, Inc., Cupertino, CA: 1990.

Carter, Daniel R. *Writing Localizable Software for the Macintosh*. Reading, MA: Addison-Wesley Publishing Company, 1991.

Hall, William S. "Adapt Your Program for Worldwide Use with Windows Internationalization Support," *Microsoft Systems Journal*, November–December 1991.

_____. "Internationalizing Windows Software," *Microsoft Windows 3.1 Developers Workshop*. Redmond, Washington: Microsoft Press, 1993, pp. 3–90. ISBN 1-55615-480-1.

IBM. *National Language Information and Design Guide—Volume 2. National Language Support Reference Manual*, 2nd ed. IBM Canada Ltd. Laboratory National Language Technical Center. North York, Ontario: Volume SE09-8002-01, March 1990.

Jones, Scott, Cynthia Kennelly, Claudia Mueller, Marcia Sweezy, Bill Thomas, and Velez. Lydia *Developing International User Information*. Bedford, MA: Digital Press, 1992. Digital Order No. EY-H894E-DP.

Microsoft. *Microsoft Windows International Handbook for Software Design*. Redmond, WA: Microsoft Corporation, 1990.

Taylor, Dave. *Global Software: Developing Applications for the International Market,* New York: Springer-Verlag, 1992.

Windows/DOS Developer's Journal 3, no. 1 (January 1992) had a number of articles on Internationalization.

An outstanding source for further reading about sorting is Denis Garneau's *Keys to Sort and Search for Culturally Expected Results.* On an ongoing basis, *Multilingual Computing Magazine and Buyer's Guide* promises to be an excellent technical resource.

Some of the references listed here relate to the Macintosh, but they contain general information about Internationalization and Localization as well as specific Macintosh information.

4 Specific Topics

4.1. INTRODUCTION

In this chapter we concentrate on the technical and translation issues involved with Internationalization and Localization. It is possible that a business decision may negate the need for the technical work. For example, after a manufacturer estimates the costs involved in modifying a Search and Replace function (see Section 2.2.5) to handle a few instances of a few German words that change form when hyphenated when they happen to occur at the end of a line, the manufacturer may well decide that it's not worth the effort. They would probably say it occurs so infrequently that they will "live" with not being able to handle it.

4.2. DESIGN ISSUES

Exactly simultaneous development in different languages is impossible, although software development clearly can include Internationalization of the code. Localization, however, must follow the development of the base case.

There are a number of specific design issues to consider: compile-time, link-time, or run-time; software product design; scheduling; character set to character set; and tools.

4.2.1. Compile-Time, Link-Time, or Run-Time?

With compile-time Internationalization, all changes are made in the source code. Clearly, the original programmers and engineers must be involved at this stage. They add routines that are knowledgeable about language and culture. The developers must work closely with translators and must do much more work with this approach, as they are really Localizing without Internationalizing first. Nevertheless, there is some merit in this approach and it should be considered; the vendor can distribute a complete object file to distributors with little if any performance degradation.

Large UNIX houses tend to use run-time language binding. This means that a UNIX application can speak in many locales. In this approach, the software product is multiply Localized, in that one software package contains all the various text files for more than one target locale. There is performance degradation due to the run-time penalty of having to look up information in a separate file for all data input or output and for how to format the various types of data. Data files that can be handled by such *globalized* software must probably be identified or *tagged* as to the formats used in its creation. This necessitates another layer of interpretation. The run-time approach may have an advantage in multilingual companies or in countries such as Switzerland. For more information on this type of approach, see the discussion of message catalogs in Appendix B.

Link-time Internationalization is somewhere in the middle. It assumes the existence of available libraries that can be added to the existing object to create an executable binary. Developers can distribute versions of their system that can be linked to create executables that understand the appropriate locale, but without the problems associated with distribution of the source. This is the approach we discuss next.

4.2.2. Software Product Design

Prepare to Internationalize first. You do this in the following way.

First, plan ahead for all variations in Localization. Decide how important each of the issues discussed in Chapter 2 is and how completely this software product will handle each of them. Plan on the settings of default options.

Next, support all necessary code pages, or characters sets, for all the Localizations planned.

Place text in resource files distinct from program code. The reason for this is that it reduces the work involved in subsequent Localizations.[1] It will allow translators' work to be focused on translation and not confused with engineering. Figure 4–1 portrays a schematic diagram of the breakdown of the program code and the text. There is no programming code in the text files nor is there any text in the program code.

There will be an invariant part of the software product—the program—and a variant part that changes according to what Localization is wanted. This variant part is often referred to as the resource files.

---

[1]There are commercial products available that claim to strip strings from code that already exists. For example, in "Foreign Language Pre-Processor and String Externalization Tools," *Developer's Preview, Windows/DOS Developer's Journal* 3, no. 1, (January 1992), Ron Burke discusses his experience with one such tool. *Computer Language* 8, no. 12 (December 1991) contains an advertisement for another such tool. In Appendix B, you can see that such a tool is even part of the HP-UX operating system.

One technical goal in development is to be able to exchange a **set** of resource files with another **set**, without having to recompile the program. Another goal is to be able to replace **one** file from the set with **a** similar file from another set without recompiling. And a third goal is to be able to replace **parts** of one resource file with similar **parts** from the corresponding file in another set without recompiling the program.

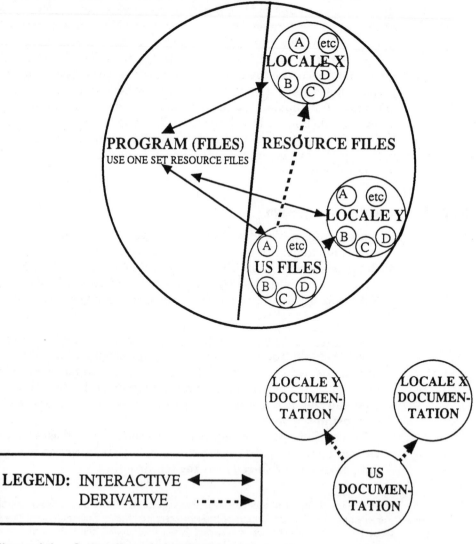

Figure 4–1. Components of a Localized Product

This idea of resource files is the crucial one in developing Internationalized software according to the modern technology of link-time binding. It allows programmers and engineers to concentrate on code and translators to focus on translation. It means that the software with all its complex logic does not have to be touched just because you want to add another language; all you have to do is translate some files.

You may have to consider special treatment for messages relating to critical hardware failures. In the event of a crash, for example, there may not be time to access a disk file and retrieve an informational message about the conditions leading to the crash. Instead, this set of messages should be available in memory where the required access time should be substantially less.

Among the messages that should be in these resource or variant files are:

All text visible to the user of the product
Custom routines that perform screen input/output
Any mnemonic shortcuts
Keystroke tables, command tables, help screens, or any other tables that may have country-dependent information—e.g., the name of the spell checker for the locale
Dialog and message boxes

When composing the messages, follow the advice given in Section 4.4.

Since strings will be of different lengths in each Localization, remove any string length dependencies from the program. Use explicit function calls like "length(cstring)," or named constants declared immediately next to the strings whose length they represent. String function should not depend on an even or odd number of bytes. Use generic routines for centering text, or for text justification in general, as the length of text will change.

You cannot always assume that your characters will need only one byte to express them. You should not use program logic that makes such an assumption if it is possible that you will be using multibyte character sets.

You may need additional space for diacritical marks.

When handling graphic objects such as bitmaps, cursors, and icons, try to avoid the use of embedded text. Text is difficult to modify when in graphic form. If you cannot avoid this, be careful about leaving enough space for translation and try to create tools to simplify the modification. Graphic objects are also language or culturally dependent. Always try to use graphic objects that represent international concepts. Do not hard code the position or size of any element on the screen or the size of dialog boxes and buttons. Remember that items will change position and size as they are translated.

Are installation and setup disks correctly identified? Do you have a detailed build procedure available? Make no assumptions about the software engineering knowledge and/or ability of the translator. If your program resides on a boot disk, will it still fit after all the resources are translated?

Develop a suite of automated tests that can also be Localized fairly easily. Even if they cover only a small portion of the software, this can pay off in the event of many Localizations.

Develop some documentation for the Localizer and translator that contains the following items (make the comments as specific as possible):

Description or outline of each source file for a general idea of its purpose.

Directions about whether or not translations of drivers are needed.

Directions about the construction of the disk if your program resides on a boot disk. Will it still fit after all the drivers are translated? The same applies for the set of disks upon which the product is supplied.

Special considerations such as space that might come up during translation.

Any data structures that must be changed to accommodate translation.

Comments describing how the translation should be done for areas where translation might be difficult.

Avoid parsing; the programming necessary to decipher input to obtain information may need to be changed with every Localization.

For MS Windows programs, put all menus, strings, and messages in the resource script (.RC) file. All dialog-box information should go in the dialog script (.DLG) file. Then there will be no need to recompile the executable program for a new Localized version of the program. Just use the Resource Compiler to relink the resources to the program. If you wish, you could incorporate the resources in an empty DLL for each locale and load them at run time. This would require a slightly different engineering approach. By having the program inspect the country and language information in WIN.INI, the program can then access the appropriate localized resource DLL.

Use *wsprintf* to incorporate variables into strings.

4.2.3. Scheduling

In the normal course of development, Localized versions were released a long time after the U.S. version was released. This appears logical; construction of the fundamental version must take place first so that there is something to translate. But the tendency recently has been to aim for simultaneous release in a number of languages or locales or to substantially shorten the time between different Localized versions. Among other things, this allows for coordinated marketing campaigns.

Simultaneous release can be achieved readily from the macroscopic point of view (months). From the microscopic point of view (measured in days or weeks), one language version does precede all the others because normally development and testing and writing documentation must, except in extremely rare circumstances, take place in one language, after which translation of the files will take place. The alternative would be simultaneous engineering development of the same program and writing of the documentation in different languages, and presumably that would lead to quite different software packages. It would be a nightmare of version control.

Nowadays, the normal procedure is to develop a version called an International English version.[2] This version incorporates all the required engineering

---

[2]You might think of the International English version as the base for the Localized American version!

features such as program code for locale date formats, currency formats, paper sizes, and so on, but all the messages, documentation, help files, and so on are in the "neutral" bland English. It is possible to test nearly all the required functionality on this version, even without the translated files. As each International English file of text is completed, it is translated.

All Localized versions stem from this International English version.

4.2.4. Character Set to Character Set

In Section 3.2.6, we described the issues that arise when you take a document from one environment to another. You may have to plan how you are going to handle *importing* and *exporting*. It will require obtaining Localized versions of the packages that you will be importing and exporting documents to and from.

4.2.5. Tools

You may have to develop and supply tools to help the Localizers and translators do their job. Among these tools can be compilers, translators (not the people who translate English into Spanish), and editors (not people either, but software also). These names are vague, but a compiler may be necessary to prepare some message files into a form that links with the invariant part of the product; a translator may just convert an ASCII file into a binary file or into a compacted version. And an editor could be of various forms—for example, one to edit embedded text in a graphic.

An especially useful tool is one that generates all text messages as they would be displayed at run-time so that translators can see how the final Localized product will look.

The Borland Resource Workshop is an example of how you would use a Resource Editor in developing an application. It makes the basic assumption (see Section 4.2.2) that the program has been divided into two parts, an invariant program part that contains all the program logic and a variant part—the resource files—that can be changed so as to modify the appearance of the program.

MS Windows' resources are data categorized by type—bitmap, cursor, dialog box, icon, string, menu, accelerator (hot key), and so on. Each piece of data is assigned a unique name or number within the type. The Workshop lets you browse, edit, view, copy, and delete certain resources.

Another type of tool could be of great use to a translator: a program that displays the file under translation in both its source and target language simultaneously and that has easy access to the glossary developed early on in the Localization project. The idea of such a simultaneous display in both languages is popular. We have seen some simple translating programs in this format for French and Spanish and the structure is attractive.

To this end, some Localizing agencies have developed their own tools. As an illustration, the INK Network offers three software products to the Product Localization industry in addition to what they use internally. First, there is INK

TextTools for *terminology management* across all Western European languages; it enables you to build and update your own translation dictionaries. Second, there is TermTracer, which allows you to integrate separate terminology dictionaries and which is available on-line. And third, there is TED, the Translation Editor, which brings together source text, translations for the relevant terms, and an editor for producing the translation.

Many Localizing agencies maintain terminology databases and dictionaries for many professional fields. It is standard operating procedure to maintain work on previous versions and editions in the expectation that work on subsequent versions will be reduced. MCB Systems of San Diego markets two products, ***XL8*** and ***Trados Translation Tools.*** *XL8* (written by International Documentation of Los Angeles) provides a translator's environment for translating strings in "C", Assembler, Pascal, Windows resource files, and Macintosh DeRez files. It provides version control and compares strings in the most recent version with strings in previous versions to determine whether a string has already been translated. The translator works on a separate station using a condensed version of XL8, receiving files from and sending files back to the manager, who works with the complete XL8. Glossaries are available. *Trados Translation Tools,* by Trados Gmbh of Germany, provides similar services for ASCII-based documentation files. It comprises ***Multiterm,*** a concept-oriented database that can manage terminology in 16 languages, a ***Text Analyzer*** to compare strings with entries in ***Multiterm,*** a text translation editor, and a *Translation memory* database. It can use "fuzzy logic" in searching for matches.

The Canadian government sells a one-million-term English–French data bank known as ***Termium*** on CD-ROM readable on a PC, as well as glossaries for, among other fields, desktop publishing and informatics. Systran (see Section 4.4.4) sells access to 20 technical glossaries and has compiled a 200,000-term Russian-English dictionary. For extremely large volumes, tens of thousands of pages, or even millions, you might have to consider machine translation services such as those offered by Systran and Logos to translation agencies who then postedit the automated translated output.

4.3. ENGINEERING ISSUES FROM CHAPTER 2

In this section we discuss how well DOS and Windows provide answers for the engineering issues discussed in Chapter 2.

From the MS Windows International Control Panel, you can choose the following countries: Australia, Austria, Belgium (Dutch and French), Brazil, Canada (English and French), Denmark, Finland, France, Germany, Iceland, Italy, Mexico, Netherlands, New Zealand, Norway, Portugal, South Korea, Spain, Sweden, Switzerland (French, German, Italian), Taiwan, United Kingdom, United States, and "Other Country."

In Windows, changing the language using the Control Panel will change the installed language module. The language values (sLanguage) in the Western European language versions of Windows (WIN.INI) are:

Language	sLanguage
Danish	dan
Dutch	nld
International English	eng
Finnish	fin
French Canadian	frc
French	fra
German	deu
Icelandic	isl
Italian	ita
Norwegian	nor
Portuguese	ptg
Spanish	esp
Spanish (modern)	esn
Swedish	sve
U.S. English	enu

4.3.1. Character Handling (and Non-American Characters)

Character sets must be available in ROM, or from the operating system or some other environment. Use the National Language Functions to prepare different character sets and have them available.

The DOS code page used in the United States and many European countries is code page 437. Many countries are starting to use code page 850, which contains fewer graphics symbols and more accented letters and special characters. Computer systems used in countries such as Norway, Denmark, and Portugal use 865 and 860, which contain more of the special characters that their languages require. Depending on the version you are using, DOS has six or nine character sets.

MS Windows supports two character sets: the ANSI character set used for most purposes, and the OEM character set, which is the IBM extended character set native to the machine using Windows. The ANSI codes from 20H through 7EH (see Section 3.2 for a description of these numbers) represent the same characters that appear in the OEM character set. The characters displayed as solid blocks are undefined characters. Windows applications normally do not use the OEM character set (except for DOS applications that run in a window).

MS Windows supports code pages by installing OEM fonts used for running DOS applications in windows and in the clipboard viewer, that correspond to the computer system's code page, and by installing the appropriate translation table for the *AnsiToOem* and *OemToAnsi* functions. If the DOS running on the computer is version 3.0 or later, Windows Setup program will use the current DOS code page. For earlier versions of DOS, the Setup program will choose a code page based on the national version of Windows.

4.3.2. Subsystems and the Character Set

Neither DOS nor Windows provides any support for this issue.

4.3.3. Importing and Exporting All the Character Set

Neither DOS nor Windows provides any support for this issue. Independently from the environment, applications should not restrict the importing and exporting of all the character set. Note that MS Windows does provide the functions *OemToAnsi* and *AnsiToOem,* but their primary function is to translate the ANSI characters used for filenames to a code page set acceptable to DOS and vice versa.

4.3.4. Sorting

Traditional American software sorting methods on a computer do not handle all the cases mentioned in Section 2.2.4 or the many more that exist. Traditional American ways had been to sort by order of the numerical equivalent of the single character.

DOS sorts according to the standard ASCII table. Depending on the version used, you'll get differences in the general character sorting. For instance, DOS 2.0 treats uppercase and lowercase separately, so that Zurich comes before aardvark in a sorted list (the technical term is *non-folded*). In DOS 3.0 and later, uppercase and lowercase letters are treated identically (or *folded*), so that aardvark comes before Zurich.

Accented letters (upper ASCII values) are treated like their nonaccented equivalents in version 3.0 and later, so that $\hat{a}$, $\acute{a}$, and $\grave{a}$ are all grouped with the letter *a*. See the discussion in Section 3.3.2 for DOS 5.0 sorting results for various values of the country code set in COUNTRY.SYS. Of the six country codes represented, three sort the same way: French French, German, and Italian. Canadian French is unique. Spanish is also unique and so is the U.S. version. It is surprising that Canadian French does not sort the same way as French French does, but then they do use different code pages. The difference centers on how they treat the extended characters. The collating sequence can be retrieved using *INT 21H subfunction 06H;* as we discuss, it is not totally correct.

Windows 3.x uses special functions (*lstrcmp* and *lstrcmpi*) to compare strings based on natural languages. These functions take into account different language alphabet orderings, diacritical marks (accents on letters), and special cases that require character compression or expansion. They rely on information in the language module that is currently installed in MS Windows. Depending on the language module installed, some characters are treated differently. For example, if the German language module is installed, the β character expands figuratively to *ss*. If the Spanish language module is installed, the character *ch* is considered a single character that sorts between *c* and *d*. Hence, these two functions should be used as a basis of your sorting routines.

4.3.5. Search and Replace

Neither DOS nor Windows provides support for Search and Replace; the application program must provide it. The two MS Windows routines *lstrcmp* and *lstrcmpi* are language sensitive and should be used as the basis of the comparision routines required in a MS Windows application's Search and Replace routine.

4.3.6. Case Conversion

DOS does not provide any assistance for case conversion, in fact, rather the reverse. There is still the holdover from the days when software was written only for the U.S. market to present all system messages and filenames in uppercase American characters, even when you have used lowercase. This can be disconcerting.

When converting lowercase letters to their uppercase equivalents, you cannot assume compiler library character and string functions work correctly for extended characters values. For instance, functions such as *isupper, islower, toupper, tolower,* and *strcmp* do not return the correct value for extended characters. These functions have to be modified to use different algorithms required by different languages.

In Windows, the case conversion functions *AnsiLower, AnsiLowerBuff, AnsiUpper,* and *AnsiUpperBuff* depend on the language module installed.

4.3.7. Word Boundaries

DOS does not provide any support for this issue. Some manufacturers provide two blanks, one for the thousands separator and one as a word delimiter. One blank is the standard word delimiter and the other is specifically used as a thousands separator. Both print or display on the monitor as a space.

In Windows 3.x the word boundary is indicated by the tmBreakChar of the TEXTMETRIC structure, which can be retrieved by using the *GetTextMetric* function. In western languages this is normally the value 32, but it may vary with other writing systems. Be wary: Some fonts may use the value zero.

Also see 4.3.25.

4.3.8. Character Boundaries

If a DOS product uses character mode for all its screen handling then a character boundary is not a problem, but if the product uses graphics mode and generates its own fonts this may be a problem if the individual characters have different widths. The software will have to keep track of where on the screen the cursor is and hence the width of the cursor, especially if the typeface changes size and style.

With Windows, the application needs to keep track of the font and its size for the characters on screen and adjust the size of the highlighted area for text selection and the placement of the cursor.

4.3.9. Hyphenation/Syllabification

DOS provides no support; it is up to the application software developer to provide the support. The application software can refer to the country code to verify it is using the correct hyphenating package. Use *INT 21H Function 65H subfunction 01H* (see Appendix M).

At start time a Windows application can, for instance, load the correct dictionary used to hyphenate by recognizing the installed language module and country code. The non-American dictionaries used to hyphenate should include irregular cases and exceptions specific to any given language. To find which language module is loaded, use *GetProfileString,* and for country code, use *GetProfileInt.*

4.3.10. Expansion of Text

The Microsoft *Windows Software Development Kit—Additional Windows Development Notes* gives the following recommendations for translating text (in menus and messages, for example):

Length of English Text (in characters)	Space Allocation (in addition to text)
1–10	200%
11–20	100%
21–30	80%
31–50	60%
51–70	40%
71 and up	30%

Neither DOS nor Windows provides support for text expansion; the application program must provide it. It is more a matter of planning and anticipating than programming.

To a certain extent, Windows provides support since Windows itself is Localized for Western European languages and strings can readily be stored in a string table as part of the resources.

4.3.11. Dialog Boxes and Menu Names Also Need Space to Grow

It's a good practice to avoid creating dense menus where most of the space is already used up in the English version. The same advice applies to help screens, error messages, title bars, and so on. For instance, the number of the help screens may increase in other languages, requiring that you adjust the help screen index values. Dialog boxes should be designed so that items can be moved freely, allowing an easy reorganization when translation occurs.

But neither DOS nor Windows provides any specific support for this, except again that Windows itself is Localized for Western European languages and treats dialogs boxes and menus as resources.

4.3.12. Accelerators

DOS does not provide support for accelerators; the application program must provide it.

In MS Windows, you can use a resource editor. If the first letter is distinct, it becomes the accelerator, otherwise you use the & sign in front of the letter you want to define as an accelerator.

Accelerator definitions should be Localizable without the need of recoding the base product each time a different language translation is required.

4.3.13. Numbered and Unnumbered Messages

Neither DOS nor Windows provides support for messages; the application program must provide it.

If you have many unnumbered messages in the software, then we strongly suggest that you go ahead and number the messages for the duration of the conversion process, and then strip the numbers out as a last step before delivery to the user.

4.3.14. Are Strings Made Up of Substrings Meaningful or Correct in Other Languages?

Neither DOS nor Windows provides support for this issue; the application program must provide it.

In Windows, the way to handle variables in messages is to use the ***wsprintf*** function and provide the appropriate logic to determine the correct string ordering for the chosen language.

4.3.15. Spell Checking

Neither DOS nor Windows provides support for spell checking; the application program must provide it.

At start time a Windows application can load the correct dictionary used to check spelling, by recognizing the installed language module and country code. ***GetProfileString*** finds which language module is loaded. The non-American dictionaries used to check spelling should include irregular cases and exceptions specific to any given language

4.3.16. Parsing Input

Neither DOS nor Windows provides support for parsing input. It is a function of the application program.

It is a good idea to avoid parsing text to obtain information. Parsing normally assumes specific syntax, and you cannot assume anything when dealing with different languages' syntax and grammar. On the other hand, if the application parses by referring to a table, then all that may be required is to translate the table.

4.3.17. The Significance of Special Characters

Neither DOS nor Windows provides any support for this issue.

4.3.18. Keyboards and Entry of Non-Keyboard Characters

Sometimes you can use two keys to enter the components of a non-American character. For example, you can enter an accent and vowel by using a *dead* key followed by the character (a *dead* key produces no input immediately on striking, but prepares an accent to be placed above the vowel—see Section E.2.1.2). We have had the experience of not being able to enter a soft hyphen at all in a product using a French keyboard. To remedy this, the developer had to specifically program the keyboard entry function for this possibility. The solution involved the use of ***Ctrl=*** where the equal sign was chosen arbitrarily (but not totally irrationally).

Pressing a dead key tells DOS to combine the accent mark with the next key you press. DOS provides for many keyboard layouts, chosen by the **keyb** command. Since keyboard layouts vary from country to country (and code page to code page), the position and combination of dead keys vary as well. The United Kingdom and the United States do not have dead keys available from the keyboard. In DOS the keyboard command (in **Autoexec.bat** if you want) selects a keyboard layout. (It replaces the **keybxx** command used in earlier versions of DOS.) The parameters are <country>, <code-page>, <kbdfile> (that is, the name of the system file that contains the keyboard layouts), and the ID that specifies a keyboard layout when a country has more than one keyboard ID (see Section 3.3.2). You can then change layouts between your selected layout and the United States one on the fly using Ctrl-Alt-F1 and Ctrl-Alt-F2.

In DOS, you can also enter characters that are not on your keyboard by using the ALT key and the numeric pad. When you enter the numerical equivalent of the character for the specific code page or character set that you are using, then this is equivalent to entering the character itself.

In Windows, dead keys act in a similar manner to those in DOS. And to enter characters that are not on your keyboard, you can use the ALT key and the numeric pad. For ANSI characters, you hold down ALT and then on the numeric pad you type zero and the three-digit code of the desired ANSI character.

In Windows, the problem regarding Internationalization is that the location of the **VK_OEM** keys changes depending on the keyboard layout chosen by the user. Windows solves this issue by using the **VkKeyScan** function to translate an ANSI character into a virtual-key code plus a shift state. Windows allows you to choose many different national layouts from the keyboard Control Panel.

4.3.19. Tracking

Neither DOS nor Windows provides support for tracking; the application program must provide it. With Windows, the function **ExtTextOut** can be used to develop a tracking routine.

4.3.20. Kerning

Neither DOS nor Windows provides support for kerning; the application program must provide it. In Windows, the application program must make the appropriate calls to routines.

4.3.21. Diacritical Marks, the Height of Characters, and Leading

DOS does not provide automatic support for this issue; the application program must provide it.

In MS Windows, the fonts supplied should provide enough internal leading for diacritical marks. If this does not occur, the font is ill-formed or corrupted. The amount of internal leading can be obtained by using the **GetTextMetrics** function and the results used in the **TextOut** function. However, there are printer drivers within Windows that must be checked for correct operation, especially if they have a native printer font mode.

4.3.22. Printers and Character Sets

Soft fonts sets should include extended characters, and the application code dealing with soft fonts should work with upper ASCII characters and map characters on different code pages to the soft fonts correctly.

Since most printers have code pages different from those used by DOS, upper ASCII characters may not print correctly. When applications use native character sets for printing and the printer does not have a mode to support them directly, all characters must be passed through a filter to convert them from IBM code points to the printer code points. Only printing characters should be sent through the filter, not control and escape sequences or graphics data. Generally, the application's printer drivers must take account of this.

Windows contains printer drivers and the appropriate character set for the locale.

4.3.23. Address Formats

No special support is provided by either the DOS or Windows environments when displaying address formats. Applications must handle the specific rules for each locale.

4.3.24. Translation of Filenames

There are some cases where the extensions of filenames probably should not be translated. It is customary to identify backup files by giving them the extension *bak;* certain graphics files have extensions such as *tif,* and *gif;* and source software program files usually identify their computer language. Preserving these conventions under Localization is worthwhile.

Translation of filenames in the DOS environment normally is limited to the use of alphanumeric characters (avoiding the use of accented letters). The file extension is also kept the same as in the U.S. version to avoid causing problems when compiling or launching a program, and for easy recognition by people who do not speak the non-American language they work on. DOS monocases all characters and removes most accents from upper ASCII values for filenames. The way these characters are mapped is a function of the current code page and country code.

If your application allows the entry of lowercase accented letters as filenames, it should convert them on the fly to the uppercase equivalant to show the user how they will be represented by the DOS file system for the code page they are currently using. The user can then decide if this name is appropriate before saving his or her work. With DOS version 3.3 or higher, *INT 21 Function 65H subfunction 04H* can be used to reference the DOS filename uppercase table.

In Windows, the easiest way to handle filenames is to use ANSI characters for

all filenames, and to use the functions *_lcreat, _lopen,* and *OpenFile* to deal
with DOS and the OEM character set. To obtain the pathname, you should use
OpenFile. The szPathName field contains characters from the OEM character
set, so it must first be converted to ANSI before it can be used as a parameter for
OpenFile. Another problem in Windows is when applications try to create filenames in ANSI that have no equivalent characters in the OEM set. The dialog
control styles **ES_OEMCONVERT** and **CBS_OEMCONVERT** solve this problem by setting parameters to convert the typed characters to valid characters
that exist in the OEM character set.

4.3.25. Numeric Formats, Separators, Negatives, and Decimal Tabs[3]

The separators needed to group numbers into groups of three are *period, comma,
apostrophe,* and *blank.* Some manufacturers provide *two* blank encodings to take
care of the ambiguity posed by a single blank. One *blank* is the standard word
delimiter and the other is specifically used as a thousands separator. Both print
and display on the monitor as a space. Windows uses the 160th character of the
ANSI character set as a non-breaking space, but DOS has no solution to offer.

The DOS COUNTRY.SYS command has no direct effect on numeric separators. It must be retrieved by using *INT 21H Function 65H Subfunction 01H,*
available in DOS version 3.3 or greater.

In Windows 3.x, there are the following settings:

sThousands determines the symbol used to separate thousands in numbers
with more than three digits; use *GetProfileString.*

sDecimal determines the character used to separate the fractional part of a
number from the integer number (for instance, the decimal comma is used
instead of a period in many European countries); use *GetProfileString.*

iDigits determines the number of decimal digits to be used in a number; use
GetProfileInt.

iLzero defines whether a decimal value less than 1.0 and greater than −1.0
should contain a leading zero; 0=no leading zero (for example, .6) and
1=leading zero (for example 0.6); use *GetProfileInt.*

On the International Control Panel, the user can choose the decimal and thousands separators and the number of decimal digits.

No special support is provided by either the DOS or Windows environments
regarding decimal tabs. Applications must handle different symbols as decimal
tabs. With Windows the application should use *GetProfileString* to retrieve the
sDecimal separator value from the International section of WIN.INI to provide a
default decimal tab character.

---

[3]If your application is written in COBOL, then the language itself provides many of the capabilities for reading and printing these variations. But COBOL has been designed with American conventions in mind and therefore is limited in recognizing other variations.

4.3.26. Arithmetic Operations, Including Rounding

No special support is provided by either the DOS or Windows environments for rounding. Applications must handle the specific rules for each locale.

4.3.27. Monetary Symbols and Currency

DOS uses the country code in the config.sys file to choose the currency symbol. The country code is a three-digit code the same as the international telephone dialing prefix for the country selected, except for the United States, which is represented by 1, and Canada, which is represented by 2. The DOS country information for the currency symbol is a five-character ASCII string and for the currency decimal places is a one-byte integer. For the currency format, the code is a one-byte integer. This information must be retrieved by using ***INT 21H Function 65H Subfunction 01H*** available in DOS version 3.3 or greater, if you want to make it available to your application.

Windows uses the sCurrency string to define the currency symbol of a country. Use ***GetProfileString***.

The setting iCurrency defines the currency format (use ***GetProfileInt***),

where   0=currency symbol prefix, no separation ($1)
         1=currency symbol suffix, no separation (1$)
         2=currency symbol prefix, one character separation ($ 1)
         3=currency symbol suffix, one character separation (1 $)

The setting iCurrDigits defines the number of digits used for the fractional part of a currency amount, and iNegCurr defines the negative currency format. Use ***GetProfileInt***.

The $ sign represents any currency symbol defined by sCurrency, the string that defines the currency symbol of the given country. Use ***GetProfileString***.

0=($1)
1=-$1
2=$-1
3=$1-
4=(1$)
5=-1$
6=1-$
7=1$-

On the International Control Panel, the user can set the currency symbol, its placement, the number of decimal digits, and the format for negative currency amounts.

4.3.28. Dates and Times

DOS uses a country code to choose the date format of a given country. The date format is a two-byte integer

where   0=USA m(month) d(day) y(year)
         1=Europe d m y
         2=Japan y m d

The DOS country information for the date separator is a two-character ASCII string.

DOS uses the country code to control the way the time is displayed. The DOS country information for the time format code is a one-byte integer

where   bit 0   0=12-hour clock and 1=24-hour clock

The time separator is a two-character ASCII string. This information must be retrieved by using ***INT 21H Function 65H Subfunction 01H,*** available in DOS version 3.3 or greater, if you want to make it available to your application.

Windows 3.x uses sShortDate to define the short date format of a country. The only values accepted are M, MM, d, dd, yy, and yyyy. Windows 2.x uses iDate to define the date format and sDate for the date separator, but they are in Windows 3.x just for compatibility.

In Windows 3.x, sLongDate can contain strings mixed with days of the week, dates, months, and years. For instance:

d MMMM, yyyy	means 9 January, 1993, for example
dddd, MMMM d, yyyy	Tuesday, March 6, 1992
M/d/yy	6/17/89
dd-MM-yyyy	18-03-1991
d "of" MMMM, yyyy	6 of September, 1960

Windows uses iTime to define the time format

where   0=12-hour clock and 1=24-hour clock

Windows also uses the following settings for time:

sTime defines the time separator, that is, the character between hours and minutes and between minutes and seconds.

s1159 defines the trailing string used for time between 00:00 and 11:59 (for example, A.M.).

s2359 defines the trailing string for times between 12:00 and 23:59 (for example, P.M.) when in the 12-hour clock format, or trailing string (GMT) for any time when in the 24-hour clock format.

The iTLZero defines whether or not the hours should have a leading zero; 0=no leading zero (9:15) and 1=leading zero (09:15).

On the International Control Panel, the user can set the date format and the time format in long and short forms.

4.3.29. Time Zones

Neither DOS nor Windows provides support for the time zone. If required, the application must provide for it.

4.3.30. Measurement Scales

When applications need to recognize both the American (English) measurement system (inches) and European metric system (meters, centimeters, etc.), a conversion factor is used between the displayed value and the internally stored value, or between the calculation value and the stored value. The selection of internal units and scale factors is very important to prevent errors from finite arithmetic. For instance, to support both inches and metric measurements, the internal units should be changed to integer thousands of millimeters to avoid truncation error when converting from and to both millimeters and inches. DOS provides no support for this.

The Windows iMeasure setting defines the measurement system selected by the user:

0=metric and 1=English. Use *GetProfileInt.*

Applications should use this setting to control measurement-dependent features. The user can choose either English or metric measurement units on the International Control Panel.

4.3.31. Page Sizes

Paper sizes vary according to the country selected. There is no particular support in DOS for paper sizes; the application must provide it.

In Windows, paper size options depend on the printer driver selected. According to the printer's options available with Windows, a wide variety of paper options is available when you set up or select your printer. The application must be able to use this information.

4.3.32. Colors

Neither DOS nor Windows provides any support for this issue.

4.3.33. Cultural Considerations

Neither DOS nor Windows provides any support for this issue.

4.3.34. Translation of Clip Art

Neither DOS nor Windows provides support for this issue.

4.3.35. Translation of Icons

Neither DOS nor Windows provides support for this issue.

4.3.36. Recognition of Translated Clip Art, Icons, and Filenames

No special support is provided by either the DOS or Windows environments.

4.3.37. Memory

As mentioned in Chapter 2 (see Section 2.2.37), Localized versions of programs may require more memory than the U.S. versions. Additionally Localized versions of DOS may have less available free memory because of the increase in string size and the necessity of using the various drivers mentioned in Section 3.3.2.

Beginning with version 4 of DOS, you can use the ***MEM*** command to display a report on memory and memory usage. If you use the ***MEM*** command with /PRO-GRAM and /DEBUG parameters, you can display a much more detailed report showing the names, sizes, and types of programs that have been loaded into memory and the portion of memory to which they have been assigned. DOS 4.0 also provides XMAEM.SYS and XMA2EMS.SYS device drivers that enable DOS and DOS applications to use memory beyond the normal maximum of 640K (655,360). DOS 5.0 uses HIMEM.SYS for extended memory and EMM386.SYS for expanded memory.

In version 3.0, Windows can run in real mode on Intel 8086, or 80286 and 80386 processor machines with less than 1 MB of memory; in standard mode on 80286 machines with 1 MB of memory or 80386 machines with less than 2 MB of memory; and in 386 enhanced mode on 80386 with 2 MB of memory. Except for real mode, Windows 3.1 does the same. In real mode, Windows and Windows applications occupy an upper area of the 640K (655,360) of conventional memory above DOS and can take advantage of any expanded memory under the Lotus-Intel-Microsoft Expanded Memory Specification 4.0 (LIM EMS 4.0). When running in standard mode, Windows can use up to 16 MB of conventional memory and extended memory. In enhanced mode, Windows supports virtual memory.

4.3.38. Non-U.S. Manufacturers and Non-American Hardware

There is no specific support in DOS for printer drivers. Windows comes with a large set of printer drivers developed by third-party developers around the world. In some cases, the Localized version supports additional printers specific to the non-American market. For example, Windows 3.0 German supports specific German printers not available with the U.S. version. For more information on non-American hardware, see Appendix E.

4.3.39. Mice

DOS does not provide any support for this issue at the user level. Mouse drivers are supplied with the mouse, and the most popular mice for the target markets should be supported. The non-U.S. versions of mouse drivers normally are Internationalized and the programmer can set a country code when interfacing his or her code to the driver. This will result in messages produced in the target language. The details can be obtained from the major mouse manufacturers' technical reference literature. If you are implementing a mouse-based DOS application, it should be tested with the drivers for the target market to ensure that implementation is correct.

The version of Windows sold in the target locale will come with a selection of mouse drivers for the popular models of mice found in the target market.

4.3.40. Setup and Installation Procedures

The setup program as well as the installation procedure should follow the same International rules used to create any application. The installation procedure may need to be changed to allow the installation of additional disks if there has been text expansion. Neither DOS nor Windows provides any particular support for this issue; you must look ahead, plan, then implement.

4.4. TRANSLATION ISSUES

Normally, you can consider translation to be a manual process, albeit one that can be substantially helped and improved by such tools as multilingual word processors, glossaries, hyphenators, thesauri, and grammar checkers. In Sections 4.4.1, 4.4.2, and 4.4.3, we assume manual translation. However, after a period of disinterest, many researchers are now studying the concept of automated translation. In Section 4.4.4 we briefly mention some of their approaches to automating the translation process itself.

4.4.1. Introduction

Keep in mind the advice we had for software in Section 4.2.2. The designer of the International English version should make the translator's job as easy as possible:

Use simple declarative sentences.
Avoid ambiguous language, humor, slang, jargon, cryptic messages.
Avoid compound adjectives.
Avoid long sentences with many ideas.
Avoid negative questions.
Avoid telegraphic style.
Avoid single word messages—"None" can have different spellings (different gender and number).
Do not create plurals by adding "s." Keep two strings, one for singular and one for plural.
Do not omit prepositions or articles from sentences.
Do not try to save space for expansion by truncating a sentence.
Consider using lists instead of a series of concepts separated by commas.
Check and correct any typographical errors.
Be as precise as possible.

Of course, Localizing or not, this is not bad advice. Its purpose is to make everything as clear as possible, and that is just as useful to any end user as to a translator.

Some organizations go so far as to standardize the technical terms that will be used. In Appendix C of their Common User Access (CUA) Guide, IBM defines a small list of user terms that are part of the CUA architecture together with their *standardized* translations into Arabic, Portuguese (both Brazilian and Portuguese), Chinese, Danish, Dutch, Finnish, French (both Parisian and Canadian), German, Hebrew, Italian, Japanese, Korean, Norwegian, Spanish, and Swedish. (See *IBM Systems Application Architecture; Common User Access; Advanced Interface Design Reference,* IBM Corporation, 1991.)[4] In many cases where there is no such standard list, the first step in translating is to develop a glossary of the technical terms and their translations for approval.

Microsoft publishes a list of Microsoft-approved terminology in English and ten other European languages for Windows, Presentation Manager, and the Macintosh in *The GUI Guide: Localizing the Graphical User Interface,* Microsoft Corporation, 1991.[5]

ISO subgroup 37 is currently working on a standard for five thousand terms in the information technology industry. The Canadian government's *Termium* is a well-known French–English aid.

4.4.2. Software

Consider the effect of terse ambiguous messages such as "Record Error" or "Card input" on someone trying to interpret them. Is "record" a noun or verb? Does the message mean that you should take note of the error or that there is an error in the record? Is "input" a noun or a verb?

Beware of unusual vocabulary in general, particularly slang, in-group references, and special characters and abbreviations.

4.4.3. Documentation

We listed the possible types of documentation in Section 2.3.2.2. The process of preparing documents for an international audience can be divided into two sequential steps:

writing text in American English for ease of understanding and use by international audiences; and
translating the text into another language.

The first step makes the documentation more comprehensible to an American-speaking international audience by reducing the vocabulary used to some basic level. Needless to say, it is impossible to define a basic set precisely; but the process of reduction includes deleting any terms that are specific to the United States and only using terms that are believed to be employed in the same way throughout the English-speaking world. Another part of the process is to make sure that the grammatical structure is rather simple: limit the use of the passive

---

[4]We guess that Appendix C will be modified in the future as there are some errors (verbs translated as nouns and so on) and the list is incomplete when compared with other computer dictionaries.

[5]And for Macintosh users, Daniel R. Carter presents some basic glossaries in Dutch, French, German, Italian, Spanish, and Swedish in Appendix B of *Writing Localizable Software for the Macintosh.*

mood; use short, direct sentences; avoid excessive use of subordinate and coordinating phrases; and express ideas and concepts as concretely as possible. Keep paragraphs short and focussed on one idea or thought.

If you follow those guidelines, you will find that the text is more accurate and more descriptive of what you are trying to say. Even if you don't translate the text for, say, financial reasons, both English-speaking and non-English-speaking readers will find it easier to read and understand what you have been trying to say.

The second step is the actual translation. Translating Internationalized (step 1) text should be easier and faster than text that has not been Internationalized. And it should be more accurate because the original text was.

Remember the following checklist when writing International documentation:

Keep the audience in mind. Again, this is normal advice to a writer; you write one way for an audience of engineers and another way for office personnel. But the application of the advice is a little more subtle in this case. References to "our headquarters location" and to the "800 toll-free number," which cannot be accessed outside the United States, should be used only when the document is designed for an American audience. We often use the term "domestic" to describe services available only in the United States. To a reader in Australia, however, "domestic" implies that service is available in Australia.

All the information on the target market audience is important. Localization does not only result in translation; it primarily means understanding and being sensitive to non-American audiences. The first thing to do is to know your audience and collect the following information about them:

Customs	Learning styles
Taboos	Presentation styles
Beliefs	Sensitivities
Values	

All are important considerations in preparing or adapting documents for an international audience. No information on such issues is irrelevant or useless.

Avoid uniquely American examples. State what something is, rather than what it is called in your part of the world. For example, "stock exchange index" is an international term. In America this is often referred to as "the Dow" and in Britain as "the FTSE 100."[6] Also, avoid the term "telephone company." Most telephone services outside the United States are provided by government Postal Telephone and Telegraph (PTT) authorities.

Be aware of cultural sensitivities. Do not use popular text and avoid religion, race, sex, politics, stereotypes, and references to parts of the body other than head, hands, and feet. For example, "left hand" is offensive in some cultures. Use "on the left" or "left side" instead.

Avoid humor. Humor is often culture specific. What is funny to you may not be readily understood in another culture, or worse, may be offensive.

---

[6]London—Financial Times Stock Exchange index; Frankfurt—DAX index; Paris—CAC 40 index; Hong Kong—Hang Seng index; Sidney—All Ordinaries index; Tokyo—Nikkei index.

Use simple sentences and simple words. Keep your sentences brief and to the point. Avoid adjectives and adverbs.

Use consistent nomenclature and style. This enhances understanding and, for documents that will be translated, assists the translator of the material.

Avoid jargon, slang, and idioms. Use terminology that everyone can understand or at least find in a reputable dictionary. Daily exposure to certain words can make it difficult to distinguish between language that pertains to your job in your region of the world and language that is clear, concise, and standard.

Use visuals liberally. But remember that not everyone reads left to right, so the intended sequence should be indicated in a graphic. This is particularly important when your document will be translated to another language.

Limit use of acronyms. Some acronyms are industry standard such as EDI, and others, such as IBM, are generally recognized only in acronym form. But many are not recognized internationally and may even have different meanings, depending on where they are used. Acronyms should be spelled out the first time they are referenced in a document, unless they are generally recognized only in acronym form.

Write large numbers in numerals. Names like billion and trillion are confusing since there are cognates in other languages that differ by a factor of a thousand. When you write 64K, do you mean sixty-four thousand (64,000), or do you mean 65,536 (2 raised to the power of 16)? Your readers and translators need to know which you mean.[7]

Use the names of months in dates. Is 10/6/92 the 10th of June, 1992, or is it the 6th of October, 1992? Writing Oct 6, 1992 and Jun 10, 1992 makes it easier for you to convey your meaning accurately.

4.4.3.1. Documentation Localization Stages

Documentation Localization stages may vary depending on the nature and the scope of each project. In general, the following stages are the most important:

Planning
Glossary development (see Section 4.4.1 for sources of standardization)
Writing
Art (graphics)

---

[7]Be particularly precise with numerical quantities; there can be problems with (false) cognates. For example, consider that the American English words *billion* and *trillion* and their cognates mean different things in different European languages, including British English.

The United Kingdom, Germany, France, Italy, and Spain use the same definitions:

	U.S.	*U.K., France, Germany, Spain, and Italy*
million	one thousand thousand	one thousand thousand
billion	one thousand million	one million million
trillion	one million million	one million million million

France uses *milliard* for the American *billion*. Germany uses *die Milliarde*.

U.K. news services often report "thousand million" to be precise; recently, newspapers in the United Kingdom have started to use the suffix *bn* to represent the American billion, as in 43.13*bn*.

Translation
Quality control
Production of the final copy.

The following are the basic steps of the translation process, which is divided into three sequential phases:

Phase 1:

Team selection
Research
Product orientation
Consultation with technical experts
Development of company-specific glossaries
Translation[8]
Stylistic and technical edit
Proofs of word-processed text

Phase 2:

Review in target market for preferred technical terminology
Incorporation of target country review changes
Edit/proof of changes
Testing/Quality Assurance
Update of glossary

Phase 3:

Type is specified and document is typeset or desktop published
At least two proofs of typesetting/desktop publishing, one for the manufacturing department and one for the documentation department
Electronically generated art work or manual paste up
Final proof of camera ready composition

The Localization of the packaging—-the box that contains all the components of a product—-should be regarded as being part of the process of writing documentation for international audiences. All the considerations on documentation translatability issues described earlier should be applied to product packaging as well as any other marketing document and collateral items such as promotional brochures, "spec-sheets," customer registration cards, quick reference cards, etc.

License agreements and copyright messages need to be modified in non-American markets. Lawyers may be able to obtain information about the law and regulations in non-American countries. Or a company's third party vendors may be

---

[8]Some sections of a software package have to be rewritten in the new language rather than translated. Tutorials that introduce the user to the program often contain many references to local customary (that is to say, American) events. Using the customary events of Bastille Day or a stroll through the Prado may make more sense than translating the activities of the Fourth of July. French telephones have different hardware than American ones, so the software may be quite different, too.

able to provide the Localization team with detailed instructions on how to modify a product's license agreement. Legal staff as well as those international marketing staff responsible for international products distribution agreements with partners should review the Localized License Agreements for correctness.

Copyright messages, usually listed on the first pages of users' manuals, have to be Localized as well. Depending on the customs of the target country considered, these copyright messages will be translated, modified, or left in the original language.

4.4.4. Automated Translation, Machine Translation (MT), and Computer-Assisted Translation (CAT)

Automated translation looms on the horizon! The idea of using computers themselves to translate from one language to another was considered very exciting in the early 1970s, but it proved too difficult a task and the excitement waned as no one made much progress. According to the director of the Center for Machine Translation at Carnegie-Mellon University, those systems picked the wrong word from 10 to 50 percent of the time, as quoted by Richard Stone in "The Education of Silicon Linguists," *Science* magazine. There is now awakened interest as computers become cheaper and more powerful. The demand for translation services grows as more and more companies take a global outlook.

As an illustration of this renewed interest, you can find simple packages available commercially and quite inexpensively, like *French Assistant, Spanish Assistant, Italian Assistant,* and *German Assistant,* produced by MicroTac Software of San Diego. These packages will translate an ASCII text file in American English (either ignoring or considering British spellings) into the target language either automatically or interactively. In the interactive mode, you may proceed sentence by sentence, comparing the sentence in the source and the target language, and modify the result immediately if you wish. You may examine the complete results in a side-by-side mode.

While in our experience the results have to be closely monitored, even in the case of simple direct sentences, they do provide a translating *environment* and, most importantly, they create the opportunity to *modify* rather than start from scratch. Additionally, they supply many fine grammatical aids. You can look up the third-person plural present perfect subjunctive of many verbs on-line, and so on. Their very existence portends greater things to come.

Another set of simple examples are the tools becoming available to assist you to write the occasional letter in French or Spanish or whatever. *Lexica,* by the Writing Tools Group of WordStar International, provides you with on-line translating thesaurus assistance in Spanish, German, French, and Dutch while you are actively working in your word processor. *Lexica* is a DOS TSR program that you can activate with a hot key while your word of interest is selected. You can set up *Lexica* in any one of the five languages, and on the fly you can change the source and target languages. In WordStar's word processor itself you can change the language of the spelling dictionary that is invoked on the fly by inserting a simple dot command into your text. Grammar checkers such as *Grammatik* by Reference Software of San Francisco are available for French as well as for English.

In the bookstore at most U.S. airports you can pick up diskettes to assist you in learning another language. For example, if you are interested in learning German, then you can choose your level of knowledge and buy a diskette that will provide you with examples and tests for that level of knowledge. A sample diskette for *German Teacher* (by MicroTutor of Frederick, Maryland) is available from the "$5 Computer Store," and you can test yourself on nouns, verbs, and so on in English to German or vice versa.

Learning Japanese has been taken to a new level by *Power Japanese,* produced by Bayware of San Mateo, California. With the package you get a headphone set to attach to your PC's parallel port. The package teaches you to read, write, and pronounce a limited set of words written in Hiragana and Katakana together with some simple grammatical structures. It provides many exercises to that end. Running under Windows 3.1, it displays characters on the screen, you can hear them pronounced, and it will analyze the component strokes. There is a drill to recognize combinations of these characters and a keyboard drill using a simulated keyboard with Japanese characters that is displayed on the screen and accessed by pointing with a mouse.

L. Chris Miller, in "Babelware for the Desktop," *Byte,* January 1993, provides a comprehensive and more detailed overview of what is available these days on PCs and work stations. The same issue contains a resource guide of machine translation software.

Of course, professional Localizers need more advanced tools in order to do their job. Our main point here is that many companies are developing packages that are quite sophisticated from the point of view of their engineering even if the product's use at this stage is limited to students and beginners.

Concurrently, academic research into the issue of translation has taken on a new life. We have discussed some tools that help both Localizers and translators in Section 4.2.5. But there is still the goal of automating the translation process itself. As reported in "Machine Translation, The Rebirth," in Mendez Translations' corporate magazine, Siemens, the University of Texas, and Louvain University are developing *METAL* (Machine Evaluation and Translation of Natural Languages), an artificial intelligence program that compares the context of words in each sentence. Muriel Vasconcellos and Eduard Houvy also survey the current state of Machine Translation and Machine-aided Translation in separate articles in the January 1993 issue of Byte magazine.

Richard Stone reports on numerous activities in "The Education of Silicon Linguists," in *Science.* There are two basic approaches according to Stone's article. In the first, the source is translated into an intermediate rigorous language first, then translated into the ultimate target. *Pangloss* (a "knowledge-based" machine translation collaboration between Carnegie-Mellon, New Mexico State, and the University of Southern California, funded by *Defense Advanced Research Projects Agency*) will parse each sentence in the source language, then send the various parts through a "concept lexicon" that is a collection of many facts about the topic. Honing in on the precise meaning of *hit,* as an illustration, the program finds the precise code for it in *Interlingua,* a generic translating language developed at Yale and Stanford in the 1970s. Finally, the word in Interlingua can be decoded into whatever target you wish.[9]

There are reports that some of these more sophisticated programs can and do translate simple documents like manuals for appliances nearly perfectly. These manuals contain very simple sentences and very precise instructions.

The second and quite unconventional approach is statistical, or "know-nothing"; Peter Brown of IBM has compiled statistics relating words in English to words in French based on the Canadian parliament's bilingual proceedings. (There are about three million sentences of this text on-line.) Then, assuming that French is a garbled version of English, a standard encryption stance, his program compares French and English sentences to compile associations in groups of three words. He is augmenting his statistics with proceedings of the European Economic Community. It appears that people's reactions to this latter approach are mixed.

Muriel Vasconcellos points out, in "Machine Translation," *Byte,* January 1993, that the quality of MT is closely tied to the amount of assistance the user is willing and able to provide. You can intervene before the translation takes place, or *pre-edit*. That means you prepare the input text in its source language and reduce lexical and structural ambiguities. If the user responds to questions during the translation, then that is *interactive editing*. And the most common intervention, *postediting*, is one where a human adds finishing touches to the output in the target language. She also points out that in many cases the output does not have to be perfect; when the subject material is time-dependent, such as weather reports or job listings, good translations as opposed to perfect ones will often suffice to communicate the gist of the message. She also believes that written-text MT systems will soon give way to the voice-based systems of tomorrow.

In the same issue of *Byte,* Eduard Hovy describes other approaches used in machine translation. *Direct* MT systems replace source-language words with target-language words using correspondence lexicons. As the lexicons grow, the systems become cumbersome and thought must be given, for example, to the value of storing separate entries for plurals of nouns and tenses of regular verbs. *Syntactic transfer* systems use *parsers* to analyze the input system and then apply linguistic and lexical rules, called *transfer rules,* to map grammatical information from one language to the other. Thus the parser will produce a *tree,* or syntactic structure of a source sentence, and another tree for the target language; then the transfer rules guide the sentence components from one tree to the other. A simple example is the relative locations of nouns and adjectives, and another is the location of the parts of verb. We have noted that in many Romance languages,

---

[9]It was reported in "The Tribal Computer Tongue" by Paul Mylrea in the *San Francisco Chronicle* of October 13, 1991 that a Bolivian mathematician called Ivan Guzman de Rojas was developing a multilingual translator where the intermediate language was not artificial like Interlingua, but real. He believes that the Aymara Indians' language had such a rigid, logical, and unambiguous structure that it is easily transformed into a computer algorithm. The article reports some of his travails in marketing his concepts to an unreceptive world.

adjectives usually follow the noun, and German is well known for placing many parts of the verb at the end of the phrase or sentence.

Interlingual systems of the type we mentioned earlier are by far the most the difficult to construct since their goal entails representing all the information every language may require with appropriate analysis and generation rules. Present implementation of all necessary components tends to be rudimentary in many semantic areas. But interlingual systems have one advantage over syntactic transfer systems in that the addition of a language requires only the rules for translation into and out of the intermediate language. For syntactic transfer systems, on the other hand, a set of rules must be developed for every other language of interest.

Commercial companies in the automated translation field have yet to generate substantial profits. Logos in Massachusetts had revenues of only five million dollars ($5,000,000) per year despite an infusion of thirty-five million dollars ($35,000,000) in venture capital; Systran Translation Systems of La Jolla, California, has revenues of three million dollars ($3,000,000) per year; and the Japanese company Worldwide Communications closed its doors in 1988. The services that these companies offer are not totally automatic; they require some assistance, particularly when confronted with ambiguous terminology. Systran, in particular, offers 27 language pairs and 20 technical glossaries. Its systems have evolved from direct transfer systems to syntactic transfer systems. Systran provides services to translating agencies and charges three thousand three hundred dollars ($3,300) per month to lease software for the first language pair such as English-French. It relies on the translating agency to postedit, a step that is considered absolutely necessary. On-line access to the main-frame database, through Systran Express, is available for 40 to 55 cents per word. Such work is oriented toward translating extremely large volumes of material, and the aim, rather than to achieve a perfect translation even of mundane technical manuals, is to increase per person hour throughput and thereby achieve overall a 30 to 40 percent decrease in translating costs. In the next couple of years, Systran intends to migrate from mainframes by rewriting its code in C and making it available on a large number of platforms.

The International Association for Machine Translation (IAMT) and the Asociation for Machine Translation in the Americas (AMTA), in Washington, DC, publishes *MT News* every four months and the *MT Yellow Pages* once a year. AMTA's address is 655 15th St. NW, Suite 310, Washington, DC 20005.

4.5. VALIDATION AND QUALITY ASSURANCE

The first version of the code to be developed is normally an "International English" version. This version should differ from other Localized versions only by the language in which the text resource files are written and by the settings of some configuration "switches" that specify which engineering rules to apply for character sets, sorting, numeric formats, and so on, as described in Chapter 2. Many people believe that most Validation and Quality Assurance processes can be applied to this version, leaving only something called linguistic testing to the resource files specific to the locale. In our view, nothing beats testing the actual localized version in a localized environment.

We should point out that the meaning of the term "quality assurance" appears to be different for translating agencies and software companies. From what we can gather, translation agencies use the term traditionally in terms of accuracy of translation; software companies mean that too, but they are also concerned about whether the software performs correctly. In this section we are taking the software companies' point of view.

There are a number of texts and manuals on quality assurance and testing. We think that Kaner, Falk, and Nguyen's *Testing Computer Software,* 2d ed., is excellent for an overall review of testing and also for a description of software development. Chapter 9 is about Localization testing. Chapter 7 of *Microsoft Windows International Handbook for Software Design,* Microsoft Corporation, 1990, also contains substantial information about testing international software.

In this section, we focus on a few points that have Internationalization aspects.

4.5.1. Has Everything to Be Translated Been Identified?

One of the more difficult tasks for developers, particularly in the case where they are Internationalizing an old product, is to ensure that they have found everything that needs to be translated. They need to isolate this material in resource files to give to the translators. They need to check that every message is made available to the translators.[10]

Since it takes time for the translators to produce their version of the messages, it might appear that developers must wait until they have completed at least a first draft of their work before they can display every message and verify that it is indeed translated. However, they can save time on this issue by producing yet another version of the messages wherein the characters are replaced with easily identifiable "rubbish" such as a series of x's. Then they run the program and inspect the messages. Messages consisting of x's have been identified, those still in English have not. Presumably these latter are in the software code, not in the resource files.

4.5.2. Some Obvious Errors to Look for First

Most American software engineers are accustomed to working in an American environment and for many, working on Internationalization and Localization projects could be their first exposure to non-American climes. They may make some simple mistakes in their first software releases, because getting other matters to work in the base case has taken priority. At first, they just are not accustomed to working with character sets other than the American ones they have been using for all their working lives.

For example, extended characters may act as unwanted word delimiters. If you

---

[10]As discussed in Section 4.2.2, tools that strip strings from already developed code are available. Some, even though not perfect, appear to assist greatly in the stripping process.

click on a word to highlight it, only part of the word between blanks and an extended character will be highlighted. We have seen this anomaly in two different companies that were Internationalizing for the first time. The general use of extended characters may be inhibited, and in particular, printing them may introduce accents and other diacritical marks that will interfere with leading. U.S. uppercase to lowercase rules may still be in use, and U.S. sorting rules may apply. Verify what happens when you use other subsystems (including the operating system or other environment), particularly what happens to the names of files when you name them with extended characters and then manipulate them.

Further problems may arise from using numbers and currencies in the formats required in different parts of the world. This can limit decimal tabulation and arithmetic operations. Dictionaries and hyphenators, as subsystems, may assume that different character sets are being used than the application does, and importing and exporting may reveal mapping and translation problems as discussed in Section 3.2.6.

In the early stages of development, it may be worthwhile to incorporate tests for such features or for the issues of Chapter 2 into a set of Quick tests for a quick look at the software's feasibility in its Localized form.

4.5.3. Testing

You should test with non-American equipment—the non-American environment and copies of the subsytems that will be used in the locale to which the product is targeted.

All characters in the character set should be verified in all the places where they will be entered, displayed, or printed. Remember that you enter these character sets on various keyboards using various drivers, and they can show up in a variety of places such as menus, dialog boxes, file names, documents, headers, footers, footnotes, endnotes, and in file list boxes. Often, a sorting order is applied to the lists displayed in these latter boxes. Normally dates and times are obtained by recourse to a procedure in the environment or operating system rather than by just entering the date, and these procedures should be checked.

The results of using a subsystem should be verified. Dictionaries, hyphenators, and the effect of DOS TSRs need to be checked. The import from and export to other software that uses another encoding schema should be verified for all characters. What happens to filenames that include extended characters when created in an application and placed under the control of the operating system or the GUI?

There may be the opportunity to compare actual operation of the Internationalized version with an un-Internationalized version in the event that the software is being changed for the international market. It would be rare indeed that no corrections were made, no features added, or that no other modifications of any type were made. Yet for large parts of the software, it may be possible to run the two versions in parallel on two machines and compare them on a feature-by-feature basis. The same test data should be used for both, if possible.

Testing a Localized product presents the same situation, in that a sibling product already exists and has probably been tested to some extent. This sibling is either the original product or the International English version. Anomalies detected during its testing phase have already been reviewed and handled in one way or another. Again, it may be possible to use the same data files, or at least to modify one set of files for use with the other, rather than to construct them from scratch. Such modifications might include different number formats, hyphenation, and so on as described in Chapter 2.

Yet another opportunity for testing exists in being able to mix resource files. In a conventionally Internationalized product, there is no reason why the software would not work with a mixture of resource files that have been Localized differently. In other words, in converting software to French, the software should "work" with a mixture of French and English resource files. It may not be very intelligible to an ultimate user; nevertheless, substituting one Localized version of a resource file for another Localized version can be a very useful procedure in debugging a piece of software. It can assist enormously in pinning down a problem that occurs in one version and not in another by systematically replacing one file from the version that doesn't work with a file from the version that does work (or vice versa).[11]

At the very least, it seems that a test suite that covers some of the basic operations and features could be very useful. Even when you are just developing another American version, it is useful to build upon the previously used test cases. They can be modified for use on the new version. With Internationalization and Localization, there is the opportunity to share the development cost of *automated* test suites. The usual argument against automating test procedures is that the time and cost of development is too high for the value obtained. On the surface, it appears worthwhile to investigate the utility of even a small test suite that can itself be Localized with each Localization.

4.5.4. Translating Back into American English

One way to verify the accuracy of translation is to have another person translate back every thousandth paragraph and then to have someone else compare the results with the original. If the two are similar, you are safe in assuming no problem; if they are not similar, then a danger flag is raised. However, as we showed in Section 2.3.1, some differences might be expected. Does *annulez* mean *cancel* or *undo?* But if there are differences, ask the translators involved what is going on, and perhaps repeat the process, increasing the sample size (try every five hundredth or hundredth paragraph and retranslate some more).

We've mentioned the possibility of using this type of sampling process to a number of a translators, who first scoff and then mention the small differences that can occur cumulatively in moving from one language to another. There is

---

[11]This procedure can be taken further. When a specific file has been isolated as the cause of the problem, you can exchange half of that file with the corresponding part from the Localized version that works. This will identify the working and nonworking halves of that file. The next step would be to exchange half of the nonworking half again so as to further narrow the range of search to a nonworking quarter. This binary search process rapidly identifies nonworking successive halves, leading eventually to the one or two lines that are the problem.

usually a story about how "the spirit is willing but the flesh is weak" ends up as "great whiskey, rotten meat" after translating from English to French to Spanish to German and back to English. They do have a point, since translation is not an exact science; except in the case of legal documents, back translation is not a common process. The process is limited in the sense that it will not verify writing styles either, but usually there is little style to talk of in software messages and documentation; it isn't great literature, and it certainly isn't poetry.

Another typical argument raised against such checking is the extra cost involved, but if you are already doing formal quality assurance, then such an activity would be part of that.

We have heard no convincing argument against using the process, and we think that on a reasonable sampling basis, it is an inexpensive way to assure oneself that the original work is correct. In an engineering sense, the process provides experimental data about possible areas of trouble; and in an administrative sense, it provides senior management with concrete statistics as evidence of accuracy or inaccuracy.

4.5.5. Beta and Other Types of Testing

It is customery in the later stages of software development to have "friendly" potential users try out the software in their normal operating environment or to verify that someone can actually take a production copy and follow the instructions to make it work. The pressures to release the product are usually intense enough at this point in development of the original version that it takes a strong character to insist that these types of test be carried out, and the pressures on the Localized versions can be even greater, as their development comes after that of the original enabled base case. Further, there can be difficulties in finding and maintaining contact with beta test sites. Consequently, these types of tests are sometimes omitted.

PART 3
Other Computers and Other Languages

5 Other Computers

5.1. INTRODUCTION

In the preceding chapters, we have dealt with the IBM PC, its principal operating system, and hardware and other environments designed for it, such as Windows. However, even though UNIX can run on a PC we have ignored it until now and we have not discussed the Macintosh computer, either. We have deliberately concentrated on one specific, although popular, computer and environment and we have concentrated on natural languages that are relatively simple to handle on that computer. But as usual, real life is far more complex, and the computer industry itself can be quite confusing.

We continue to focus on the simple languages in this chapter—those whose characters require one byte and that are written left to right. In Chapter 6, we discuss the more complex languages, a great many of which are to be found in Asia and the Near East. Some of the complexities to be found are single-byte bidirectional strings (text made up of single-byte characters, but both left to right and right to left) and double-byte characters.

A number of factors contribute to the difficulty of understanding the computer industry and create confusion about it. First, the machine upon which the industry is based is complicated. It is a complex electronic and mechanical device, and knowing what makes it tick is technically quite difficult. We think that is clear from our discussions up to now, although we have tried to make some sense out of it for you.

Second, in real life there are hundreds of computers and thousands of operating systems and probably millions of software packages. Relatively few are compatible with each other and competition is fierce.[1] Claims that one system is better than another abound and some of the claims even have merit. And third, the rate of change in the computer industry is so great that your knowledge can be out of date in months and certainly within years.[2] So even if something really were "best" today, it may not have been so six months ago and probably won't be so six months from now.

In this chapter and its related appendixes we discuss some of the other computers and operating systems and how they approach the issues of Internationalization and Localization. Again, we will be restrictive; we will discuss two that are at opposite ends of the spectrum from a user's point of view. The first, UNIX, is very complex both in its development and in its use. It was an evolutionary improvement over existing technology. We characterize it as an attempt to reinvent computing and to avoid all the mistakes that were made up until then. While the creators have to a large extent succeeded, by their diversity, they have created a technology that mystifies many people.

The second, the Macintosh, is simple to use. It was revolutionary in that its use of a graphic user interface introduced a dramatic shift in the way people used computers. The Macintosh brought the use of computers within the reach of the abilities of ordinary people, leaving the technical matters unobtrusive. Very few users of a Macintosh know that an operating system exists and they do not want to know nor do they need to know. This is truly startling to any computer user of as little as ten years ago.

Up until now, we have been discussing how people in different countries can use the same software products on the same computer. Introducing another operating system and another computer creates a new dimension of understanding or confusion. Despite its rational technical base, the computer world has very strong emotional undercurrents within it. It may sound trivial to a noncomputer professional as to what kind of machine and what kind of operating system you use, but the computer world is so broad and so deep that there are many sophisticated computer users who do not, cannot, or will not understand what other sophisticated computer users may be doing. The users of some systems may develop a surprisingly strong attachment to their environment and a surprisingly strong disdain for someone else's. To nonbelievers they can exhibit what appears to be extraordinary arrogance. There can be considerable antagonism.

5.2. THE UNIX WORLD

We do not think it possible to discuss UNIX without an excursion into how it was developed. Much of the complexity, and much of the difficulty in understanding it

---

[1] For example, consider the character sets we have discussed. EBCDIC, ASCII and its derived code pages, and ANSI are all different. We will be discussing even more, those for UNIX and for the Macintosh. All different.

[2] The apocryphal advertisement in the computer industry is that if the development of cars proceeded as quickly as the development of computer hardware and software, then you should have been able to buy a Rolls Royce that did 250,000 miles per gallon for a dollar—ten years ago!

stems from this equally complex history. The complexity of the environment reflects the complexity of the structure that built it.

5.2.1. History of UNIX

UNIX is a very powerful operating system with tools that many other operating systems imitate and incorporate. It is very difficult to learn and its commands are cryptic.[3] And it is also an environment that needs some knowledge of its development in order to understand it. That is partially because it comes in many varieties.

We have heard of the following varieties of UNIX: AIX, Amiga3000, UX, A/UX, BSD4.3, Mach3.x, OSF/1, OSF/2, SCO/XENIX, SCO/UNIX Sys V, Sun OS, UNIX III, UNIX V, XENIX, and VAX/VMS. There may be more.

UNIX is almost like English in that there are so many varieties of it as a result of all the different institutions involved in its development and despite all attempts to set standards. A UNIX developer, proficient in one variety, probably has to learn a new version to work somewhere else. The learning process is not that hard; he or she just looks for the particular equivalent syntax and grammar that is used in the new variety. All that is necessary is learning new syntax. For example, the *mail* command ***mailx*** in System V is ***mail*** in the Berkeley system.

The original impetus behind UNIX was scientific; now there is an attempt to make it palatable to the commercial world. The story behind the development of UNIX is complex; it is full of rival institutions, including scientific laboratories in the private sector, universities, and commercial giants, all coming forth with different versions that compete with each other, and yet there is some form of cooperation in the definition of standards and joint work from consortiums.

While many institutions make changes to UNIX or to their own version, many standards are still proposed and accepted. Naturally, many institutions develop versions that conform to the standards and that also have what are commonly called *extensions*.

Here is the story of UNIX as we best we can discern it. Ken Thompson of Bell Labs developed the first version of UNIX on a PDP-7 in 1969. The first licensed release took place in 1976 (Version 6) and the first portable version (Version 7) was available in 1978. Since then, starting in 1979, Bill Joy introduced a set of "Berkeley enhancements" and by 1986 we had Berkeley 4.3 *BSD* (Berkeley Software Distribution). In 1983, AT&T marketed System V as an industry standard. System V (the specifications are known as "sysvid") is a recognized standard in the UNIX world. AT&T's publication defining the System V interface is known colloquially as the "blue" or "purple" book. Microsoft developed *XENIX* in 1984.

There are cooperative efforts; Peggy King lists 15 collaborative groups in *Danc-*

---

[3]The commands, of course, do make sense, but they are not as intuitive as in other systems. You read, display, and join a file with ***cat*** from *concatenate;* you print a file with ***lp*** from *line printer;* you read and write to tapes with ***tar*** from *tape archive;* and you list the files in a directory with ***ls*** from *list.* We do not think there's any excuse for calling an important command ***grep*** even if it is an acronym and is so good that manufacturers for other operating environments have copied the name.

ing with the Enemy. The first, starting in 1984, was European, and was called BISON after the initials of the members: Bull, ICL, Siemens, Olivetti, and Nixdorf. This evolved into X/OPEN in 1988 and is dedicated to producing application portability standards in a series called *XPG.* It now includes some U.S. manufacturers and has also adopted POSIX standards.

Then there is *OSF,* the Open Software Foundation, started by Apollo, IBM, Digital Equipment Corporation, Hewlett-Packard Company, Groupe Bull, and Siemens AG in 1988. It is a nonprofit research and development organization dedicated to the development of a standards-based open software environment. Apollo is now merged into Hewlett-Packard.

Sun and AT&T started another consortium in response, this group is now known as *UNIX International.* Current membership includes the rest of the computing industry giants such as Amdahl, AT&T, Control Data, Data General, Fujitsu, ICI, Intel, Motorola, NCR, NEC, Olivetti, Prime, Sun, Texas Instruments, Toshiba, and Unisys.[4] There are presently about 150 members of this consortium.

Despite the bickering (some call it out-and-out war) between these latter two groups, both System V.4 (AT&T's latest release of UNIX) and OSF/1 (the first release of OSF's UNIX-*based* operating system) conform to *POSIX* (a set of standards developed by the U.S. Institute of Electronics and Electrical Engineers— see Section 7.2).

There are two GUIs under development, the Open Software Foundation's *Motif* and the Sun/AT&T's *Open Look.* Both are based on *X* (developed at M.I.T.), sometimes known as *X-Windows,* a network client server software for UNIX Graphical User Interfaces (GUI) that was developed at M.I.T. under Project Athena in 1986.

Motif, released in 1989, incorporates technologies from DEC (toolkit and User Interface language), Microsoft (Presentation Manager), and Hewlett-Packard (3-D appearance). Open Look provides three toolkits to facilitate building Open Look-compliant applications; *NeWs, XView* and *Xt+.*

A number of communications services are available to UNIX shops: *UUNET* provides low-cost access to electronic mail, *netnews,* public-domain software, and standards information.[5] *USENET* is a global network, built using a UNIX facility called *uucp* (UNIX to UNIX copy) that allows UNIX users to read and exchange information electronically and *INTERNET* a *DARPA* (Defense Advanced Research Projects Agency) is a network built using Internet protocols.

Many claim that UNIX's ability to network is one of its outstanding advantages. That ability makes it ideal as the basis of on-line stock-trading systems. And since it is closely associated with the hardware, it is ideal for developing the real-time systems to be found in such military applications as avionics and weapons control.

OSF has now committed to using concepts used in the *MACH* interface; funded by DARPA, the original work was performed at Carnegie-Mellon University.

---

[4]UNIX System Laboratory, Inc. (USL) develops and distributes UNIX. USL was part of AT&T until December 1992 when Novell Inc. purchased USL for about $360 million in stock.

[5]UNIX has a poor reputation for data security, partially due to the emphasis on networking machines. Networking also carries with it an added vulnerability to the proliferation of viruses. One virus, in fact, spread through the use of mail! However, everyone is now aware of this vulnerability and presumably has taken measures.

OSF will use the MACH kernel. One version will replace an interface that IBM was developing. The goal of a Tenon Systems version is to provide seamless integration of UNIX and MacOS for the entire Macintosh family of computers, support true multitasking to run simultaneous standard and Macintosh applications, and provide a Macintosh "look and feel."[6]

USL sells only source code rights to UNIX, so users must wait until the hardware vendors have finished their work of porting (and compiling) the new source codes to their machines.

Across the UNIX spectrum, there are some uniform and some similar terms. The *kernel* is the set of programs that corresponds to the firmware we discuss in Section D.6.1, and the *shell* is the interface between the user and the kernel. Each user has a shell that interprets commands. There are many auxiliary commands that augment the operating system but are not part of it. Such commands include ***cat, sort, lp, mail*** and ***awk*** (the syntax may vary slightly).

The directory structure is a tree, and there are many standard file directories:

/usr
/usr/lib
/bin
/dev
/etc

As a user, you are usually assigned a *home* directory that you log on to.

5.2.2. Technical Aspects—Issues Supported

We will mostly discuss Hewlett-Packard's version of UNIX—HP-UX. HPNLS is the Native Language Support provided by HP-UX. It reduces or eliminates the barriers that would make HP-UX difficult to use in a non-English language. It conforms to a collection of standards specified by the X/OPEN Portability Guide (XPG), Issue 2 and 3, IEEE 1003.1 (POSIX), and ANSI C, as well as HP-added enhancements.[7] For a more detailed discussion, see Appendix B.

There is specific support for the following issues.

5.2.2.1. Character Handling (and Non-American Characters)

UNIX-based systems have traditionally used the ASCII code set to express American English. Before Internationalization and Localization was popular, the 7-bit ASCII codes were used, that is, the low end (000–127). This has been expanded to include the high end (128–255). But not all UNIX commands are updated yet for the 8-bit code set. ***Mail*** still relies on the 7-bit code that is embedded in the 8-bit code.

HP supplies a number of 8-bit code sets and supports ISO sets on such peripher-

---

[6]The Macintosh version of UNIX is known as A/UX.
[7]Actually, XPG/2 adopted HPNLS.

als as printers, plotters, and terminals. The International Organization for Standardization (ISO) recognizes a series of 8-bit sets called ISO-8859 that can support European, Middle Eastern, and other alphabetic languages. The first in the series is ISO-8859/1, then there is ISO-8859/2, and so on through ISO-8859/9. The ISO-8859/1 is often called Latin/1. See Appendix J for illustrations of these sets.

HP supports the following 8-bit locales and sets:

Langid	Lang=	Code Set	Language
00	n-computer	ASCII	no NLS—based on 7-bit set
01	american	ROMAN8	American English
02	c-french	ROMAN8	Canadian French
03	danish	ROMAN8	Danish
04	dutch	ROMAN8	Dutch
05	english	ROMAN8	English
06	finnish	ROMAN8	Finnish
07	french	ROMAN8	French
08	german	ROMAN8	German
09	italian	ROMAN8	Italian
10	norwegian	ROMAN8	Norwegian
11	portuguese	ROMAN8	Portuguese
12	spanish	ROMAN8	Spanish
13	swedish	ROMAN8	Swedish
14	icelandic	ROMAN8	Icelandic
61	greek	GREEK8	Greek
99	C		Computer
100	POSIX		Posix default
101	american.iso88591	ISO8859-1	American English
102	c-french.iso88591	ISO8859-1	Canadian French
103	danish.iso88591	ISO8859-1	Danish
104	dutch.iso88591	ISO8859-1	Dutch
105	english.iso88591	ISO8859-1	English
106	finnish.iso88591	ISO8859-1	Finnish
107	french.iso88591	ISO8859-1	French
108	german.iso88591	ISO8859-1	German
109	italian.iso88591	ISO8859-1	Italian
110	norwegian.iso88591	ISO8859-1	Norwegian
111	portuguese.iso88591	ISO8859-1	Portuguese
112	spanish.iso88591	ISO8859-1	Spanish
113	swedish.iso88591	ISO8859-1	Swedish
114	icelandic.iso88591	ISO8859-1	Icelandic
142	czech	ISO8859-2	Czechoslovakian
143	hungarian	ISO8859-2	Hungarian
144	polish	ISO8859-2	Polish
145	rumanian	ISO8859-2	Rumanian
146	serbocroatian	ISO8859-2	Serbo-Croatian
148	slovene	ISO8859-2	Slavic (Slovenia)
180	russian	ISO8859-5	Russian
181	bulgarian	ISO8859-5	Bulgarian
321	greek.iso88597	ISO8859-7	Greek

Figure 5–1 shows ROMAN8 and GREEK8 character sets, while Appendix L shows the complete set and Appendix J shows the ISO character sets.

As of September 1992, HP plans to use ("is moving as fast as they can") ISO-8859/1, 8859/2, and 8859/5.[8] HP is also working on using ISO-8859/6 and 8859/8; work integrating these latter two takes longer, as they involve bidirectional considerations.

There is provision for other sets: the Langids 901–999 are reserved for user-defined languages.

5.2.2.2. Sorting

The routine *localedef* (see Appendix B) builds six categories of data. A *category* is composed of one or more *statements,* each starting with a *keyword* followed by one or more *expressions,* where expressions are sets of well-formed character-code metacharacters, strings, and constants. There are four types of legal expression—ctype, shift, collate, and info.

One of the categories of data is:

LC_COLLATE   affects the behavior of regular expressions and the NLS string collation functions (*string,* and *regexp*)

5.2.2.3. Case Conversion

Another category of data that *localedef* handles is:

LC_CTYPE   affects the behavior of regular expressions, character classification, and conversion functions (*ctype, conv,* and *regexp*). It also affects the behavior of all routines that process multibyte characters (*multibyte* and *nl_tools16*).

5.2.2.4. Numbered and Unnumbered Messages

If you are developing applications for a locale that already exists, then your main concern is to ensure that your messages are distinct from the program. HP provides a message *catalog* to assist in this process. You can verify that your locale exists already in a number of ways. The *-d* option for *localedef* prints out all the information about the locale. Or you can look at the readable /usr/lib/nls/config file.

5.2.2.5. Printers and Character Sets

The *lp* and *lpstat* commands print hard copy and provide information about the specific printers and classes of printers.

---

[8]As per a phone call with Hewlett-Packard.

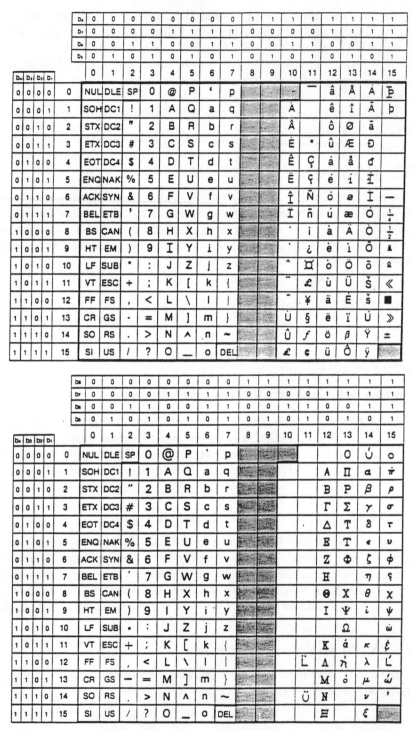

Figure 5-1. HP-UX Character Sets: Roman8 (above) and Greek 8 (below).
Copyright © 1990 Hewlett-Packard Company. Reproduced with permission.

5.2.2.6. Keyboards and Entry of Non-Keyboard Characters

The **stty** command sets up the keyboard; there is no specific support for dealing with non-keyboard characters.

5.2.2.7. Numeric Formats, Separators, Negatives, and Decimal Tabs

Another category of data that *localedef* handles is:

LC_NUMERIC   affects the handling of the radix character in the formatted input/output functions (*printf, scanf,* and *vprintf*) and the conversion functions (*evct* and *strtod*). It also affects the numeric values in the *localeconv* structure.

localeconv( )   formats numeric functions such as currency symbols, decimal point character, indicator for location of currency symbol and collation/sorting, and so on. Specifically, it sets:

decimal_point   (the same as RADIXCHAR)
thousands_sep
grouping   (these three data are in the LC_NUMERIC category)

No special support is provided regarding decimal tabs. Applications should be flexible enough to handle different symbols as decimal tabs. For instance, your application should recognize a comma as a decimal tab in French.

5.2.2.8. Monetary Symbols and Currency

Another category of data that *localedef* handles is:

LC_MONETARY   affects the behavior of functions that handle monetary values (*localeconv*)

5.2.2.9. Dates and Times

Another category of data that *localedef* handles is:

LC_TIME   affects the behavior of time conversion functions (*strftime*).
strftime( )   formats date and time. It converts the contents of a tm structure to a formatted data and time string.[9] It operates on all the data in the LC_TIME category of data and percentage.

5.2.2.10. Time Zones

UNIX provides for setting the time zone during installation of the operating system.

5.2.2.11. Page sizes

You can set page sizes in the UNIX formatters **troff** and **nroff.**

---

[9]The routine strftime can modify most variables to do with time. See footnote 3 in Appendix B.

5.2.3. Technical Aspects—Issues Not Supported

There is no specific support for the following:

Subsystems and the character set
Importing and exporting all the character set
Search and Replace
Word boundaries
Character boundaries
Hyphenation/syllabification
Expansion of text
Dialog boxes and menu names also need space to grow
Meaningful values for accelerators
Are strings made up of substrings meaningful or correct in other languages?
Non-American spell checkers (It is customary for American UNIX systems to
    have a spell checker.)
Parsing input
The significance of special characters
Kerning
Tracking
Diacritical marks, the height of characters, and leading.
Address formats
Translation of filenames. (UNIX allows up to (and including) 32 characters in a
    filename.)
Arithmetic operations, including rounding
Measurement scales
Colors
Cultural considerations
Translation of clip art
Translation of icons
Recognition of translated clip art, icons, and files
Memory
Non-U.S. manufacturers and non-American hardware
Mice
Setup and installation procedures

5.3. UNIX REFERENCE MATERIAL

For further reading, we recommend:

Hewlett-Packard's HP-UX Release 7.0 of September 1990.
Hewlett-Packard. *Native Language Support: HP-UX Concepts and Tutorials. HP 9000
    Series 300/800 Computers.* HP Part Number 97089-90058, First Edition September
    1989.
Hewlett-Packard. *Native Language Support: User's Guide HP 9000 Computers.* HP Part
    Number B2355-90036, August 1992.

5.4. THE MACINTOSH WORLD

As we claimed in Section 5.2, the complexity of the environment reflects the complexity of the organization that built it. In the case of the Macintosh, the user finds a simple-to-use environment constructed by a simple organization.

5.4.1. History of Apple and Macintosh

By contrast with the UNIX story, the history of Apple Corporation and the Macintosh seems to be a sea of tranquility interrupted only by rivers of calm and peace. Clearly the building of such an industrial giant in such a short time has not really been peaceful; in fact, the installation of a company chairman with no computer industry experience in place of one of the founders did indeed signal a classic fight between the founders and supporters of the professional manager style. The founders lost and the professional manager is in charge of the ship. There have been other upheavals and reorganizations; and there has been one important shift in pricing the machines in the direction of lower prices. Nevertheless, from our point of view as outsiders and users, we need only to deal with one developer—the Apple Corporation.

The appearance of the first Macintoshes was a revolutionary step in the use of computers and in the *interface* between users and computers. Although Xerox Corporation's Palo Alto Research Center (PARC) pioneered the design and the interface, Xerox did not enforce its patents and copyrights and it was left to the small Apple Computer company to patent a version. All that the interface did was to make it easy for the nonprofessional human being to use a computer and produce superb looking documents without much training and certainly without any knowledge of operating systems and files and command languages and so on. Even to this day, many users don't know a thing about the operating system; they don't need to and they don't care, either. The catch was that Macintoshes cost significantly more than IBM PCs. In 1990, Apple produced cheaper Macintoshes. The essence of the new approach was that the Macintosh was a graphical, or bit-mapped, machine from the very beginning and almost from the "inside out."

Not surprisingly, this led to two camps complete with different jargon in the computer community, the Macintoshes and the non-Macintoshes. In fact, we still find it difficult to talk technical jargon with Macintosh users; those items taken for granted as shoptalk in the non-Macintosh world appear to be unknown in the Macintosh world. And non-Macintosh people find it hard to believe that you are really working intellectually by moving a mouse and its cursor around and clicking and double-clicking it. You don't have to spend time learning a bizarre collection of commands to use the Macintosh, so how can there be any intellectual content?

Nevertheless, there is a level at which the Macintosh does operate as a character-based machine for programmers and engineers; the languages used traditionally are PASCAL with C becoming more popular. However, bit manipulation, window and dialog-box manipulation, and fonts and scripts are introduced at such a low level and there are so many resources for performing mundane tasks (such as opening and closing a window) that a programmer can incorporate into his or her program, that many Macintosh applications appear on the surface to be very similar to each other. Indeed, in our experience, if you can run one application, you can run them all.

In 1991, Apple's revenues from outside North America were greater than its U.S. revenue for the first time, following a trend of the last five years. Apple has actively pursued overseas opportunities and maintains international developer contacts on every continent.

5.4.2. Technical Aspects—Issues Supported

The Macintosh series of computers is based on Motorola's 68000 chip family.

So many resources are available on the Macintosh that programming is much simpler than on other machines. You can modify many of the functions so that your windows and menus and dialog boxes are all derivatives of the masters (or objects) supplied by Apple. Apple has devoted a great deal of effort to making Localization straightforward and relatively simple. In most cases (we mean very close to 100 percent), it is necessary only to extract, translate, and restore resource files.

A script is defined as a "writing system," a collection of all the elements that characterize the written form of a human language, such as Roman, Japanese, and Arabic. As part of system software, the Script Manager supplies routines that provide crucial services for the character representation, text direction, contextual forms, diacritical marks, lowercase and uppercase characters, character reordering, word demarcation, text alignment, dates, time, and numbers as dictated by a given script (e.g., Japanese, Hebrew, American English) and in some cases by the country as well.

The Macintosh script systems are collections of software facilities that work with the Script Manager to provide for basic differences between writing systems, such as character sets, fonts, keyboards, text collation, and word breaks. Examples of script systems are Roman, Japanese, Arabic, Traditional Chinese, Simplified Chinese, Hebrew, Cyrillic, Thai, and Korean.

Introduced in 1986, the Script Manager has been updated and, according to Greg Williams in his article "Plan It for the Planet," as of February 1991 Apple supports no fewer than 29 versions of Localized system software, each of which is "fueled" by one of six script systems. As a result, the Macintosh works in at least one of the major languages in 215 countries.

The Macintosh worldwide system software consists of the Macintosh Script Management System (the Script Manager and one or more script systems) and the International Utilities Package, international resources, keyboard resources, and certain keyboard-handling routines. A spoken language that may be written in more than one script is treated on the Macintosh as several languages, one for each script in which the language is written. For instance, Malaysian can be written in either Roman or Arabic script. The Macintosh Script Management System distinguishes the written versions with languages codes, such as langMalayRoman and langMalayArabic.

The Macintosh Script Management System also addresses worldwide differences with the concept of regions. For instance, German is used in Germany, Austria, Switzerland, the Netherlands, the northeast part of Italy, and so on. Each of these areas may have different conventions for time, date, and number formats. A number, called a region code, is then used to designate a region that is smaller or larger than a country, but that shares the characteristics described. Localized versions of the Macintosh system software combine information specific to scripts, languages, and regions. The Macintosh system software is now available in numerous Localized versions: American, Arabic, Australian, British, Croatian, Danish, Dutch, Farsi, Finnish, French, French Belgian and Luxembourgian, French Canadian, French Swiss, German, German Swiss, Greek, Hebrew, Hindi (India), Icelandic, Irish, Italian, Japanese, Korean, Maltese, Norwegian, Portuguese, Simplified Chinese, Spanish, Swedish, Thai, Traditional Chinese, and Turkish.

The Script Manager available with System Software version 7.0 provides additional features besides standard routines for the manipulation of ordinary text, a means to make your application work with many writing systems, and access to the International Utilities Package to provide Localizable date, time, and number conversion. Worldscript, released with System 7.1 in October 1992, expands the Macintosh's capabilities even further; unfortunately, it was released too late for us to report on it in this book.

The new features available with System Software version 7.0 are reflected in its ability to:

Retrieve font and style information in each script's local variables

Determine if a double-byte script system is installed

Obtain a pointer to the current 'KCHR' resource (the resource that specifies the mapping of virtual key codes to character codes, for instance, ASCII)

Determine the current region code

Obtain improved information on word boundaries for word selection and line breaking

Perform more sophisticated and faster word selection and word wrap

Truncate and substitute text in a way that improves its adaptation to different scripts and languages

Perform uppercase and lowercase conversion more easily

Strip diacritical marks

Handle fully justified text with intercharacter spacing and multiple style runs on a line, using special scaling if desired

Create simple script systems that use the Roman Script System

Use the keyboard menu to select keyboard layouts

Install and remove multiple scripts, keyboards and fonts

Use new KeyScript verbs to select the next available keyboard within a script to restrict the available keyboards temporarily

With multiple script systems installed, you can switch back and forth between different scripts.

In the following Sections 5.4.2.1 through 5.4.2.23, *itl* refers to an *International Utilities Package* resource. *KCHR, kcs#, kcs4,* and *kcs8* resources are keyboard resources.

5.4.2.1. Character Handling (and Non-American Characters)

Apple Computer presents a number of character sets that are chosen by Localizing the operating system. There is an extended ASCII character set and built-in International Utilities. A Script Manager supports non-Roman scripts such as Arabic, Hebrew, Japanese, and Chinese. Apple claims that since everything is done in graphics on the Macintosh, that the Macintosh is ready to support most languages (Williams, *Competing in Worldwide Market*).

Asian code sets can support ideographic languages such as Japanese, Korean, and Chinese. In these languages, each word is written using one or more unique ideographic characters. There are thousands of such symbols in these languages and most characters require two or more bytes. Using double bytes provides for up to 65,536 possibilities. When using these double-byte characters, you should not infuse one byte with meaning.

The Macintosh always has at least two script systems present when a non-Roman script system is installed. With System Software version 7.0, a script systems may be installed as a *secondary script* or as a *primary script,* (also called *system script*) which affects system defaults and is the script used in dialog boxes, menus, and alerts. With System Software version 7.0, the user installs each non-Roman *script system* with an *Installer* that allows users to install the script as a primary or secondary script. The Finder also allows users to add or remove secondary script systems—it permits users to move a collection of script resources into the System file. There are script resources, keyboard resources, and font resources. A script-configuration control panel lets users specify different features in a script system, such as the calendar system to be used.

Apple Computer's *Guide to Macintosh Software Localization* portrays the following character sets:

Roman	Greek
Arabic (including characters for Urdu, Farsi, and Malay)	Hebrew
	Icelandic
Central European	Japanese
Traditional Chinese	Korean
Croatian	Thai
Cyrillic	Turkish

Figure 5–2 shows the Roman and Greek character sets. Appendix K portrays all the sets. Since Arabic and Hebrew have alternative glyphs, Figure K–8 shows these. The Western European languages use the Roman character set.

The Script Manager has always supported the simultaneous use of more than one non-Roman script, but with System Software version 7.0 it is easier for users to install multiple script systems, and these script systems function properly even though they are not the system script. This is very handy when your application needs to support multiple languages. For instance, word processors may tag a text run with a language attribute similarly to style attributes: this language tag can govern the behavior of hyphenators and spell checkers, for example.

	0x	1x	2x	3x	4x	5x	6x	7x	8x	9x	Ax	Bx	Cx	Dx	Ex	Fx
x0	NUL	DLE	SP	0	@	P	`	p	Ä	ê	†	∞	¿	–	‡
x1	SOH	DC1	!	1	A	Q	a	q	Å	ë	°	±	¡	—	·	Ò
x2	STX	DC2	"	2	B	R	b	r	Ç	í	¢	≤	¬	"	,	Ú
x3	ETX	DC3	#	3	C	S	c	s	É	ì	£	≥	√	"	„	Û
x4	EOT	DC4	$	4	D	T	d	t	Ñ	î	§	¥	ƒ	'	‰	Ù
x5	ENQ	NAK	%	5	E	U	e	u	Ö	ï	•	µ	≈	'	Â	ı
x6	ACK	SYN	&	6	F	V	f	v	Ü	ñ	¶	∂	Δ	÷	Ê	ˆ
x7	BEL	ETB	'	7	G	W	g	w	á	ó	ß	Σ	«	◊	Á	˜
x8	BS	CAN	(	8	H	X	h	x	à	ò	®	∏	»	ÿ	Ë	¯
x9	HT	EM	)	9	I	Y	i	y	â	ô	©	π	…	Ÿ	È	˘
xA	LF	SUB	*	:	J	Z	j	z	ä	ö	™	∫	NBSP	/	Í	˙
xB	VT	ESC	+	;	K	[	k	{	ã	õ	´	ª	À	¤	Î	°
xC	FF	FS	,	<	L	\	l	|	å	ú	¨	º	Ã	‹	Ï	¸
xD	CR	GS	-	=	M	]	m	}	ç	ù	≠	Ω	Õ	›	Ì	˝
xE	SO	RS	.	>	N	^	n	~	é	û	Æ	æ	Œ	fi	Ó	˛
xF	SI	US	/	?	O	_	o	DEL	è	ü	Ø	ø	œ	fl	Ô	ˇ

	0x	1x	2x	3x	4x	5x	6x	7x	8x	9x	Ax	Bx	Cx	Dx	Ex	Fx
x0	NUL	DLE	SP	0	@	P	`	p	Ä	ê		°	῏	Π	ΰ	π
x1	SOH	DC1	!	1	A	Q	a	q	Å	ë	´	±	Α	Ρ	α	ϱ
x2	STX	DC2	"	2	B	R	b	r	Ç	í	΄	²	Β	Σ	β	ς
x3	ETX	DC3	#	3	C	S	c	s	É	ì	£	³	Γ	Τ	γ	σ
x4	EOT	DC4	$	4	D	T	d	t	Ñ	î	®	΄	Δ	Υ	δ	τ
x5	ENQ	NAK	%	5	E	U	e	u	Ö	ï	÷	῀	Ε	Φ	ε	υ
x6	ACK	SYN	&	6	F	V	f	v	Ü	ñ	¦	Ά	Ζ	Χ	ζ	φ
x7	BEL	ETB	'	7	G	W	g	w	á	ó	§	·	Η	Ψ	η	χ
x8	BS	CAN	(	8	H	X	h	x	à	ò	¨	Έ	Θ	Ω	θ	ψ
x9	HT	EM	)	9	I	Y	i	y	â	ô	©	Ή	Ι	Ϊ	ι	ω
xA	LF	SUB	*	:	J	Z	j	z	ä	ö	™	Ί	Κ	Ϋ	ϰ	ϊ
xB	VT	ESC	+	;	K	[	k	{	ã	õ	«	»	Λ	ά	λ	ϋ
xC	FF	FS	,	<	L	\	l	|	å	ú	¬	Ό	Μ	έ	μ	ό
xD	CR	GS	-	=	M	]	m	}	ç	ù	–	½	Ν	ή	ν	ύ
xE	SO	RS	.	>	N	^	n	~	é	û	‰	Ύ	Ξ	ί	ξ	ώ
xF	SI	US	/	?	O	_	o	DEL	è	ü	—	Ώ	Ο	ΐ	ο	o

Figure 5–2. Macintosh Character Sets: Roman (above) and Greek (below)

5.4.2.2. Sorting

The Macintosh has collating sequences for American, Arabic, British, Chinese, Croatian, Czech, Danish, Dutch, Faroese, Finnish, Flemish, all French, all German, Greek, Hebrew, Hungarian, International (English), Italian, Japanese, Korean, Norwegian, Persian, Polish, Portuguese, Spanish, Swedish, and Turkish.

Sorting order is specified with a primary order and a secondary order. The primary order is by *class;* for example, sorting all forms of *a*, then sorting within the class. There are allowances for expansion, contraction, ignoring characters, and exceptions such as *Mc* and *St*.

The International Utilities Package in System Software version 7.0 includes new routines that allow an application to supply 'int2' or 'int4' resources more easily, call sorting routines with explicit specification of an 'itl2' resource handle, sort strings that may be in different scripts or languages, and obtain tables from an 'itl2' or 'itl4' resource. The ***IUScriptOrder, IULangOrder, IUStringOrder,*** and ***IUTextOrder*** functions provide interscript and interlanguage sorting. The ***IUScriptOrder*** function takes a pair of script codes and returns –1, 1, or 0 depending on whether text in the first script should be sorted before, after, or in the same place as text in the second script. The system script is always sorted first.

The ***IULangOrder*** function takes a pair of language codes and returns –1, 1, or 0 depending on whether text in the first language should be sorted before, after, or in the same place as text in the second language. The language codes iuScriptCurLang and iuScriptDefLang are not valid for ***IULangOrder*** because no script is specified. Languages that belong to different scripts are sorted in the same order as the scripts to which they belong.

5.4.2.3 Search and Replace

The ***ReplaceText*** function allows for substitution of text in all scripts.

5.4.2.4. Case Conversion

Each 'itl2' resource contains the International Utilities package sorting hooks and routines and tables for character type, case conversion, and word breaks. With System Software version 7.0, it also includes length information for the code and tables it contains. The new set of routines available from both assembly and high-level languages provides Localizable lowercasing, uppercasing, and stripping of diacritical marks. Use UpperText and LowerText procedures.

5.4.2.5. Word Boundaries

NFindWord in the Script Manager determines word boundaries.
Each 'itl2' resource contains the International Utilities package sorting hooks and routines and tables for character type, case conversion, and word breaks. With System Software version 7.0, the 'itl2' resource also includes length information for the code and tables it contains.

5.4.2.6. Character Boundaries

CharByte, CharType, and *ParsTable* get data pertaining to specific characters.

5.4.2.7. Dialog Boxes and Menu Names Also Need Space to Grow

Text in dialog boxes is self-centering.

5.4.2.8. Meaningful Values for Accelerators

The Macintosh resources also support this issue. Several keyboard equivalents are reserved for use with worldwide versions of system software, Localized keyboards, and keyboard layouts. These keyboard equivalents have actions that do not correspond directly to menu commands. Applications that make extensive use of keyboard equivalents should guarantee alternative methods of gaining access to functions, in order to avoid keyboard equivalents that use the space bar in combination with the command key and other modifier keys, since these combinations may be reserved and used by the Script Manager and various script systems.

It is customary to preserve certain traditional commands for popular or common functions and not to Localize them. *Save, Copy, Paste, Cut,* and *Open* are usually left as *Command S, Command C, Command V, Command X,* and *Command O.*

5.4.2.9. Parsing Input

The *IntlTokenize* function allows your application to recognize tokens without making assumptions that depend on a particular script. For instance, a single token for "less than or equal to" may have two representations in the U.S. system software. But in the Japanese system software, only one representation is possible. The application does not need to be aware of the difference, because the tokenizer identifies the different elements in an arbitrary string of text by using Localized information from the 'itl4' resource.

5.4.2.10. Tracking

System 7.0 provides many functions for manipulating text in any system.

5.4.2.11. Diacritical Marks, the Height of Characters, and Leading

System 7.0 provides many functions for manipulating text in any system.

5.4.2.12. Measurement Scales

As explained earlier, each 'itl0' resource contains short date and time formats and formats for currency and numbers and the preferred unit of measurement.

5.4.2.13.Keyboards and Entry of Non-Keyboard Characters

On the Macintosh as supplied in the United States, you can use the desk accessory (DA) *key caps,* which allows the user to examine the effect of multiple keys. Often, in the American character set with an American keyboard, accents and diacritical marks can be found by using the *option* key together with *c* for ç, *e* for the acute accent, ' for the grave accent, *i* for circumflex, *u* for umlaut, and *n* for tilde.

With System Software version 7.0, a *keyboard* menu is displayed with a list of all the keyboard resources in the system. *KCHR, kcs#, kcs4,* and *kcs8* are keyboard resources. The last three define keyboard color icons; the first defines the keyboard layout. If a particular KCHR is inconsistent with the script system (for example, if a Japanese KCHR resource is present in a system that has only the Roman Script System), then it does not display. Key Caps will appear as per the active script system.

A keyboard Control Panel allows users to specify a particular keyboard layout.

5.4.2.14. Printers and Character Sets

The Macintosh provides substantial support for printers and character sets. The Script Manager PrintAction procedure allows the printer driver to be independent of the particular scripts being used. Each PrintAction procedure does the tasks appropriate for its script system. Keep in mind, though, that if you use the wrong LaserWriter driver for a script system, characters will map incorrectly because the drivers are Localized and have different encodings.

5.4.2.15. Numeric Formats, Separators, Negatives, and Decimal Tabs

The Script Manager supplements the Standard Apple Numerics Environment (SANE) and allows applications to display formatted numbers and read both formatted and simple numbers, even though the numbers and the format strings may have been entered using different Localized system software.

Each installed script has one or more 'itl0' resources. The resource ID for each 'itl0' resource is in the script's resource number range. The default 'itl0' resource for a script is specified by the script's 'itlb' resource, which specifies font and style information for the script and other script initialization data. Each 'itl0' resource specifies number format (decimal separator, thousands separator, and list separator), currency format (currency symbol and position, leading or trailing zeroes, and how to show negative numbers), short date format, time format, and region code for this particular 'itl0' resource.

5.4.2.16. Monetary Symbols and Currency

The 'itl0' resource also handles formats for currency. In particular, currency symbol and position, leading or trailing zeroes, and how to show negatives.

5.4.2.17. Dates and Times

The Macintosh extended date routines can handle a range of roughly 35,000 years. As mentioned earlier, each 'itl0' resource also contains short date and time formats. The basic 'itl1' resource provides information on long date formats: the order, the elements to include, the names of the days and months, and how to abbreviate the names.

This basic format presents some limitations. For instance, it assumes that 7 day names and 12 month names are sufficient, which is not true for certain calendars such as the Jewish calendar, which can sometimes have 13 months. Another limitation is that day and month names are abbreviated by simply truncating the names to a fixed length, which does not work for certain languages.

With System Software version 7.0, the 'itl1' resource can be optionally extended to contain a list of extra day names for calendars with more than 7 days, a list of extra month names for calendars with more than 12 months, a list of abbreviated day names, a list of abbreviated month names, and a list of additional date separators.

With System Software version 7.0, the 'itl1' resource has also been extended to contain an optional calendar code. Multiple calendars may be available on some systems, and it is necessary to identify the particular calendar for use with the 'itl1' resource.

5.4.2.18. Time Zones

You can access the stored location (latitude and longitude) and time zone of the Macintosh from parameter RAM. The MAP control panel allows users to specify the location of their Macintosh computer.

5.4.2.19. Page Sizes

There is extensive support for international paper sizes (A4, A3, A5, etc.) on printers compatible with the Macintosh.

5.4.2.20. Colors

There is no specific support for choosing colors. With System Software version 7.0, a keyboard color icon family is available to specify the small icon that corresponds to each 'KCHR' resource. There are some differences between the color icon family for keyboards and the color icon families used elsewhere in the Macintosh Operating System. These keyboard icon types ('kcs#', 'kcs4', and 'kcs8') are used in the keyboard control panel and in the keyboard menu when it is displayed on some Localized versions of the system software.

5.4.2.21. Memory

The item that corresponds to a TSR is an *init*. It is possible for the user to specify the amount of memory available, and for any application this cannot be below a specific amount. Strings in separate resources are not allocated to the system heap, and when Localizing within the Roman alphabet, there would be virtually no change in memory requirements.

5.4.2.22. Non-U.S. Manufacturers and Non-American Hardware

At present, this issue is not a factor in the Macintosh world. Apple produces all its hardware or has it manufactured under its control.

5.4.2.23. Mice

The Macintosh family supports many different types of hardware, including mouse devices. These devices are supported through hardware interfaces that include SCSI (Small Computer System Interface), ADB (Apple Desktop Bus), and SCC (Serial Communications Chip).

5.4.3. Technical Aspects—Issues Not Supported

The Macintosh offers no specific support for the following; applications must explicitly provide for these situations:

Subsystems and the character set
Importing and exporting all the character set
Arithmetic operations, including rounding
Address formats
Hyphenation/syllabification
Kerning
Non-American spell checkers
Expansion of text
Numbered and unnumbered messages
Are strings made up of substrings meaningful or correct in other languages?
Translation of clip art
Translation of icons
Translation of filenames (The Macintosh allows up to (and including) 31 characters, including blanks and many special characters.)
Recognition of translated clip art, icons, and files
Cultural considerations
Setup and installation procedures

5.5. MACINTOSH REFERENCE MATERIAL

For further reading, we recommend:

Apple Computer, Inc., *Inside Macintosh,* Vol. 6. Reading, MA: Addison-Wesley Publishing Company, preliminary release, October 1990.

Apple Computer, Inc., *Guide to Macintosh Software Localization.* Reading, MA: Addison-Wesley Publishing Company, 1992.

Apple Computer, Inc., *Software Development for International Markets: A Technical Reference.* APDA Draft. Cupertino, CA: Apple Computer, Inc., 1988. A7G0016.

Apple Computer, Inc., *Worldwide Software Development Overview*. Cupertino, CA: Apple Computer, Inc., 1990.

Carter, Daniel R. *Writing Localizable Software for the Macintosh*. Reading, MA: Addison-Wesley Publishing Company, 1991.

Microsoft. *Microsoft Windows International Handbook for Software Design,* Redmond, WA: Microsoft Corporation, 1990.

6 Other Languages

6.1. INTRODUCTION

So far we have dealt with languages with characters that can be expressed in one computer byte, like American English.[1] These languages are also "left to right." For us in the West, that makes these languages comparatively simple to manipulate on computers. But there are more complex languages, a great many of which are to be found in Asia and the Near East.[2] In this chapter we discuss some of the extra concepts and approaches required to take account of them.

Some Asian "ideographic" languages do not delimit words by spaces or punctuation. For cursive scripts like Arabic, Farsi, and Urdu there is a marked difference in the widths of the letters and proportional spacing is required for printing.

---

[1]There are some curiosities even within these. For example, Maltese is an Arabic-based language written in Latin script, and Serbian and Croatian, written respectively in Latin and Cyrillic scripts, are "the same" orally. Ladino is old Spanish written in Turkish script. We are dealing with the *written* forms of languages here, and the concept of language and region is adequate to distinguish between them.

[2]Computers, up until now, have not been geared to handle these complexities. A case in point is Japan. In utter contrast to Japan's well-deserved reputation for manufacturing and marketing high-quality consumer electronics and computer equipment throughout the world, the *use* of such equipment in Japanese industry and organizations is surprisingly limited in comparison with their use in other developed societies. This must be due to the difficulties of handling Japanese characters; faxes, on the other hand, which allow for handwritten characters, are very popular. However, John Riley in "Japanese Computing: An In-Depth Overview of a Modern Industrial Revolution," *Multilingual Computing Magazine and Buyer's Guide,* says that the Japanese are beginning to make substantial use of the personal computer.

Descenders may be much greater in these languages than in others. Some characters require more space than Roman characters. We should also mention that we cannot even rely on numbers or numerals to have the same glyph, as do the Western European languages. Other languages contain numerical glyphs that we would not recognize, one from the other.

According to *Inside Macintosh*, Vol. 6, by Apple Computer, Inc., even the order in which characters within a word are written differs from the order in which the characters are spoken in Devanagari. Some of the ways in which a user might want to sort Chinese can be by the number of strokes required to represent the character, the radical (root) of the character, or the number of strokes added to the radical, or the numeric value of the character as represented in a character set.

We can say that there are four classes of languages for the computer engineer to look at:

Simple—the "Roman" languages that we have discussed so far
Contextual—ones in which the forms of characters depend on the context
Multibyte—languages with more than 256 characters
Directional—languages written in other than left-to-right/top-to-bottom style.

In some languages, characters have different forms depending on the context. This occurs in handwritten or cursive English even, where some characters may take a different form depending on whether they are the initial characters of a word or not. In (otherwise rather straightforward) Greek, sigma or σ has that form in the middle and beginning of a word, but is written (almost) like *s* at the end of a word. So the name of the character *sigma* is written in lowercase as σιγμα whereas the last letter in Ελλας is also sigma. In more exotic languages, such as Arabic, ligatures are very common, thereby changing the form of more than one character depending on the position in the word.

Some languages, like Japanese, Korean, and Chinese, have more characters than can be accommodated in one byte. In these languages, each word is written using one or more unique ideographic characters. There are thousands of such symbols in these languages and it takes more than one byte to contain and distinguish so many characters. Multibyte (that is, a mixture of double-byte and single-byte) languages raise some very challenging questions. Using two bytes provides for up to 65,536 possibilities, and Asian code sets must support ideographic languages such as Japanese, Korean, and Chinese. When using these double-byte characters, you cannot infuse one byte with meaning. There may be no "natural order" to characters vis-à-vis sorting and no uppercase forms as distinct from lowercase.

How can you design a keyboard or other input device to handle four or five thousand or ten thousand characters? Physically, where would you locate the keys and how would you label them? Can a user really make sense of it, or do you need a Ph.D. in Oriental Studies on top of your Ph.D. in Computer Science combined with a photographic memory? Clearly the computer world has already taken one approach to the problem by saying there will be two or more bytes to contain a character. That still leaves the question of designing a keyboard with, say, 256 possible entries and some way of recognizing that a combination of one or two or three or more inputs represents, let's say, the two thousand, one hundred and forty-first character. Can anyone remember all that sufficiently well to attain some adequate level of fluency? The question of "how fast can you type" now gets some unbelievably low answers![3]

One approach is to have the computer assist the user by displaying various aids on the screen. If you can input a radical or root character from the keyboard, then point to and choose additional strokes that would complete your desired character from a group that is displayed on the screen, then perhaps you can input text that is both intelligible to the machine and to a human. A popular method to enter Kanji (Japanese ideographs) is to use a phonetic representation of the ideograph entered either in Latin characters or in the Katakana syllabary. A choice of phonetically similar ideographs is then presented, from which the user may select the correct one.

Another approach is pen-based systems where the machine-human interface takes on completely new dimensions. You do not use a keyboard in this approach, but instead use hardware devices that allow you essentially to handwrite your input and leave it to the operating system to interpret the input and convert it to the more conventional bytes and computer words that we have discussed.

The Roman languages are written left to right/top to bottom. Clearly there are, in this form of analysis, seven other possibilities, but we have only heard of languages using the following:

left to right/top to bottom
right to left/top to bottom
top to bottom/right to left

In some cases, we must deal with bidirectional, but still single-byte languages, where one line of, say Hebrew or Arabic, written right to left may contain interspersed English written left to right. That raises issues that U.S. programmers do not ordinarily concern themselves with. The issue of *directionality* refers to the direction that the language is normally read, as well as to the order of characters in a file. Latin is left to right, and non-Latin is right to left. *Order* can relate to the keyboard—the order in which the user enters keystrokes—or the screen—the order in which characters are displayed. Another term for this concept/process is *text-rendering*. *Backing-store order* refers to the order in which character codes are stored in memory, and *display order* refers to the order in which characters are portrayed on a device.

6.2. THE PC WORLD

6.2.1. Introduction

In Japan, the personal computer market is dominated by five major personal computer architectures:

---

[3]Nevertheless, there are newspapers printed daily in many of these languages, so the issues we raise can be overcome. There are several varieties of keyboard in Japan, for example: the JIS, the New JIS, the Thumb Shift (by Fujitsu), and the M-style (NEC). The details of such keyboards are beyond the scope of this introductory book.

NEC 9800 series and Epson compatibles
Toshiba J-3100
IBM AX
Fujitsu
IBM PS/5

The Japanese marketplace is problematic for the software company endeavoring to release a package there for two main reasons. The first reason is that in Japan one has to deal with a character set of over six thousand glyphs, and designing hardware and software to cope with this is difficult. The second is that the PC market sector is fragmented among the five manufacturers, each with hardware platforms significantly different from the others and, with the exception of the AX series, they are all significantly different from the base IBM PC architecture. Fortunately, they all run a variety of MS-DOS 3.21j.[4]

When Localizing for the Japanese market, besides taking into account the normal cultural issues such as currency, date formats, and so on, you must consider the fact that written Japanese uses two native character sets, Katakana and Hiragana, plus Chinese-based characters, Kanji, Latin characters, and Arabic numerals, as well as punctuation and general symbols, with a total of over six thousand characters. ASCII, a 7-bit code allowing 128 unique patterns, is not up to the task of conveying all this information.

To create a character set this large requires rethinking the representation of the character set. This was achieved by defining a *Double-Byte Character,* or *DBC,* set. A *Double-Byte Character* set uses exactly two bytes (16 bits) of storage and enables alignment of character and cursor to be maintained. A *Double-Byte Character* set permits 64K (65,536) codes, more than enough to handle all Japanese codes and allow room for expansion.

In Japan, early computers ignored Japanese and adhered strictly to ASCII standards.[5] The Japanese Industry Standard (JIS) was the first Japanese character set standard in Japan. To maintain compatibility a double-byte character, on/off escape sequence was built in to allow the single-byte and the double-byte codes to coexist. Microsoft then developed SJIS (Shift JIS) to make it easier to port DOS. This standard separated the DBC first byte ranges and the ASCII single-byte characters so that the need for the DBC on/off mechanism was eliminated.

---

[4]Japanese DOS version numbers differ from manufacturer to manufacturer. The current version of Japanese DOS is 3.21j, but NEC markets it as version 3.3 and Epson markets it as version 4.0.

[5]The following code pages are mentioned for the languages listed:

Language	Country Code	Code Page and Keyboard
Arabic	785	864, 850
Chinese (simplified)	086	936, 437 ch
Chinese (traditional)	088	938, 437 tn
Hebrew	972	862, 850 -
Japan	081	932, 437 ja
Korea	082	934, 437 ko

Code pages 862 and 864 are available only with DOS version 4 installed with a country-specific supplement.

Code pages 932, 934, 936, and 938 are valid only with the Asian edition of DOS version 4 running on a computer manufactured for use in Asia.

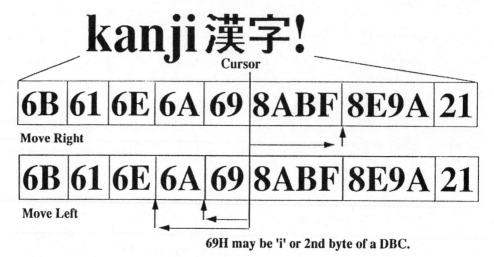

Figure 6–1.   Cursor Movement

To allow compatibility with ASCII a technique had to be devised to allow *Single-Byte Characters (SBC)* to be represented along with the Japanese Double-Byte Characters. The first standard, *JIS* (Japanese Industry Standard), defined over six thousand characters. Because the ASCII and DBC codes overlapped, an escape sequence to turn on and off the DBC was built in to allow the two to coexist.

Microsoft could not port MS-DOS to JIS easily, so a new standard based on JIS was developed. This new standard, *SJIS* (Shift Japanese Industry Standard), separated the DBC first byte ranges and the ASCII characters to different code space.[6] This works as follows: ASCII is assigned its normal code space of 0H through 7FH, and Katakana is assigned A0H through DFH.[7] The first byte of the DBC is found in the space 81H to 9FH and E0H to EFH. The second byte of the DBC is found in the ranges of 40H through 7EH and 80H through FCH. Hence, if a byte contains a character in the range of 81H to 9FH or E0H to EFH, it indicates that it is the first half of a double-byte character. You must take into account that the second byte range of the SJIS overlaps the first byte range and check that this is really the first byte and not the second byte. See Figure 6–1.

It works the same way with the other character sets. It is a matter of keeping track of the character entities and whether they are double-byte entities or single-byte entities. This leads to complications with cursor movements, insertion, deletion, and string searches. Suitable algorithms need to be used to take account of DBC-SBC issues.[8] See Figure 6–2.

---

[6]Shift JIS indicates that the JIS code space has been shifted to allow the coexistence of ASCII, double-byte characters, and the single-byte half-width Katakana characters.

[7]These hexadecimal numbers are the locations of characters within the character set table and also are the numerical equivalents of the characters.

[8]See John Nelson, *Windows/DOS Developer's Journal*, 3, no. 1, "Japanese Double Byte Character Processing," (January 1992), pp. 23–34.

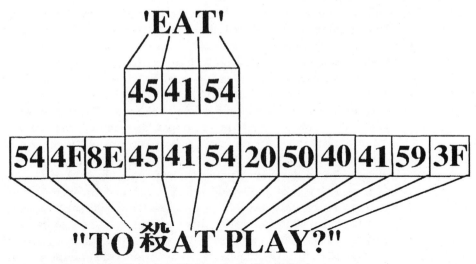

Figure 6–2.   Search Substring 'Eat' Produces Illegal Find

Screen display is complicated because of the DBC-SBC issue. It is important to realize that a DBC is a single distinct unit and that Japanese video controllers tend to operate on this premise. If bytes from a misaligned DBC are found in video memory, the interpretation of video memory by the video controller will be either totally or partially corrupted. Each screen line should start with either a SBC or the first byte of a DBC and similarly end with a SBC or the last byte of a DBC. The display width of a DBC is twice the width of a SBC, hence the cursor for a DBC is twice the width as for a SBC. If the cursor is placed on the second byte of a DBC, the cursor disappears and remains hidden until the cursor is moved or the byte at the cursor is changed to a SBC or the first byte of a DBC. The application should be designed to ensure the cursor does not fall on an "illegal byte." If the system uses text windows, then it must take care not to garble VIDEO RAM by clearing and/or saving the overlapped screen area with halves of DBCs at the windows boundaries.

The large number of characters available in written Japanese requires a reasonable method of keyboard entry.[9] This is achieved by using an *Input Method* or *Front End Processor, (FEP)*. The FEP permits the user to enter sequences of phonetic or alphabetic (Latin) characters that can then be modified and translated in several ways to find the correct DBC. The FEP can operate transparently to the application or can be partially or fully controlled within the program. The FEP is hooked into the hardware keyboard interrupt and captures key scan codes and buffers the characters internally for possible translation by the user. The FEP uses the 25th screen line to display the buffered input and the possible transla-

---

[9]Some argue there is no reasonable method to enter as complicated a written language as Japanese and that the perfection of pen entry character recognition systems will lead to higher market penetration in Japan.

tion functions and conversion. Once the user accepts the translated string, the DBC is placed in the keyboard buffer for the application to retrieve. If the FEP is turned off, the keyboard can be used for entering SBC English or SBC Katakana characters, depending on the shift state of the kana key. For the programmer there are several other complications involving the FEP, but these issues are better covered elsewhere (see footnote 8).

In Japan, about 60 percent of the PCs that are sold use hardware developed by NEC.[10] This hardware is unique to Japan and cannot run software developed elsewhere unless the software is rewritten. The rest of the market is fragmented among a number of different manufacturers using a variety of operating systems.

If you are targeting your product for the widest base of installed systems, the dominance of the NEC 9800 series can be considered a major problem when Localizing for the Japanese market. The NEC 9800 series uses INTEL chips ranging from the 8086 to 80846. This series of machines comes with a choice of two video cards of 640 × 400 resolution and 1120 × 750 resolution. The majority of the installed base has the normal resolution video adapter, and unless your application specifically needs the higher resolution, it may be advisable to consider Localizing it for the normal resolution NEC monitor. The ROM BIOS calls that this computer uses are different from those used in the IBM PCs and their clones, and the video display adapter works in a manner different from any found elsewhere in the world of IBM PCs and their clones.

The major differences as far as the programmer is concerned is that the NEC 9800 series BIOS has differences in the interrupt vectors and the structure of the video RAM, *VRAM*. The keyboard interrupt vectors are changed from *int* 16H to *int* 18H, and share *int* 18H with the video interrupt, which has been relocated from *int* 10H to *int* 18H. The NEC 9800 series also uses *int* 1AH instead of *int* 17H for printer service routines. Almost all Japanese printers support JIS, but before a DBC is sent to the printer the character must be translated from SJIS to JIS. The NEC 9800 series BIOS does not support this task, and the conversion must be performed by the application.

The IBM PC interleaves character and attribute bytes in *VRAM*, but the NEC 9800 series does things totally differently by storing the characters and their attributes in separate memory blocks. The character part of the NEC *VRAM* consists of 8KB starting at location A000H, and the attribute part is the 8KB (8,192 bytes) block starting at A2000H. Further complications arise from the way the NEC video Controller handles the DBCs. It wants them to be JIS, but since the DOS is using SJIS, they have to be converted to JIS and then manipulated further to get them into the right format for the video controller.

The recommended technical strategy, as a learning step, may be to Localize your application on the AX (Architecture Extended), as it is the only Japanese PC compatible with the IBM PC/AT. Once you are satisfied with the results of this Localization operation, you can then move your code to other platforms and concentrate on the hardware differences that need to be taken account of in the program code. The AX, although it is compatible with the IBM PC/AT, has exten-

---

[10]"IBM to Supply Hitachi with Language PCs," *Financial Times,* 27 December 1991.

sions to support the Japanese language. The AX operates in two modes: Japanese and English. The AX has a screen mode not found in the PC/AT, mode *53H INT 10H,* the AX Japanese graphics mode. This can be used to check for an AX. When the English mode is active, the Japanese extensions are disabled. For those without access to an AX, Sanyo of Japan has produced a program called AX VGA/S, which emulates the AX on an 80386 IBM AT with VGA.

Microsoft has Localized MS Windows into Japanese, and this brings a much needed element of device independence to programming for the Japanese market. Windows 3.1J was shipped in May 1993.

A group of 22 Japanese companies have entered into an alliance with IBM to form the Open Architecture Developers' Group (OADG). This group's intention is to market computers in Japan based on the architecture of IBM PCs and to promote the use of DOS/V. DOS/V is an operating system derived from the MS-DOS that IBM markets in Japan. DOS/V is capable of running software developed for ordinary IBM PCs as well as Japanese language applications. If this development proves fruitful and obtains a significant market share, then the road to Localization for Japan may be made a little less bumpy. The combination of Japanese Windows 3.1J running on the different versions of DOS/V will eliminate an application's dependence on the hardware platform.

Ken Lunde's *Understanding Japanese Information Processing* presents an extraordinarily comprehensive survey of technical issues in the Japanese market.

6.2.2. Routines

The Kana-Kanji conversion system for MS-DOS must include a front-end processor for Japanese input for converting keystrokes into Japanese, and a Kana-Kanji conversion module for controlling the Japanese conversion process from an application.

As for Chinese, there are at least 12 "well-known" methods of input for Chinese language programs, according to Pacific Rim Connections' *Catalogue of International Computer Software and Hardware Services.* There are variations within the 12 methods. The methods are Pinyin, Radical Input Method (RIM), G. B. Code, Row-Column Code, Telegraph Code, Four-Corner Code, Jianzi Shima, Bopomofo, Cangjie, Jian Yie, Big 5, and Chinese National System (CNS).

6.2.3. Windows 3.0/3.1

In addition to the routines that we mention in Section 3.3.3, there are two other functions of use for stepping through a character string, namely *AnsiNext* and *AnsiPrev.* According to Leslie Gardenswartz in "Japanese and Windows," *Windows/DOS Developer's Journal,* Vol. 3, no. 1 (January 1992), a version of Japanese Windows that will run on an ordinary IBM AT is in beta-test as of January 1992. The Japanese are accustomed to denoting a menu hot key by showing it in parentheses after the Japanese glyphs, and the sorting routines are not perfect; for example, they treat a double-byte *A* differently than a single-byte *A.*

There is also an Input Method Editor (IME), and you do not have to modify Windows programs to use it.

6.2.4. Character Sets

For Chinese software, you should assume code page 936 (People's Republic of China) or code page 938 (Taiwan). The code pages for Japanese and Korean are 932 and 934, respectively. Windows NT will use Unicode (see Section 3.2.5).

6.3. THE UNIX WORLD

6.3.1. Introduction

Edge's *Work-Group Computing Report* (10 December 1991) 1, no. 29 p. 10(1) contains an announcement that MIPS has introduced an international version of its RISC/OS, or UNIX-based operating system, and a Japanese country kit with a Japanese language interface for MIPS workstations and servers. The user simply has to type in the phonetic sound of the character, and it is automatically converted to the appropriate Kanji character. HP supplies an Input Method for HP-UX, *NLIO*.

There may be some confusion with C standards in light of the close connection between C and the UNIX operating system (which is also written in C). One objective that HP has in International program design is to support programmers in developing applications that are code-set independent. The *Worldwide Portability Interface (WPI)* automatically converts data to/from its internal coding to/from *wide* characters. The *wide* character representation is more convenient because it offers a single data type for all languages.

HP suggests the following procedure:

Convert *char* data types to *wchar_t*
Use:

wscmp	instead of	*strcmp*
iswdigit	instead of	*isdigit*
fgetwc	instead of	*fgetc*

The WPI has 11 routines that can identify all the traits of characters for all supported languages. The function **wctype** in the HP-UX reference lists these routines and provides information about them. There are further Internationalized routines for character and string processing (16), upshifting and downshifting (2), character identification (11), numeric formatting (3), and data and time (2). For input and output, there is an additional feature in the conversion character that allows you to specify the order of substrings as well as wide character conversion routines.

6.3.2. Character Sets

HP has the following character sets for these more complicated languages:

Langid	Lang=	Code Set	Language
41	katakana	KANA8	Katakana
51	arabic	ARABIC8	Arabic
52	arabic-w	ARABIC8	Western Arabic
71	hebrew	HEBREW8	Hebrew
81	turkish	TURKISH8	Turkish
301	arabic.iso88596	ISO8859-6	Arabic
341	hebrew.iso88598	ISO8859-8	Hebrew
361	turkish.iso88599	ISO8859-9	Turkish

HP also supports the following multibyte character sets for alphabets of more than 256 characters:

Langid	Lang=	Code Set	Language
201	chinese-s	PRC15	Simplified Chinese
211	chinese-t	ROC15	Traditional Chinese
212	chinese-t.big5	BIG5	Traditional Chinese
221	japanese	JAPAN15	Japanese (Shift-JIS)
222	japanese.euc	JAPANEUC	Japanese
231	korean	KOREA15	Korean

UJIS and *japanese.euc.* are the same. Despite the inclusion of the characters *15* in their names, PRC15, ROC15, JAPAN15, and KOREA15 are 16-bit character sets.

We mentioned that HP is also working on using ISO character sets. These include ISO-8859/6 and 8859/8 (see Appendix J for illustrations), but work integrating these latter two takes longer as they involve bidirectional considerations.

There is provision for other sets: Langids 901–999 are reserved for user-defined languages. To define a language, use the routine *localedef* as described in Appendix B, Sections B.3.1. and B.3.2.

KANA8's first 128 characters are the same as JASCII (the same as ASCII except that the set substitutes ¥ for \) and the last 128 characters are available for Katakana. For Asian languages some HP peripherals support five HP-16 character sets that are compatible with the five HP-15 sets we listed. It is necessary to use *NLIO* (Native Language Input/Output) to convert between HP-15 and HP-16 during input and output. *NLIO* is needed with some Asian terminals to provide the input method by which a user can input multibyte characters using a conventional keyboard. It provides input methods for Japanese, Korean, and Chinese.

HP does not yet support top-to-bottom aspects of languages; Chinese is handled right to left.

6.3.3. Routines

The function ***iconv*** operates on files and converts characters from one code set to another.

In Hewlett-Packard's HP-UX Release 7.0 of September 1990, a number of routines are available for handling multibyte characters. Included are:

mblen()	determines the number of bytes in a multibyte character
mbtowc(),	determines the number of bytes in a multibyte character, determines code value of type wchar_t, and stores code in object pointed to by pwc
mbtowcs(),	converts a sequence of multibyte characters from the array pointed to by s into a sequence of corresponding codes and stores these codes into the array pointed to by pwcs
wctomb(),	determines the number of bytes needed to represent the multibyte character whose value is wchar and stores the multibyte character representation in the array object pointed to by s
wctombs(),	converts a sequence of codes from the array pointed to by pwcs into a sequence of multibyte characters and stores them into the array pointed to by s

There are some Macro Calls that take the place of byte pointer operations:

Macro Call	Byte Pointer Analog
CHARAT(p)	(*p)
ADVANCE(p)	(p++)
CHARADV(p)	(*p++)
WCHAR(c,p)	(*p=c)
WCHARADV(c,p)	(*p++=c)

These macros operate on byte pointers, but since they call *mbtowc* (which replaces *FIRSTof2* and *SECof2*), they work on multibyte characters.

The LC_TYPE category setting Locale (see Section 5.2.2.3) determines the behavior of the multibyte character and string functions.

The environment variable *LANGOPTS* is concerned with *mode* and *order*. Mode can be left to right or right to left, and order can be the order in which the user enters keystrokes or the order in which characters are displayed.

Two commands are available in HP-UX to manage data directionality: **forder** and **strord.** The command **forder** converts the order of characters in a file from screen order to keyboard order or vice versa. The command **strord** will convert the order of characters from keyboard to screen order in special cases.

6.4. THE MACINTOSH WORLD

6.4.1. Introduction

The Macintosh System Software offers a very flexible architecture for developing applications that can support more than one script. The Japanese system software is the combination of the U.S. system software, which includes the Roman Script System, the Macintosh Operating System, the Toolbox, and so on, and KanjiTalk, the Japanese Script System, all of which are Localized for Japan.

6.4.2. Character Representation

As described in Chapter 5, the Script Manager allows different script systems to be installed, maintains global data structures, supports switching keyboards between different scripts, provides many utilities, and provides a standard interface for programmatic access to script systems.

Available script systems include Roman, Japanese, Arabic, Traditional Chinese, Simplified Chinese, Hebrew, Cyrillic, Thai, Korean, and scripts for India, Bangladesh, Devangari, Bengali, Gurmukhi, Gujarati, and more. These script systems supply fonts, ways to represent various keyboards, text collation, word breaks, and the formatting of dates, times, and numbers. Some of these script systems include special routines for handling exceedingly large character sets, which have comprehensive procedures for character in out, and for handling bidirectional or contextual text.

Scripts such as Japanese Hiragana and Katakana are syllabic: contrary to alphabetic scripts, in which the characters symbolize the phonemic elements in the language, the characters in syllabic scripts stand for syllables in the language. Katakana and Hiragana, together usually called Kana, consist of symbols that, with the exception of the single-vowel letters and the letter *n*, represent a single consonant sound followed by a vowel sound. Katakana and Hiragana's phonetic characters represent the entire Japanese alphabet of sounds, based on five vowels.

Other scripts such as Japanese Kanji, Chinese Hanzi, and Korean Hanja, include ideographic characters. The pronunciation of these ideographic characters depends on the meaning of words. For instance, the pronunciation of some Japanese Kanji characters derived from the Chinese characters, while others originated as the language evolved, so that a word can be pronounced in different ways according to how it is used. The Macintosh Script Manager routines, as described later, allow applications to run without knowing if one- or two-byte codes are being used, as long as the application is written to allow two-byte codes. The capability to represent contextual forms required to correctly display Arabic text, for instance, is also handled by the Script Manager. Glyphs, the displayed forms representing characters, may have very different shapes in relation to where they occur within a word. Also, certain characters may be combined to compose a new form (called ligature) when they occur together. Ligatures are handled by the Script Manager and are required for the correct display of Arabic text, as are characters that change form depending on what other characters are nearby.

Scripts such as Chinese, Japanese, and Korean have no case distinction. Diacritical marks, the signs modifying the value or sound of characters, may indicate different things in different languages. For instance, in Arabic certain diacritical marks specify the doubling of consonants, and in Vietnamese may indicate pitch. Rules for text ordering may vary considerably from language to language. Languages such as Cyrillic, Greek, Arabic, and Hebrew do not make a distinction between phonetic and writing order for vowels and other marks, while Southeast Asian scripts such as Devanagari treat phonetic and writing order as two separate conventions. Also, Asian scripts such as Japanese and Thai generally do not have any word delimiters. In all these cases, the Script Manager offers a sophisticated method to handle all of the described variances among different languages.

The Unicode Standard by the Unicode Consortium, portrays the Unicode Encoding to the Macintosh character mappings. Apple is a member of the consortium and intends eventually to use Unicode.

6.4.3. Text Direction

In Roman scripts, characters are written from left to right on horizontal lines of characters written from top to bottom. In Chinese, characters may be written from top to bottom on vertical lines that run from right to left. In Japanese, characters traditionally run from top to bottom on vertical lines of characters written from left to right. Today, many Japanese books are also written from left to right on a horizontal line. The Korean language, which consists of two types of characters, Hangeul and Hanja, is written from top to bottom in vertical columns that run from left to right. Nowadays, many Korean books are written from left to right on a horizontal line without Chinese characters. Arabic and Hebrew have many characters written from right to left, but the horizontal lines of text are still written from top to bottom. The Macintosh Script Manager provides the ability to write from right to left, to mix right-to-left and left-to-right directional text within lines and blocks of text, and to use ideographic text.

6.4.4. Routines

The Script Manager routines make it possible to write applications independently of the particular script in use. The Script Manager text handling routines are based on the concept of *runs,* that is, consecutive text with the same attributes, including *style runs, script runs,* and *direction runs.* A *style run* is a sequence of text all in the same font, size, style, color, and script. A *script run* is a sequence of text in the same script, and a *direction run* is a sequence of text with characters having the same direction.

Script Manager can handle the following:

Text Direction	enter a mix of scripts that naturally have different direction on the same line—e.g., English and Hebrew
Character Representation	two bytes per character
Contextual Forms	characters that change shape depending on what precedes and succeeds—e.g., Arabic
Comparison Order and Sorting	
Word Delimiters (space, period)	
Text Justification	
Date, Time, and Numbers	

See Chapter 5 and Appendix C for more details, along with Apple's *Inside Macintosh, Volume 6; Software Development for International Markets: A Technical Reference, APDA Draft;* and the *Guide to Macintosh Software Localization* and

Worldwide Software Development Overview. Apart from being very complete and comprehensive reference manuals, they provide excellent general information.

General guidelines available from Apple recommend the use of the International Utilities Package for:

date/time, unit measure, and currency formats
string comparison and sorting routines

You must be careful about using high-level language routines such as printf, scanf, Readln, and Writeln because they probably assume single-byte character sets, whereas Quick Draw, Script Manager, and International Utilities traps do not.

In "Plan It for the Planet," by Greg Williams, he suggests considering the following sequence for steps in Localizing in the Macintosh world:

If the difference between the original and new (Localized) versions of the systems are limited to number, currency, time and date format, and a slightly different character set, then use of the International Utilities Package may be sufficient with Localized system software.

TextEdit may be the next tool to consider if your software handles only simple text messages to and from the user. Even with this limited application of nonprogrammer energy, Arabic text interspersed with English can be bidirectional.

Use Script Manager if your program handles moderately complex manipulations of text. You will probably need it if handling both Roman and non-Roman scripts.

It is possible that you will need to develop your own routines if your text-handling is very complex.

6.4.5. Text Manipulation

TextEdit supports different script systems. TextEdit allows the user to edit and display text in multiple scripts and styles when a non-Roman script system is in use. TextEdit automatically handles text with more than one script, style, and direction. For instance, you can mix English text (left-to-right direction) with Arabic text (right-to-left direction) in the same line. TextEdit also supports text alignment and provides routines to support fully justified text.

Another resource editor you can use is "Resorcerer" by Mathemaesthetics. According to Douglas McKenna of Mathemaesthetics, there are two ways to create resources. One way is to compile a text file containing descriptions of resources written in a data declaration language. In general, using a data declaration language is error-prone and time consuming because it forces you to know the internal formats of the resources. The other way of creating resources is to use a resource editing application, such as Resorcerer, to create and maintain the project resource file. Resorcerer has many editors within it dedicated to editing the most common standard resource types, such as dialogs, menus, strings, string lists, icons, color lookup tables, resource templates, versions, and so on. Since the editors know the structures of these commonly used resources, the user does not need to worry about the internal form of the resource data. Some useful features supported by Resorcerer include strings editable in any font, screen copying capabilities for all graphic resources, Value Converter, which lets you see and convert between binary, hex, octal, and most standard Mac 32-bit types, general 32-bit Hex editor, powerful color menu editor, custom editor compatible with ResEdit 'TMPL' resources, and so on.

As a rule, localizers use the MPW (Macintosh Programmers Workshop) Editor to extract the translatable resources and to build the Localized version.

The APDA (Apple Programmers and Developers Association) distributes AppleGlot, a stand-alone resource editor. It extracts strings and places them in a structured text file, much as DeRez does. A translator can translate the text using any word processor. AppleGlot then restores the translated text in the same resource locations as their originals. An important feature is that it can work with glossaries, replacing already translated strings with translations made previously. This can reduce the translation effort in later versions.

7 Standards and Standards Organizations

7.1. INTRODUCTION

The concept of standards is an ancient one. From the earliest times civilizations used standards to ensure good communication of concepts and to impart some honesty in commerce. The cubit, a unit of measure used in ancient Egypt, is one of the oldest known standards. It was based on the length of the forearm of a certain Pharaoh. This length was copied to a black granite master from which copies were made. These copies were to be used in the ancient equivalent of the surveying and construction industries. Today physical standards are based on a document that describes a theoretical ideal but may still use a model as a reference point.

There are two pertinent definitions of *standard* in *Webster's* dictionary:

something established for use as a rule or basis of comparison in measuring or judging quantity, content, extent, value, quality, etc.; as *standards* of weight and measurement are fixed by the government.

anything recognized as correct by common consent, by approved custom, or by those most competent to decide; a model, a type, a pattern, a criterion.

We call standards imposed the first way *de jure* standards and those imposed the second way *de facto*. Many de facto standards evolve into de jure standards.

We interact subconsciously with *de jure* standards in everyday life when, for example, buying a pound of meat, both in terms of quantity and grade or quality. Normally we take it for granted that, no matter where we are, the State enforces its local standards. It is difficult to imagine a social life in the absence of such standards.

In the United States and many other countries, standards in the software computer industry are enforced only when dealing directly with government contracts or in mission-critical tasks.[1] The enforcement procedure is to specify that the product must conform with a certain standard or the bid will not even be considered.

Something can become so popular that it becomes a *de facto* standard because it is immediately perceived, recognized, and accepted as a solution or a way of doing something that many people in a community had been trying to resolve for some time. A product sometimes fills an unarticulated need to the extent that the pioneer's brand name becomes a generic name for the product. There are "Xeroxes" and "Kleenexes," to name a couple. Rolls Royces and Mercedes cars are commonly accepted de facto standards of excellence in automotive engineering.

In the computer world, our machine of interest, the IBM PC, was so widely accepted in the marketplace that it became a de facto standard because it brought computer power to the average person. A thriving software industry developed around it and some say that it would not have been a success but for a spreadsheet program, *1-2-3,* which itself was a de facto standard for a short time.[2] Earlier examples of de facto standards are FORTRAN, a programming language that helped engineers and mathematicians solve scientific problems, and COBOL, a programming language that helped accountants to develop large-scale accounting systems. A more modern example is the language C; in its early days a book (*The C Programming Language,* 1978) by Brian W. Kernighan and Dennis M. Ritchie defined the standard for C.

The history of FORTRAN and COBOL and also C shows an evolution away from their de facto status to a de jure status as the American National Standards Institute (ANSI) developed standards so that different manufacturers of the language compilers would produce similar, if not identical, versions of the language.[3] ANSI is not a government body with legal enforcement powers, but rather an organization that coordinates and maintains standards for a number of industries. While not enforceable with the power of law, such standards clearly have economic clout because consumers can understand what an individual manufacturer is offering.[4] Because of this value of efficient and clear communications, most manufacturers of software follow the recommended set of standards if feasible with the technology available.

---

[1]Mission-critical system: A system where life or safety could be involved, for instance, a train control system or insulin pump. There are many government regulations in such cases, even though private industry makes the products.

[2]Remember hardware sales can and have been driven by software demands on the part of the consumer.

[3]We think the reverse takes place when a manufacturer, as so often happens, produces a version that is a *superset* of the standard. By that, the manufacturer means that its version does everything that the standard calls for, *and a little bit more.* If the manufacturer is influential enough, or the change is popular enough, then there is a new de facto standard. If not, then this version becomes one of presumably several slightly incompatible and nonstandard versions.

[4]Sometimes a statute will incorporate a coordinating organization's standard or refer to it as the base document. In that manner, the standard will then have the force of law.

Standards also provide, among other things, a basis by which one computer manufacturer can plan to connect its computer to another and thus provide for the transfer of data, software, and information in general; this allows entry into another manufacturer's market domain.

The computer industry has learned that there is a benefit in developing and publishing standards well in advance of the appearance of any working hardware or software environment. Published standards then serve as *specifications,* particularly for operating system and other environments, and as constraints as well. The existence of specifications provides the opportunity to work on both the development of the hardware and its software before the environment is ready.

For example, at the moment, in our field of interest, many manufacturers plan to support the *ISO 10646* or *Unicode* standard for character sets.[5] The combined standard ISO 10646 and Unicode 1.1 was adopted as an international standard by member countries in June 1992. Microsoft has been building provisions for it into the yet-to-be-released Windows 4.0. and Windows NT. There has been sufficient progress in developing the Unicode standard to permit the integration of its core concepts into such products during their development.

Standards are not permanent. They can be superseded by newer standards and technical advances can render them obsolete or otherwise useless. Formal standards also evolve over time. As an illustration, note that there has been a progression in standards over the years for character sets. Originally companies had their own character sets, but this inhibited communication between computer systems. The introduction and acceptance of ASCII (although because of its large installed base IBM continued to use EBCDIC) was a major step in *compatibility* between computers.

As we implied in Chapter 3, ASCII was originally a 7-bit code set that could support only 127 characters, specifically the 52 lower- and uppercase letters in the alphabet, the ten numeric symbols, various control codes, punctuation, mathematical operators, and a very limited number of accents. This did not provide any support for non-American languages. With the release of the IBM PC, IBM developed an 8-bit derivative of ASCII called PC 8, which used the codes between 128 and 256 to represent additional graphic characters and some accented characters. Since it is not possible to represent all non-American characters in this space, the concept of code page switching was developed, whereby the relevant page of information could be substituted for the appropriate national language.

Then ANSI developed its own 8-bit ASCII code and the International Organization for Standardization developed a range of 8-bit character code sets supporting English and the other European languages plus Hebrew and Arabic. None of these directly addressed the issue of collating sequences, but the ability to provide support for non-English languages improved. Standards for ideographic languages such as Japanese and the varieties of Chinese have been normally set by the national governments and interpreted by the various hardware and operating system manufacturers to fit the engineering realities. These ideographic lan-

---

[5]ISO 10646 is a four-byte encoding and Unicode is a two-byte compression of that.

guages use several different multibyte encodings, for example, the Japanese JIS standard—X 0208—encoded as SJIS and UJIS.

We have implied that standards in the software industry are useful in facilitating clear communication. But this is not always the case when dealing with systems that handle multiple natural languages. In the UNIX area, we believe the proliferation of standards adds to the confusion of someone trying to understand it. See the discussion on the history of UNIX in Chapter 5.

7.2. ORGANIZATIONS

While the concept of a standard is simple, appealing, and of obvious value, in practice the real world of standards is very confusing because of the proliferation of groups issuing standards, the number of topics, and the number of standards that they issue. (There is even an adage that the nicest thing about standards is that there are so many to choose from!) Most countries have at least one organization that is recognized as being responsible for defining national standards or for enforcing them. The national organization may be a governmental agency or it may be a trade association. There are international, regional, and worldwide organizations that will coordinate the work of individual national organizations. Of these latter, the most influential is:

ISO   International Organization for Standardization

Some of the national organizations that issue standards are:

AFNOR   Association Française de Normalisation
ANSI   American National Standards Institute
ASMO   Arab Standards and Metrology Organization
BSI   British Standards Institute
CAS   China Association for Standards
CCITT   Consultative Committee for International Telephone and Telegraph
CSA   Canadian Standards Association
DIN   Deutsches Institut für Normung (German)
ECMA   European Computer Manufacturers Association
FIPS   Federal Information Processing Standards
IEC   International Electrotechnical Commission
IEEE   Institute of Electrical and Electronics Engineers
JSA   Japanese Standards Association
NNI   Nederlands Normalisatie-instutuut
SCC   Standards Council of Canada
SFS   Soumen Standardisomisliitto (Finland)

Three other organizations of interest are LISA (Localization Industry Standards Association), the Unicode Consortium, and the Secretary of State for Canada. Appendix G contains a list of all of these organizations together with their addresses.

The ISO is the principal coordinating body for standards. In many countries the local standards are directly based on ISO standards in totality. In others, such as the United States, the ISO standards may be adopted with reservations about certain parts of the standard after approval by the local standards body. The national version of a standard will often have the same number as the ISO's version. Make sure that you have the complete appropriate standard and not some version truncated by your own national body.[6]

Normally, a national body formulates, proposes, and sponsors a standard. Once ISO sees a proposal for a standard as useful, it sets up international consultations. A committee of experts, or *TAG* (Technical Advisory Group), based on their experience in a certain area can define a *de jure* standard. Based on their knowledge of what can be accomplished now, within the limitations of the present technology, and what would be useful to have accomplished, they will define the specifications known as a standard.

In the United States, ANSI membership consists of over 1,100 companies, 250 organizations, and 30 government agencies. It is the official U.S. representative to the ISO and the IEC. ANSI requires standards-developing organizations to reaffirm their standards every five years. You may purchase many ISO and IEC standards through ANSI. In our experience, this is more expensive than buying them directly from ISO. In the early stages of development, there are Working Drafts (WDs), Committee Drafts (CDs), Draft International Standards (DISs), and then International Standards (ISs). The more information you can provide in the form of document numbers, or the draft's name, or the name of the standards group responsible for the document, the better your chance of identifying it to ISO or to ANSI.

There is a hodgepodge of standards, and they tend to have some system dependency as manufacturers adopt them to fit their needs or become impatient for the development of suitable standards for their needs and their customers' needs. The world of standards is bureaucratic and it is difficult to get a good grasp on the current status of standards.

7.3. ISSUES FROM CHAPTER 2

Standards are useful for creating enabled and Localized software. The main standards of concern to the software translator are those applying to non-American characters.

---

[6]While doing research for this book, we received letters from standards organizations that did not conform with the published standard printer paper sizes for those countries or that used different monetary formats. We don't know if these were singular aberrations of these organizations or whether it was general practice to disregard their own standards. Since we have not had much occasion to study standards in detail and have generally found the world of standards to be confusing, this was not surprising. Based on our experience, we advise you to tread carefully. Treat many published standards with caution and also ask your distributor in your target country to inform you of the actual practices in their locale.

7.3.1. Non-American Characters

Currently there is a multiplicity of standards for character sets. We hope this multiplicity will be rationalized in the future with the widespread adoption of Unicode. Following are the standards for character sets that we will discuss:

ISO-8559/1–8559/9	8-bit Single-Byte Coded Graphic Character Sets
ISO10646/UNICODE	
ISO-646	Information Processing—7-bit Coded Character Set for Information Interchange
ASMO 449, ECMA-114	
ANSI X3.4	American National Standard Code for Information
Interchange	
JIS X 0208–1990	Code of the Japanese Graphic Character Set for Information Interchange
JIS X 0212–1990	Supplementary Code of the Japanese Graphic Character Set for Information Interchange
ANSI Standard X3. 159	C Programming Language Standard 98:991990
-1987 ISO/1EC	

7.3.1.1 IBM PC ISO-8559: 8-Bit Single-Byte Coded Graphic Character Sets

These sets extend ISO-646 for the major European languages and Arabic and Hebrew. The characters in the range 00H to A0H (we remind you that these hexadecimal numbers represent a range of characters within the character set, see Section 3.2) are the same in each set, while the variant part is from A1H to FFH. The range 00H to 1FH is called the C0 range (these are the first two columns) and is used for control characters. The range 80H to 9FH is the C1 range and is meant for control characters defined by other ISO standards. Manufacturers have rarely taken advantage of this, although the so-called Windows ANSI character set actually uses the ISO-8859/1 set with the addition of several characters in the C1 space. The ISO-8859 Latin Alphabets Nos. 1 through 5 supply different extended characters in their variant code area so they can be used with a wide variety of languages. The other sets' characters are self-evident from their titles:

ISO-8859/1 Part 1: Latin alphabet No. 1
ISO-8859/2 Part 2: Latin alphabet No. 2
ISO-8859/3 Part 3: Latin alphabet No. 3
ISO-8859/4 Part 4: Latin alphabet No. 4
ISO-8859/5 Part 5: Latin/Cyrillic alphabet
ISO-8859/6 Part 6: Latin/Arabic alphabet
ISO-8859/7 Part 7: Latin/Greek alphabet
ISO-8859/8 Part 8: Latin/Hebrew alphabet
ISO-8859/9 Part 9: Latin alphabet No. 5

Figure 7–1 shows ISO-8859/1 and 8859/5, while Appendix J shows all these character sets.

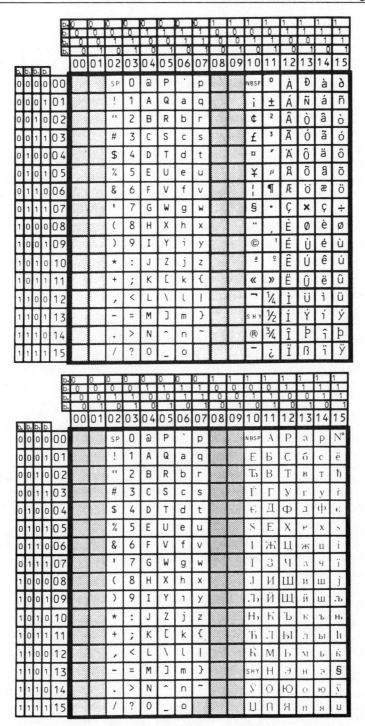

Figure 7-1. ISO Character Sets: ISO-8859/1—Latin 1 (above) and ISO-8859/5—Latin/Cyrillic (below)

7.3.1.2. ISO10646/UNICODE

ISO 10646 is a 32-bit character set that has been combined with Unicode 1.1, which is a 16-bit universal character set adopted in 1992 by various manufacturers in a consortium. The combined standard was adopted in June 1992. ISO has been working on the Universal Character Set (UCS) since 1984. It is a four-byte standard with a two-byte subset "Basic Multilingual Plane" (BMP). The BMP in the final version of the UCS (ISO10646) is identical to Unicode.

Unicode is based on having each character represented by two bytes, and there are 65,536 different codes available for characters.[7] This large number of characters makes it theoretically possible to incorporate a code for most characters in all modern written human languages and still have some unused codes available for private special purposes.

As with other character sets, each character has a numerical equivalent starting at zero. According to the Unicode Consortium's *The Unicode Standard* of 1991, ASCII is at the low end, then the various European Latin code sets and various other languages such as Devanagari and the ideographic character sets of Chinese, Japanese, and Korean.[8] Prior to this, languages such as Devanagari were poorly supported or not supported at all.

Unicode also includes a wide selection of specialized characters for mathematics, commerce, graphics, and so on. In the Unicode standard, mappings are provided between Unicode and various existing standards to enable transfer of data between systems that support Unicode and others that support the older standards. Unicode contains a Private Use Area for those end users and software developers who need a special set of characters for their application programs.

---

[7]There is one inherent problem in using a double-byte character set as a standard, and that is the problem of little-endian and big-endian computer word formats used in different computer systems. (A little-endian computer word is one in which the bytes at lower addresses have lowest significance. This is analogous to writing 14 as 41 but reading 41 with the understanding that it is 4 + (1 × 10). A big-endian computer word is the converse of this.) To enable systems that use different byte orders to read Unicode plain text format files, the file must start with a Byte Order Mark (BOM) as the first single wide character in a Unicode plain text format file. This enables a system reading the Unicode file to determine the byte order of the file and if necessary to convert the byte order to the receiving system's native byte order. The BOM is FEFF. If the system sees FFFE (the reverse byte order of the BOM), it indicates that the byte order of the Unicode plain text file is the reverse of the receiving system and should be processed accordingly.

[8]Han characters are the characters that originated among the Chinese to write the Chinese language. These are now used in China, Japan, and Korea. Each character represents a word, not just a sound, and developed from ideographic principles. The Han ideographs of Chinese, Japanese, and Korean have been culled from various national standards. Because all three language groups use a considerable number of Han ideographs in common, there are variants for certain characters and these are encoded separately. A total of 22 Han standards were folded into one for the Han component of Unicode.

There were approximately 119,000 characters covered by these national standards. After separating out cognate characters, 21,001 characters remained to be encoded in Unicode. The decisions on which characters were slight variants and could be left out of Unicode were based primarily on guidelines published by JIS, the Chinese proposal for common Han character encoding, ISO/JTC1/WG2/N480, and recommendations from the University of Toronto. In addition, the Japanese syllabic Katakana and Hiragana are also given their own code space along with Hanguel.

Outside of these applications the codes in this area are not defined. Unicode is a character encoding, the actual representation of the characters on screen or hard copy as glyphs are left to the operating system and/or the application developer. Culturally expected sorting is left to the operating system/application developer.

The Unicode Standard by the Unicode Consortium portrays the Unicode Encoding to ISO-8859, Windows Character Sets, Macintosh Character Sets, PC Code Page (including some Asian ones, single-byte and double-byte), and EBCDIC mappings. It also outlines the procedure for proposing another character. Being a private organization, the consortium does not involve the protracted processes of the more common standards organizations.

7.3.1.3. ISO-646: Information Processing—7-Bit Coded Character Set for Information Interchange

This standard provides an international set of interpretations for the 128 code values 00 to 7F. These are intended to be Localized into national standard codes.

7.3.1.4. ASMO 449, ECMA-114

Equivalent to ISO-8859-6, this is the encoding for the basic Arabic characters.

7.3.1.5. ANSI X3.4 American National Standard Code for Information Interchange

This is the ubiquitous ASCII, the U.S. Localized version of ISO-646. This standard provides interpretations for the 128 code values 00 to 7F.

7.3.1.6. JIS X 0208–1990: Code of the Japanese Graphic Character Set for Information Interchange[9]

This character set supplies the encoding for Hiragana and Katakana, the Japanese syllabary characters. It consists of two levels: level 1 encodes 524 non-Kanji and 2,965 Kanji characters: level 2 adds 3,390 Kanji characters to JIS level 1, but it is ordered by radical order and stroke.

7.3.1.7. JIS X 0212–1990: Supplementary Code of the Japanese Graphic Character Set for Information Interchange

Level 3 increases the size of the X 0208 set by 5,801 Kanji characters, and 245 non-Kanji characters and the characters are also ordered by how they are written. JIS is based on a 7-bit system that requires special escape sequences to enter DBCS mode.

---

[9]Ken Lunde, *Understanding Japanese Information Processing,* O'Reilly and Associates, Inc., 1993, ISBN 1-56592-043-0, has a very comprehensive collection of Japanese character encodings.

7.3.1.8. ANSI Standard X3.159-1989 / ISO 9899:1990, C Programming Language

This is currently the only standard programming language that provides support in its specification for international features such as multibyte character sets, wide character sets, and locales. If the compiler manufacturer says it supports only the "C" locale, this means the *setlocale* function has no effect and does not alter the cultural behavior of the other libraries.

7.3.1.9. IBM PC

The DOS code pages discussed in Chapter 3 are the de facto standard for this machine.

7.3.2. What Standards Handle and Do Not Handle

We know of some standard for the following Localization issues.

7.3.2.1. Address Formats

Country names are used to tell the operating system for which culture the system is expected to supply information. Generally these have been standardized by the ISO and use the standard name aids in communication.

ISO-3116   Code Set for the Representation of Names of Countries
ISO-639   Code Set for the Representation of Names of Languages

Address formats vary from country to country and the local standards can be obtained from the Postal Service of the country in question. This information may be available from the embassy or consulate.

7.3.2.2. Monetary Symbols and Currency

An attempt had been made to introduce an international standard for currency separators by the International Conference on Weights and Measures. This group recommends that the thousands separator should be a space instead of a comma or period. There has been resistance to this in many countries that still use their traditional separators of either a comma or period. Line breaks should not be permitted to occur in currency strings, that is, the application should treat currency delimiters correctly as internal to the currency string.

ISO-4217   Codes for the Representation of Currency and Funds

Besides the international symbol for a currency, which is designed to consist of three uppercase letters in the range A to Z, the culturally more natural form should be used in end-user software. For example, U.S. dollars are represented in the normal cultural sense as $123.46, while in international form that amount is represented as USD 123.46. Similarly, Danes write 100kr, but the international form is 100DKK. The Swiss use SFr, and the international standard is CHF.

7.3.2.3. Dates and Times

According to ISO 3307 and ISO 1000, the decimal digits representing "fractions of a second" and "seconds" should be separated by the same character that represents the decimal separator for the locale. The fractions can be tenths of a second, hundredths, or thousandths of a second.

7.3.2.4. Time Zones

Time zone names tend to be a local cultural device; the standard way to communicate time zone differences is by how many hours plus or minus Coordinated Universal Time (i.e., Greenwich mean time) the originating locales time is.

This standard should be implemented so that the user can choose the appropriate time format for his or her locale. In the case of document transmission, where time zone stamping is important, the application should permit the registration of how many hours plus or minus Coordinated Universal Time the originating locale's time is.

7.3.2.5. Hyphenation/Syllabification

Standards for hyphenation/syllabification vary from language to language and may depend on common grammatical usage, while in some countries the rules are strictly laid down by an organization such as l'Académie française in France. Apart from that and the German *Duden,* we know of no standard for this.

7.3.2.6. Case Conversion

Case conversion depends on the character set/code page being used. Not all character sets support case conversion (e.g., Han, or Arabic-based sets). These sets should ignore monocasing (converting from one case to another), while those such as ISO-8859/1 or code page 437 should support it. Note that even in these sets there are characters that are naturally monocases (e.g., the numbers) and monocasing is ignored for them.

7.3.2.7. Measurement Scales

Nearly all countries in the world use the metric system for measurements. This standard is based on the Systeme International d'Unités (SI units). In the United States everyday measures are based on the (old) English system of measurement, although in some technical areas metric units may be found. In Great Britain, Australia, and New Zealand there is a mixture of Imperial measurements and metric units in everyday use, though in industry the units used are metric.

The ANSI standard is ANSI X3.50–1986.

7.3.2.8. Page Sizes

The main defining standard for metric sizes is DIN 66008. Most countries in the world tend to use formats based on the A and B metric sizes. See Appendix A.

7.3.2.9. Keyboards and Entry of Non-Keyboard Characters

Following are some keyboard standards:

IBM keyboards are de facto standards.
Macintosh keyboards are de facto standards.
QWERTY is a de facto standard in the United States and some other English-
speaking countries.

There is an alternative keyboard available in the United States—the Dvorak. In contrast to the qwerty, which was designed for use on typewriters and was intentionally slow on some characters, the Dvorak was designed for more rapid key entry.

7.3.2.10. Memory

There is a de facto standard LIM (Lotus, Intel, Microsoft) EMS 4.0 for expanded memory on IBM PC's and clones and XMS for accessing extended memory.

7.3.2.11. Sorting

Both Duden and DIN 5007 specify a German character sequence. They are slightly different. DIN 5007 sorts diphthongs with the unumlauted vowels and is intended for use with lists of proper names, for example, telephone directories. We know of no other standards for sorting.

7.3.2.12. Items for Which We Know No Standards

There are many Localization issues that standards do not handle. We know of no formal standard for the following:

Numeric formats, separators, negatives and decimal tabs
Arithmetic operations, including rounding
Kerning
Tracking
Diacritical marks, the height of characters, and leading
Non-American spell checkers
Search and Replace
Expansion of text
Dialog boxes and menu names also need space to grow
Meaningful values for hot keys
Numbered and unnumbered messages
Are strings made up of substrings meaningful or correct in other languages?
Parsing input
Translation of clip art
Translation of icons
Translation of filenames
Recognition of translated clip art, icons, and files
Mice

Colors
Cultural considerations
Word boundaries
Character boundaries
The significance of special characters
Subsystems and the character set
Importing and exporting all the character set
Non-U.S. manufacturers and non-American hardware
Setup and installation procedures

7.4. LOCALIZATION INDUSTRY STANDARDS ASSOCIATION (LISA)

Some European Localization agencies have taken the initiative to promote standardization in technical terminology by organizing technical seminars, forums, and so on with some of their biggest customers, such as Microsoft, IBM, Lotus, and Apple. The aim is to have most of the involved companies meet, discuss common problems, and agree on a standard terminology (or at least a compromise among the different companies' preferences) for the translator and end user's benefit.

LISA is currently working to standardize five thousand terms for the Information Technology industry. LISA is an international nonprofit organization of users and vendors of translation services, dedicated to improving the industry through meeting together to discuss and establish standards, discuss common problems, distribute information to others, and attempt to raise the overall recognition and image of the product Localization industry. It is headquartered in Geneva, Switzerland. Primarily, LISA provides a forum for members; it meets four times a year and organizes subgroups to address specific areas of concern. Apple Computer Europe, Alpnet, Berlitz International, Digital Equipment, IBM/European Language Services, ICL/UK, INK International, Lotus International, Mendez Translations, Microsoft/International Product Group, NCR France, Oracle Europe, Rank Xerox Language Center Europe, Sequent Computer Systems Europe, and Softrans International are the charter members/managing board. LISA has made a provision for Associate Membership by subscription at USD 800 per year.[10] Associate members will receive the LISA-newsletter, invitations to participate in LISA sponsored projects, workshops, and seminars, and an invitation, on a fee basis, to attend an annual meeting.

Members of LISA recently approved the LISA Terminology Interchange Format, for terminology and terminology interchange, which is being proposed to the ISO Technical Committee/37.

7.5. GUIDELINES

Besides standards, there is a wide variety of *guidelines* developed by different computer industry leaders. For example, if you are developing for the Macintosh

---

[10]*USD* is the standard way of expressing U.S. dollars.

there are recommended user guidelines, such as Macintosh User Graphical Interface Guidelines. Likewise, IBM has the SAA CUA guidelines for developing applications that can be used across the hardware and software platforms that they and some of their competitors produce. Similarly, Microsoft Windows has user interface guidelines that are based on the SAA CUA from IBM. These guidelines should be treated as a standard and be followed as closely as possible unless there is a pressing need to deviate from them.

7.6. ISO 9000 AND ISO 9660

Recently ISO has published an important series of standards called the ISO 9000 series. In the United States it was adopted as ANSI/ASQC Q90. (ASQC is the American Society for Quality Control.) Five separate standards, ISO 9000, ISO 9001, ISO 9002, ISO 9003, and ISO 9004, comprise the overall ISO 9000 standard. ISO 9000 sets out the basic requirements to be met by establishing, documenting, and maintaining a quality-management system that demonstrates a commitment to quality to customers and an ability to supply their quality needs.

ISO 9000	Guidelines for selection and use of the appropriate part of the ISO 9000 series
ISO 9000-3	Guidelines for the application of ISO 9001 to the development, supply, and maintenance of software
ISO 9001	Guidelines for design/development, production, and servicing
ISO 9002	Guidelines for production and installation
ISO 9003	Guidelines for final inspection and test
ISO 9004	Guidelines for quality management and quality system elements

The basic process is similar to that used for accrediting schools, colleges, universities, and hospitals. Just as the knowledge that an institution is accredited is supposed to make you feel that it is reputable and therefore trustworthy, so the information that a company is *registered* is supposed to be a sign that a company is reputable and trustworthy. The fact that a supplier or company is *registered* demonstrates that it conforms to ISO 9000 standards; it has been audited by accredited assessors, has passed the audit, and can be listed in a country's directory of firms in compliance with the standard.

Clearly, the assessors performing the audits are themselves trained and audited in their own process of accreditation. In the United States, the ASQC will play a significant part in this higher-level process of accreditation. In turn, their accredited assessors will register individual suppliers and companies. The ASQC is also a prime source of detailed information about the ISO series and many other quality issues.

ISO 9660 is ISO's file format for CD-ROMs. Many CD manufacturers have adopted it so as to make their disks compatible with a large variety of computers.

PART 4
Business Aspects

8 Logistics, Roles, and Responsibilities

8.1. INTRODUCTION

In previous sections of this book and in Appendix D we discuss software product development. The result of all that development is a "master" set of disks and publishing proofs from which we can manufacture individual copies of a software product for sale.[1] Distribution obviously takes place in the target country, but where and how should development, Internationalization and Localization, and manufacturing take place? Do other organizations have an interest in the choice? What are the issues to consider in making the decisions?[2]

Before discussing where the production work should take place, we want to say a few words on the factors that we think play an important role in the Localization process: time, cost, resource availability, and accuracy.

Localized versions of software have an enormous advantage over the U.S. version, and end users prefer a Localized version even if sold at a premium price in comparison to the U.S. version. Multiple Localized versions may be needed in countries where more than one language is officially spoken (Switzerland, Bel-

---

[1]*Software*, by the way, is not sold. Its use is *licensed*. U.S. manufacturers have taken the same approach in their overseas operations. A license can be for source code or executable code and is normally based on the number of computers, users, or CPUs, that will use the copy. Apart from the legal technicality, everything else about the transaction between the end user and the producer is like a sale. It looks like a sale, it acts like a sale, people talk about sales volumes, and so on, but it isn't a sale.

[2]Please bear in mind that this book is addressed primarily to U.S. organizations interested in Internationalization and Localization of software for distribution in Canada and Western Europe. It is also assumed that these U.S. organizations will carry out the original software development in U.S. English and will conduct whatever quality assurance they consider necessary.

gium, and Canada). Developers that can provide multilingual versions of a product will have a competitive advantage over companies that do not, and they will be regarded as more appealing by distributors in those multilingual markets.

Many people are involved in a product Localization process, such as staff for product development, Localization, documentation, marketing, sales, and technical support. Some of these people may be located in different places, often far from each other. External organizations such as distributors, joint venture partners, and Localization agencies may also be involved, and the coordination of all their efforts can be complex.

8.2. TIME

You can save time by Localizing in the United States where the development takes place, since communication is easy and quick. This is not always possible; occasionally Localization must take place in the locale in which the Localized software is to be marketed (the target locale), and in some cases Localization is carried out at a place that is close neither to the developing organization nor to the target locale. The time that is saved in communication may be lost if an equivalent (or greater) amount of time is needed for U.S. engineers to learn what they need to know about the target locale.

Problems arise when Localization is handled by third-party vendors, external translation agencies, subsidiaries, or distributors distant from the developing organization. Problems can be exacerbated if Localization takes place in another country. Many companies have experienced delays due to their physical separation from the Localizer.

8.3. ORGANIZATION

The overall cost of Internationalization and Localization depends on a large number of factors. Different companies implement the Localization process in different ways. Usually the goal is to minimize production time and cost while meeting the organization's quality standards. Some companies have been extremely successful in Localizing their products by:

> setting up long-standing business relationships with a worldwide network of reliable distributors, subsidiaries, joint venture partners, and third-party Localization agencies;
> developing Internationalized versions of software at the parent company;
> creating small development and Localization teams in the largest markets; and
> learning from their own past experiences, and from the successes and failures of their competitors.

The result of a successful combination of all these factors is a worldwide product strategy. This can enable a company to build and introduce products Localized in several languages in different countries concurrently.

8.4. AVAILABILITY OF RESOURCES

Since translating into your own native tongue is one of the comparatively simple modes of translation, it is generally easier to find translators in the country where the Localized product will be sold. Companies Localizing in the United States can experience difficulties in finding a translator in the language and the locale required, at the exact time that they need one. In addition, the target locale will provide easier access to Localized versions of equipment, operating systems, and other related software such as word processors that provide input for desktop publishing programs.

8.5. ACCURACY

While finding native speakers is obviously easier in the target locale than in the United States, there is no guarantee that a translation done in the country where the product will be sold is more accurate than a translation done at the company's headquarters. Several factors are involved, including the linguistic and technical competence of the translator, experience of the translator, knowledge of the particular product to be Localized, working environment, project management, time frame, and motivation.

Accuracy also depends on the timeliness and precision of the information given to all of the parties to the Localization process. These include the translator, the Localization team, subsidiaries, partners, distributors, translation agencies, technical support staff, and the marketing and sales force. The greater the distances between these groups, the more difficult it is to pass on information and corrections promptly. Last-minute changes can be very difficult to handle.

8.6. GEOGRAPHY

Broadly speaking, the work necessary to produce an Internationalized and Localized software product may be distributed geographically as follows:

Develop	Internationalize	Localize	Manufacture
U.S.	U.S.	U.S.	U.S.
U.S.	U.S.	Target Locale	Target Locale
U.S. and Target	U.S. and Target	Target Locale	Target Locale

In practice, it is not always easy to determine where some aspect of the work is actually done. If the manufacturer has a network of computers that encompasses many target countries including the United States, and if development work and Localization work are transmitted routinely from place to place, then it's not possible to state unequivocally that the development and Localization work is being done in one place or the other, since the two processes are so closely intertwined. A Quality Assurance engineer in the United States might routinely check the work of a translator in Spain and send anomaly reports from the United States to Spain for correction.

There is a large variety of hybrid situations where the Internationalization and Localization process can be partially done in the United States and partially done by subsidiaries in target countries. To complicate the scenario, software companies may also contract with outside Localization agencies that will handle the Localization in the country where the product is to be sold.

There is no such a thing as a perfect model you can apply to your company at any time. Each situation has to be carefully evaluated according to variables such as the company's size, the nature of its business, the products and technology sold, the organization of subsidiaries and distributors, market sizes, market potentials, and so on, to find the Internationalization and Localization model that is most appropriate to your organization. Whatever model you adopt today may need to be changed as the market changes.

The rationale for choosing a Localizer in the target locale is more or less the converse of the rationale for choosing one close to your development location. But you will have more difficulty in communicating with a Localizer in your target locale for a number of reasons. For example, California office hours overlap with European office hours only for about an hour in the Pacific morning, so that phone calls need to be made at those times. They overlap with Asian office hours in the late afternoon, but due to the International Date Line, you are limited to four days a week (your Friday is their Saturday). Faxes are, of course, quite rapid—but they are still faxes. Sending packages back and forth by a carrier such as DHL will take about three or four days to Europe. Occasionally, there will be a delay, or a package may be mislaid. Decisions based on communication will therefore take much longer. You will have less control in general and over schedules in particular.

It is almost impossible to overstate the difficulties of communicating over such long distances and between people in different cultures. It is our experience that few people understand the need to be both precise and complete in their communication, particularly written communication, and even fewer will take the time and expend the energy required in ongoing matters that appear routine.

It helps to have a data communication link, but this has to work perfectly in order that characters, particularly control characters such as "carriage return," are not stripped from files. Moreover, you should also consider the cost of sending large files back and forth over the ocean. A direct PC-to-PC file transfer can be quite an experience (and expensive, too), if you consider the phone line problems you may have when trying to transmit some data to your Spanish office, for example. Unless you decide to keep your international data exchange to a minimum, you definitely need more sophisticated file transfer methods, for instance a public BBS with mailbox capability such as CompuServe or Apple Link that allows you to upload your files and then retrieve them at a later time, removing the time difference problem.[3]

---

[3]However, it was not clear to us at our time of writing how CompuServe handled extended characters, because its character set is limited to the lower ASCII set; at least it requires that the high bit be stripped according to Red Ryder 10.0 Documentation, "Using International or Special Character Sets," p. 70. (This should not be a problem with binary transfers.) As of July 8, 1992, CompuServe is testing a 256-bit ASCII character set. Which one, we don't know, and local U.S. CompuServe personnel can't tell us. The German language CompuServe Interface Managers (CIMs) operate in 7-bit ASCII and users substitute diphthongs such as *ue* for the character *ü*. Many users in the Foreign Language Forum (GO FLEFO) recommend the use of the routine CFLIP, available in the library.

Even working at a distance in the United States raises minor issues concerning work schedules. It is customary for many Southern states to celebrate Robert E. Lee's birthday, a factor you may not consider when planning a business trip since it is not a national holiday. Europeans take many more vacations and holidays than their American counterparts, and Europe in particular is famous or notorious for shutting down in August. Such sources as Letts' *Timeplan Diary* recommend avoiding business visits to France and Spain from July through September. In Arab countries, it is difficult to do business during *Ramadan*.

8.6.1. Model 1: All Work Done in the United States

In this first model the Internationalization and Localization process takes place in the United States, and the software company is completely responsible for it and for the manufactured product. This approach is effective for companies that are new to international business and want to control every phase of the process. Obviously, you'll need staff that is competent to handle all of the activities that are involved in Internationalization and Localization.

If you choose a Localizer whose place of business is close to your own, you can confidently expect the same level of communication that you would get with any other local supplier. You could expect to have about the same level of control, too. What you might also expect is that the Localizer, being distant from the target locale, may not be quite as up-to-date as a Localizer working in the actual target country. Your Localizer may not be able to inform you about the popular platforms of the moment (the computer business is a very fast-moving one), it may not have close ties with local distributors, and the Localizer's staff may be out of touch with the current culture of the target locale.

Since languages and cultures are "living things," constantly evolving, it is more difficult for translators living in the United States to keep informed about the latest trends in the computer business in the target locale, even if it is their native soil, unless they spend much of their time travelling and working in their own country as well as in the United States. New technical terms are created all the time, and sometimes technical terms borrowed from other cultures can become so popular in the target language that the terms are no longer perceived as "borrowed terms."

And lastly, access to non-American hardware and software will be difficult. The lack of such equipment can be a serious impediment to development and quality assurance of software.

8.6.2. Model 2: Development and Internationalization in the United States and Localization and Manufacture in the Target Country

In this second model the Internationalization is handled in the United States by the developer, while others located at the target locale are in charge of the Localization process. In this case you need to seek organizations that have Localization groups and that have experience in translating and adapting products for the local market. Your collaborators also need to be very responsive in providing you with Localization requirements, market information, feedback on product features, and so on at the very early stage of your international product development cycle. Your access to target hardware and software is better and therefore development and testing will be better directed.

If your organization is sufficiently large, you might want to establish a European subsidiary office to coordinate and support Localizations in individual countries.

In either case, should the Localizer discover anomalies, there can be some delay in getting them to the attention of the developer and communicating their resolution back to the Localizer. In the latter stages of development, when there may be daily updates and releases, delays can result in overloading the communication system.

8.6.3. Model 3: Development in Both the United States and the Target Locale, and Localization and Manufacture in the Target Locale

In this model, the software company has a network of collaborators that have expertise in developing international products as well as in Localizing products. The development group in each collaborator is actually co-developing the product with its U.S. counterpart. In one sense, the U.S. developer acts as a supervisor of the development work done in the target locale to ensure that all of the desired features are included and that the quality is up to its standards. This allows a faster international product development process and an easier implementation of the requirements of each local market. Communication between the development and Localization group is facilitated in this case, since both groups are in the same local organization.

You will need a method of software configuration control for the various Localized releases you'll send to your translation sites overseas, particularly when working on several Localized versions at once. However, the advantage of Localizing in the target country is that your Localizer will know the local computer scene, the local distributors, and the local reviewers very well and will be able to offer up-to-date advice about many issues. Your Localizer may also be able to handle local technical support issues very quickly.

8.7. BUSINESS RELATIONSHIPS

Unless your company is already involved extensively in Canadian and European enterprises and has branches or subsidiaries throughout Western Europe, you will have to develop relationships with various collaborators in other countries. These collaborators will include some or all of the following: software developers, Internationalizers, Localizers, translators, marketers, manufacturers, and distributors. Your relationship to any of these may be a simple contract, a joint venture, equity participation, or any of many other possible business arrangements.

The most critical issue when doing international business is to find the right collaborator and to establish a successful business relationship. U.S. Government agencies such as the Department of Commerce, foreign consulates, computer associations, platform-specific development and marketing support organizations, international trade associations, and publications offer general marketing information on target markets as well as lists of distributors, consultants, representatives, and so on whom you can contact.

Choose your international colleagues carefully; you don't have to sign up with the first one that you find. Take time to investigate the different possibilities you have in the markets you want to target, talk to local experts, local press people, distributors working for your competitors, and visit local trade shows. Most important of all, check to see if the potential collaborators you want to contact are familiar with your products and if your products fit with their overall line of products.

Potential collaborators will want information about you. Be prepared to give them a description of your company, its history, past and recent successes, your product line, customers, market size, and competitors. Explain the benefits they will derive from working with you.

Distributors may expect you to suggest pricing strategy (dealer and distributor margins, licenses, volume discounts, etc.), as well as ideas for promotions and product introduction. It is your responsibility to make sure that the distributors (and any other collaborators, for that matter) understand what you expect from them—the type of role and business relationship you want to establish with them. Any issues you can resolve with your future colleagues prior to the first draft of the contract can avoid wasting time and money.

8.7.1. Distribution Channels

There are several distribution channels, other than subsidiaries or sole distributors, that software companies can evaluate before committing to a particular one. Establishing a *joint venture* overseas is a fast way to get started at fairly low risk. Joint venture arrangements seem common among international distributors. The advantage of using these worldwide (inexplicably called Pan European) distributors is their buying power and stocking capabilities. The disadvantage is that it is unlikely that these organizations can maintain equal capabilities in all their markets.

Use of direct mail systems for software, popular in the United States, is increasing overseas. It can work successfully if products lend themselves to mail-order marketing. However, the cost involved in acting as the local distributor can be high. When the product does not require any support, is low priced, and is not sold through international distributors and mass market organizations, the mail-order system can work well for overseas distribution.

Some U.S. distributors now act as international distribution houses as well. The advantage of this solution is the distributor's strength in terms of price and buying power. The disadvantage is the lack of focus on product lines and market diversification. Since U.S. distributors tend to fear competition from international distributors, they frequently try to force developers to allow worldwide distribution rights.

Other still fairly new distribution approaches include electronic and CD ROM and hard drive distribution. Electronic distribution seems quite logical for software products. In the United States there are several bulletin boards that provide this service. The Minitel system provides this service in France (see Glossary). Low-priced software products (under $200) benefit the most from this type of distribution.

CD ROM and hard drive distribution can work well for products that do not need manuals. It also seems very effective for selling products by letting customers test the software prior to purchase. However, this approach may become a burden when pre-sale support is needed or when some of the software is not included with the product as a bundle; for instance, the seller might not have exclusive rights to sell all the products in the bundle.

8.7.2. Contract Negotiation

Even if you are not new to international business, it is always a good idea to consult a lawyer who specializes in international business. When negotiating a contract with a distributor, there will always be many legal issues to deal with, such as copyrights and trademarks, local licenses, and local import and export restrictions. Potential collaborators should be investigated thoroughly, and legal and financial issues must be considered as well as staff, market share, goals, history, and so on.

U.S. headquarters (including its counsel) must be responsible for negotiating any contract with any potential collaborator. Any initial oral agreement should be closely followed by a written contract. This process avoids confusion and unnecessary delays in getting your Localized products into the market. Some companies have experienced an unacceptable deterioration in quality because a collaborator has cut costs too much when it was responsible for Localization costs, either in part or completely.

8.7.3. Relationship with Your Distributors

The success of the relationship with your distributors depends a great deal on how well you and the distributors do business together and how much you share the same goals. The contract between you and a distributor should clearly contain all the details of how business will be conducted: payment terms, minimum order quantities, the bounds of the marketing territory you are giving, shipping and receiving procedures, stock rotation, pricing, general contract terms, causes for termination, how to handle customers' returns and defective products, warranties, product registration policies, and technical support issues.

To avoid misunderstandings later on, the contract must be specific as to who owns the inventory, how long the agreement will last, and how to handle the potential dissolution of the agreement. Being clear at the time a contract is signed will increase the likelihood that the ensuing relationship will be mutually beneficial and satisfactory.

An important component of any contract with a distributor is the statement of your marketing expectations. Set realistic goals, reward exceptional performance, and be flexible. Work with your distributors to identify market opportunities. Business practices are different in different countries. For example, in France, after a day-long meeting with your distributor, it is not uncommon to conclude a deal at a dinner table rather than in an office. Be prepared to travel extensively; a face-to-face meeting and a warm handshake can do much more than calls, faxes, and daily correspondence with your distributors. Once you have selected a distributor, trust that person's judgment; he or she knows the market better than you do. Your distributor's success will be your success.

It is a real challenge to understand people who are many miles away and who do not necessarily share your culture and social values, and to make them enthusiastic about your products and motivated to work hard on your behalf. A carefully written and clearly understood contract can be a major contribution to mutual understanding.

8.7.4. Marketing Issues

Since the software industry is a fast-moving one, companies that do not have a good understanding of the latest trends in the target market risk Localizing their products poorly.

If the marketing of a Localized software product is to be a success, it is essential that both you and your distributor work on the same marketing and sales goals. It is equally essential that you and your distributors agree on the shares of the proceeds that each party is to receive. You, the manufacturer, are responsible only for Localizing the software and for delivering the master disks. The distributor does all the rest (he or she may find translators/Localizers for you also); that person will create an entire marketing and distribution package, finalize a distribution plan, and be responsible for product positioning, packaging, pricing, and advertising. In other words, your distributor will create your product's image for you. In such a case your return should be in the range of 15 to 20 percent of your distributor's profit. It is therefore critical that you and your distributor agree in advance and in specific contract terms, on all these issues to avoid unpleasant surprises and perhaps even the failure of the product.

When a company has sufficient in-house expertise to fully Localize a product itself (software, manuals, collateral, packaging), then it can collect up to 40 percent of the distributor's profits. This time, though, the company has made quite an investment up-front to translate, manufacture, ship, and stock the product.

Normally, the retail price of American software products in Europe is 25 to 30 percent higher than it is in the United States. We cannot find any justification for this that makes sense to us. The most common reason we have heard is that European end users expect such services as telephone assistance, on-line help, and immediate access to updated versions of the product they bought. In the United States, the manufacturer often provides these services and presumably must cover the costs involved. We can't believe that it makes such a difference in cost as to who provides the service. In Europe, the distributor becomes the strategic party who knows best how to meet customers' expectations.

In contrast to what happens in the United States, where the developer is responsible for deciding product advertising and public relations, European distributors invest time and money to position a Localized product through press conferences, newsletters, and advertising. For this reason it's not unusual for U.S. companies to offer their distributors exclusive distribution rights and higher margins.

8.7.5. Ownership of the Localized Product—Intellectual Property Laws

Copyright and patent laws vary from country to country, even though there are international agreements in both areas. As a result, be sure to consult appropriate legal advisors before entering into any agreements regarding any aspect of the production, distribution, or marketing of any software product.

The ownership of any Localized product should be fully discussed with your non-American collaborators when any part of the work of Localization is being done by any outside entity, and the results of the discussion should be included in any contract that is negotiated between the parties. Normally, the developer who owns the base product from which the Localized version is derived wants to own the Localized version as well, but in some countries such as France, the translator will own the copyright to the translated material unless otherwise specified. If the developer maintains rights to the Localized version then the copyright message will only mention the translator's and distributor's names as the translator and distributor. The laws vary from country to country.

There are cases when the development of a Localized product is handled entirely by a local entity to meet a special customization requested by an important customer. In this case, an agreement between you and the distributor should specify clearly who owns what.

8.7.6. Gray Marketing and Piracy

Gray marketing happens when a product is acquired outside the channel authorized to distribute it. For example, if you buy a car or an expensive watch in Europe and import it yourself to this country, you are becoming part of a gray market for that product. Most non-American manufacturers have already set up a sales, marketing, and support organization here. Similarly, non-American software resellers that bypass their authorized distributors to purchase a product directly from U.S. companies contribute to or cause a gray marketing problem.

U.S. companies react in different ways to minimize the problem of gray marketing: they prohibit their domestic distributors from selling abroad, sign exclusive contracts with non-American distributors, reevaluate and adjust margins granted to their non-American distributors to reflect value added to the product by the distributors, and make new product releases available in the target markets at the same time the new releases are announced in the United States. Localization can reduce the consumers' incentives to buy gray-market versions of a software product because of the availability of local support and ease of use of the official version.

Piracy is much greater in some overseas locations than in others. The economic incentives are reputed to be higher with higher software prices and lower per capita incomes in many areas. Regulation of the distribution and sale of unauthorized copyrighted material is more lax in many parts of the world. Pakistan, Hong Kong, and Saudi Arabia are rumored to be great sources for pirated copies of software. Some governments are also taking actions to diminish the problem. For instance, the Government in Brazil, in addition to removing import restrictions, has approved very strict antipiracy rules that will be officially enforced by the end of 1992.[4]

8.8. LOGISTICS

8.8.1. Some Actual Cases

In the last few years, some U.S. companies (for example, DEC) have had Localization centers in France, England, and Germany, while many companies (Borland, Claris, Lotus, Microsoft, and Retix) have worked out of Ireland.[5] Prior to its acquisition by Borland, Ashton-Tate had a Development Center in Singapore translating into 15 European languages. Chile and India also are sources of well-educated and comparatively lower-paid work forces.

8.8.2. International Technical Support

Some problems with software that is marketed overseas surface at headquarters in the shape of a forlorn fax from San Marino or Liechtenstein. The turnaround time for an overseas user who has encountered a problem can be quite long. Lucky ones can communicate well enough in English to say "Mayday" (or should it be "M'aidez"?). Those who do not find it so easy to communicate are in a worse situation.

It should go without saying that a manufacturer who has realized the potential of Localized software has given some thought to how users may be supported. A high level of technical support has actually become the competitive edge for many companies. The level of technical support that customers expect from vendors today is much higher than it was in the past, according to the latest statistics published by associations such as the Software Publishers' Association. In a more and more competitive environment, good technical support becomes critical to the success of a product.

---

[4]We do not know how they will be enforced.

[5]According to an article by Barry O'Keefe of *The Irish Times,* extracted in the June 1992 issue of *World Press,* Ireland is consciously attempting to become the "Software Capital" of Europe. With the advent of ASK, Inc. there are six out of the world's top ten software companies with offices there, to take advantage of Ireland's English-speaking, well-educated work force. Seven thousand (7,000) people contribute USD 2.5 billion (the article doesn't say if this is an American or English billion and they only differ by a factor of one thousand) or 10 percent of total exports. However, we hear rumors that at least one large U.S. company is centralizing its Localization activities back in the home office in the United States.

It is necessary to have staff that is technically competent to understand problems that arise after a software product is in general use, but that can communicate at the user's level of experience and in the user's language, to give advice on how to handle a problem.

When volume in one locale does not warrant a technical support staff for that target country alone, you can consider regional support that answers questions and provides support to several target countries within the region. For example, a technical support department in Brussels, London, Dublin, or Frankfurt might service all of Western Europe. Many companies have adopted this solution, which allows an extensive geographical coverage and good leverage of existing resources.

Among the advantages to companies with a high level of international technical support is the ease with which they obtain feedback from users. This feedback can then be used to decide on product features for future versions of that product.

8.8.3. Maintenance and Repairs of Anomalies

Normally, the responsibility for software maintenance and the repair of anomalies is specified in the agreements you have with your non-American collaborators. Maintenance may be performed either by the U.S. developer or by the non-American entity that Localized the product in the target locale.

Software is not "bug" free (a bug is any problem found in a product), and "quiet releases" (releases that fix a certain number of "bugs") are quite common in any product life cycle. International companies find it necessary to quickly address problems reported by their international end users through their normal channels (distributors, third-party vendors, subsidiaries, etc.). For large international corporations the process of certifying "bug fixes" can take some time because of divided responsibilities within any large company. For instance, if a bug fix has not been approved by a European branch office after being tested by the development group in the U.S. organization, then it has to be reworked until the U.S. organization obtains final approval from the local branch.

8.9. ROLES AND RESPONSIBILITIES

There are many different tasks that arise in the course of Internationalizing and Localizing a software package. There are engineering tasks or translation tasks, and frequently both, that must be addressed in dealing with text strings, messages and dialog boxes that are part of the user interface, text in clip art and icons, filenames, "readme" files, messages in on-line Help, copyright messages, manuals (including covers), supplements and collateral material, license agreements, quick reference cards, registration cards, boxes and promotional materials that are part of the box, slipcovers, and labels for the disks containing the software product.

The responsible parties may be in more than one organization. The software developer's engineers may Internationalize the software, perhaps in consultation with Localizers, and then the Localizer will Localize while the developer's Quality Assurance staff verifies that work. The developer's software engineers will address any anomalies found in this process. After the product is manufactured, marketers and distributors will market and distribute the Localized product. During the entire process, it is quite likely that the software developer will consult with the manufacturer of the computer on which the software is to operate, the developer of the operating system of that computer, or the developer of its Graphic User Interface as questions arise.

8.9.1. The Localizer

Ideally, a Localizer should combine both technical and linguistic talents. He or she must be able to talk the language of the software developer. Some of the skills expected from the personnel who deal with Localization are:

Engineering:

Familiarity with computers in general, with specific platforms in particular, and with the type of software to be Localized.

Translation:

Knowledge of the target country and sensitivity to language and cultural concerns.
Absolute fluency in the target country's version of the language, and some familiarity with computers in general, and with the specific platform in particular, is useful even for documentation translation, not just software.

The Localizer performs the engineering function and manages the software during the process of conversion. The Localizer supervises the translator and uses any necessary tools to verify and validate the functionality of the Localized product.

8.9.2. The Translator

The translator's main responsibility is to translate text. To this end, the translator should be a native speaker of the target language. The translator works under the direction of the Localizer and alerts engineers to potential cultural problems or issues.

Organizations offering translation services have started to address such important issues as the standardization of technical terms. The translator has to accept the terminology dictated by the software developer and the Localizer and use it consistently throughout the work.[6]

8.10. QUALIFICATIONS OF A LOCALIZING AGENCY

Some of the largest translation companies have technical professionals (software engineers, linguists, etc.) who have the know-how to make the technical side of the Localization process much easier and productive for nontechnical translators. These types of agencies we call Localizing agencies. Appendix F contains a list of some of the more experienced ones in European languages.

---

[6]This is particularly true on the Macintosh, where users have come to expect a consistent, predictable interface as a matter of course and deviations stick out like a sore thumb.

If you are contracting with a Localizer, there are some qualities and qualifications that you should look for in addition to price and a proven track record. A contractor may be expected to be familiar with the general environment in which the software runs (for example, IBM PCs, Networks, Windows, Macintosh, or UNIX, preferably with the manufacturer's version of those environments) and may also be expected to provide necessary education, training, and technical support to any subcontractors. Further, in many cases, the Localizer would be expected to have the necessary equipment to run the software. It is not unusual for software developers to expect some validation of the translated material. This requires some computer knowledge and background.[7]

Software companies often provide their Localizers with tools to go with their Internationalized products to combine components into the form that executes on a machine. Often these tools are primitive or a little "shaky"; they are intended for internal use in the development process and are not for sale to the public. The developer does not devote a great deal of effort to make them perfect. The use of such tools, or having the background necessary to use them or even to make them work, is primarily a software engineering function.

There are tools available on the market that allow you to modify/translate a special type of file, such as a resource file, containing text strings. These tools tend to be targeted to developers and programmers and require a certain level of technical competence. Some of these tools are so low-level that you can easily find yourself in difficulty if you don't know how to use them.

A Localizing agency is expected to have expertise in the business of translating text. In a very real sense, this is an agency's bread and butter. You would expect them to be successful at it and to have translated text for many kinds of clients in addition to software developers. Many Localizers have developed considerable expertise in managing terminology and they maintain extensive databases developed in the course of their experience in translating from one language to another. Localization agencies with experience in translating into many languages, not just one or two, may effect some economies of scale because the overhead of learning and familiarization with the product can be spread over a number of Localizations rather than just one.

8.11. STANDARDS IN EUROPE AND IN AMERICA

American manufacturers should investigate the Europeans' point of view about the standards pertaining to their products. There will probably be a different set. We would recommend checking with the target country's local consulate at an early stage for information about the current state of pertinent standards.

Some people believe that Europeans take standards more seriously than do Americans; they take a more rigid approach, one that results in less room for individual initiative. In, say, standards relating to the ergonomics of computer

---

[7]Some large software companies expecting long-term relationships with Localizers will divide up their Localization work between two or more Localization agencies. This keeps the agencies on their toes.

hardware, disagreement between Europeans and Americans centers on the inclusion of *shall* compared to *should*.

There can be two major consequences of this conservatism. First, government procurement procedures may require that products meet certain standards, just as in the United States. Their standards may be stricter.

Second, in product liability law, a manufacturer's defense against charges of defective products can be substantially bolstered by demonstrating that the manufacturer has proceeded according to normal and reasonable practice within the industry. Conforming to standards that prevail locally can be part of such a demonstration.

Of growing importance is ISO 9000. It appears that many potential Europea, customers will look for suppliers who are certified under its procedures. It is a requirement for doing business in the European Community starting in 1993. See Section 7.6 for a brief discussion.

8.12. REFERENCE MATERIAL

Greentree Associates (in Boston, MA) produces the *SPA International Resource Guide and Directory,* which contains the names and addresses of many organizations, consultants, Localizers, lawyers, and translators interested and experienced in the software Localization process. It is published semi-annually. The MZ Group (in San Francisco, CA) publishes the *Macintosh Service Directory* quarterly. Subsidized by Apple, it contains many advertisements by many providers on the Macintosh. The RM Publishing Corporation (in Rolling Hills Estates, CA) publishes the *International Software Report* monthly and provides international news focused on software.

9 Cost Considerations

9.1. INTRODUCTION

In this chapter we discuss some of the costs that are involved in Localizing and marketing a software product.

There are many paths by which an organization can reach a decision to develop and market a software product. We will mention here only a very few of the many considerations that may apply to such a decision.

The anticipated sales volume and the planned selling price (that is, the net received by the developer), along with the expected total development cost, are essential for a decision that is based on the return on the investment.

For example, although you might be willing to invest a substantial amount in developing a French version of a software product for France where the market may be large (France's population in 1989 was 56 million), you probably would not want to put as much into developing a French version for Québec (with a population of only 7 million). If a product is developed for France, it would not be unreasonable, on financial grounds, to ignore the linguistic differences (upper-case accented vowels and probably a small number of differences in vocabulary) in your product, and to attempt to sell the same version in both France and Quebec. The only differences between the French and the Canadian packages might be the registration card's return address, some references to setting the locale in the operating system, and some references about how to get technical support.

Many other reasons may underlie a decision to develop and market a particular product. A product may be offered at a price very much greater than that required for a satisfactory return on investment if it is thought that customers will buy it, as a means for offsetting investment losses that may have resulted from products that did not achieve an acceptable return. Alternatively, a product may be developed simply to fill in a line of products and to shut out possible competition, even if it is a "loss leader" or if the expected return is not as high as might be considered "normal" by the developer.

Whatever path is followed in reaching a decision to produce a particular software package, good business practice requires the developer to have a realistic understanding of the costs of development. While a developer may be familiar with the costs involved in producing a package for the U.S. market, that person may not be quite as familiar with the additional cost considerations that arise in the course of preparing a software product for an international market.

9.2. COSTS TO BUILD INTERNATIONAL PRODUCTS

Internationalized or Localized products incur costs that do not arise in the development of a product designed to be offered only in the U.S. market. These additional costs include the costs of Internationalization, Localization, translation, freight, customs duties and taxes, and technical support. They can be estimated reasonably well and will provide management with the information it needs to make realistic development decisions. Note that there are times when Internationalization or Localization is applied to a product already in the U.S. market. In such a case, the costs of making a product available in the international market will be incremental to the costs already incurred.

Costs to build international products may vary according to the type of product and the platform on which it is to operate. Cost will also depend on the Localization process you select, as well as on market and economic conditions. If the product is not already in existence, costs will include expenditures for development (specifications, design, programming, quality assurance, documentation, Internationalization and Localization, maintenance), manufacturing (including the cost of materials), distribution, technical support, marketing (product launch, publicity, advertising), legal fees, taxes, and the ever-present overhead.

9.2.1. Development Costs

When developing a product for the international market, you must discuss the product specifications not only with the product developers, but also with the marketers (both domestic and from the locations in which you plan to sell the product) and any outside parties that will have any part in the development, manufacture, distribution, or marketing of the product. The process of "freezing" the product's features may take quite some time, but it is important that all the interested parties clearly understand the specifications of the product before a single line of code is written. Of course, it is even better if all parties agree on the specifications and the features that they describe, but this is not always possible; sooner or later a decision is made, and the responsibility for it lies with the developer.

Changing the features of a software product after programmers have started writing code can be costly, particularly if you develop under the Windows environment, since at the time of this writing experienced Windows programmers are expensive and difficult to find. Testers, technical writers, Localizers, and translators rely on the product specifications to complete their tasks, and if the specifications are unclear or out of date, time will be wasted. Of course there are times when circumstances require that the specifications for a software product be changed. When this happens there will be additional costs, and time will be lost, but these are unavoidable.

Costs to ensure that your Internationalized and Localized products perform as required by their specifications can be reduced if the Localizers in the target locale, distributors, and marketers participate throughout the cycle from development to end-user delivery. It is also helpful if target locale people provide technical support and resources in so-called "beta tests."[1] A beta test is extremely useful when the product under development involves country-specific hardware (e.g., printers) not available in the United States. Testing a translated product to find typographical errors and other linguistic problems should be performed by the target locale people, if possible.

9.2.2. Translation Costs

Prices for translation can vary considerably among different translation agencies both in the United States and in other countries. In 1989 there were about 120 translation agencies located in the Silicon Valley of California. Typically these are small businesses generating about $500,000 in revenues per year that have been in operation for five or six years. Their prices for translating technical documentation can range from 15 to 40 cents per word, or as much as $100 a page. Translation firms located in the Silicon Valley focus on the software Localization business due to the concentration there of computer companies that seek to customize their products for the international marketplace.

Abroad, prices for translation vary between 15 and 40 cents per word depending on the language.[2] Prices depend on the particular cultural and economic conditions in each country. For instance, translators in Sweden usually belong to unions that establish the minimum price for translation services. You will probably not be able to find any translator there working as a freelancer who will accept less than the union rate.

Some agencies may charge more for the translation of language that is part of the software (menus, dialog boxes, and messages in the user interface of a product) than for the translation of manuals. For translation tasks such as resizing dialog boxes, preparing screen dumps, compiling help files, translating text in icons or bitmap images, translating and customizing sample files, templates, and on-line documentation (tutorial), you are usually charged an hourly rate that can vary from

---

[1]In a beta test, a product is provided to a group of selected end users for them to use in a real environment and to identify anomalies that have not been detected in testing done by the developer.

[2]See Appendix F for a list and brief description of some of the larger Localization agencies that work with European languages.

$35 up to $200. For proofreading and linguistic testing you are also charged an hourly rate. Hourly rates for desktop publishing can vary from $35 up to $150, while per-page rates can vary from $40 to $50. Some agencies offer a volume discount if your product is to be Localized into more than one language.

If a U.S. developer wants a target locale translator to manage a translation project, especially one requiring translation into more than one language, additional costs will accrue. U.S developers that do not have the resources to manage several Localization projects at the same time can benefit from this coordination service.

9.2.3. Internationalization and Localization of an Already Existing Product

If the product you want to Localize is to be translated into more than one language, you have to decide if you want to Internationalize it first, a step that can reduce the overall costs. Without the Internationalization process, the Localization of your product has to start from scratch with each translated version, and no development leverage may be possible. Skipping the Internationalization step is effective only when you need to translate a product as quickly as possible, and no other translated versions of the same product are anticipated.

9.2.4. Internationalization and Localization of a New Product

When developing a new product that you plan to offer on the international market, you will be well advised to include in the original development work the features that are necessary to make it international. This will avoid additional costs for rewriting code to add the international features at some time farther along in the development cycle. A product designed to be capable of Internationalization and, consequently, Localization will allow you to reach a worldwide customer base at the same time you release your product in the United States.

Your marketing staff should develop the list of countries in which the new product is to be sold. Even though no translation is required at the time the English International version is released, the basic product needs to be able to support the different character sets, input/output methods, and national conventions (date, time, currency, list separator, measurement system, and numeric values) of all the targeted countries. The additional advantage is that the cost of any translated version produced in the future will be less than the cost of Localizing without this preparation.

9.2.5. Marketing Costs and Revenue

Software developers (at least those that produce retail packages) normally sell their products through distributors. The distributors buy the products at a substantial discount of the list price. In the international arena, the distributor's discount tends to be much higher than in the United States, perhaps as much as 60 or 70 percent. It is the international distributor and not the developer who is expected to pay the marketing costs. Again, it is the norm for the international distributor to charge substantially more than the U.S. list price, perhaps by a factor of two.

The marketing of products overseas is almost as expensive as it is in the United States. For instance, the average cost of marketing and advertising for a six-month period to introduce a product in France is about $150,000 (compared with $250,000 for a low-end launch in the United States[3]). If the U.S. list price is $200, and the distributor pays $60 for it, and sells it for $300, then he must sell 625 just to cover the introduction cost (150,000 divided by 240). The developer recovers only $60 per unit or $37,500 (60 multiplied by 625) from this arrangement. This may cover the incremental development, Localization, and manufacturing costs for a low-end shrink-wrapped desktop publishing program.

9.2.6. Manufacturing Costs

More and more companies are now using outside manufacturing services to avoid the overhead and the fixed costs of developing a manufacturing division of their own. There are many companies in the United States and abroad that offer a wide variety of services (and prices). The more common services obtained from outside suppliers by U.S developers are printing and packaging, media production, assembly, quality assurance and control, scheduling, and order filling. Translation service, design work, and collateral materials printing are also available.

Manufacturing operations in Ireland and Taiwan, where there are excellent tax incentives, can reduce manufacturing costs for U.S. companies. Using off-shore manufacturing agents is becoming more popular since shipping is expensive, as are the value-added taxes (VAT) your distributors need to pay to receive your products. If a problem with the product develops, it may take quite some time to return the product to the United States, complete the necessary paperwork, and ship the replacement. Offshore manufacturing companies can be useful in these situations.

9.3. CUSTOMS DUTIES AND TAXES

Be sure you get as much information as you can on customs duties and taxes specific to the countries you target. People with whom you work in the countries in which your product is sold can help you find out what the specific regulations are. Someone in your own offices should also be familiar with customs duties and taxes for all the countries in which you market your products. They must also keep up with changes to rules and regulations. Foreign consulates and trade associations can help you with general issues in this area. One of the best sources is the U.S. Department of Commerce, International Trade Administration.

According to the European Community desk at the U.S. Department of Commerce, International Trade Administration, Washington, DC (202-482-2905),

---

[3]This is an off-the-cuff figure quoted by a professional marketer in a U.S. software publishing company.

there are no customs duties on software products imported into any of the member countries of the European Community. However, all EC member countries use a value added tax that is assessed at the time of entry into the country.

The VAT for software, as a percentage of the United States wholesale price, in January 1993, is:

Belgium 19.5%	Italy 19%
Denmark 25%	Luxembourg 15%
France 18.6%	Netherlands 17.5%
Germany 14%	Portugal 16%
Greece 18%	Spain 15%
Ireland 21%	U.K. 17.5%

There is as yet no provision for equalization of VAT between the member countries of the European Community, and to our knowledge there are no longer any duties between member countries.

One of the reasons to export a few master disks rather than large numbers of manufactured products to your partners overseas is to reduce the VAT expenses that your international business partners would have to pay. It is also an incentive to manufacture locally.

9.4. IMPORT AND EXPORT REGULATIONS

The United States controls the kinds of software that can be exported. Software that has to do with intelligence or espionage activities, encryption procedures, and military applications is subject to the most control. With the demise of the Cold War, the rationale for the controls has undergone some changes. However, in 1993 Apple Computer, due to U.S. government requirements, had any customer receiving APDA products certify that they would not knowingly export products to Afghanistan, Albania, Bulgaria, Cambodia, Cuba, Czechoslovakia, Estonia, Hungary, Iraq, Laos, Latvia, Libya, Lithuania, Mongolian People's Republic, North Korea, People's Republic of China, Romania, Serbia, countries of the old U.S.S.R., and Vietnam.

In 1990 the Department of Commerce proposed a new regulation, *general license,* that eliminated individual validated licensing requirements on approximately $30 billion of annual U.S. exports to COCOM countries (COCOM consists of 17 nations, including NATO, except for Iceland and including Australia and Japan). There are now two types of export licenses: general and validated. Most of the computer product exports are considered under the general license category, so that no specific licensing is required before products are shipped. A general license has now been established for exports to Australia, Belgium, Denmark, Finland, France, Germany, Greece, Italy, Japan, Luxembourg, the Netherlands, Norway, Portugal, Spain, Switzerland, Turkey, and the United Kingdom. Products that require a validated license can be found in the Export Administration regulations provided by the Department of Commerce, Office of Export Administration.

In July 1992, the National Security Agency loosened controls on encryption procedures. While continuing restrictions on Data Encryption Standard (DES), much control was shifted from the State Department to the Commerce Department on a case-by-case basis. Commerce Department rules are considered to be less stringent than the rules for weapons exports that the State Department uses. Software products that use encryption must still be submitted for review. A major issue is the length of the key used in the encryption. Those submitted to the NSA will be answered in seven days by fax rather than the weeks and months it took previously.

An example of how import/export regulations vary depending on the country you target is that any software package imported into Spain needs to be approved by the Spanish government before it can be distributed. In the case of France, imported software packages must be fully translated before the products can be sold. (This probably means translated rather than Localized, but it is difficult to imagine a full translation without some Localization. Presumably such matters as numeric formats and sorting orders are not specified.)

Since selling overseas always involves risk, you should seek financial advice through your own bank and government agencies. Another good source of helpful information is the Software Publishers' Association International Resource Guide and Directory.

It is all too easy to make expensive mistakes. In 1991 Digital Equipment Corporation was fined $2.4 million by the Commerce Department, the largest penalty ever for export-control violations, for shipping computer products without formal national security authorization.

9.5. REPATRIATION OF FUNDS

A major consideration for any developer interested in doing international business is how to repatriate funds paid by business associates in a non-American country. Some companies use a standby letter of credit by which a distributor secures a line of credit from a bank and the bank guarantees it. When you work with a distributor (or any other agency overseas) for the first time, it is wise to protect yourself with a specific payment terms policy. When the distributor has proved to be a reliable associate for the long run, the bounds of the agreement can be expanded and better terms can be granted.

9.6. FREIGHT COSTS

You need to understand how much it will cost you to ship the Localized product to distributors. This will depend, of course, on the location of the manufacturing facility.

A typical software package might weigh 1 kilo and contain five 5 1/2- and five 3 1/2-inch disks. On a 500-kilo (1,100-pound) shipment from San Francisco, airport to airport, freight rates for handling on the same day that you call, could be as follows.[4]

---

[4]Quote from Circle Freight International, South San Francisco, CA, for Paris, Madrid, Rome, and Frankfurt on May 11, 1993.

Paris	$960—@ $1.92 per kilogram
Madrid	$1,015—@ $2.03 per kilogram
Rome	$1,265—@ $2.53 per kilogram
Mexico	$990—@ $0.99 per kilogram
Buenos Aires	$1,145—@ $2.29 per kilogram
São Paolo	$1,400—@ $ 2.80 per kilogram

A freight forwarder often uses a national airline such as Iberia or Lufthansa and will usually manage to deliver the material in three to four days. It can be cheaper if you can wait a few days to allow the freight forwarder to bundle the shipment into a larger one. Often the freight forwarder has a branch or an affiliate of some kind who can pick up the shipment at the airport, clear the package through customs, and deliver it to the consignee.

Other freight costs include:

For exporter:

Documentation charge per shipment—$15–$25
Inland freight—from your site to airport in the U.S.

For consignee:

Pick up, clear customs
Inland freight from airport to destination

Bear in mind that freight and postal rates change regularly.

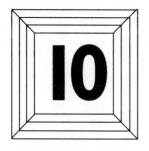

10 Going the Other Way: Europe to America

10.1. INTRODUCTION

America is a magnet. It offers a rich, sophisticated, developed market for computer software.[1,2] Computers abound in homes and in businesses. There are millions on millions of fluent computer users and probably millions of sophisticated designers, programmers, and engineers. Distribution channels, computer-oriented publications, and advertising are well-developed and can provide marketing statistics by the ton.

The United States is a large homogeneous market where one language will serve all.[3] Provided that you have Localized your product into the correct American variety of English and not into British, and your product is useful, then only

---

[1] Some people claim (e.g., Michael J. Weiss in *The Clustering of America,* New York: Tilden Press, Harper & Row, 1989) that, given your ZIP code, they can tell what you ate for breakfast, what you read while eating it, what TV program kept you up late, and what vehicle carried you to work.

[2] Of course, America is a marketing magnet for everything, apparently. The powers-that-be have even agreed to play the 1994 World Cup in the United States! This truly global contest of national soccer teams rivets nearly every non-American to the television to watch a sport that is quite minor in this country.

[3] There is also a significant Spanish-speaking market in California, Florida, New York, Texas, and the Southwest. There are Asian markets to match—Chinese, Japanese, and Vietnamese on the West Coast. California state law has made English the official language of the state and all businesses must deal with Federal and State officials on English-language forms. But California election ballots are written in English, Spanish, and Chinese. And while the Library of Congress will not assign card numbers to books translated from English or some foreign language into another foreign language, translations into Spanish are accepted. From time to time, word processor developers will target the Spanish-speaking communities as potential markets for the Localized Spanish versions of their products.

your marketing ability will limit your sales.[4] The field of applications is large; you name it and there is probably a market for it. Further, you can repatriate revenues without any problems arising, except for the ubiquitous Internal Revenue Service that will want its share of your profits.

The odds are that you will be in the strange situation of developing products on American equipment probably using American development tools such as programming languages even for your home market. As a software developer, you will have been exposed to American methods and procedures. If you use non-American equipment (obviously, we don't mean foreign manufactures or clones of American products), you will have to convert to American equipment and environments in order to have any size market at all.

Most of the issues that we discussed in Chapters 8 and 9 have their counterpart in introducing products to the United States.

10.2. MARKET

The U.S. market seems an easy target for European developers attracted by a stable financial environment and high economic potential. Other markets such as China, India, Russia, and Spanish Latin America still represent more of a risk for investors. Many of their economies are in the throes of dismantling communism, struggling under the burden of enormous debt or runaway inflation, or operating in unstable political environments.

10.2.1. IBM PC

Considered a popular standard, IBM PC machines appeal to a large audience of various ages and educational levels. The PC boom started in the United States much earlier than in other geographical areas. Intel 80286 processor machines are now considered obsolete, and 486 machines are replacing the 386.

---

[4]Choose the correct variety of English. English, of course, is perhaps the language with the greatest number of varieties. Varieties exist in the United States, Canada, Australia, the Caribbean, South Africa, New Zealand, Kenya, Nigeria, England, Scotland, Ireland, India, and Pakistan—to name some. While most educated people from these countries can easily converse with each other on most topics, there are certainly specialized vocabularies (sports and business, for example) within each region that are unintelligible to inhabitants of other countries. Do you know that a chinaman is a left-hander's googly, itself a leg-break delivered with an off-break action? These terms are in the vocabulary of all cricket-loving Commonwealth people, but in few others'.

It will be evident then that while there are many similarities among the variants of English, there are also substantial cultural differences that are reflected in the language. Many run-of-the-mill words and phrases have different meanings; to use a word with alternative meanings can be embarrassing, particularly if it involves one of the many that are innocuous in one English and slightly vulgar or off-color in another.

English itself is the second language of choice in many other countries and in many professions forming an unofficial world language. This is hardly surprising, considering the enormous influence of the British Empire succeeded immediately by the dominance of the United States and the enormous scientific, technical, and engineering advances made during these two periods of dominance by parts of the English-speaking world. Choosing the exact vocabulary in translation doesn't strike us as an easy task.

10.2.1.1. DOS

Many people in the computer industry think that DOS is at the end of its product cycle due to the enormous success of Windows, but Version 5.0 seems to have received good acceptance and Microsoft introduced Version 6.0 in April 1993. IBM is planning its own DOS 6.0, and Novell is to release DR DOS 7.0. DOS is still popular, and many applications are still developed to run under it; OS/2 is attractive to the many corporate users.

10.2.1.2. Windows

Nine million Windows 3.0 have been sold worldwide since it was introduced. Clearly, Windows is becoming the most used platform by developers of PC software. By March 1993 about 13 million copies of Windows 3.1 had been sold.

10.2.2. Macintosh

The Macintosh environment is very popular in the United States. In its early days, it was considerably more expensive than the IBM PC, but its ease of use made it the favorite of many nonprofessional computer users. Now that Windows provides a similar enviroment on the PC, it will be interesting to see how Macintosh applications will compete. Claris, Apple's software development company, is porting strategic applications to Windows. The converse is true; many Windows applications turn up on the Macintosh.

10.3. IMPORT REGULATIONS

Imported hardware must conform to such U.S. regulations as those established by the Consumers' Protection Agency (CPA)—for example, on radiation emissions—and the Federal Communications Commission (FCC). All hardware must be marked clearly in English with the country of origin (according to U.S. Customs). Imported software cannot violate any existing trademark or copyright agreements in force between the United States and the country from which you are importing. The medium—normally floppy disks—must also be clearly identified in English with the country of origin.

10.4. CUSTOMS AND EXCISE

The duty on floppy disks is infinitesimal.[5] Duty is assessed on the basis of the area of the recorded material at the rate of 9.5 *cents* per square meter. A double-sided 5 1/4-inch disk is 0.018 (rounded from 0.01755) square meters and a 3 1/2-inch disk is 0.008 square meters; thus the duty on the large floppy is negligible

---

[5]The tariff number for software on floppy disks is 8524.90.40806.

at $0.00171 and on the smaller it is an even more negligible $0.00076. We don't even know how to say those amounts, so consider them in terms of $17.10 and $7.60 per ten thousand disks.[6] If your product has ten disks, then U.S. Customs duty adds about one cent to the cost of sales.

Documentation is considered part of the package—manuals are not counted for duty. Separately packaged, they are considered as books and therefore are free, too.

10.5. OTHER COSTS

Other costs will include Inland Freight Fee, from your pick-up site to the airport, Freight, Documentation Charges (about $15 to $25 per load), handling charges clearing Customs at the airport, and Inland Freight Charge to Consignee.

10.6. DISTRIBUTORS

Traditional distribution channels here in the United States don't usually provide additional services as republishers in Europe do. The number of services is limited. For instance, the manufacturer typically provides marketing funds for advertising and publicity, not the distributor as in Europe. Any consideration on how to choose the right distribution channel and partner suggested in Chapters 8 and 9 is applicable here as well.

10.7. LOCALIZERS

You have the same considerations as the Americans exporting to Europe; you have a tradeoff of incurring communication problems during Localization at a distance from your main developers against the advantages of up-to-date local knowledge and assistance in marketing your product.

In the Silicon Valley, there are many small translation companies (about 120 in 1989) with annual revenues on the average of $500,000 per year. Alpnet and Berlitz Translations have substantial operations here in the United States, and AT&T is offering software Localization services (see Appendix F). INK/Donnelly Language Solutions has opened East and West Coast offices.

10.8. TECHNICAL SUPPORT

Basing your technical support here means your phone bill will be much less than running phones across the Atlantic. You should have faster response to cus-

---

[6]Per a telephone call with U.S. Customs on February 27, 1992. We even compute the smaller disk area to be more like 0.007 square meters at most, but we won't argue about it. However, Customs does bother to collect it.

tomers plus an outpost for gathering user information about your product's performance and suitability for the market. Technical support is a way of differentiating your products from the competition. Basically, Americans will prefer to deal with local Americans rather than distant Europeans.

10.9. MAINTENANCE

You have the same considerations as the Americans exporting to Europe. Depending on how you set up the development process and how you Localize and distribute your products, you should consider the most cost-effective solution to maintain your product lines. You might benefit sometimes from having a U.S. office that can put in a full day's work at a different time than the European's full day, due to the time differences.

10.10. OWNERSHIP

The United States has finally, as of March 1, 1989, signed the Berne Convention for the Protection of Literary and Artistic works. The works of foreign authors from nations that are also members of the Berne Union are protected.

10.11. COMPETITION

You name it, we've got it. In one form or another, pretty much whatever you want to import to the United States has rivals already developed and on the market. Your competition will be of all kinds. There are still programmers working away in garages and attics in their spare time hoping to emulate the success stories of Bill Gates, Steve Jobs and Steve Wozniak, and Hewlett and Packard. There are enormous companies with well-established track records in development, manufacturing, marketing, advertising, and distribution.

10.12. ACCOUNTING PRACTICES[7]

There are accounting procedures and practices in some European countries that are unacceptable in the United States unless you have made special arrangements beforehand. For example, we have seen Swiss invoices with terms of 60 days 2%, 90 days net. Such an invoice is laughable in the United States (unless

---

[7]We verified these accounting practices with the Chief Financial Officer of a California company with substantial overseas operations. Originally European himself, he snorted with derision at the normal practices of the institutions that handle wire transfers and at the Accounts Payable procedures of many of his European customers. He has found Californian institutions that handle wire transfers efficiently and quickly and so bypasses New York.

you are paying rather than receiving). It is normal in the United States to quote terms of 2%10, net/30, meaning that you get 2 percent off the value of the invoice for paying within 10 days, rather than 60, and that the invoice is due in 30 days, not 90. All consumer and small business billing in the United States operates on this basis. The phone company, credit card companies, landlords—everyone—charges monthly.[8]

Anyone expecting to operate in the United States must pay their bills monthly. If you don't, then you are just making work for accounting auditors; for your routine expenses like rent and phone, you would have two or three intervening invoices to keep track of in your pending file. Large organizations like state governments and insurance companies may delay payments to you, but this is considered to be the result of incompetence. They are too big and powerful to fight and it is almost impossible to find an employee who admits to being responsible.

Europeans should also take note that many New York banks that handle wire transfers are notorious for taking inexplicable amounts of time to handle such simple matters as a wire transfer. They can take as long as 20 days and come up with lame excuses for it in the face of modern technology. In addition, they charge fees to both parties. Such delays must be planned for in handling payments to U.S. suppliers. From time to time, though, you do hear of methods of payment that reflect the use of modern technology and that are reasonably quick.

---

[8]We have seen MasterCard charges made in France on May 17 appear on the next American statement with a cutoff date of May 18.

Paper Sizes

A.1. AMERICAN

Paper	Inches	Millimeters
A0	35 × 45	889 × 1143
A1	23 × 35	584 × 889
A2	17 × 22	432 × 559
A3	11 × 17	279 × 432 (ledger)
A4	8.5 × 11	216 × 279 (letter)
A5	5.5 × 18.5	140 × 216
A6	4.25 × 5.5	108 × 140
A7	3.5 × 4.25	88.9 × 108
International Fanfold		210 mm × 12 inches
Computer Paper	14 × 11	336 × 279
U.S. Legal	8.5 × 14	216 × 336

A.2. EUROPEAN ISO-JISA SERIES

The biggest size of paper is A0, with an area of one square meter and with sides that are in the ratio of one to the square root of two. Smaller sizes are derived by dividing the next larger format into two equal pieces. DIN66008 is the standard.

Paper	Inches	Millimeters
A0	33.1 × 46.8	841 × 1189
A1	23.4 × 33.1	594 × 841
A2	16.5 × 23.4	420 × 594
A3	11.7 × 16.5	297 × 420
A3 continuous	13.5 × 12	342.9 × 304.8
A4	8.25 × 11.66	210 × 297
A4 continuous	8.25 × 12	210 × 304.8
A5	5.8 × 8.25	148 × 210
A6	4.1 × 5.8	105 × 148
A7	2.9 × 4.1	74 × 105

Folders	Inches	Millimeters
B0		1000 × 1414
B1		707 × 1414
B2		500 × 707
B3		353 × 500
B4	9.84 × 13.89	250 × 353
B5	6.93 × 9.84	176 × 250
B6	4.92 × 6.93	125 × 176
B7		88 × 125
B8		62 × 88
B9		44 × 62

Envelopes	Inches	Millimeters
C0		917 × 1297
C1		648 × 917
C2		458 × 648
C3		324 × 458
C4		229 × 324
C5		162 × 229
C6		114 × 162
C6-long		114 × 228
C7		81 × 114
C8		58 × 81

A.3. JAPANESE JISA SERIES[1]

Paper	Inches	Millimeter
B0	40.47 × 57.3	1034 × 1456
B1	28.7 × 40.6	728 × 1030
B2	20.3 × 28.7	515 × 728
B3	14.3 × 20.3	364 × 515
B4	10.1 × 14.3	257 × 364 or
B4	9.83 × 13.87	250 × 352
B5	7.2 × 10.1	182 × 257 or
B5	6.93 × 19.83	176 × 250
B6	5.0 × 7.2	128 × 182
B7	3.6 × 5.0	91 × 128

[1]The Japanese Standards Association used European A4 paper in its correspondence with us.

UNIX

B.I. INTRODUCTION

In this appendix we discuss the support that UNIX provides for someone wanting to Localize software for a Western European language. Hewlett-Packard's *Native Language Support; User's Guide HP 9000 Computers,* published in August 1992, describes the Native Language Support provided by HP-UX. For more information, refer to it and to the HP-UX reference manual. We provide an overview in this appendix, but there are far more details and some recommendations that we have not included. If you actually want to Internationalize in the UNIX world, you will have to refer to the manual. For an overview of what goes on with more complicated languages, see Chapter 6.

The HP-UX Native Language Support (NLS) reduces or eliminates the barriers that would make HP-UX difficult to use in a non-English language. It conforms to standards specified by the X/OPEN Portability Guide (XPG), Issues 2 (actually, this derives from HPNLS, Hewlett-Packard Native Language Support) and 3, IEEE 1003.1 (POSIX), and ANSI C, as well as HP added enhancements. The language-sensitive areas of functionality are:

Character handling
Character classification such as printable, alphabetic, numeric, etc.
Shifting
Collating
Directionality
    Mode: left to right, right to left, and vertical columns
    Order: keyboard and screen. They can be different: keyboard order refers to the order in which characters are entered on a keyboard; screen order refers to the order in which characters are displayed or printed.

When there is no Native Language Support, there is a default locale called *C*.

NLS also provides a messaging facility for extracting hard-coded strings from an application source code and storing them externally to the code. Utilities are provided that aid the translation of messages by putting them in a *catalog*. At run time, the program accesses messages in that catalog where the messages are in the desired language.

For the UNIX operating system itself, this poses a fairly large order, as there are about 13,000 messages.

B.2. CHARACTER SETS

The ASCII code set has traditionally been used on UNIX-based systems to express American English. Before Internationalization and Localization were popular, the 7-bit ASCII codes were used, that is, the low end 000–127. This has been expanded to include the high end 128–255. But not all UNIX commands are updated yet for the 8-bit code set. *Mail,* for example, still relies on the 7-bit code that is embedded in the 8-bit code.

HP supplies a number of 8-bit code sets (see Appendix L) and supports the ISO sets on such peripherals as printers, plotters, and terminals. HP supports the following 8-bit locales/sets:

Langid	Lang=	Code Set	Language
00	n-computer	ASCII	no NLS—based on 7-bit set
01	american	ROMAN8	American English
02	c-french	ROMAN8	Canadian French
03	danish	ROMAN8	Danish
04	dutch	ROMAN8	Dutch
05	english	ROMAN8	English
06	finnish	ROMAN8	Finnish
07	french	ROMAN8	French
08	german	ROMAN8	German
09	italian	ROMAN8	Italian
10	norwegian	ROMAN8	Norwegian
11	portuguese	ROMAN8	Portuguese
12	spanish	ROMAN8	Spanish
13	swedish	ROMAN8	Swedish
14	icelandic	ROMAN8	Icelandic
41	katakana	KANA8	Katakana
51	arabic	ARABIC8	Arabic
52	arabic-w	ARABIC8	Western Arabic
61	greek	GREEK8	Greek
71	hebrew	HEBREW8	Hebrew
81	turkish	TURKISH8	Turkish
91	thai	THAI8	Thai
99	C		Computer
100	POSIX		Posix default
101	american.iso88591	ISO8859-1	American English

102	c-french.iso88591	ISO8859-1	Canadian French
103	danish.iso88591	ISO8859-1	Danish
104	dutch.iso88591	ISO8859-1	Dutch
105	english.iso88591	ISO8859-1	English
106	finnish.iso88591	ISO8859-1	Finnish
107	french.iso88591	ISO8859-1	French
108	german.iso88591	ISO8859-1	German
109	italian.iso88591	ISO8859-1	Italian
110	norwegian.iso88591	ISO8859-1	Norwegian
111	portuguese.iso88591	ISO8859-1	Portuguese
112	spanish.iso88591	ISO8859-1	Spanish
113	swedish.iso88591	ISO8859-1	Swedish
114	icelandic.iso88591	ISO8859-1	Icelandic
142	czech	ISO8859-2	Czechoslovakian
143	hungarian	ISO8859-2	Hungarian
144	polish	ISO8859-2	Polish
145	rumanian	ISO8859-2	Rumanian
146	serbocroatian	ISO8859-2	Serbo-Croatian
148	slovene	ISO8859-2	Slavic (Slovenia)
180	russian	ISO8859-5	Russian
181	bulgarian	ISO8859-5	Bulgarian
301	arabic.iso88596	ISO8859-6	Arabic
321	greek.iso88597	ISO8859-7	Greek
341	hebrew.iso88598	ISO8859-8	Hebrew
361	turkish.iso88599	ISO8859-9	Turkish

HP also supports the following multibyte character sets for alphabets of more than 256 characters:

Langid	Lang-	Code Set	Language
201	chinese-s	PRC15	Simplified Chinese
211	chinese-t	ROC15	Traditional Chinese
212	chinese-t.big5	BIG5	Traditional Chinese
221	japanese	JAPAN15	Japanese (Shift JIS)
222	japanese.euc	JAPANEUC	Japanese
231	korean	KOREA15	Korean

Note that japanese.euc and UJIS are the same. And, despite the inclusion of the characters *15* in their names, PRC15, ROC15, JAPAN15, and KOREA15 are 16-bit character sets. Finally, there is provision for other sets: Langid 901–999 are reserved for user-defined languages.

As of September 1992, HP plans to use ("is moving as fast as they can") ISO-8859/1, -8859/2, and -8859/5. HP is also working on using ISO-8859/6 and -8859/8; work integrating these latter two takes longer, as they involve bidirectional considerations.

To define a language, use the routine *localedef* described in Sections B.3.1. and B.3.2. The command **iconv** operates on files and converts characters from one code set to another.

B.3. PREPARATION

B.3.1. Routines

In Hewlett-Packard's HP-UX Release 7.0 of September 1990, a number of routines are available for building a locale or parts of a locale.[1] Included are:

localedef	sets up the language environment as specified by an input file. It reads a "localedef script" from the input file, creates a file called locale.def, and installs this file in the appropriate directory. There are six *categories* of data (see Section B.3.2) in the locale.def file. If a category is not specified, then it sets up the default "C" for that locale.
setlocale ()	sets, queries, or restores that aspect of a program's locale as specified by the *category* argument. A program's locale refers to those areas of the program's Native Language Support (NLS) environment for which the values of *category* have been defined.
strftime()	formats date and time. It converts the contents of a tm structure to a formatted data and time string.[2] It operates on all the data in the LC_TIME category of data and percentage.
nlsinfo()	can be used to display the native language support information including the categories of data. It can display information about what languages are currently supported.
localeconv()	formats numeric functions such as currency symbols, decimal point character, indicator for location of currency symbol and collation/sorting, and so on. Specifically, it sets :

decimal_point   (the same as RADIXCHAR)
thousands_sep
grouping   (these three data are in the
                 LC_NUMERIC category)

and the functions listed under LC_MONETARY, except for *crncystr.*

nl_langinfo	(replaces langinfo) returns a pointer to a string containing information relevant to a particular language or cultural area as defined in the program's locale.
nl_tools 16	collection of tools to process 16-bit characters.

---

[1]We are excluding a discussion of all the flags that pertain to each function. For a complete discussion, see the HP-UX Release 7.0 manual of September 1989.

[2]The routine strftime can modify all of the following: locale's abbreviated weekday name, full weekday name, abbreviated month name, full month name and appropriate date and time representation, day of the month as a decimal number, locale's combined Emperor/Era name, locale's Emperor/Era year, hour as a decimal number (24 hour and 12 hour), day of the year as a decimal number, month as a decimal number, minute as a decimal number, new-line character, locale's Emperor/Era name, locale's Emperor/Era year, locale's equivalent of either *am* or *pm*, second as a decimal number, tab character, week number of the year and weekday as decimal number, locale's appropriate date representation and appropriate time representation, year without century as a decimal number, year with century as a decimal number, time zone, and percentage.

A number of routines are available for handling multibyte characters. Included are:

mblen()	determines the number of bytes in a multibyte character
mbtowc()	determines the number of bytes in a multibyte character, determines code value of type wchar_t, and stores code in object pointed to by pwc
mbtowcs()	converts a sequence of multibyte characters from the array pointed to by s into a sequence of corresponding codes and stores these codes into the array pointed to by pwcs
wctomb()	determines the number of bytes needed to represent the multibyte character whose value is wchar and stores the multibyte character representation in the array object pointed to by s
wctombs()	converts a sequence of codes from the array pointed to by pwcs into a sequence of multibyte characters and stores them into the array pointed to by s

There are some *macro calls* that take the place of byte pointer operations:

Macro Call	Byte Pointer Analog
CHARAT(p)	(*p)
ADVANCE(p)	(p++)
CHARADV(p)	(*p++)
WCHAR(c,p)	(*p=c)
WCHARADV(c,p)	(*p++=c)

These macros operate on byte pointers, but since they call *mbtowc* (which replaces *FIRSTof2* and *SECof2*), they work on multibyte characters.

One objective that HP has in International program design is to support programmers in developing applications that are code-set independent. The *Worldwide Portability Interface (WPI)* automatically converts data to/from its internal coding to/from *wide* characters. The *wide* character representation is more convenient because it offers a single data type for all languages. HP suggests the following procedure:

Convert *char* data types to *wchar_t*
Use:

wscmp	instead of	*strcmp*
iswdigit	instead of	*isdigit*
fgetwc	instead of	*fgetc*

If there is no parallel routine, you can use *wcstombs* to convert wide character data to multibyte.

The environment variable **LANGOPTS** is concerned with *mode* and *order*. Mode can be left to right or right to left and order can be the order in which the user enters keystrokes or the order in which characters are displayed.

Two commands are available in HP-UX to manage data directionality, **forder** and **strord.** The command **forder** converts the order of characters in a file from screen order to keyboard order or vice versa. The command **strord** will convert the order of characters from keyboard to screen order in special cases.

The LC_TYPE category setting Locale (see Section B.3.2) determines the behavior of the multibyte character and string functions.

A large number of lower-level commands have been Internationalized and are available to work with Localized programs. See Appendix C of Hewlett-Packard's *Native Language Support*.

B.3.2. Data

The routine *localedef* (see Section B.3.1) builds six categories of data. A *category* is composed of one or more *statements,* each starting with a *keyword* followed by one or more *expressions,* where expressions are sets of well-formed character-code metacharacters, strings, and constants. There are four types of legal expression—ctype, shift, collate, and info.

The categories of data are:

LC_ALL — affects the behavior of all other categories, as well as all *nl_langinfo*.

LC_COLLATE — affects the behavior of regular expressions and the NLS string collation functions (see *string* and *regexp*).

LC_CTYPE — affects the behavior of regular expressions, character classification, and conversion functions (*ctype, conv,* and *regexp*). It also affects the behavior of all routines that process multibyte characters (see *nl_tools 16*).

LC_MONETARY — affects the behavior of functions that handle monetary values (see *localeconv*)

LC_MESSAGES — affects affirmative and negative response expressions.

LC_NUMERIC — affects the handling of the radix character in the formatted input/output functions (*printf, scanf,* and *vprintf*) and the conversion functions (see *evct* and *strtod*). It also affects the numeric values in the *localeconv* structure.

LC_TIME — affects the behavior of time conversion functions (see *strftime*).

The statements must come between the category tags and the end of the category. These are denoted by:

LC_ALL — and END LC_ALL
LC_CTYPE — and END LC_CTYPE
LC_COLLATE — and END LC_COLLATE
LC_MONETARY — and END LC_MONETARY
LC_MESSAGES — and END LC_MESSAGES
LC_NUMERIC — and END LC_NUMERIC
LC_TIME — and END LC_TIME

One keyword—*modifier*—can be used in any category. It is a string identifying the name of the modifier. There are some keywords that do not belong to any category of data:

revision   string identifying the revision number of the locale.def file.

langname   string identifying the name of the language. It follows the naming convention of the LANG environment variable.

langid   decimal number identifying the language id. Used as a shortcut to identification by some routines.[3] It is required by localedef.

Following are the keywords for each of the six categories:

LC_ALL—affects the behavior of all other categories, as well as all *nl_langinfo.*

yesexpr   string identifying affirmative response for yes/no questions

noexpr   string identifying negative response for yes/no questions

direction   string identifying text direction

context   string indicating character context analysis—null indicates no analysis, *1* indicates Arabic context analysis required

All except 'context' are langinfo items.

LC_COLLATE—affects the behavior of regular expressions and the NLS string collation functions.

sequence   sequence of character codes for collation.[4,5]

Collate expressions following the keyword represent a sequence of character codes that define a collation order. Each character code in the sequence is assigned an ascending sequence number. Collate expressions include single character-code constants, character-code ranges, character-code priority sets, two-to-one character-code pairs, one-to-two character-code pairs, and character-code don't-care sets.

LC_CTYPE—affects the behavior of regular expressions, character classification, and conversion functions. It also affects the behavior of all routines that process multibyte characters.

Must be followed by ctype expressions:

isupper   character codes classified as uppercase letters

islower   character codes classified as lowercase letters

isdigit   character codes classified as numeric

isspace   character codes classified as spacing (delimiter) characters

ispunct   character codes classified as punctuation characters

iscntrl   character codes classified as control characters

isblank   character codes classified as printable space characters that must also be defined in *isspace*

---

[3]As of February 1992, full NLS support is not available for all HP-UX commands. See the *International Support* section of specific commands.

[4]It is possible to represent one-to-two and two-to-one character-code pairs using left and right brackets and angle brackets respectively in the sequence. This allows the collating sequence to handle the sorting issues outlined in Section 2.2.4, including a "don't care" arrangement.

[5]There is a further collating order distinction, that between *folded* and *nonfolded*. In folded sequences, uppercase characters are intermixed with lowercase characters, and in nonfolded sequences, lowercase characters come after *all* uppercase characters

isxdigit   character codes classified as hexadecimal digits

isfirst   character codes classified as the first bytes of two-byte characters

issecond   character codes classified as the second bytes of two-byte characters

Must be followed by shift expressions:

ul   relationships between uppercase and lowercase characters for languages that have a one-to-one relationship

toupper   lowercase to uppercase relationships

tolower   uppercase to lowercase relationships: *toupper* and *tolower* are used only for languages that do not have a one-to-one relationship between uppercase and lowercase characters

langinfo items:

bytes_char   string containing the maximum number of bytes per character for the character set used for a specified language

alt_punct   string mapped into the ASCII equivalent string b ! " # $ % & ' ( ) * + , - . / : ; < = > ? @ [\ ] ^ _ ' { | } ~, where b is a blank

LC_MESSAGES—affects the behavior of affirmative and negative string expressions

yesexpr   defines the affirmative response for yes/no questions (replaces yesstr)

noexpr   defines the negative response for yes/no questions (replaces nostr)

LC_MONETARY—affects the behavior of functions that handle monetary values.

int_curr_symbol   international currency symbol applicable to current locale as per ISO 4217

currency symbol   local currency symbol applicable to current locale

mon_decimal_point   decimal point used to format monetary symbols

mon_thousands-sep   separator for groups of digits to the left of the decimal point in formatted monetary

mon_grouping   string indicating the size of each group of digits in formatted monetary quantities

positive_sign   the string used to indicate a nonnegative-valued formatted monetary quantity

negative_sign   the string used to indicate a negative-valued formatted monetary quantity

int_frac_digits   the number of fractional digits (to the right of the decimal point) to be displayed in an internationally formatted monetary quantity

frac_digits   the number of fractional digits (to the right of the decimal point) to be displayed in a locally formatted monetary quantity

p_cs_precedes   set to 1 or 0 if the currency_symbol respectively precedes or succeeds the value for a nonnegative formatted monetary quantity

p_sep_by_space	set to 1 or 0 if the currency_symbol respectively is or is not separated by a space from the value for a nonnegative formatted monetary quantity
n_cs_precedes	set to 1 or 0 if the currency_symbol respectively precedes or succeeds the value for a negative formatted monetary quantity
n_sep_by_space	set to 1 or 0 if the currency_symbol respectively is or is not separated by a space from the value for a negative formatted monetary quantity
p_sign_posn	set to a value indicating the positioning of the positive sign for a nonnegative formatted monetary quantity
n_sign_posn	set to a value indicating the positioning of the positive sign for a negative formatted monetary quantity

langinfo items:

crncystr	string for specifying the currency

LC_NUMERIC—affects the handling of the radix character in the formatted input/output functions and the conversion functions. It also affects the numeric values in the *localeconv* structure.

grouping	for size of each group of digits in formatted nonmonetary form

langinfo items:

decimal_point	same as RADIXCHAR
thousands_sep	
alt_digits	string mapped into the ASCII string '0123456789b+-.,eE' where b is a blank

LC_TIME—affects the behavior of time conversion functions.

These keywords except *era* are identical to their corresponding *langinfo* items.

d_t_fmt	
d_fmt	
t_fmt	
day_1 to day_7	
abday_1 to abday_7	
mon_1 to mon_7	
abmon_1 to abmon_7	
am_str	
pm_str	
year_unit	
mon_unit	
day_unit	
hour_unit	
min_unit	
sec_unit	
era_fmt	
era	names and dates of eras or emperors

Info expressions follow all *langinfo*-type, *lconv*-type, and *era* keywords. Each expression is a string.

The expressions following the *langinfo*-type keywords define the strings associated with the items in *langinfo*. Each expression consists of a string to be associated with the item identified by the keyword.

The expressions following the *lconv*-type keywords define the strings associated with members of the *lconv* struct in *localeconv* (see Section B.3.1). Each expression consists of a string to be associated with the member identified by the keyword.

Each expression following the keyword *era* defines how the years are counted and displayed for one era (or emperor's reign).

B.3.3. Directories and Files

The following files contain NLS information for HP-UX:

/usr/lib/nls	NLS information is in this directory.
/usr/lib/nls/config	A readable ASCII file that identifies currently installed locales including those created by *localedef*. It contains locale names and their corresponding locale-ID numbers.
/usr/lib/nls/*locale*	Each installed *locale* has this directory. It can include subdirectories for *terr* or *codeset*.
/usr/lib/nls/*locale* / *locale.def.*	Locale-dependent processing information.
/usr/lib/nls/*locale* / *.cat*	Localized message catalog files.

B.4. OPERATION

B.4.1. Development

If you are developing applications for a locale that already exists, then your main concern is to ensure that your messages are distinct from the program. HP provides a message *catalog* to assist in this process. You can verify that your locale already exists in a number of ways. The **-d** option for *localedef* prints out all the information about the locale. Or you can look at the readable /usr/lib/nls/config file.

To prepare a program for Localization, you first strip out the messages from the program, place them in a message catalog after translation, and then replace them in the program with appropriate calls to access the messages in their catalog. In the description that follows, remember that it is a convention to name files with the name of the program but with different extensions.[6] For example, the message and catalog files for the program *abc.c* are *abc.msg* and *abc.cat*.

To strip messages, HP supplies the routine *findstr*, which copies all strings into a specified *str* file. You probably then need to edit this file because not all strings are messages. For example, some strings are used as type specifiers in

---

[6]Use of this convention allows for automation of the process using the **make** command.

commands such as ***fopen.*** After making these modifications, you then use *insertmsg,* which produces a *msg* file. This assigns a message number to each string in the message file and writes the numbered messages out in a format suitable for use as a catalog. It also creates a version of the original source code in which each string identified in the string file is replaced by a ***catgets*** call with the assigned message number and the name of the new source file, which is the name of the original program prefixed with *nl_.*

You might want to edit the message catalog by grouping messages in the *msg* file and placing them in sets. Messages consist of numbers followed by a space, then by the text, and ending with a new\line. You can intersperse messages with comments (for the translator, for example) whose format is *$space* followed by *text,* and you can group messages with a *$set* line.

You create the catalog with a ***gencat*** command such as

```
gencat abc.c abc.msg
```

There is some slight editing necessary on the new source code. ***Catgets*** accesses the catalog, but you must open the catalog first with a ***catopen*** command and close it with a ***catclose*** call. The command ***dumpmsg*** will list the messages in a message catalog.

Environment variables include LANG, the set LC_CTYPE, LC_COLLATE, LC_MESSAGES, LC_MONETARY, LC_NUMERIC, and LC_TIME described in Section B.3.2, NLSPATH, and LANGOPTS.

General format of the locale name in the environment variable LANG is "lang_terr.codeset"

> where lang = "en,"
> "fr,"
> "ja,"
> "de," etc.

(Refer to ISO 639 Code Set for the Representation of Names of Languages)

> and terr= "US,"
> "JP,"
> "NL,"
> "ES," etc.

(Refer to ISO 3116 Code Set for the Representation of Names of Countries)

> and codeset = "ASCII"
> "88591"
> "SJIS" (Shift Japanese Information Standard)
> "UJIS" (Japanese Limited EUC—Extended UNIX Code)

Examples:

```
setenv LANG fr_FR.88591 (French, France)

setenv LANG ja_JP.SJIS (Japanese, Japan)
```

UNIX is multiuser. An individual user (even one user using more than one shell) can also set the environment. For example, in the Korn shell, the user could type:

LANG=fr_FR.88591

for French in France.

NLSPATH allows a user to change the naming and locations of message catalogs. *LANGOPTS* is concerned with *mode* and *order*. Mode can be left to right or right to left, and order can be the order in which the user enters keystrokes or the order in which characters are displayed. We discuss these more in Chapter 6.

B.4.2. Error Checking

In addition to normal error checking and the procedures that we mention in Section 4.5 of Chapter 4, you should check for missing catalogs, overwritten messages in memory, wrong settings for environment variables, and routines that may strip the eighth bit.

B.4.3. Interaction with C

C has its own standards for dealing with multiple-byte characters. See Section 7.3.1.8 in Chapter 7.

APPENDIX C

Macintosh

C.I. INTRODUCTION

In this appendix we give an overview of how the Macintosh provides support for someone wanting to Localize software. Also refer to Chapter 6 for what goes on with more complicated languages. Good technical references are Apple's *Worldwide Software Development Overview* and Apple's *Guide to Macintosh Software Localization*. When you actually Internationalize and Localize, you will need them. Daniel R. Carter gives a very good example in *Writing Localizable Software for the Macintosh*.

Suffice it to say that Apple has built in Internationalization and Localization concerns to such an extent that the technical manuals even mention Localizing Japanese Script Systems for use in a French version of the Macintosh. The Macintosh has been carefully designed so that Localization is quite readily achieved. Apple has developed the concept of *Worldwide Software*. To qualify as such, an application must satisfy two criteria:

It must be possible to Localize the application's interface for any language just by editing its resource files; and

Each Localized version must be able to support the user's natural way of writing, whether Roman letters, Chinese characters, or any one of the world's 27 writing forms.

C.2. CHARACTER SETS

As shown in Appendix K, there are character sets for:

Roman	Icelandic
Arabic	Japanese
Central European	Korean
Chinese	Thai
Croatian	Turkish
Cyrillic	Arabic Encoding
Greek	Hebrew Encoding
Hebrew	

Western languages use the Roman character set

C.3. PREPARATION

There are two types of resources, system and application.

With system software version 7.0, the user installs each non-Roman *script system* with an *Installer* that allows users to install the script as a primary or secondary script. The Finder also allows users to add or remove secondary script systems; it permits users to move a collection of script resources into the System file. When moving a collection of script resources, it transfers the resources specified by the script's *itl0, itl1, itl2, itl4,* optional *itl5, KCAP, KMAP, KSWP, KCHR, kcs#, kcs4,* and *kcs8* resources. So there are script resources, keyboard resources, and font resources.

The application resource types are for dialog and alert boxes, item lists, icons, menus, strings, document windows, fonts, pictures, and sounds.

C.3.1. Routines

Drawing Text

Char2Pixel & NChar2Pixel	Finds the screen position of carets and selection points, given the text and length
Pixel2Char	Finds the nearest text-string offset that corresponds to a pixel width in the displayed text
Drawjust & NDrawjust	Draws the given text at the current pen location in the current font, style, and size
MeasureJust	Measures text that may be fully justified
FindWord	Returns two offsets in the offset table that specify the boundaries of the word selected by the offset and leadingEdge
HiliteText	Finds the characters between two offsets that should be highlighted

Date and Time Utilities

(The Script Manager uses an extended time-in-seconds format called a Long-DateTime and an extended calendar-date format called a LongDateRec.)

String2Date	Sets the appropriate fields in a LongDateRec from the text representation of a date

String2Time	Sets the appropriate fields in a LongDateRec from the text representation of a time
LongDate2Secs	Converts a LongDateRec to a LongDateTime
LongSecs2Date	Converts a LongDateTime to a LongDateRec
IULDateString	Takes a LongDateTime and returns a formatted text string of the date only
IULTimeString	Takes a LongDateTime and returns a formatted text string of the time only
ToggleDate	Modifies a LongDateTime (time-in-seconds) by changing the second, minute, hour, A.M./P.M., day, month, or year fields of the corresponding LongDateRec field.
ValidDate	Checks the validity of a LongDateRec
Readlocation	Reads the machine's geographic location and time zone from the data stored in its parameter RAM
Writelocation	Writes the machine's geographic location and time zone to the parameter RAM

Formatting Text

FindScriptRun	In text with both Roman and non-Roman scripts, shows how to break mixed text into separate runs of Roman and non-Roman text
PortionText	Indicates the correct proportion of justification to be allocated to one run of text in a line when compared to other text.
GetFormatOrder	For a given line of text, tells in what order format runs should be drawn based on the line direction.
StyledLineBreak	Breaks a line on a word boundary.

Modifying Text

LwrText	Provides Localizable lowercasing of text (up to 32 KB in length; planned for System 7.0)
StripText	Provides Localizable stripping of diacritical marks (up to 32 KB in length; planned for System 7.0)
Transliterate	Converts the given text to the closest approximation in a different script or type of character; also performs uppercasing and lowercasing

Number Utilities

| FormatStr2X | Reads a text representation of a number (with the formatting associated with a given human language) and creates the correct extended floating-point number |
| FormatX2Str | Creates a text representation of a number according to the current script's formatting of numbers |

Other

GetEnvirons	Retrieves global variables maintained for all scripts
SetEnvirons	Sets global variables maintained for all scripts
GetScript	Retrieves local variables and routine vectors maintained for the specified script

SetScript	Sets local variables and routine vectors maintained for the specified script
GetDefFontSize	Returns size of the current default size
GetSysFont	Returns identification number of current system font
GetAppFont	Returns identification number of current application font
GetMBarHeight	Returns height of menu bar as required to hold menu titles in current font
GetSysJust	Returns the value of a global variable that represents the direction in which lines written in the system script are justified
SetSysJust	Sets a global variable that represents the direction in which lines written in the system script are justified
KeyScript	Sets the keyboard script, changes the keyboard layout to that of the new keyboard script, and draws the script icon for the new keyboard script
FontScript	Returns the script code for the font script
Font2Script	Translates a font identification number into a script code
IntlScript	Returns the script code for the International Utilities script
CharByte	Checks the byte length of the specified character
CharType	Returns more information about the specified character
ParseTable	Builds a table indicating byte length for all characters in a string

C.3.2. Localization Tools

Apple's *Software Development for International Markets: A Technical Reference* says the tools most necessary for localization are the Localizer, ResEdit, and FEdit Plus.

The Localizer disk contains Installer scripts (a specific version for each version of the System file) used to install keyboard and international resources into a system file.

ResEdit is an interactive, graphics-based editor that can be used to edit the resources in your files. It can display data in either hexadecimal or formatted fields. The generic way of editing a resource is to fill in the fields of a dialog box. The layout of these dialog boxes is determined from a template (TMPL) in the ResEdit resource file. There are some templates supplied and you can add your own.

You can also edit the *finf* resource, which controls the fonts used in your application. And you can edit the text and paper sizes in the Page Setup dialog.

FEdit Plus is a byte editor that can be used to translate text that is embedded in code and to change the boot blocks of a disk. It displays only in hexadecimal.

There is also a stand-alone Macintosh program, AppleGlot, that extracts all the strings from an application so that a translator can work on them without any programming expertise, then replaces them in the application's resource files.

You can also use Resorcerer by Mathemaesthetics, Incorporated to edit your resources and design interfaces (see Section 6.4.5).

If you use parts of the Localizer in your software, then you need to obtain a license from Apple. Installation is straightforward, consisting of selecting the version or country name to be installed and clicking an Install button. International resources are available (as of 1988) for the following languages:

American	Greek
Australian	Icelandic
British	Norwegian
Canadian French	Portuguese
Danish	Spanish
Dutch	Swedish
Finnish	Swiss French
Flemish	Swiss German
French	Turkish
German	

C.4. OPERATION

C.4.1. Development

On the whole, consider Internationalization to be done; you only have to Localize. Install the appropriate script supplied by Apple. Then, depending on how complex and different your application is, use the International Utilities, ResEdit, and then the Script Manager to Localize. If that doesn't do everything, then you will have to program the remaining differences yourself.

C.4.2. Use

Use the mouse to double-click and choose your keyboard layout, script, and so on.

The Basic Concepts of Computers: Software

D.1 INTRODUCTION

This appendix is addressed to those who are not familiar with computers and have not been exposed to computer terminology. It will not make you an expert, but it will make it easier for you to understand the material in this book.

You might think that computers compute. There was a time when that was all they did. Nowadays, computers are all-purpose machines that do many things other than compute or calculate.[1] They can be used to produce and edit sounds and pictures, for example. For our purposes in this appendix, we are interested in computers as they are used to manipulate characters and strings of characters, or text. In Appendix E, we discuss the components from a hardware point of view.

A computer is an electro-mechanical device that consists of a number of pieces of hardware, shown schematically in Figure D-1. These pieces are as follows:

Keyboard   Basically the standard typewriter keyboard with the addition of some keys that cause the computer to perform special functions. This is one of the two basic devices by means of which the computer operator tells the machine what to do.

Mouse   A device the operator moves by hand to move an arrow (or some other indicator) around on the screen so that some

---

[1]Just as originally, a *typewriter* was the *person* who wrote type, a *computer* was the *person* who *computed*. What did they compute? They computed tables of various kinds—logarithms and trigonometric functions, to name two. Such tables were published as aids to professionals who needed to make extensive calculations. In the early days of typewriting and computing, the machines replaced such aids and aides, and took their names.

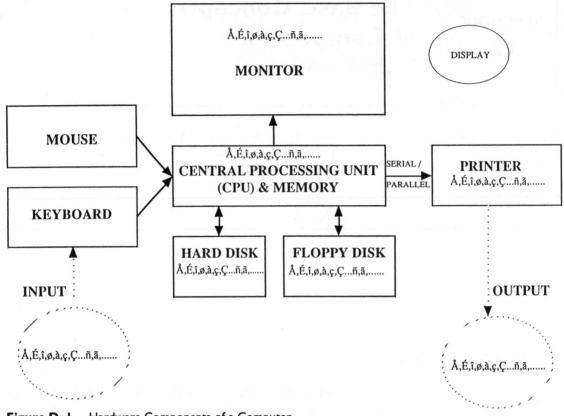

Figure D–1.   Hardware Components of a Computer

other action can be taken on the screen at a place of the operator's choice.

Monitor
: A televisionlike screen on which information is presented to the operator and on which the actions ordered by the operator are reflected.

CPU/Memory
: This is the heart of the machine. The central processing unit (CPU) carries out the instructions given it by the operator or by a *program*. Every CPU has associated with it a *memory*, which is a set of numbered locations into which data can be inserted or *stored*. Typically, the memories in modern computers are large, being able to store one to twenty or so millions of individual pieces of information. Access to this type of memory, either to store or to retrieve information, is very rapid, commonly in fractions of a microsecond. Storing an item of information in any type of memory is called "writing" and extracting an item is called "reading."

Hard Disk
: A recording medium that is usually a permanent part of a particular computer. A hard disk is a form of memory slower than that associated with the CPU but capable of storing

	many millions of items (20 million to 500 million and more) of information. In some machines the contents of the CPU memory are erased when the machine is turned off. This is not the case with the hard disk or the floppy disk (see next item). Both hard and floppy disks are sometimes referred to (loosely) as disk drives.
Floppy Disk	A portable recordable medium on which you can store and retrieve computer files and therefore copy and transport them from one computer to another. Similar to the hard disk but of smaller capacity (from half a million to a million-and-a-half items of information). Floppy disks are not permanent components of any particular computer and are used to introduce new programs or data, and to store information away from the computer for backup in the event of a computer failure.
Printer	A device for producing hard copy of text and graphics from a computer.

A computer operates under the control of a series of commands known as a *program*. Programs generically are called software, to differentiate them from the computer hardware. When a program operates, the computer carries out the instructions that make up the program.

Normally, the computer examines the instructions in a program in the order of their appearance. It proceeds from the first to the second to the third, and so on. However, one of the most important features of modern computers is that they can make decisions such as: "If the number in memory location X is positive, proceed to the next instruction; if it is negative, proceed to instruction number N." Examples of instructions that might appear in a program are:

Scan the keyboard to determine which key or combination of keys has been pressed.

Read the contents of some portion of the hard disk and write it into some specified portion of the CPU memory.

Write some specified portion of memory onto a specified location of the hard disk.

Print the contents of some section of the memory.

Display the contents of some section (or sections) of memory on the monitor screen.

Add the contents of some specified part of the memory to the contents of some other specified part of the memory and place the sum in yet another specified part of the memory.

Test the contents of some memory location to see if the number represented is positive, negative, or zero.

Proceed to a specific instruction.

Carry out an instruction in some particular location of memory or with some particular name.

The contents of memory, either the CPU memory or the disks, is called data. Each program that controls the computer determines whether a particular item of data is to be considered a number or an instruction. The next section discusses the basic organization of data.

D.2. BITS, NIBBLES, BYTES, AND WORDS

All the data operated on in a computer or stored in any of its memories is in the form of a number consisting of either the digit 1 or the digit 0. These are called *bits,* an abbreviation of *bi*nary dig*its*. Computers are built around numbers represented by bits since it is much easier to make a device, such as an electronic switch, that is either *on* or *off* than to make one that has the ten different positions that would be needed to represent a decimal digit.

We learn the decimal form of number representation at our mothers' knee, but numbers can also be represented in binary form, using only the digits 0 and 1. Our usual number system, using the digits 0 through 9, is called the decimal system, that is, a system using the base of 10; the system using only the two digits 0 and 1 is called the binary system, which uses the base 2.[2]

While the computer is busily using the binary system, this fact is usually of no particular concern to a computer user and only becomes important to a computer programmer at the very lowest and most detailed level of programming or of error detection and correction.

Since the rules of arithmetic apply to numbers however they may be represented, a computer user need not care, or even know, how the computer he or she is using looks at numbers.

A single digit, a 0 or a 1, is, as noted, called a *bit*. A group of 4 bits, which it is sometimes a convenient group for a computer to handle, is called a *nibble*. Eight bits, or two nibbles, is called a *byte*. Computer memories are usually measured by the number of bytes they can retain.

Computers are commonly designed to handle groups of 8 or 16 or 32 bits at a time. Such groups are referred to as *words*. In a 32-bit computer, data is handled 32 bits at a time, while a 16-bit computer handles data at only 16 bits at a time. In transferring data from one place to another on the computer, the computer looks, as instructed, for information at certain addresses. The addresses refer to the locations of words. On a 32-bit computer, an instruction to read a word from a specific location on the hard disk is an instruction to read the collection of 32 bits starting at that specific address.

The decimal system has the advantage that in a single digit we can represent ten values, zero through nine. In the binary system, a single digit can represent only two values, zero and one.

D.3. PROGRAMS AND DATA

All of the information in a computer, or entered into it from any external point, is stored in the form of "ones" and "zeroes." One feature that makes an electronic computer more than just a fast adding machine is that it is designed so that at

---

[2]Any number can be used as the base of a number system. A *ternary* system uses the digits 0, 1, and 2. Systems using 4, 5, and so on and even as many as 60 digits have been used in one society or another. Our clocks, based on twelve numbers, are on the duo-decimal system. Hours have 60 minutes and circles have 360 degrees. Our decimal system is only one of many systems, and not always the most useful, as computers have so forcefully demonstrated.

some times during its operation it considers a set of "ones" and "zeroes" (which may consist of only a few or, alternatively, many "words" worth of "ones" and "zeroes") as instructions that it is to carry out, while at other times it will view a set of words as data on which the instructions are to act. A second feature that distinguishes the modern computer is that a set of words that are considered instructions at one time may be considered data at another.[3] It is this ability of the computer to modify the instructions that it is executing that gives it its full power.

The sets of instructions that are written for the computer to carry out are called *programs,* and the people who write them, *programmers.*

While all programs end up finally as groups of words consisting of "ones" and "zeroes," writing programs with only those two characters is incredibly cumbersome and error-prone. While early computers were indeed programmed that way, from the very beginning programmers recognized the need to develop what are now called "higher-level languages" so that they could write instructions more concisely. Any higher language must be submitted to an intermediate program that will convert the higher-level language into the "ones" and "zeroes" that the computer requires. A number of intermediate programs have been written, called variously "assemblers" or "compilers."[4] When a programmer writes a program in a higher-level language, it is first either assembled or compiled. After this step the program is ready to be executed; that is, it is available to operate on data to provide the desired outcome.

There are many programming languages, some quite elementary and some of very high sophistication. Some appear, when written, to be collections of unintelligible symbols. Others appear very close to a written language like English or French. Programmers commonly write their programs one instruction at a time within a text editor. Programs are frequently described as being of, say, "fifty lines of code" or, perhaps, of "a hundred thousand lines of code." (In this sense, the word "code" is a holdover from earlier days when one line usually did one thing; now a line of what is still called code may carry out a very large number of logical or arithmetic steps.) Computer programs in the space program, where an enormous number of quantities regarding the condition and position of a space vehicle must be known at a very rapid rate, can consist of millions of lines of code.[5] See Section D.6 for a discussion of various types of software programs.

As programs have grown in size, computers have had to increase in speed so

---

[3]An example of the treatment of an instruction as data is the following: You are finding the sums of several sets of numbers. When you have added the first set, you tell the computer to store the sum in memory location X. You then modify that instruction (that is, you treat it as a number) by adding one to the X so that the next time that instruction is executed, when you have found the sum of the second set of numbers, it will store that sum in memory location $X + 1$. This is repeated so that the same group of instructions can add many sets of numbers, placing the sum of each set in a different memory location without having to duplicate the adding and storing instructions as many times as there are columns of numbers to add.

[4]There is a difference between "assemblers" and "compilers" that need not detain us here; all intermediate programs take a higher-level language and convert it so that the computer can execute it. Whether a program is assembled or compiled is of no concern to the programmer; what a programmer wants is a program that runs.

[5]It is an enormous tribute to the writers and testers of these programs, where a small error can result in a tragic catastrophe, that they have worked as well as they have.

that these huge programs can be carried out in reasonable times. Early computers, built with electro-mechanical rather than electronic switches, could carry out a few hundred instructions per second. The introduction of electronic switching increased speeds into the thousands and tens of thousands of instructions per second. As transistor and computer chip technologies have progressed, speeds have risen into the millions of instructions per second (called *mips*) and are now well into the billions of operations per second (*bips*). However fast a computer can be made, a problem can be proposed that requires yet more speed and greater memory capacity.

D.4. FILES AND FILE DIRECTORIES

Since it is usually the case with modern computers that several (sometimes many) programs are stored in the computer at the same time and that bodies of data pertinent to different programs are also stored, it is convenient to organize both programs and data in ways that make them easy to handle. Computer designers took a hint from the fact that offices usually store their information in file cabinets in which many file folders are arranged in some logical order. Computers normally provide the facility to create as many files as are considered necessary. Programs or data or both can be put into any file and convenient names can be assigned to these files.

Computers have a flexibility that offices do not; files can be created inside other files, and still further files can be created inside these new files. For example, it might be found useful to create a file called Correspondence, and to put into it a set of files called Correspondence 1991, Correspondence 1992, and so on, into each of which the individual documents would be filed. Going still further, it might be useful to have in each year's file a further file folder for Letters Sent and another for Letters Received. This sort of folder in a folder can be continued almost indefinitely; Letters Sent can have in it file folders for Letters Sent Outside U.S. and Letters Sent Within U.S. As a matter of terminology, collections or clusters of files are called *directories*.

A computer user does not have to know the physical location of a file or a directory; the computer program that controls basic computer operations keeps track of the names of all files and where they are physically located in any of the various possible storage media. If a user wants a particular item, he or she might call for the file Correspondence/Correspondence 1991/Letters Sent/Letters Sent Within U.S./Letter to John Smith of Jan 12. This series of names used to locate a particular document is called a *path*. Every document in a computer can be found using the appropriate path.

Note that in the previous example, the user did not have to know the physical whereabouts of the Letter to John Smith. Finding the physical location is taken care of by the basic program that controls the computer. This basic program is called the *operating system*. Almost all operating systems provide a facility that allows a user to locate a particular file or document even if he or she does not know the exact path name.

The contents of any file are up to the user. As a user becomes more familiar with a particular machine, he or she will develop his or her own style of file structure and filenames. When files are being constructed for access by many users, agreement must be reached early in the development of these files as to what the naming conventions will be.

It is not unusual to keep programs, data, and text in different files, sometimes even in different directories. This is usually done for ease of access or modification. Sometimes the amount of data is so vast, as in the account files for a bank or the billing files for a public utility, yet different portions must be easily retrieved for different purposes, that the data are stored in a set of related files called a *database*. A database consists of sets of files that may be accessed by different keys or indices in conjunction with one another.

A text file, such as a word processing document like a letter, consists of a number of characters interspersed with special characters that cause the succeeding characters to appear on the next line (analogous to the line feed function of a typewriter) and terminated with special characters that the printing or display program recognizes as indicating the end of the document.[6] Text files written under the control of one word processing program have the limitation that some other word processing program may not be able to interpret them since the various special characters that are used might be different.

D.5. CODES

Earlier we noted that all of the data stored and manipulated by a computer is represented by "ones" and "zeroes," and that the computer is able to tell when a series of such digits is to be considered an instruction to be carried out or as data on which an instruction is to operate. Note that during the development phase of a program, its source code can serve as data to other programs such as a compiler. A compiler will take the program source code as input data and translate it to another form as output data. The interpretation and translation of the components of a program is carried out according to very strict and precise rules that are outside our area of interest. Computer people say that the program is written in a language, and that is an apt description. However, the form of the language is an engineering or mathematical one and is not to be confused with the natural languages that are of interest to us.

At the lowest level, the number *1A* in the first byte of a word may be interpreted[7] as an instruction such as "Add the contents of the word at the address given in the third nibble (first after the first byte) of this word to the word at the address given in the fourth nibble." This operation could have a mnemonic code, too, such as *AR*. The characters *19 (CR)* could mean "compare the contents of the

---

[6]This is a conventional description of file formats commonly found in character-based computers before the advent of Graphic User Interfaces.

[7]Thank God for the passive voice! We don't know *who* or *what* is doing the interpreting and therefore cannot say.

words at the two addresses in the third and fourth nibbles." And so on. There might be as many as three or four hundred operations in the *instruction set*. There could be long instructions and short instructions, where long instructions take more than 16 bits to complete and are to be found in 32-bit word machines.

The sequence of instructions at this level is a software program. Ultimately, no matter how high a level an engineer programs in, the program instructions are compiled and translated and assembled and linked into such a set of instructions in this type of code. As we discussed earlier, it is far easier and more productive to program in higher-level languages whose form is similar to mathematical or engineering terminology than in this very detailed coding language.

One level higher, you find symbolic codes such as *CLA* for *Clear and add, JMP* for *Jump* (transfer program control to a specified location in the program), and so on.

For computer data and information, a number of coding schemes have been developed so that computer users can use a byte as a specific character. Interpreted one way, then, a byte can be part of a program instruction, interpreted another way it can have a numerical value, and interpreted yet another way a byte can *represent a character*.[8] For example, there has been common agreement—a de facto standard—among the manufacturers of many high-level languages to represent fractional numbers in words in certain ways. These are numbers with decimal "points." Normally, the procedure was to store the floating-point number (as it was called) as a binary number in something akin to scientific or engineering notation. That is, the number would be represented as a decimal number with the decimal "point" in a specific place and there would be a multiplier of powers of ten. How all this was stored in one word and retrieved was up to the compiler for the language in question. Clearly, the more bits in the word, the greater the precision could be.

But we are interested in yet a different interpretation. Earlier we talked of bytes and words as having numerical integer values. Associated with each numerical value is a character, and this association represents the code. Software programs that are to manipulate alphabetic characters must recognize the code. It is the interpretation and manipulation of the *data* as symbols and glyphs that is of interest to us in this book. In a very real sense, in this book we discuss how to manipulate the software programs themselves so that they will in turn manipulate the new codes or characters necessary for Internationalization and Localization.

The collection of coding schemes for all the possible contents of a data-byte or a data-word is known as a *character set*. In the computer world there are *single-byte* character sets and *double-byte* character sets. In this book, we discuss many character sets from the point of view of their international potential. In books

---

[8]A numeral is a "pictorial" representation of a number. Strictly speaking, it is not a number itself, just the representation of one. Since it is not a number, there are only a few computer languages such as COBOL that provide for arithmetic operations on these numerals. But by sacrificing the time required to decode the pictorial representation of a number into a numerical value and back again in all operations, COBOL was routinely able to achieve a large order of precision, far greater precision than other high-level languages of its era, and suitable enough to make it the main language for accounting applications.

about printing on a computer, you would find others, such as Postscript, Ventura, and Framemaker.

D.6. TYPES OF SOFTWARE

There are quite a few varieties of software. They range from very low level (the "closest" to the machine) to high level (the "closest" to natural language and mathematical statements and "pseudo" English). As a very rough rule of thumb, higher-level software incorporates the power and the capabilities of lower-level software quite succinctly.

This ability to incorporate lower levels is quite significant. For example, it allows a programmer writing an accounting program (applications software) to concentrate on debits and credits and nearly ignore the mechanics of how to store the accounting information on disk. Similarly, an aeronautical engineer can focus on the flow of air around a rudder. To store the information on a disk at any time, all the programmer need do is incorporate a simple statement such as *write file,* and the detail of actually recording the information on disk at a specific location is taken care of by procedures in lower-level software. A *compiler* takes care of introducing the actual lower-level procedures for *write file.*

From our point of view, the significance is that higher-level programs can both take advantage of capabilities in lower-level programs and be constrained by the limits of these capabilities. Writing programs in a high-level language such as Pascal means you can take advantage of the support of your operating system, which in turn takes advantage of lower-level programs; on the other hand, if these don't do what you want them to do, then you have a problem at the Pascal level of coding whatever it is that you want. You just may not have the tools to do it.

To illustrate this concept, consider the case where you want your program to display or print the time that your program writes a report. Your program can access the system clock in the format provided by the operating system. If the operating system provides it in the format that you want, you have nothing else to do before having the program display it. If it is not in the format that you want, then your program must manipulate it so that it is in the desired format.

You might also be confronting the task of Internationalizing and Localizing one of the lower-level types of system. The lower the level, the more you have to build into the software rather than rely on functions being available for use.

D.6.1. Firmware

Firmware is the lowest level language of all. In our principal context of the IBM PC, it is also known by the name of *ROM/BIOS.* It is mysterious to 99 percent of users, including programmers and engineers; it is "halfway between hardware and software." It is used when you start the machine or "boot" it; it passes data between the various components of the machine and supplies fundamental operating functions to the operating system. Some of the functions can involve the details of reading and writing data from and to the hard disk or to the floppy disk. The details would involve specific and precise commands to write or read so many bits at a precise address.

Its Internationalization and Localization functions are minimal since it is written in numerical code that can hardly be related to any natural language. On the other hand, it must provide one character set; in the United States, for the PC, it is normally code page 437.

D.6.2. Operating Systems

On the next higher level we have operating systems. You use a very cryptic English, in English acronyms or in a shorthand that normally has some mnemonic value in English, in order to interact with an operating system, and those attributes make the machine somewhat more intelligible to users than dealing with symbols or even numbers. A reasonably sophisticated user can "set environment," configure the machine, manage memory and storage, change character sets, and use firmware functions to read and write and store data without knowing the insides of those functions. References to locations where data is to be found are in symbolic terms and the internals of the functions would translate these symbolic addresses into the precise addresses required. If users know what they want to do, they can use a function to do it without knowing the details of how it is done.

Packaged with the operating system are tools such as compilers, interpreters, editors, and various utilities such as functions that "find files," and so on. Compilers and interpreters translate higher-level languages into lower-level code (see Section D.6.5). Operating systems can be very sophisticated and can offer programmers and engineers a comprehensive set of tools to increase their productivity, or they may be quite bare bones. One of the more powerful systems is *UNIX* (the name derives from UNICS, an acronym for Uniplexed Information and Computing Service), which provides an ability to string commands together, offers a control procedure for maintaining different versions of code in a coherent form, and offers a procedure to control the links between different parts of a complex software product. UNIX, developed at AT&T, quickly found a home in universities and research institutions; in the past couple of years, there has been a strong drive to make it more palatable for commercial users.

Some operating systems also include protocols for communications between machines near and far; other systems can link similar machines together in networks. UNIX offers an "e-mail" system as part of the *OS* (Operating System); on other machines a separate product is required. Machines and user terminals can be linked together so that many users can use one CPU (Central Processing Unit—see Appendix E) or many CPUs can be linked in a network. It all depends on the basic purpose of the machine and on whether you prefer cabbages to Brussels sprouts (one large computer serving many dumb terminals or many more-or-less equally sized computers on a network).

The ideas used in one operating system are often incorporated in later versions of other operating systems. For example, later versions of *DOS* for the IBM PC incorporate many ideas originally found in UNIX.

Our machine of interest, the IBM PC, uses an operating system called *DOS* (Disk Operating System).[9] There are many manufacturers of DOS, including IBM, which produces PC-DOS, Microsoft Corporation, which produces MS-DOS, and Digital Research Corporation, which produces DR DOS. All the manufacturers' versions perform the same functions generally, but there may be some differences in detail. This system has undergone many revisions starting with its original release of DOS 1.0; the latest versions available of PC-DOS is version 5.0 and of MS-DOS is version 6.0. As we have seen, DOS provides for character sets or code pages in addition to the one provided by ROM/BIOS.

The operating systems for large machines used for such purposes as processing millions of transactions per day, or providing 24-hour-a-day service of some kind to millions of users are very complex.

When you start a computer, it comes up under the control of its operating system. Many operating systems provide the ability to transfer control to a file that sets operating parameters and that even allows an application to take over control.

D.6.3. Graphic User Interfaces and Other Operating Environments

A fairly recent development has been to interpose another layer of software between the programmer and engineer to provide functions that the operating system doesn't, or to provide an easier access to the power of the operating system without a necessity for learning another language.

As we hinted above, UNIX is a very powerful operating system with tools that many other operating systems incorporate. But it is very difficult to learn and its commands are very cryptic. In fact, it almost encourages users to live in a world of jargon that is incomprehensible to other humans. On the other hand, Apple Computer made their machines far easier to use and received enormous acclaim for this step. Apple made the use of Graphical User Interfaces popular. It allowed users to dispense with arcane text and point at representations of files with a mouse.

Some manufacturers are therefore interposing "graphical interfaces" between the user and the operating system. In many cases, concurrent with this development, they are providing capabilities that previously would have been part of the OS command line, but are now part of the graphic interface.

In the UNIX world, there are now two interfaces, the Open Software Foundation's Motif and the Sun/AT&T's Open Look. Both are based on X-Windows, a network client server software for UNIX Graphical User Interfaces (GUI).

In the DOS world of the IBM PC, most later versions of DOS include a shell that is easier to use than DOS itself, and Microsoft is presenting Windows, a powerful graphical interface. Microsoft is selling an enormous number of copies of Windows and it is rapidly becoming a de facto standard in the PC world. Windows provides far more extensive Internationalization capabilities than DOS.

Many of these GUIs are related to each other even though they run on different platforms. According to Tim Bajarin in "Industry Insight: Windows' Future Still Haunted by Apple Lawsuit" (*Bay Area Computer Currents,* January 28–Feb-

---

[9]There is another operating system called DOS; IBM used it on its larger computers a few years ago.

ruary 10, 1992, p. 19), Xerox's Palo Alto Research Center developed an interface, but never enforced its many copyrights; Apple developed a version of the PARC GUI and copyrighted it in Apple Corporation's name for use on the Macintosh.[10] Microsoft obtained a license in 1985 for 179 features for use in Windows 1.0 in the IBM PC world. Microsoft in turn sublicensed this GUI to Hewlett-Packard for use in its New Wave GUI and also used in its Presentation Manager in OS/2. IBM also has a license from Apple to use the GUI in its UNIX product.

D.6.4. Applications

Computer applications are all around us in today's world. Computers are used for all kinds of tasks. In this section, we just want to mention a few ways in which the applications can be classified.

A distinction that is decreasing in importance as hardware gets cheaper is the one between scientific and commercial applications. In the former, typically many numbers are manipulated, possibly in very complex ways, to obtain a few results; this has been called number crunching. On the other hand, in massive accounting systems, many transactions are manipulated to obtain many simple results. The hardware requirements for the former involved powerful CPUs and little need for memory and storage devices, while the latter required the reverse.

Some systems operate in real time. Examples are equipment for monitoring patients in hospitals; plane, car, and hotel reservations systems; information retrieval systems operating worldwide; and many mechanical control systems for planes and machines. Other systems like billing systems can operate so that statements for customers, say, can be prepared without the need for instant response. This latter way of operating is called *batch mode*.

Someone writing a document in a word processing package, making a spread-sheet model, or laying out a brochure in a desktop publishing package is operating in an *interactive mode* with the computer.

An application that runs under DOS can use any of the character sets provided by DOS. One running under Windows can use its Internationalization features.

D.6.5. Programming Languages

From our point of view, "programming languages" and "applications" are indistinguishable. Engineers and programmers use any of about two hundred languages to write their applications. Some languages are designed to make certain products easier to develop, and some languages are to be found in one form or another on many machines, while some are to be found on only one or two. Some languages are necessary for writing lower-level software.

Programming has traditionally been an undisciplined activity, but it is now becoming more of an engineering craft. It can be very complex, and the difficulties of coordinating and managing the development work of many programmers

---

[10]At least two other companies, Viewstar in Emeryville, California, and Metaphor in Redwood City, California, use derivatives of the PARC GUI. Neither is as well known as Apple Corporation.

and engineers are far greater than you might assume. They are so great, in fact, that even though most of the people involved are intelligent and can be quite experienced, software development projects are usually behind schedule and over budget. Another interesting fact is that about 60 percent of the overall U.S. programming budget is devoted to maintenance, where mistakes and omissions in the original code are corrected.

There is some interest in developing design languages, the use of which would eliminate programming per se. The idea is that with sufficiently precise design, it should then be a mechanical task to translate the design into some form that operates and controls a computer. From another point of view, of course, you could say that doing so is simply moving the programming function to another location in the software development process.

The mechanical process of writing program code is to write the code in the programming language of choice, then submit it to a compiler that scans it for correctness and translates it into the code that can actually run the computer. There is a similar process of *interpretation* that translates the code step-by-step as it operates; this process can be helpful in the early stages of development wherein the program looks "correct" but isn't doing what you had hoped it would do. Code as written by the programmer is called *source code,* while code that can actually execute on the machine is called *object code* or *binary.*

Once the program has compiled, it is *linked* or *bound* with other parts that have undergone the same process and then it *runs.* It is even possible in some instances to "attach" some parts at run-time. This process is called *late-binding.* The purpose of binding is to allocate symbolic addresses for functions and data all relative to each of the components, so that the program counter can find its way through the logic of the combined software program.

Some programming languages contain libraries of special functions that the programmer can include in the code, many allow you to include blocks of code with the use of a single statement and that code can be used over and over again in different programs.

Some programming languages are designed to make it easy to process lists, others are designed for making scientific-type calculations, others for accounting, and still others for easy maintenance

The lowest level of language, the closest to the machine, is called *assembler.* This language is quite cryptic, and while it deals normally with symbols or variables, the instructions for any of about 100 basic operations are limited to two or three characters in length. (Assembly code is assembled in computer terminology, not compiled.)

Higher-level languages include SAS, LISP, FORTRAN, BASIC, COBOL, Pascal, Algol, FORTH, MODULA-2 and -3, SPL/3000, APL, ADA, B, BCPL, RPG, SNOBOL, RATFOR, JOVIAL, AUTOLISP, OBERON, SMALLTALK, C, and C++.[11] Because you can use more characters in these languages for the names of functions and variables (they can be longer than equivalents in assembly language), it is possible that a layperson could make some sense of the code by try-

---

[11]Yes, there was a *B* language, used internally at Bell Labs, part of AT&T.

ing to read it. SAS is very useful for statistical work, LISP for processing lists, FORTRAN for scientific work, and COBOL for the accuracy required in accounting. Pascal was the original language of choice on the Macintosh machines, and C is being used more and more. To use these languages on any machine, you must make sure the operating system contains the appropriate compiler, or some third-party manufacturer must provide one.

A very popular language nowadays is C; in some of its various dialects, it can perform both low-level operations at the bit level and, more normally, perform at a high level. It's possible to write some programs in a language like C; that in part is almost indistinguishable from Pascal. However, Pascal allows for more manipulation of data structures than does C.

A recent development in the IBM PC world has been the use of object-oriented code. This code allows a user to reuse code that has already been developed for a specific purpose. The fact that graphical interfaces allow less sophisticated users to perform more complicated functions has provided more impetus to the use of object-oriented code. This code, available at the moment in C++/Windows, Object Vision, Visual Basic, and in object-oriented Pascal, provides for easier manipulation of the standard objects like icons and windows that are to be found in the graphically oriented products of today.

When you use a GUI, the act of programming object-oriented code can take the form of moving objects around on a screen with a mouse, in sharp contrast to the traditional method of editing large blocks of text characters. The programming text or code associated with object-oriented code is automatically moved with the object.[12] This facility can lead to enormous increases in programmer productivity and a decrease in programming errors since the code is being *reused*. On the other hand, traditional programmers do find it hard to believe that this is programming. To them, the mechanics of programming consist of writing streams of text in a computer language with references to files, data, displays, and printing, and with logical branches depending on the values of events and data. Moving objects around with a mouse pointer has the appearance of playing a game. For many years, Macintosh programmers have enjoyed this feature to the consternation of their IBM colleagues. At last, the IBMers have their chance to play and be productive at the same time too.

D.6.6. Miscellaneous: Macros and 4GLs

There are other ways of programming, such as setting up or recording and playing back a sequence of keystrokes. That is to say, rather than writing in something like a natural language or in some cryptic series of codes or moving objects around on forms, you can record a series of keystrokes that are commands to a software package and constitute *macros*. Macros are a series of elementary steps

---

[12]This code cannot be translated or Localized. Therefore, a non-American who uses this method of programming and who wants to see the code developed must still cope with a programming language that is based in American English. For example, the code will contain *IF* (rather than *SI*), *CASE*, *PRINT*, *WRITE*, *READ*, *INPUT*, and so on rather than their translations. Abbreviations for functions will be American abbreviations or terms such as *ROUND*, *DAY*, *PMT*, *PV*, *FV*, and so on.

for the application that can be invoked time and time again by one command. Many packages such as Lotus 1-2-3 provide a capability to develop macros.

Other products and applications provide for a kind of programming in a language that is special to the application. For example, fourth-generation languages *(4GLs)* are to found with many databases. *NOMAD* on large machines provides for interaction with FORTRAN and COBOL, as well as having its own language; the *IMAGE* database on the HP3000 can be programmed in *QUIZ/QUICK;* and *dBASE, FOXPRO,* and *CLIPPER* manipulate dBASE databases on the IBM PC. *Paradox* has its own programming language called *PAL.* On the Macintosh, you can program *Hypercard,* a primitive yet powerful filing system.

At first glance, many of these languages look alike. An experienced programmer can usually intuit what a program in another language is supposed to be doing, be it displaying something on the screen, accepting input from the keyboard, printing, or even conforming to some logic. It is also good programming practice these days to be quite liberal with *comments* in the code; the presence of such comments proves to be quite beneficial, especially to maintenance programmers.

D.7. SOFTWARE PRODUCTION PROCESS

In this section we discuss how software is produced with an eye to Internationalization and Localization. We have indicated before that this is a sequential process; first, Internationalization, which enables the second, Localization. The first is almost totally engineering, the second a combination of engineering and translation. You can Localize a product without first going through the Internationalization process. However, this approach doesn't allow you to leverage the work you need to do to Localize a product in the event you have to Localize it for several countries.

We describe the basic functions that occur in the production process. Our treatment is somewhat superficial and does not reflect any of the passions and emotions displayed as internal deadlines approach, and are missed, and budget constraints are reached and passed. None of us has ever seen the idealized sanitized process described in many textbooks; we are more familiar with the kind of events that Kaner et al. describe in *Testing Computer Software.* Two hundred unresolved anomalies two weeks before the date of release to Manufacturing concentrates the mind wonderfully, as the saying goes.

To some extent, we paint an idealized picture of the process. Since this is not a book on development, we will dwell more on the additional work that Internationalization and Localization require. The minimum goal of the Localized package is to be able to process all the extended characters. A local user must be able to input all the characters in his or her language, display them on the screen, and print them for a reasonable machine configuration in the user's country. If you cannot do that for a locale, forget about all the other issues and abandon the attempt!

Managing software development is sometimes like trying to manage chaos, where changes are the only constants. In our experience, the software industry is one of constantly underestimated time and cost budgets, of pressure from senior management, of missed deadlines and cost overruns.

In our simplified version of the process, we distinguish five departments actively involved in the process of developing a Localized software product: International Sales and Marketing, Development (including Software Quality Assurance), Documentation, Maintenance, and Technical Support. For the moment we ignore the manufacturing process and consider only the development of the intellectual component, resulting in masters that may be reproduced for sales copies.

D.7.1. International Sales and Marketing

This department's most important role is to market and sell the product in the appropriate local marketplace. It must develop logistics for shipping the product. But it also must serve as a conduit between the developers and documenters on one hand and the market on the other.

One of International Sales and Marketing's major roles is to contribute international and local points of view in developing user specifications. To accomplish this, the marketers obtain information on local practices and preferences in the use of software and work with the software developers to resolve questions of style. They find distributors and act as liaison with them, and they may find Localizers.

They can also find and develop relations with potential beta-test customers. Again, International Sales and Marketing is the channel through which anomalies discovered by the beta-test users are reported to the Software Quality Assurance department for inclusion in the anomaly tracking system and ultimate disposition.

This department will also run international technical support services (see Section 8.8.2).

D.7.2. Development and Software Quality Assurance

Development is the department where programmers and engineers produce the actual software. They participate in the specification process, they design how the software will operate, and they produce the programming code. The Software Quality Assurance department tests the product under development and validates that the software works. Software Quality Assurance and Development work closely together. Software Quality Assurance finds anomalies, reports them to Development, and keeps track of them. Then Development addresses them in its next internal release and Software Quality Assurance verifies the repairs while continuing its search for new anomalies.

In our context, developers will look at Internationalization first, then at Localizing (see Section 4.2.3). Clearly, the developers should have access to the non-American equipment and environments for their work.

D.7.3. Documentation

The Documentation department produces all the documents associated with the software. Normally, this includes warranties, manuals, supplements, on-line help, boxes, slipcovers, registration card, stickers, readme files, and disk labels. The documentation itself is part of the product and often is as substantial as the software component. This part needs to be tested for quality, in addition to the usual editing. Someone needs to verify that the instructions for the installation and use of the product are correct. It is necessary to develop and apply Quality Assurance tests to documentation as well as to edit and proofread. The so-called *conformity test* focuses on testing the manual against software to find any discrepancy that needs to be corrected. People in the Documentation department often actually use the product so that they can learn about what they are going to describe. Usually, they begin their work with an early release of the product, one that contains abundant errors. Documentation writers serve as de facto testers of the product and provide the Software Quality Assurance department with information about any anomalies they counter.

D.7.4. Maintenance

Once the software product is released to market, the Maintenance department assumes responsibility from the Development department. Programmers make repairs and provide enhancements.

D.7.5. Technical Support

The Technical Support department receives the telephone calls from customers working with the released software product who have questions about the software. Clearly, the Technical Support group must be familiar with the features of the new software product and must be able to communicate with the user. Just as clearly, apart from speaking a mutual language, they must be familiar with the users' languages and cultural issues.

The Basic Concepts of Computers: Hardware

E.I. INTRODUCTION

You might ask what the purpose of discussing hardware is in a book that deals with software. Well, software drives or controls hardware, and unless the software can drive the hardware to display or print the extended characters necessary for other languages, then the total exercise is one in futility. Further, the manipulation of messages or *text strings* that are in the software in such procedures as sorting, or in formatting their display on the screen or printer or into a form that can be transferred to another computer, all takes place in the hardware. Thus some basic knowledge of a computer is useful so as to understand hardware constraints and to have a grasp of the terms you may have to translate.

In this section, we again use the IBM PC as the machine of interest. It is relatively simple in its design, but many of its basic principles apply to other systems. Logically, you can think of the machine as follows:

A digital computer is a programmable device that can move data and transform them by performing various arithmetic and logic processes.

A personal computer consists of several physical modules; the keyboard, the monitor, and the system unit. The system unit contains within it the power supply and the motherboard and it can contain different options boards. The motherboard consists of the central processing unit (CPU), the logic necessary for the CPU to communicate with other system components such as the primary memory storage in random access memory (RAM), the ROM BIOS, the bus, and attached devices such as disk drives, video cards (that drive monitors), and ports.

E.2. HARDWARE COMPONENTS

E.2.1. Keyboards

The keyboard is traditionally the major way for the user to interact with a computer. As its name implies, it is a mechanism by which a user presses a key and initiates a signal that the computer can interpret as the code for a character.

The key in each position when pressed emits a specific unique *scan code*. The *BIOS* translates this scan code into a character code value for use by the system unit. For systems that do not use U.S. English, KEYB.COM is used to intercept the scan codes and remap them to represent the correct country keyboard layout. Hence it is possible to use a U.S. keyboard with a non-American layout, though you lose the extra key (see Section E.2.1.2).

See Figure E.1, which shows the layout of a U.S. and a French keyboard.

E.2.1.1. Function Keys

Function keys are labeled F1 through F10, except on the 101 keyboard where there are 12 function keys. At the DOS command line level they are used for sim-

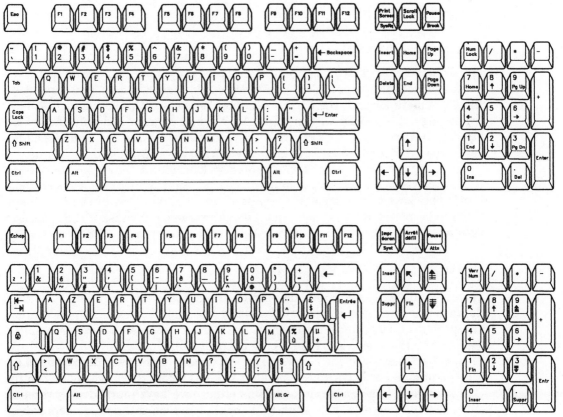

Figure E-1. U.S. (above) and Foreign (below) Keyboards 101 and 102

ple line editing functions. In application software they can be assigned by the designers to represent commonly needed commands. For example, F1 is quite often used to represent Help. In translating it is important to make sure that the function keys still maintain their designed purpose and that any messages they generate when pressed are correctly displayed.

E.2.1.2. Dead Keys

In many non-English languages some of the characters that a language requires are accented (e.g., *è* or *ö)*. Some of these characters (also called extended characters) are assigned places on the keyboard. For example, on the Spanish keyboard, *ñ* is found where the U.S. keyboard has *L*.

Frequently, since there are not enough keys to provide all the accented characters, DOS uses dead keys to combine accent marks. A dead key is one that just represents accent marks. The dead key does not produce an immediate result and does not cause the cursor to move on the screen, but it tells DOS to combine the accent mark with the next key pressed. On the French keyboard you type *ô* by pressing the dead key for the circumflex *^*, then pressing the *o* key. If you press a dead key, then a key that cannot be combined with a dead key, the result is an error response from DOS. The error response is usually a beep from the system's speaker.

E.2.1.3. U.S. Keyboards

The de facto standard layout for the U.S. keyboard is the *QWERTY* layout with some minor changes, such as the addition of function, alt, control, escape, and cursor keys and the numeric keypad. There have been three revisions of this keyboard.

The original keyboard with the IBM PC/XT had 83 keys and only the left *alt* key. The next revision, with the IBM AT, included the *sysrq* key to make an 84-key keyboard. Both of these keyboards are referred to as Standard keyboards.

The final revision and the most common one found today is the 101-key Enhanced Keyboard, where the numeric keypad and cursor pad have been separated. This keyboard is an ANSI standard. These differences in the features of the U.S. keyboard designs should not affect the translator's task if the American base software has been properly designed to take account of the differences.

E.2.1.4. Non-American Keyboards

The main difference between a non-American keyboard and the U.S. keyboard is the layout of the "typewriter keys," namely the alpha characters, punctuation, and graphical characters. Further, you can enter accented characters using a dead key for the accent and then typing the character.

On the 102 keyboard the right alt key will usually be marked *altgr*. And there is an additional key between the left shift key and where there is a "Z" key on the U.S. keyboard. Non-American keyboards often have keys marked with three or four characters on each key. With an enhanced keyboard the characters can be entered as follows: To type the upper left character, press the shift key and the character key. Use the key combinations described in the following table to type the lower right and upper right characters. The national layout of the keyboard is controlled by KEYB.COM and code page switching (see Section 3.3.2).

Key Combinations	Characters
Character Key Only	Lower Left Character
Shift + Character Key	Upper Left Character
AltGr + Character Key	Lower Right Character[1]
Alt + Shift + Character	Upper Right Character

E.2.2. Monitors and Video Adapter Cards

There are several different video adapters and monitors in use on the IBM PC and compatible systems. The video adapter "drives" the monitor. All PC video adapters use memory-mapped displays. An image of the screen is built in video memory, then the video circuitry reads it and translates it into the appropriate signals to control one or more electron guns in the monitor. Software may be designed to recognize and output information to some or all of these devices.

The video adapter card and monitor must be matched for type to work correctly. The coarsest electrical distinction that can be made is between digital (TTL, transistor-transistor logic) and analog, according to the manner in which the video adapter transmits information to the monitor.

E.2.2.1. Digital Adapters and Monitors

In digital adapters, intensity and color (if available) data are communicated to the monitor via a digital code. The discrete number of intensities and colors depends on the number of available bits allowed for each screen location.

E.2.2.1.1. Monochrome Display Adapter (MDA) and Monitor

The MDA was the original display adapter on the first IBM PC systems. It is a monochrome text device able to display 80 columns by 25 lines of alphanumeric data or text only. It can display characters with the following attributes:

high intensity
blinking
inverse
underlined

Many modern software packages no longer support the MDA because its display features are limited. Since it is hardwired for only one code page there is no code page switching.

The MDA uses a monochrome TTL (transistor-transistor logic) monitor.

---

[1]With a Standard Keyboard the lower-right character is entered using the alt + character key for Denmark, Norway, and Finland. For Canada use alt + shift + character key, and for all other layouts use alt + ctrl + character key.

E.2.2.1.2. Hercules Monochrome Graphics Adapter and Monitor

The Hercules Monochrome Graphics Adapter rectifies some of the deficiencies of the MDA. It has a mode compatible with the MDA plus its own native 720 × 348 bit-mapped graphics mode that can produce crisp monochrome graphic images. This graphics mode is not directly supported by the ROM BIOS, and software intended to work with it must supply its own special drivers and supply its own graphics mode character sets.

The Hercules Monochrome Graphics Adapter uses the same type of monochrome TTL monitor as the MDA and will display graphics like circles and ellipses when the HMGA is in graphics mode.

E.2.2.1.3. Color Graphics Adapter (CGA) and Monitor

The Color Graphics Adapter adds a color graphics capability. Its resolution in text mode is far less than the MDA, as its character cells are 8 x 8 as compared with the MDA's 9 x 14 character cell. The CGA has a graphics resolution of 320 x 200 with four colors or 640 x 200 with two colors.

CGA has access only to the lower ASCII set in ROM when in graphics mode. The CGA can use only its own hardware code page (typically 437). Fortunately, it is obsolete. If you want to support it in enabled software, ideally you should create your own fonts and render them in graphics mode.

The Color Graphics Adapter works with a TTL color graphics monitor. This monitor can display a maximum of 16 different colors, although the CGA in graphics mode can transmit only 4 colors, chosen from a palette of 16, to it at a time.

E.2.2.1.4. High-Resolution Color Graphics Adapter (CGA) and Monitor

Certain models of PCs sold by Olivetti and AT&T use a variation of the CGA—the high-resolution CGA—which has a maximum graphics resolution of 640 × 400.

The monitor is similar to the CGA monitor but supports 400 horizontal scan lines maximum instead of 200.

E.2.2.1.5. Enhanced Graphics Adapter (EGA) and Monitor

The EGA has both more and higher resolution modes than the CGA. It can use the routine DISPLAY.SYS to download font tables through code page switching. The EGA has a monochrome compatible text mode and graphics modes of 640 × 350 with a choice of 16 colors out of 64. It also supports the various CGA modes.

The EGA monitor is a color TTL device and can display a maximum of 64 colors. The character set may be changed by code page switching using DISPLAY.SYS.

E.2.2.2. Analog Adapters and Monitors

In analog adapters, intensity and color (if available) data are communicated to the monitor via an analog signal whose strength is derived from the digital data. The household rotary light dimmer, for example, is a simple analog device in which the light intensity depends on how much the knob is turned.

In an analog video adapter the independent variables are the three primary colors red, green, and blue, each transmitted via a separate conductor. Each color is infinitely variable in theory, but there are practical considerations and cost that limit the number of colors.

There is currently one mainstream analog video display adapter available for the IBM PC and compatible computers, the Video Graphics Array (VGA).

E.2.2.2.1. Video Graphics Array (VGA) and Monitor

The Video Graphics Array, as it is called when part of an IBM PS/2 motherboard, or Video Graphics Adapter as an adapter card, can transmit a maximum of 256 (2^8) colors simultaneously from a palette of 262,144 (2^{18}) colors.

The VGA is backwardly compatible in its modes with the MDA, CGA, and EGA cards. It has a maximum resolution of 640 × 480 with 256 colors. The character set may changed by code page switching using DISPLAY.SYS.

There is an extension to the VGA standard called Super VGA. This mode has a resolution of 800 × 600. Some manufacturers provide a 1024 × 768 resolution mode.

The VGA uses an analog monitor capable of displaying an infinite number of colors, though in reality it is limited by the display adapter. VGA monitors also are available in monochrome, in which case they remap the colors as 64 shades of gray. The VGA can detect whether it is connected to a color or monochrome VGA monitor.

E.2.3. System Unit

The system unit contains the power supply, the motherboard, and different option boards. The motherboard contains the central processing unit, the memory, the bus, and drivers for storage and output devices.

The control and arithmetic and logical processing unit form what is known as the central processing unit or processor. Sometimes, there is a secondary unit called a coprocessor.

E.2.3.1. The Central Processing Unit (CPU) and Coprocessor

The CPU controls the flow of information in the computer, interprets encoded instructions, and performs arithmetic and logic instructions. The CPU fetches and then executes an instruction. The major classes of instructions are memory access, and arithmetic and logical.

E.2.3.1.1. Memory Access Instructions

A memory access instruction either retrieves from or transmits information to internal fast memory (register), external memory (RAM), or a *port* (connected to a device such as a hard disk drive or keyboard). The CPU will also respond to external events called *interrupt requests*. If its interrupt request lines are used to service requests from external devices (e.g., keyboard input) that cannot wait for it to finish its current task, the processor saves its current state, serves the interrupt request, restores its state, and then continues with the task that was interrupted.

E.2.3.1.2. Arithmetic and Logical Instructions

An arithmetic and logical instruction performs simple integer arithmetic or logical operations on data.

The data and instructions are accessed by the CPU from the memory subsystem, providing instantly accessible storage for data and instructions. Similarly, intermediate results can be passed to the memory subsystem. The memory storage subsystem consists of RAM and ROM memory. Computers also have floppy and hard disk drives for storage that provide relatively slow permanent storage for large amounts of information, but these are actually input/output devices and not part of the memory subsystem.

Coprocessors perform some functions that the CPU doesn't handle quickly. In the PC, the CPU normally can perform only integer arithmetic (the exception is the INTEL 80486). There is usually a socket on the motherboard that can be filled with a numeric coprocessor chip. This chip is dedicated to performing floating-point mathematical operations. Programs such as spreadsheets and engineering design programs that use floating-point mathematics can perform such operations by emulating them in software. But unless the program is designed to detect the numeric coprocessor, the ability of this chip to speed up these operations will not be used.[2] In nearly all cases where a coprocessor is used in a system, it reduces the load on the CPU and speeds up the general functioning of the system.

The speed of the system is affected by the clock speed. The clock speed is the rate at which the internal mechanism of the CPU works, and it is affected by the internal word size of the CPU and the external word size of the system bus. The speed is also affected by how fast the RAM memory is. RAM is volatile and must be actively refreshed. The faster this refresh cycle is, the quicker a particular location in RAM can be accessed. Lastly, CPU speed depends on word size. Generally, the larger the word size the more information can be processed at one time and the faster its throughput.

E.2.3.2. Memory

CPU chips have different word sizes. The IBM/PC and XT and their clones are based on the INTEL 8088. The IBM AT uses the 80286. Some IBM/AT clones use the 80836 and the 80486.

The INTEL 8088 has an internal word size of 16 bits, but it has an 8-bit data bus, which means that when it needs to communicate with the outside world it has to break the data into 8-bit pieces to move it through the narrow 8-bit data bus. The PC/AT, which uses the 80286, has a 16-bit data bus, hence it is not slowed down by having to convert between its internal and external word size. The bus is the multiwire circuitry that carries data, controlling signals, and electrical power. The 80386 and 80486 have 32-bit buses, but in systems designed with them that are also to be IBM PC/AT compatible, the bus slots used for interfacing adapters are 16 bits. Some systems do provide a proprietary 32-bit slot for use with proprietary high-speed memory access cards.

Because PC/MS-DOS was designed as the operating system for the original IBM PC that used the INTEL 8088, the memory usage characteristics are dominated by

---

[2]Other systems such as the Amiga have special coprocessor chips to enhance the speed at which graphics objects are manipulated.

this underlying fact. The INTEL 8088 can address a maximum of 1 megabyte (1,048,576 bytes) of memory at one time. But because of design considerations only 640K of the 1 MB of address space is available for software, including the operating system. The rest of the address space is used by system software (ROM BIOS), memory used for the video display, and memory used for other peripherals.

When 80286, 80386, and 80486 machines are started, they emulate the 8086, but they can be switched to modes with enhanced instruction sets and the ability to address much more memory. These features are not used directly by DOS, but may be found in extensions to it and in software running under some less common operating systems that run on IBM/ATs and their clones.

The memory found in a PC is of two types, RAM and ROM.

E.2.3.2.1. RAM

Random Access Memory (RAM) can be both read from and written to. RAM is volatile and provides short-term storage while the computer is turned on. RAM is the memory used to store the program's data and instructions. The processor will also use RAM to store intermediate results to be used later in the execution of the program, at which time the processor will retrieve this information from RAM. Video adapters also use RAM to store their memory maps.

As mentioned, DOS can directly access only 640K bytes of memory even when running on a system with a processor that is capable of addressing more memory. To overcome this limitation, two methods have been introduced, *expanded memory* and *extended memory*.

Expanded memory uses memory that is not part of the PC's addressable 1 MB. It instead uses an unused 64K (65,536) segment of memory near the top of the PC's addressable memory. This section of memory contains the addresses of memory outside the PC's normal address space and is accessed through the use of a special driver. A program that is designed to work with expanded memory can use this additional memory to store data. The latest standard for expanded memory is LIM 4.0.

Extended memory can be used only on machines equipped with 80286 or higher chips, and it enables these machines to use the memory above 1 MB. The most common use is for an electronic or virtual RAM disk. There is a specification for accessing extended memory called XMS (eXtended Memory Specification), and this is used by HIMEM.SYS and other extended memory managers. HIMEM.SYS is required when running Microsoft Windows 3.x in standard or enhanced mode; Windows can directly access up to 16 MB of extended memory.

E.2.3.2.2. ROM

Read Only Memory (ROM) is memory that can only be read. The only time it is written to is during the manufacturing process, when it is loaded with its data and/or program. ROM can be found in several places in a computer system. These places include the character generator ROM on certain types of video adapters, printers, and the ROM BIOS.

The ROM BIOS is a permanent read-only memory, and it contains the basic input/output system that controls the fundamental interactions of the computer and its subsystems. It is known generically as *firmware* (see Section D.6.1). The operating system can then access these primitive interactions to provide a higher level of services to the application or user. The ROM BIOS acts as a layer between the operating system and the hardware. This also means a manufacturer can hide the physical details of the hardware from the operating system and the application software.

The ROM BIOS has a published series of entry points for services that stay constant. You can also make extensions of the ROM BIOS for devices that are developed at a later date. For example, VGA adapters have their own ROM BIOS extensions that seamlessly integrate with the ROM BIOS the computer was manufactured with.

When a CPU in the 8088 family is started or reset, it automatically starts program execution at address FFFF:0000 first.[3] This is a function of the design of the processor. The ROM BIOS memory location at FFFF:0000 is a jump instruction to the beginning of the hardware test routines and the ROM startup code.

E.2.3.3. Storage (Input and Output)

Because RAM is volatile and may need to be used by another program, disk drives are used to store data and information. Information stored on disk, on magnetic surfaces, remains intact until you deliberately alter it.

The file system on PC disks is hierarchical. There is a root directory that can contain files and subdirectories. In turn the subdirectories can contain more files and subdirectories and so on until the disk is filled. The maximum amount of space on a disk that is available to a user may be limited by some overhead associated with each directory and each file created. The reason this limitation occurs is twofold.

One reason is because each disk is divided into clusters. The size of a cluster varies depending on the capacity of the drive. For example, if you are using a hard drive that is formatted so that the cluster size is 4,096 bytes and you save a file that is 20,500 bytes long, this file will need six clusters or 24,576 bytes of storage, resulting in a waste of 4,076 bytes. As you can see, this can result in a significant amount of wasted storage. Disks with different capacities have different cluster sizes.

The other reason is that DOS limits the maximum number of files and directory entries in the root directory. The maximum number of root directory entries for a hard disk is 512; 1.2 MB and 1.44 MB disks can hold 224 entries, and 360K and 720K disks can have 112 entries.

Subdirectories are not limited in the number of files they can contain, as long as there is space on the disk. The subdirectory maintains a table of entries as a separate file rather than as a fixed part of the disk. If you observe a good hierarchical directory structure you should not run into this limitation.

The most important aspect for a user is what constitutes a legal filename. The following characters can appear in a legal filename: the letters *A* through *Z;* the

---

[3]This number is an address stated in hexadecimal arithmetic that refers to the relative location or position in RAM.

numerals *0* through *9;* the characters *' ~ ` ! @ # $ % ^ & ( ) _ - {* and *}* and high-bit characters (with ASCII values over 127).

This last item means that non-American characters can be supported in filenames. The filename can consist of a maximum of 11 characters including a filename extension of a maximum of 3 characters, for example, ENGLISH.DOC (the period is not part of the name; it merely indicates to DOS that an extension follows the name). Directories follow similar naming conventions. Because Microsoft Windows uses DOS's underlying file system the same naming rules apply.

In addition, the following reserved words should not be used as file or directory names; CLOCK$, CON, AUX, PRN, NUL, COM1, COM2, COM3, COM4, LPT1, LPT2, and LPT3.

There are two types of disk drive, hard disks and floppy disks.

Information on disks is stored on concentric tracks. Each track can hold a certain amount of information. The more tracks a disk has, the more information the disk can hold.

E.2.3.3.1. Hard Disks

A hard disk is sometimes called a fixed disk because it remains in the system. Hard disks store information on one or more rigid disks stacked in a sealed case.

The maximum amount of information that can be accessed on a fixed disk is 32 MB for versions 2.0 through 3.3 of DOS. This limitation is due to the way DOS created the table that served as the file "index" for the disk. For disks larger than 32 MB, DOS 3.3 and later versions contained procedures for creating logical drives on the hard disk.

For DOS 4.0 and 5.0, the maximum logical drive size was increased to 256 MB.

E.2.3.3.2. Floppy Disks

The magnetic surface of a floppy disk is on a thin flexible disk inside a protective cover. Like the hard disk, the floppy disk stores information on concentric tracks, but not as densely, and because there is only one disk the total storage is less. Floppy disks can be removed from their drives and are the most common method in the PC world for transferring programs and data files from one machine to another.

Floppy disks come in two forms, 5 1/4 inch and 3 1/2 inch. Most floppy disks are double-sided, that is, both sides are used for storing information. (There is an older obsolete format for single-sided 5 1/4-inch disks. You may occasionally come across these if you are asked to work with files that were put into storage some years ago.)

Double-sided double-density 5 1/4-inch disks store 360K bytes (362,496 bytes) of information maximum. High-density 5 1/4-inch disks can store 1.2 MB (1,213,952 bytes). The high-density drive can also format a disk as a 360K disk.

IBM/PC and XTs and their clones normally have double-density drives and ATs have high-density drives. If a 360K disk is formatted on a high-density drive, you may have difficulty using it on a double-density drive because the high-density drive write head creates narrower tracks than the double-density drive. Hence it is normally better to format a 360K disk on a double-density drive thus allowing both double-density and high-density 5 1/4-inch drives to read it.

The 3 1/2-inch disk drive comes in 720K (730,112) and 1.44 MB (1,457,664) capacities. The 1.44 MB drive can format, read, and write both 720 and 1.44 disks. Because the disk casing of the 1.44 MB disk has two holes and the 720K disk has only one, the 1.44 MB drive can discern which type of disk has been inserted and treat it accordingly.

As with the 5 1/4-inch drives, the names *double density* and *high density* are applied to the 3 1/2-inch drives. The double density is the 720K and the high density is the 1.44 MB drive.

E.2.3.4. Control

The control subsystem coordinates the overall activity of the CPU with its environment. In the IBM PC and its clones the CPU's control subsystem is assisted by two external additions. One, the DMA (direct memory access) controller, assists with memory accesses by freeing up the CPU by performing memory accesses for it. The other, the interrupt controller, similarly assists the CPU by checking for interrupts and then passing them to the CPU. The use of such controllers decreases the direct workload for the CPU.

E.2.4. Printers

To obtain a permanent human readable hard copy of work produced, you usually use a printer. The most common types of printers are 9-pin and 24-pin dot-matrix printers, laser printers, ink-jet printers, PostScript printers, and plotters.

Printers can operate in either serial or parallel mode (see Section E.6).

E.2.4.1. Dot-Matrix Printers

The dot-matrix printer uses a print head consisting of a vertical row of print hammers. The print head moves horizontally back and forth across the page generating a vertical bar of dot patterns at each column position by striking a ribbon and thereby serially generating characters or part of a graphic image.

In text mode, a character is produced in response to a stream of codes sent to a printer. These codes indicate attributes such as underline, bold, italic, and superscript, as well as the actual character to be printed at a given position.

There are two major groups of printer control codes used. These are the IBM and EPSON control codes, and they each have subsets within them.

Some other dot-matrix printer manufacturers have their own printer control codes and they have to be taken into account when designing printer driver engines and the printer drivers for specific makes and models of printers. In text mode, dot-matrix printers have a limited number of font styles and sizes and language capabilities.

The language capability of the printer is changed by altering a switch setting or sometimes by sending a control code. You can overcome these limitations by driving the printer in graphics mode. The fancy output that is produced by desktop publishing packages is achieved in this manner.

Using the graphics mode frees the printer from relying on its native character set in ROM and permits the use of many different fonts supplied as software and representing diverse languages not found in the specific printer's native character sets. The graphic image is generated by taking the image of the page represented in memory and dividing it into bands that are fed to the printer so that the individual hammers of the printer are driven to produce the appropriate image.

Because different models of printers have different control codes to set them in graphics mode and different physical characteristics (e.g., the minimum distance the print head can move horizontally or vertically), the driver must include special algorithms to take account of the physical characteristics in order to maintain the correct representation of the page as to aspect ratio and dimensions.

Dot-matrix printers have two main feed mechanisms:

1. *Tractor* or *pin feed* uses special paper with perforations on the edge that are engaged by a feed mechanism. The page length of this paper even in international sizes is based on U.S. sizes because the bulk of the printers were originally designed by American manufacturers with no regard to non-American sensibilities.
2. *Cut sheet* uses paper in a similar manner to a typewriter. Occasionally you may come across a cut sheet printer with an auto cut sheet paper feeder.

E.2.4.2. Laser Printers

Laser printers may sound like daunting and magical devices, but they are simply another form of raster device with a more sophisticated imaging device than a hammer and ribbon.

The basis of laser printing is the effect that shining a bright light on a drum coated with a photoelectric material has. The spots that are exposed to the light become highly charged. A beam of light "paints" a charged image on the drum one row at a time and a motor advances the drum as each row is completed. This results in a highly charged electrostatic image of the page on the drum compared to the background potential. The drum passes over a container of toner and the charged areas on the drum attract the toner. The area of the drum that has passed over the toner is then brought in touch with a piece of paper that has passed over a corona wire imbuing it with an even larger electrostatic charge. The toner transfers itself to the paper because of the potential gradient, and heated rollers fuse the toner to the page. The drum then rotates past a discharge wire to remove any remaining charge, a scraper cleans the drum of any toner traces, and the drum is ready to process the next image.

Most laser printers have an unprintable area at the top and bottom of the page and occasionally at the right and left margins. You may need to take this into account when enabling a printer driver to handle metric size page formatting.

The native font sets are in the printer's own ROM, but some laser printers allow so-called soft fonts to be downloaded into them and some can use fonts from cartridges. To achieve more diversity in size and selection of fonts, the laser printer can be driven in graphics mode.

The most common control code set is Hewlett-Packard Printer Control Language (HPCL). This consists of a sophisticated escape control language.

Canon and some other manufacturers have their own languages, but many emulate one of the five versions of HPCL. PostScript (see Section E.2.4.4) is gaining popularity as a printer control language because it provides a common interface to many different printers.

E.2.4.3. Ink-Jet Printers

Ink-jet printers use a set of very fine nozzles to spray a pattern of ink droplets on a page. They can be considered analogs of the dot-matrix printer, but they produce higher quality output and are much quieter. The control languages usually are based on HPCL or EPSON escape sequences.

E.2.4.4. PostScript Printers

PostScript is a page description language used for page layout, graphics, and scalable font descriptions. A dedicated printer has a built-in interpreter to create the bit image that is being described by PostScript. Add-on cartridges are available for many non-PostScript laser printers. Many of the new color thermal transfer printers use PostScript. PostScript has its own character set. You should make sure the drivers correctly map the character code points to the PostScript code points.

E.2.5. Mouse

The mouse is a pointing device that is moved across a surface. In response to this movement a cursor is moved across the screen. Depending on the supporting software, the cursor may change shape based on the region of the screen it is in to indicate the context in which it is operating. The system can read the position of the cursor relative to its starting position, and when a button is clicked on an active screen area (e.g., in selecting from a menu), this activity is communicated to the software package. If the menu selection box changes size due to Localization, then it must be designed so that the hot area of the menu box changes appropriately. The hot area or hot box is an area on the screen where clicking the mouse causes a response.

E.3. FONTS

A font is a complete set of letters, numbers, symbols, and punctuation marks all in the same style and size (although scalable fonts do not include size). *Multilingual Computing Magazine and Buyer's Guide* contains advertisements for computer fonts in seemingly hundreds of exotic and esoteric languages.

E.3.1. Native Fonts

Native fonts are the font sets contained in the character ROM set of the printer or display adapter. Printers quite often have more than one native font set available. These fonts are stored in ROM as bit-map images. (PostScript printers' native fonts are scalable fonts.)

E.3.2. Scalable Fonts

Scalable fonts consist of a mathematical description of a font in terms of the relationship between plotted points. The size of the font can be adjusted on the fly (that is to say, on demand) to any size within a given maximum and minimum because the font includes these formulae.

The fonts also quite often treat *italics* and **bold** as attributes and create these on the fly as well. These fonts are displayed on the screen in graphics mode and may be printed.

Programs such as Adobe Type Manager, which runs under Microsoft Windows 3.x, provide these capabilities. Some scalable fonts come in cartridges and take advantage of built-in features of the specific printer control language (the HPIII printer uses HPCL5, for example), but unless an equivalent scalable screen font is available it may not be possible to display the characters on the screen.

E.3.3. Downloadable Fonts

Many printers permit programs to download fonts to them as bit maps to be used instead of their native fonts. Others permit both bit-map and scalable fonts to be downloaded to them.

E.4. MODES

Both printers and video adapters can normally operate in two modes, graphics mode and character mode. Only the Monochrome Display Adapter and obsolete daisy-wheel printers work solely in character mode. For both video and printer output devices, the software designer will have designed fonts around the concept of a character box when they are driven in graphics mode.

E.4.1. Graphics Mode

Graphics mode, otherwise known as all points addressable, works by addressing each point on the screen individually. Each point is called a *PEL* or *pixel,* both of which are abbreviations for "picture element."

The number of bits necessary to address each pixel depends on the video adapter and the graphics mode it is operating in. The adapter interprets the bit map of the image in memory and turns the appropriate pixel on or off. Pictures and scalable fonts are displayed in graphics mode. Most graphics-capable video adapters also provide for the display of their internal character sets.

E.4.2. Character Mode

In character mode the monitor displays text only. This text is generated by bit maps of characters contained in the character generator. EGA and VGA permit user-defined bit maps to be downloaded so as to enable additional character sets to be displayed. Under DOS this is usually achieved using code page switching and DISPLAY.SYS.

The characters are drawn in character cells, which are two-dimensional boxes where the representation of the character is drawn. Different video adapters and printers have different native character boxes. The maximum size of the character within each box is slightly smaller than the box so there will be a little space around each displayed character. There are two exceptions: first, in the CGA character cell, a lowercase letter with a descender (*g, j, p, q, y*) will touch the top of an uppercase letter directly below it. And second, in all modes the line drawing characters in the IBM extended character set will butt up against related symbols in adjoining boxes.

The main character cell sizes (in pixels) are:

CGA	8H × 8V
MONO	9H × 14V
EGA	8H × 14V
VGA	8H × 16V
VGA	9H × 16V

If the software is going to be using the built-in text mode character ability of an adapter, certain adapters may be more suitable than others because of their inherently better image quality.

Printing uses a similar principle to character boxes when using native fonts, and the cell sizes depend on the particular make and model of printer.

E.5. DRIVERS

A driver is a piece of software that allows the program (either the operating system or an application) to communicate with a device in a standard way. In the computer world a device may be tangible, such as a monitor or printer, or an abstraction such as a virtual disk drive that is created in memory to emulate an extremely fast disk drive.

Since many device drivers are available in Internationalized and Localized formats, the Localized versions may require differing amounts of memory than the U.S. version.

E.5.1. Printer Drivers

Printers are produced in many different makes and models. Normally a printer from one manufacturer will have control codes in common with earlier models, but as more features are added the control set is increased.

The driver replaces any control codes used by the program for its own internal use with the specific codes used by a printer. It also uses special algorithms to take account of the physical characteristics of the printer to maintain the correct representation of the page as to aspect ratio and dimensions.

In graphics modes the driver should also attempt to represent tonal representations as faithfully as possible.

In Internationalization and Localization you should be sure that any messages produced by or related to the printer drivers are translated and that the printer is using native fonts that include the extended characters for the languages in question. It may be necessary to adjust page length and width algorithms to provide their metric equivalents.

E.5.2. Mouse Drivers

The application program uses a driver to communicate with the mouse. The mouse driver is provided by the mouse manufacturer and sometimes contains messages. Normally, in the non-American marketplace, a Localized version that displays appropriate messages on loading is available. The message language chosen for display depends on the country code and/or code page.

The mouse driver initializes the mouse with a known screen coordinate and keeps track of where the mouse pointer is. It also notifies the system when a mouse button has been depressed or released. Additional functions are available but they are mainly of concern to programmers.

E.5.3. Miscellaneous Drivers

Drivers can be created for devices that did not exist when DOS was created, such as CD ROMs. These drivers enable the device to use simple DOS commands to interact with the user and also mean that an application programmer need not know the internal details of the device.

E.6. PORTS

Serial ports transmit information sequentially and usually include some form of error detection technique. Some printers are serial devices. When serial devices are used in the DOS system, the *mode* command must be used to set the correct parameters for the serial port to match the characteristics of the serial device to which it is attached. These parameters include speed of transmission and error correction.

Parallel ports send information 8 bits at a time. They are normally used when communicating with a printer. More data can be transmitted in a given time using parallel ports but at the cost of using more wires than in a serial cable.

E.7. OTHER PERIPHERALS

Other peripheral devices include tape drives, CD readers, and scanners.

E.7.1. Tapes

For archival purposes on PCs and other small computers, tape cartridges are used to back up the data on hard disks. This is a quick and efficient method to save a copy of the contents of the disk in case of hard disk failure or some disaster such as fire. The tapes ideally should be kept in a site secured against fire or water damage and should not be exposed to strong magnetic fields such as those generated by power transformers. That way, if serious problems occur with the data currently in use, then it is possible to restore previous versions of the data from these backup files.

Mainframes and most large computers have traditionally used large reels of tape for data storage and as an intermediate, less expensive, form of memory. As they have been in use for many years, there has been considerable evolution in their design. There are 8-track versions, 9-track versions and considerable variation in density, known as bits per inch, or BPI. The last time that any of us worked on a mainframe, BPIs had reached the levels of 800 and 1,600. They, too, are being replaced with tape cartridges.

UNIX systems use a stream cartridge tape for backup and for transferring data from one machine to another one that is connected to it. The UNIX command for reading and writing it in various formats is *tar,* which stands for "tape archive."

E.7.2. CD ROMs

CD ROMs are optical disks similar to those used in compact disk music players and laser video players. They can store a large quantity of information, much greater than conventional tapes and disks, and this data can be used directly off the CD or loaded onto a hard disk as an intermediate step. The CD ROM medium is an efficient method of distributing computerized reference materials because it can store so much information.

As the name implies, normally you can only read from CD ROMs. There is a form of CD that a user can write to once and read many times (WORM drives). This can be useful if you need to archive a large quantity of material, and then need to be able to access it and play it back in a nonsequential or random fashion.

E.7.3. Scanners

Scanners are used to input written, typed, or graphical material into a computerized system for storage or manipulation. Certain software in conjunction with a scanned image can translate text in a limited range of fonts into ASCII with reasonable accuracy.

E.8. NON-AMERICAN HARDWARE

When distributing your product outside the United States, you may need to test and support the operation of your software on non-American hardware. In general, many European computers are provided only with 3 1/2-inch floppy drives. Some computers have more than 640K (65,5360) bytes of base memory and so on those machines you should make sure your software can run in that memory. The VGA is not as popular in many countries as it is here in the United States. Be prepared to support EGA, CGA, and Hercules standards.

Since the hardware situation changes rapidly, you should ask your local partner for the latest information. It can be expensive and complicated to obtain foreign hardware for use here, particularly Japanese.

E.8.1. Amstrad

Amstrad is a U.K. computer manufacturer. It makes an IBM clone.

KEYB.COM in MS-DOS 5.0 does not work correctly with 1.4 revision or earlier ROMs. This has been corrected by ROM upgrades.

E.8.2. Olivetti

Olivetti is an Italian computer manufacturer. It makes an IBM clone, among other machines. Olivetti in some models uses the CGA 400 video adapter card.

E.8.3. Japanese Computers

See Section 6.2 for information on Japanese computers. Japanese computers are notorious in terms of cost; however, with the introduction of DOS/V and Windows 3.1J, market prices are expected to decrease.

E.9. NON-AMERICAN VERSIONS OF HARDWARE AVAILABLE IN THE UNITED STATES

E.9.1. Printers

Some of the early dot-matrix printers (e.g., the EPSON MX-80) do not have the built-in ability to change national character sets. Such printers were Localized for each market and you must test whether the native character set works correctly for these printers. If you intend to support such a printer in a Localized version of software, you must either acquire a Localized version of the printer for testing or ask your partner in the target locale to test it for you. If your product drives the printer in a pure graphics mode this should be less of a worry.

Production of these Localized but non-Internationalized printers ceased some years ago. Their use is therefore decreasing, but the decision on whether to provide for their support depends on their current popularity in the target locale's marketplace.

E.9.1. Monochrome Display Adapters

Monochrome Display Adapters may have different character generator ROM sets depending on country of distribution. For example, the ASCII characters 155 and 157 appear as slashed *O*'s (ø) if you have the Norwegian/Danish video ROM.

Alphabetic List of Localizers with Experience in Western European Languages

The Localizers themselves provided us this information at our request; we have not verified it independently, although we have worked with many of them.

ALPNET is headquartered in Salt Lake City, Utah, with major production offices in London, Stuttgart, Paris, Madrid, Barcelona, Montreal, Hong Kong, Singapore, and 12 other locations throughout Europe, Asia, and North America. ALPNET was formed in 1988 by the merger of Automated Language Processing Systems and five established translation companies throughout the world. This merger brought together high-tech translation technology with over 60 years of history and experience in the translation industry. ALPNET employs over 225 full-time people and has a translation capability of over 2,000 tested and qualified linguists. ALPNET is a publicly owned company whose shares are traded on the NASDAQ market under the trading symbol AILP, with 1991 revenues of $US 23 million. ALPNET provides translation services into all currently written languages, in addition to providing state of the art multilanguage desk top publishing, as well as interpretation and other related services. ALPNET can be contacted in London (tel 011-44-81-688-3852 or fax 011-44-81-688-8888) or in the United States at (tel) (801)-265-3300 or (fax) (801)-265-3310.

ALPNET's partial client listing includes AEG, Apple, AT&T, Bull MTS, Compaq, Cullinet, Digital Equipment, Epson, Fujitsu, Grundig, Hayes, Hewlett-Packard, Honeywell Bull, IBM, ICL, Informix, MicroPro, Microsoft, Migent, NCR, Nixdorf, Novell, Pansophic, Philips, Rank Xerox, Siemens, Texas Instruments, Unisys, WANG, and WordPerfect in the computer hardware and software industries.

AT&T, one of the world's largest and most global corporations, offers full-service Localization, translation, and multiplatform desktop publishing services through its Language Line business unit in Monterey, California. It has a close relationship with the prestigious Translation Department of the Monterey Institute of International Studies. In addition, it uses AT&T's worldwide telecommunications network to unite hundreds of tested translators, Localizers, and other linguists around the globe. Situated near Silicon Valley, Language Line has easy access to the engineering expertise needed to Localize sophisticated programs, including not only consumer software but also vertical market applications and software embedded in medical, measuring, industrial, and other devices. Projects range from simple text replacement to system-level programming and re-engineering, as well as double-byte enabling for Asian languages. In addition, the California location has helped it build a large customer base from the globally minded companies that populate the San Diego–Santa Clara–Redmond high-technology corridor. Other customers can be found worldwide. AT&T representatives were not at liberty to disclose their income from software Localization.

Part of Language Line's mission is to couple linguistic expertise with real-world tools. As a result of their multiyear technology partnership with Bell Labs, they have developed TermWorks(sm), a state-of-the-art Localization, translation-reuse, and terminology management tool. You may receive information about AT&T's Localization services by contacting sales manager Bob Steiner at 800-648-0874 or fax 800-648-0875. Other Language Line services include over-the-phone interpretation in over 140 languages, 24 hours a day. For information about over-the-phone interpretation, call 800-752-6096.

Berlitz Translation Services, part of Berlitz International, has 30 translation centers in 18 countries: 7 in North America, 18 in Europe, 3 in Latin America, and 2 in Asia. It employs over 200 project and language managers, resident software engineers, and senior translators, and it maintains a network of more than 2,000 contract native-fluent translation experts. Berlitz International's revenues, for all divisions including schools and books, were $260 million in 1991 and its stock is traded on the New York Stock Exchange. On November 27, 1992, Berlitz announced a renegotiated merger agreement with Japan's Fukutake Publishing Company that gives Fukutake a 67 percent stake in the company. Berlitz Translation Services' revenue was about $32 million. Berlitz International was founded in 1878 and Berlitz Translation Services was created in 1984. It supports PCs, OS/2, Windows, Macintosh, and UNIX. You may contact the company by calling Joseph McLaughlin, National Sales Director (tel 1-212-777-7878 or fax 1-212-505-9975).

BOTS Gmbh is headquartered in Munich with subsidiaries in Paris, Barcelona, the United Kingdom, Italy, and Switzerland and partner offices in Scandinavia, Portugal, Benelux, and Eastern Europe. It employs a large network of full-time and freelance specialist translators, and its revenues were about $US 6 million in 1991. It was founded in 1945 and specializes in multilingual software Localization, especially products requiring high levels of software engineering expertise. You may contact BOTS Gmbh by calling Peter C. Jacques, President, or Jürgen Leschner, Technical Manager (tel 011-49-89-24-71-34-0 or fax 011-49-89-24-71-34-14).

The INK Network, now known as R. R. Donnelly Language Solutions, is headquartered in Amsterdam with offices in Barcelona, Brussels, Copenhagen, Luxembourg, Madrid, Oslo, Paris, Stuttgart, and Uppsala (Sweden). It employs a bit over 200 people and had revenues of about $US 18 million in 1991. The network is 12 years old and specializes in DOS, Macintosh, Windows, DEC, IBM AS/400, and UNIX Localizations. Recently, INK merged with the Documentation Services Group of R. R. Donnelly & Sons Company of Chicago. You may contact INK by calling Jaap van der Meer at the Amsterdam office (tel 011-31-20-5114610 or fax 011-31-20-5114611). They have opened a California office (tel (408)-748-1881 or fax (408)-748-1151).

INK's customer list includes Borland/Ashton-Tate, Bull, Digital Equipment, Fujitsu, IBM, ICL, Lotus, Microsoft, Oracle, Philips, Ricoh, Siemens, and Software Publishing Corp (SPC), to name the largest.

Mendez Translations is headquartered in Brussels with offices in Neuilly-sur-Seine in France, Madrid, Düsseldorf, Milan, and Maastricht (Holland). The company has relationships with translating agencies in Sweden and Israel. It employs 300 people and had revenues of about $US 12 million in 1991. The company is 21 years old and specializes in software Localization. You may contact Mendez Transactions by calling José Mendez, Marketing Director, in Brussels (tel 011-32-2-647-27-00 or fax 011-32-2-647-55-50).

Mendez's customer list includes Aldus Europe, Agfa Gevaert, Atlas Copco, BASF, Canon, Commission of the European Community, Compaq Computer, Du Pont de Nemours, Esso, Exxon Chemical International, General Electric CGR, Honeywell, Lanier, Levi-Strauss Europe, L'Oréal, Lufthansa, 3M Corporation, Management Center Europe, McCann Erickson, McDonald, Microsoft Corporation, Mobil Oil, Morton Thiokol, Proctor & Gamble, Rover, Rubson, Sharp, Shell, Siemens, Smith Kline Biologicals, Solvay & Cie, S.W.I.F.T., Symbol Technologies, Teradyne, Vista Chemical, and Volvo.

Names and Addresses of Standards Organizations

We compiled this information from IBM's *National Language Information and Design Guide—Volume 1. Designing Enabled Products Rules and Information Guide* and Juliussen and Juliussen's *The 1992 Computer Industry Almanac,* and from correspondence and via phone calls to some consulates.

AFNOR Association Française de Normalisation
    Tour Europe
    Cedex 7
    92080 Paris La Défense
    France

ANSI—American National Standards Institute
    1430 Broadway
    New York, NY 10018

ASMO—Arab Standards and Metrology Organization
    PO Box 926161
    Amman
    Jordan

BSI—British Standards Institute
    2 Park Street
    London W1 A2BS
    England
    011-44-71-629-9000 (phone)

CAS—China Association for Standards
    P.O. Box 820
    Beijing
    China

CCITT—Consultative Committee for International Telephone and Telegraph
2, rue de Varembe
CH-1211 Geneva 20
Switzerland

CSA—Canadian Standards Association
178 Rexdale Blvd.
Rexdale, Ontario M9W 1R3
Canada

DIN—Deutsches Institut für Normung
Burggrafenstrasse 4-10
Postfach 1107
D-1000 Berlin 30
Germany

ECMA—European Computer Manufacturers Association
114 Rue du Rhône
CH-1204 Geneva
Switzerland

FIPS—Federal Information Processing Standards
U.S. National Bureau of Standards
Institute for Computer Sciences and Technology
Gaithersburg, MD 20899

IEC—International Electrotechnical Commission
3, rue de Verambe
CH-1211, Geneva 20
Switzerland

ISO—International Organization for Standardization
1, rue de Verambe
Casa Postale 56
CH-1211 Geneva 20
Switzerland

JSA—Japanese Standards Association
1-24, Akasaka 4
Minato-ku, Tokyo 107
Japan

NNI—Nederlands Normalisatie-Instutuut
Kalfjeslaan, P.O. Box 5059
2600 GB Delft
Holland

SFS—Soumen Standardisomisliitto (Finland)
P.O. Box 205, SF-00121
Helsinki
Finland

SCC—Standards Council of Canada
International Standardizations Branch
2000 Argentina Road, Suite 2-401
Missassauga, Ontario, L5N 1V8
Canada

IEEE—Institute of Electrical and Electronics Engineers
345 East 47th Street
New York, NY 10017-2394

LISA—Localization Industry Standards Association
9B Chemin Castan
CH-1224 Chêne-Bougeries
Switzerland
011-41-22-349-2222 (phone)
011-41-22-349-8977 (fax)

Unicode Incorporated
c/o Metaphor Computer Systems
1965 Charleston Avenue
Mountain View, CA 94043

Department of the Secretary of State of Canada
Terminology & Linguistics Services Directorate
Promotion and Client Services Division
Ottawa, Ontario K1A 0M5
Canada
819-997-9727 (phone)
819-994-3670 (fax)

ASQC—American Society for Quality Control
611 East Wisconsin Avenue
P.O. Box 3005
Milwaukee, Wisconsin 53201-3005
414-272-8575 (phone)
800-248-1946 (fax)

OADG—Open Architecture Developers Group
Kohwa-Nittoh Bldg. 8F
3-17-9 Tsukiji, Chuuou-ku
Tokyo, Japan 105
011-81-3-3541-4874 (phone)
011-81-3-3545-2463 (fax)

WordPerfect 5.1 Character Sets

There are 13 WordPerfect 5.1 character sets available to users (within the sets, individual characters are numbered starting with count 000). The sets are in the form of tables of various sizes; the addresses increase by row and are in decimal format.

The following character sets are shown in Figures H-1, H-2, H-3, and H-4.:

Set	Name and Number of Characters (starting at 000)
0	ASCII (to 126)[1]
1	Multinational 1 (to 233)
2	Multinational 2 (to 27)
3	Box Drawing (to 87)
4	Typographic Symbols (to 84)
5	Iconic Symbols (to 34)
6	Mathematic/Scientific (to 234)
7	Mathematic/Scientific Extension (to 228)
8	Greek (to 226)
9	Hebrew (to 43)
10	Cyrillic (to 147)
11	Hiragana and Katakana (to 184)
12	user-defined—made up of user-chosen characters from the others.

---

[1]While the reference material in the Word Perfect Developers' Guide clearly shows 126, this might be 127. The character set is called ASCII, a fact that leads one to believe it should have 128 characters, labeled 000 through 127.

```
            0 1 2 3 4 5 6 7 8 9 0 1 2 3 4 5 6 7 8 9 0 1 2 3 4 5 6 7 8 9
                                  1                   2
  0
 30            ! " # $ % & ' ( ) * + , - . / 0 1 2 3 4 5 6 7 8 9 : ;
 60        < = > ? @ A B C D E F G H I J K L M N O P Q R S T U V W X Y
 90        Z [ \ ] ^ _ ` a b c d e f g h i j k l m n o p q r s t u v w
120        x y z { | } ~
```

Table 0 (top): character set grid.

Table 1 (middle): diacritical and accented character set grid.

Table 2 (bottom): diacritical mark character set grid.

Figure H–1. WordPerfect 5.1 Character Sets: Tables 0 (top), 1 (middle), and 2 (bottom)

Figure H–2. WordPerfect 5.1 Character Sets: Tables 3 (top), 4 (second row), 5 (third row), and 6 (bottom)

Figure H–3. WordPerfect Character Sets: Tables 7 (top), 8 (middle), and 9 (bottom)

Figure H–4. WordPerfect 5.1 Character Sets: Tables 10 (top), 11 (middle), and 12 (bottom). Table 12 is an example of a user-defined set obtained using a postscript printer driver.

DOS Code Pages

DOS character sets are called code pages and are presented in the form of a 16 by 16 matrix or table. The columns are in increasing order from left to right. Each character is assigned a location within the table. This location or address is its numerical equivalent. Addresses start at 000 in the upper left cell and increase along each vertical column in groups of 16 to the largest address of 255 in the lower right cell. In the tables shown, addresses are in both decimal and hexadecimal format; for example, the first two columns, on the left, cover the range 000 to 31 or 00H to 1FH.

The following code pages are shown in Figures I–1, I–2, and I–3.

Figure I–1: 437, 850

Figure I–2: 852, 860

Figure I–3: 863, 865

1		0	16	32	48	64	80	96	112	128	144	160	176	192	208	224	240
	2A→ ↓B	0-	1-	2-	3-	4-	5-	6-	7-	8-	9-	A-	B-	C-	D-	E-	F-
0	-0		►		0	@	P	`	p	Ç	É	á	▓	└	╨	α	≡
1	-1	☺	◄	!	1	A	Q	a	q	ü	æ	í	▒	┴	╤	β	±
2	-2	●	↕	"	2	B	R	b	r	é	Æ	ó	▓	┬	╥	Γ	≥
3	-3	♥	‼	#	3	C	S	c	s	â	ô	ú	│	├	╙	π	≤
4	-4	♦	¶	$	4	D	T	d	t	ä	ö	ñ	┤	─	╘	Σ	⌠
5	-5	♣	§	%	5	E	U	e	u	à	ò	Ñ	╡	┼	╒	σ	⌡
6	-6	♠	▬	&	6	F	V	f	v	å	û	ª	╢	╞	╓	µ	÷
7	-7	•	↨	'	7	G	W	g	w	ç	ù	º	╖	╟	╫	τ	≈
8	-8	◘	↑	(	8	H	X	h	x	ê	ÿ	¿	╕	╚	╪	Φ	°
9	-9	○	↓	)	9	I	Y	i	y	ë	Ö	⌐	╣	╔	┘	Θ	∙
10	-A	◙	→	*	:	J	Z	j	z	è	Ü	¬	║	╩	┌	Ω	·
11	-B	♂	←	+	;	K	[	k	{	ï	¢	½	╗	╦	█	δ	√
12	-C	♀	∟	,	<	L	\	l			î	£	¼	╝	╠	▄	∞	ⁿ
13	-D	♪	↔	-	=	M	]	m	}	ì	¥	¡	╜	═	▐	φ	²
14	-E	♫	▲	.	>	N	^	n	~	Ä	₧	«	╛	╬	▌	ε	■
15	-F	☼	▼	/	?	O	_	o	⌂	Å	ƒ	»	┐	╧	▀	∩	

1		0	16	32	48	64	80	96	112	128	144	160	176	192	208	224	240
	2A→ ↓B	0-	1-	2-	3-	4-	5-	6-	7-	8-	9-	A-	B-	C-	D-	E-	F-
0	-0		►		0	@	P	`	p	Ç	É	á	▓	└	ð	Ó	-
1	-1	☺	◄	!	1	A	Q	a	q	ü	æ	í	▒	┴	Ð	β	±
2	-2	●	↕	"	2	B	R	b	r	é	Æ	ó	▓	┬	Ê	Ô	=
3	-3	♥	‼	#	3	C	S	c	s	â	ô	ú	│	├	Ë	Ò	¾
4	-4	♦	¶	$	4	D	T	d	t	ä	ö	ñ	┤	─	È	õ	¶
5	-5	♣	§	%	5	E	U	e	u	à	ò	Ñ	Á	┼	ı	Õ	§
6	-6	♠	▬	&	6	F	V	f	v	å	û	ª	Â	ã	Í	µ	÷
7	-7	•	↨	'	7	G	W	g	w	ç	ù	º	À	Ã	Î	þ	¸
8	-8	◘	↑	(	8	H	X	h	x	ê	ÿ	¿	©	╚	Ï	Þ	°
9	-9	○	↓	)	9	I	Y	i	y	ë	Ö	®	╣	╔	┘	Ú	¨
10	-A	◙	→	*	:	J	Z	j	z	è	Ü	¬	║	╩	┌	Û	·
11	-B	♂	←	+	;	K	[	k	{	ï	ø	½	╗	╦	█	Ù	¹
12	-C	♀	∟	,	<	L	\	l			î	£	¼	╝	╠	▄	ý	³
13	-D	♪	↔	-	=	M	]	m	}	ì	Ø	¡	¢	═	¦	Ý	²
14	-E	♫	▲	.	>	N	^	n	~	Ä	×	«	¥	╬	Ì	¯	■
15	-F	☼	▼	/	?	O	_	o	⌂	Å	ƒ	»	¬	¤	▀	´	

Figure I–I. DOS Code Pages: 437—U.S. English (above) and 850—Multilingual (Latin I) (below)

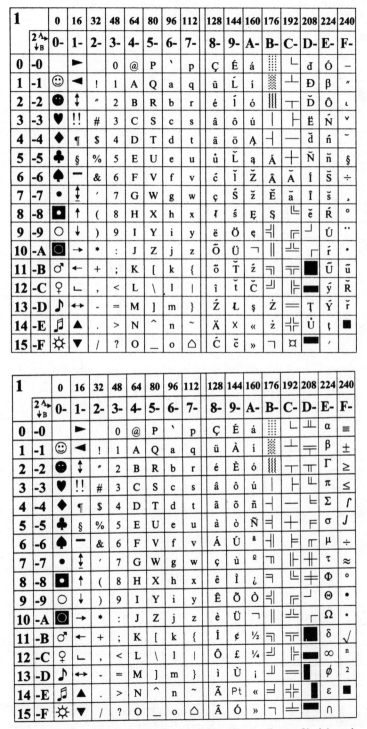

Figure I–2. DOS Code Pages: 852—Slavic (Latin 2) (above) and 860—Portugal (below)

1 / 2A↓B	0 / 0-	16 / 1-	32 / 2-	48 / 3-	64 / 4-	80 / 5-	96 / 6-	112 / 7-	128 / 8-	144 / 9-	160 / A-	176 / B-	192 / C-	208 / D-	224 / E-	240 / F-
0 / -0		►		0	@	P	`	p	Ç	É	¦	░	└	╨	α	≡
1 / -1	☺	◄	!	1	A	Q	a	q	ü	È	´	▒	┴	╤	β	±
2 / -2	☻	↕	"	2	B	R	b	r	é	Ê	ó	▓	┬	╥	Γ	≥
3 / -3	♥	‼	#	3	C	S	c	s	â	ô	ú	│	├	╙	π	≤
4 / -4	♦	¶	$	4	D	T	d	t	Â	Ë	¨	┤	─	╘	Σ	⌠
5 / -5	♣	§	%	5	E	U	e	u	à	Ï	¸	╡	┼	╒	σ	⌡
6 / -6	♠	▬	&	6	F	V	f	v	¶	û	³	╢	╞	╓	µ	÷
7 / -7	•	↨	'	7	G	W	g	w	ç	ù	¯	╖	╟	╫	τ	≈
8 / -8	◘	↑	(	8	H	X	h	x	ê	¤	Î	╕	└	╪	Φ	°
9 / -9	○	↓	)	9	I	Y	i	y	ë	Ô	┌	╣	╔	╛	Θ	∙
10 / -A	◙	→	*	:	J	Z	j	z	è	Ü	¬	║	╩	╒	Ω	·
11 / -B	♂	←	+	;	K	[	k	{	ï	¢	½	╗	╦	█	δ	√
12 / -C	♀	∟	,	<	L	\	l	¦	î	£	¼	╝	╠	▄	∞	ⁿ
13 / -D	♪	↔	-	=	M	]	m	}	=	Ù	¾	╜	═	█	ø	²
14 / -E	♫	▲	.	>	N	^	n	~	À	Û	«	╛	╬	█	ε	■
15 / -F	☼	▼	/	?	O	_	o	△	§	ƒ	»	┐	╧	█	∩	

Decimal Value → / ↓ (Hex Value)	0 / 0	16 / 1	32 / 2	48 / 3	64 / 4	80 / 5	96 / 6	112 / 7	128 / 8	144 / 9	160 / A	176 / B	192 / C	208 / D	224 / E	240 / F
0 / 0		►		0	@	P	`	p	Ç	É	á	░	└	╨	α	≡
1 / 1	☺	◄	!	1	A	Q	a	q	ü	œ	í	▒	┴	╤	β	±
2 / 2	☻	↕	"	2	B	R	b	r	é	Æ	ó	▓	┬	╥	Γ	≥
3 / 3	♥	‼	#	3	C	S	c	s	â	ô	ú	│	├	╙	π	≤
4 / 4	♦	¶	$	4	D	T	d	t	ä	ö	ñ	┤	─	╘	Σ	⌠
5 / 5	♣	§	%	5	E	U	e	u	à	ò	Ñ	╡	┼	╒	σ	⌡
6 / 6	♠	▬	&	6	F	V	f	v	å	û	ª	╢	╞	╓	µ	÷
7 / 7	•	↨	'	7	G	W	g	w	ç	ù	º	╖	╟	╫	τ	≈
8 / 8	◘	↑	(	8	H	X	h	x	ê	ÿ	¿	╕	└	╪	Φ	°
9 / 9	○	↓	)	9	I	Y	i	y	ë	Ö	⌐	╣	╔	╛	Θ	∙
10 / A	◙	→	*	:	J	Z	j	z	è	Ü	¬	║	╩	╒	Ω	·
11 / B	♂	←	+	;	K	(	k	{	ï	ø	½	╗	╦	█	δ	√
12 / C	♀	∟	,	<	L	\	l	¦	î	£	¼	╝	╠	▄	∞	ⁿ
13 / D	♪	↔	-	=	M	)	m	}	ì	Ø	¡	╜	═	█	ø	²
14 / E	♫	▲	.	>	N	^	n	~	Ä	Pt	«	╛	╬	█	ε	■
15 / F	☼	▼	/	?	O	_	o	⌂	Å	ƒ	»	┐	╧	█	∩	

Figure I–3.   DOS Code Pages: 863—Canadian French (above) and 865—Nordic (below)

ISO Character Sets

ISO character sets are in the form of a 16 by 16 matrix or table. The columns are in increasing order from left to right. Each character is assigned a location within the table. This location or address is its numerical equivalent. Addresses start at 000 in the upper left cell and increase along each vertical column in groups of 16 to the largest address of 255 in the lower right cell. The addresses are in hexadecimal format; for example, the first two columns, on the left, cover the range 000 to 01F where F = 15.

The following character sets are shown in Figures J–1, J–2, J–3, J–4, and J–5.

J–1: ISO-8859/1—Latin 1; ISO-8859/2—Latin 2

J–2: ISO-8859/3—Latin 3; ISO-8859/4—Latin 4

J–3: ISO-8859/5—Latin/Cyrillic; ISO-8859/6—Latin/Arabic

J–4: ISO-8859/7—Latin/Greek; ISO-8859/8—Latin/Hebrew

J–5: ISO-8859/9—Latin 5

	00	01	02	03	04	05	06	07	08	09	10	11	12	13	14	15
00			SP	0	@	P	`	p			NBSP	°	À	Ð	à	ð
01			!	1	A	Q	a	q			¡	±	Á	Ñ	á	ñ
02			"	2	B	R	b	r			¢	²	Â	Ò	â	ò
03			#	3	C	S	c	s			£	³	Ã	Ó	ã	ó
04			$	4	D	T	d	t			¤	´	Ä	Ô	ä	ô
05			%	5	E	U	e	u			¥	µ	Å	Õ	å	õ
06			&	6	F	V	f	v			¦	¶	Æ	Ö	æ	ö
07			'	7	G	W	g	w			§	·	Ç	×	ç	÷
08			(	8	H	X	h	x			¨	¸	È	Ø	è	ø
09			)	9	I	Y	i	y			©	¹	É	Ù	é	ù
10			*	:	J	Z	j	z			ª	º	Ê	Ú	ê	ú
11			+	;	K	[	k	{			«	»	Ë	Û	ë	û
12			,	<	L	\	l	|			¬	¼	Ì	Ü	ì	ü
13			-	=	M	]	m	}			SHY	½	Í	Ý	í	ý
14			.	>	N	^	n	~			®	¾	Î	Þ	î	þ
15			/	?	O	_	o				¯	¿	Ï	ß	ï	ÿ

	00	01	02	03	04	05	06	07	08	09	10	11	12	13	14	15
00			SP	0	@	P	`	p			NBSP	°	Ŕ	Ð	ŕ	đ
01			!	1	A	Q	a	q			Ą	˛	Á	Ń	á	ń
02			"	2	B	R	b	r			˘	˛	Â	Ň	â	ň
03			#	3	C	S	c	s			Ł	ł	Ă	Ó	ă	ó
04			$	4	D	T	d	t			¤	´	Ä	Ô	ä	ô
05			%	5	E	U	e	u			Ľ	ˇ	Ĺ	Ő	ĺ	ő
06			&	6	F	V	f	v			Ś	ś	Ć	Ö	ć	ö
07			'	7	G	W	g	w			§	ˇ	Ç	×	ç	÷
08			(	8	H	X	h	x			¨	˛	Č	Ř	č	ř
09			)	9	I	Y	i	y			Š	š	É	Ů	é	ů
10			*	:	J	Z	j	z			Ş	ş	Ę	Ú	ę	ú
11			+	;	K	[	k	{			Ť	ť	Ë	Ű	ë	ű
12			,	<	L	\	l	|			Ź	ź	Ě	Ü	ě	ü
13			-	=	M	]	m	}			SHY	˝	Í	Ý	í	ý
14			.	>	N	^	n	~			Ž	ž	Î	Ţ	î	ţ
15			/	?	O	_	o				Ż	ż	Ď	ß	ď	˙

Figure J–1. ISO Character Sets: ISO-8859/1—Latin 1 (above) and ISO-8859/2—Latin 2 (below)

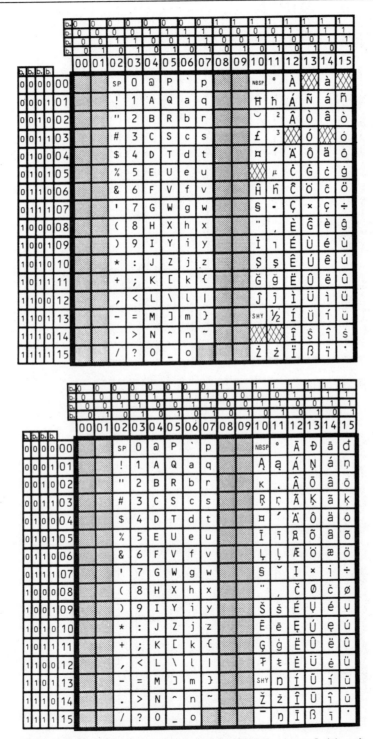

Figure J–2. ISO Character Sets: ISO-8859/3—Latin 3 (above) and ISO-8859/4—Latin 4 (below)

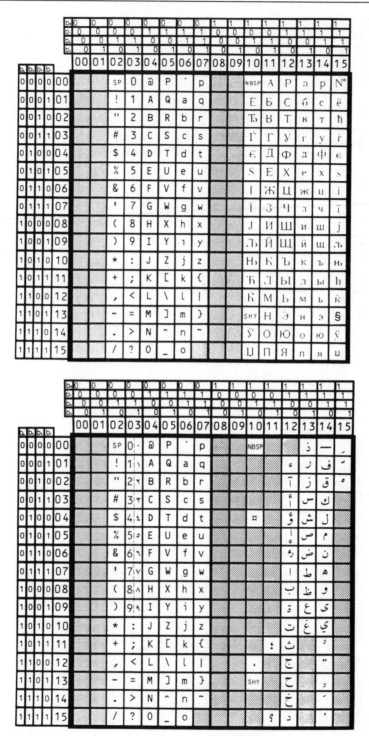

Figure J–3. ISO Character Sets: ISO-8859/5—Latin/Cyrillic (above) and ISO-8859/6—Latin/Arabic (below)

Figure J–4. ISO Character Sets: ISO-8859/7—Latin/Greek (above) and ISO-8859/8—Latin/Hebrew (below)

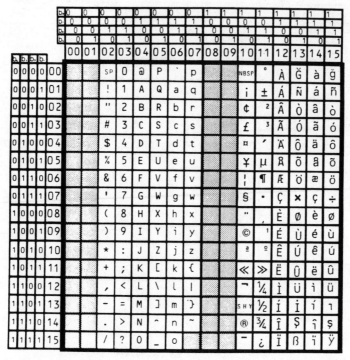

Figure J–5.   ISO Character Sets: ISO-8859/9—Latin 5

Macintosh
Character Sets

Macintosh character sets are in the form of a 16 by 16 matrix or table. The columns are in increasing order from left to right. Each character is assigned a location within the table. This location or address is its numerical equivalent. Addresses start at 000 in the upper left cell and increase along each vertical column in groups of 16 to the largest address of 255 in the lower right cell. The addresses are in hexadecimal format; for example, the first two columns, on the left, cover the range 000 to 01F.

The following character sets are shown in Figures K–1 through K–8.

K–1: Roman

K–2: Arabic and Central European

K–3: Chinese and Croatian

K–4: Cyrillic and Greek

K–5: Hebrew and Icelandic

K–6: Japanese and Korean

K–7: Thai and Turkish

K–8: Arabic and Hebrew. The Arabic and Hebrew encodings in Figure K–8 are alternatives to those in K–2 and K–5.

	0x	1x	2x	3x	4x	5x	6x	7x	8x	9x	Ax	Bx	Cx	Dx	Ex	Fx
x0	NUL	DLE	SP	0	@	P	`	p	Ä	ê	†	∞	¿	–	‡	
x1	SOH	DC1	!	1	A	Q	a	q	Å	ë	°	±	¡	—	·	Ò
x2	STX	DC2	"	2	B	R	b	r	Ç	í	¢	≤	¬	"	‚	Ú
x3	ETX	DC3	#	3	C	S	c	s	É	ì	£	≥	√	"	„	Û
x4	EOT	DC4	$	4	D	T	d	t	Ñ	î	§	¥	ƒ	'	‰	Ù
x5	ENQ	NAK	%	5	E	U	e	u	Ö	ï	•	µ	≈	'	Â	ı
x6	ACK	SYN	&	6	F	V	f	v	Ü	ñ	¶	∂	Δ	÷	Ê	^
x7	BEL	ETB	'	7	G	W	g	w	á	ó	ß	Σ	«	◊	Á	~
x8	BS	CAN	(	8	H	X	h	x	à	ò	®	Π	»	ÿ	Ë	¯
x9	HT	EM	)	9	I	Y	i	y	â	ô	©	π	…	Ÿ	È	˘
xA	LF	SUB	*	:	J	Z	j	z	ä	ö	™	∫	NBSP	/	Í	˙
xB	VT	ESC	+	;	K	[	k	{	ã	õ	´	ª	À	⁄	Î	˚
xC	FF	FS	,	<	L	\	l	|	å	ú	¨	º	Ã	‹	Ï	¸
xD	CR	GS	-	=	M	]	m	}	ç	ù	≠	Ω	Õ	›	Ì	˝
xE	SO	RS	.	>	N	^	n	~	é	û	Æ	æ	Œ	fi	Ó	˛
xF	SI	US	/	?	O	_	o	DEL	è	ü	Ø	ø	œ	fl	Ô	ˇ

Figure K–1.   Macintosh Character Sets: Roman

	0x	1x	2x	3x	4x	5x	6x	7x	8x	9x	Ax	Bx	Cx	Dx	Ex	Fx
x0	NUL	DLE	SP	0	@	P	`	p	Ä	ê	RLSP	.	*	ذ	ـ	ً
x1	SOH	DC1	!	1	A	Q	a	q	NBSP	ë	!	١	ء	ر	ف	ٌ
x2	STX	DC2	"	2	B	R	b	r	Ç	…	"	٢	آ	ز	ق	ْ
x3	ETX	DC3	#	3	C	S	c	s	É	ì	#	٣	أ	س	ك	پ
x4	EOT	DC4	$	4	D	T	d	t	Ñ	î	$	٤	ؤ	ش	ل	ت
x5	ENQ	NAK	%	5	E	U	e	u	Ö	ï	٪	٥	إ	ص	م	چ
x6	ACK	SYN	&	6	F	V	f	v	Ü	ñ	&	٦	ئ	ض	ن	ه
x7	BEL	ETB	'	7	G	W	g	w	á	ó	'	٧	ا	ط	ه	ق
x8	BS	CAN	(	8	H	X	h	x	à	»	)	٨	ب	ظ	و	گ
x9	HT	EM	)	9	I	Y	i	ẏ	â	ô	(	٩	ة	ع	ى	ڈ
xA	LF	SUB	*	:	J	Z	j	z	ä	ö	×	:	ت	غ	ي	ژ
xB	VT	ESC	+	;	K	[	k	{	ں	÷	+	؛	ث	]	ٰ	}
xC	FF	FS	,	<	L	\	l	|	«	ú	،	>	ج	\	ٕ	|
xD	CR	GS	-	=	M	]	m	}	ç	ù	—	=	ح	[	ٖ	{
xE	SO	RS	.	>	N	^	n	~	é	û	.	<	خ	^	ٓ	ڑ
xF	SI	US	/	?	O	_	o	DEL	è	ü	/	؟	د	ـ	ٗ	ع

	0x	1x	2x	3x	4x	5x	6x	7x	8x	9x	Ax	Bx	Cx	Dx	Ex	Fx
x0	NUL	DLE	SP	0	@	P	`	p	Ä	ź	†	¡	ņ	–	ŗ	ū
x1	SOH	DC1	!	1	A	Q	a	q	Ā	Ď	°	Ī	Ń	—	Š	Ů
x2	STX	DC2	"	2	B	R	b	r	ā	í	Ę	≤	¬	"	,	Ú
x3	ETX	DC3	#	3	C	S	c	s	É	đ	£	≥	√	"	„	ů
x4	EOT	DC4	$	4	D	T	d	t	Ą	Ē	§	ī	ń	'	š	Ű
x5	ENQ	NAK	%	5	E	U	e	u	Ö	ē	•	Ķ	Ň	'	Ś	ú
x6	ACK	SYN	&	6	F	V	f	v	Ü	Ė	¶	∂	Δ	÷	ś	Ų
x7	BEL	ETB	'	7	G	W	g	w	á	ó	ß	Σ	«	◊	Á	ų
x8	BS	CAN	(	8	H	X	h	x	ą	ė	®	ł	»	ō	Ť	Ý
x9	HT	EM	)	9	I	Y	i	y	Č	ô	©	Ļ	…	Ŕ	ť	ý
xA	LF	SUB	*	:	J	Z	j	z	ä	ö	TM	ļ	NBSP	ŕ	Í	ķ
xB	VT	ESC	+	;	K	[	k	{	č	õ	ę	Ľ	ň	Ř	Ž	Ż
xC	FF	FS	,	<	L	\	l	|	Ć	ú	¨	ľ	Ő	‹	ž	Ł
xD	CR	GS	-	=	M	]	m	}	ć	Ě	≠	Ĺ	Ō	›	Ū	ż
xE	SO	RS	.	>	N	^	n	~	é	ě	ġ	ĺ	õ	ř	Ó	Ģ
xF	SI	US	/	?	O	_	o	DEL	Ź	ü	Į	Ņ	Ō	Ŗ	Ô	ˇ

Figure K–2. Macintosh Character Sets: Arabic (above) and Central European (below)

	0x	1x	2x	3x	4x	5x	6x	7x	8x	9x	Ax	Bx	Cx	Dx	Ex	Fx
x0	NUL	DLE	SP	0	@	P	`	p	§	DB	DB	∞				
x1	SOH	⌘	!	1	A	Q	a	q		DB	DB	°				
x2	STX	✓	"	2	B	R	b	r		DB	DB	¢				
x3	ETX	◆	#	3	C	S	c	s		DB	DB	£				
x4	EOT		$	4	D	T	d	t		DB	DB	¥				
x5	ENQ	NAK	%	5	E	U	e	u		DB	DB	¶	T6			
x6	ACK	SYN	&	6	F	V	f	v		DB	DB	∂	T7			
x7	BEL	ETB	'	7	G	W	g	w		DB	DB	ƒ	T8			
x8	BS	CAN	(	8	H	X	h	x		DB	DB	Δ	T9			
x9	HT	EM	)	9	I	Y	i	y		DB	DB	π	...			
xA	LF	SUB	*	:	J	Z	j	z		DB	DB	_	NBSP			
xB	VT	ESC	+	;	K	[	k	{		DB	DB	—	•			
xC	FF	FS	,	<	L	\	l	|		DB	DB	"				
xD	CR	GS	-	=	M	]	m	}		DB	DB	"				®
xE	SO	RS	.	>	N	^	n	~		DB	DB	'		.		©
xF	S1	US	/	?	O	_	o	DEL		DB	DB	'				TM

	0x	1x	2x	3x	4x	5x	6x	7x	8x	9x	Ax	Bx	Cx	Dx	Ex	Fx
x0	NUL	DLE	SP	0	@	P	`	p	Ä	ê	†	∞	¿	Đ	–	ð
x1	SOH	DC1	!	1	A	Q	a	q	Å	ë	°	±	¡	—		
x2	STX	DC2	"	2	B	R	b	r	Ç	í	¢	≤	¬	"		
x3	ETX	DC3	#	3	C	S	c	s	É	ì	£	≥	√	"		
x4	EOT	DC4	$	4	D	T	d	t	Ñ	î	§	¥	ƒ	'		
x5	ENQ	NAK	%	5	E	U	e	u	Ö	ï	•	μ	≈	'		
x6	ACK	SYN	&	6	F	V	f	v	Ü	ñ	¶	∂	Ć	÷	ć	
x7	BEL	ETB	'	7	G	W	g	w	á	ó	ß	Σ	«	◊		
x8	BS	CAN	(	8	H	X	h	x	à	ò	®	∏	Č		č	
x9	HT	EM	)	9	I	Y	i	y	â	ô	Ş	ş	...	©		π
xA	LF	SUB	*	:	J	Z	j	z	ä	ö	™	∫	NBSP			
xB	VT	ESC	+	;	K	[	k	{	ã	õ	´	a	À			
xC	FF	FS	,	<	L	\	l	|	å	ú	¨	o	Ã			
xD	CR	GS	-	=	M	]	m	}	ç	ù	≠	Ω	Õ			
xE	SO	RS	.	>	N	^	n	~	é	û	Ž	ž	Œ	Æ		æ
xF	S1	US	/	?	O	_	o	DEL	è	ü	Ø	ø	œ	»		

Figure K–3.   Macintosh Character Sets: Chinese (above) and Croatian (below)

	0x	1x	2x	3x	4x	5x	6x	7x	8x	9x	Ax	Bx	Cx	Dx	Ex	Fx
x0	NUL	DLE	SP	0	@	P	`	p	А	Р	†	∞	ј	–	a	р
x1	SOH	⌘	!	1	A	Q	a	q	Б	С	°	±	ѕ	—	б	с
x2	STX	✓	"	2	B	R	b	r	В	Т	¢	≤·	¬	"	в	т
x3	ETX	◆	#	3	C	S	c	s	Г	У	£	≥	√	"	г	у
x4	EOT		$	4	D	T	d	t	Д	Ф	§	¥	ƒ	˙	д	ф
x5	ENQ	NAK	%	5	E	U	e	u	Е	Х	•	µ	≈	'	е	х
x6	ACK	SYN	&	6	F	V	f	v	Ж	Ц	¶	∂	Δ	÷	ж	ц
x7	BEL	ETB	'	7	G	W	g	w	З	Ч	І	Ј	«	„	з	ч
x8	BS	CAN	(	8	H	X	h	x	И	Ш	®	Є	»	Ў	и	ш
x9	HT	EM	)	9	I	Y	i	y	Й	Щ	©	є	…	ў	й	щ
xA	LF	SUB	*	:	J	Z	j	z	К	Ъ	™	Ї	NBSP	Џ	к	ъ
xB	VT	ESC	+	;	K	[	k	{	Л	Ы	Ђ	ї	Ћ	џ	л	ы
xC	FF	FS	,	<	L	\	l	|	М	Ь	ђ	Љ	ħ	№	м	ь
xD	CR	GS	-	=	M	]	m	}	Н	Э	≠	љ	Ќ	Ё	н	э
xE	SO	RS	.	>	N	^	n	~	О	Ю	Ѓ	Њ	ќ	ё	о	ю
xF	S1	US	/	?	O	_	o	DEL	П	Я	ѓ	њ	ѕ	s	я	¤

	0x	1x	2x	3x	4x	5x	6x	7x	8x	9x	Ax	Bx	Cx	Dx	Ex	Fx
x0	NUL	DLE	SP	0	@	P	`	p	Ä	ê		°	ῖ	Π	ΰ	π
x1	SOH	DC1	!	1	A	Q	a	q	Å	ë	ˈ	±	Α	Ρ	α	ϱ
x2	STX	DC2	"	2	B	R	b	r	Ç	í	ʼ	²	Β	…	β	ς
x3	ETX	DC3	#	3	C	S	c	s	É	ì	£	³	Γ	Σ	γ	σ
x4	EOT	DC4	$	4	D	T	d	t	Ñ	î	®	΄	Δ	Τ	δ	τ
x5	ENQ	NAK	%	5	E	U	e	u	Ö	ï	÷	῀	Ε	Υ	ε	υ
x6	ACK	SYN	&	6	F	V	f	v	Ü	ñ	¡	Ά	Ζ	Φ	ζ	φ
x7	BEL	ETB	'	7	G	W	g	w	á	ó	§	·	Η	Χ	η	χ
x8	BS	CAN	(	8	H	X	h	x	à	ò	¨	Έ	Θ	ψ	θ	ψ
x9	HT	EM	)	9	I	Y	i	y	â	ô	©	Ή	Ι	Ω	ι	ω
xA	LF	SUB	*	:	J	Z	j	z	ä	ö	™	Ί	Κ	Ϊ	χ	ϊ
xB	VT	ESC	+	;	K	[	k	{	ã	õ	«	»	Λ	Ύ	λ	ϋ
xC	FF	FS	,	<	L	\	l	|	å	ú	¬	Ό	Μ	ά	μ	ό
xD	CR	GS	-	=	M	]	m	}	ç	ù	-	½	Ν	έ	ν	ύ
xE	SO	RS	.	>	N	^	n	~	é	û	‰	Ύ	Ξ	ή	ξ	ώ
xF	S1	US	/	?	O	_	o	DEL	è	ü	—	Ώ	Ο	ί	o	ο

Figure K–4. Macintosh Character Sets: Cyrillic (above) and Greek (below)

	0x	1x	2x	3x	4x	5x	6x	7x	8x	9x	Ax	Bx	Cx	Dx	Ex	Fx
x0	NUL	DLE	SP	0	@	P	`	p	Ä	ê	RLSP	0	ל	–	א	נ
x1	SOH	DC1	!	1	A	Q	a	q	ﬔ	ë	!	1	„	—	ב	ס
x2	STX	DC2	"	2	B	R	b	r	Ç	í	"	2		"	ג	ע
x3	ETX	DC3	#	3	C	S	c	s	É	ì	#	3		"	ד	ף
x4	EOT	DC4	$	4	D	T	d	t	Ñ	î	$	4		'	ה	פ
x5	ENQ	NAK	%	5	E	U	e	u	Ö	ï	%	5		'	ו	ץ
x6	ACK	SYN	&	6	F	V	f	v	Ü	ñ	₪	6	.	שׂ	ז	צ
x7	BEL	ETB	'	7	G	W	g	w	á	ó	'	7	ִ	שׁ	ח	ק
x8	BS	CAN	(	8	H	X	h	x	à	ò	(	8	ֻ	\	ט	ר
x9	HT	EM	)	9	I	Y	i	y	â	ô	)	9	…	ֹ	י	שׁ
xA	LF	SUB	*	:	J	Z	j	z	ä	ö	NBSP	:		ֲ	ך	ת
xB	VT	ESC	+	;	K	[	k	{	ã	õ	+	;	ָ	ֳ	כ	}
xC	FF	FS	,	<	L	\	l	|	å	ú	,	<	ַ	ֱ	ל	]
xD	CR	GS	-	=	M	]	m	}	ç	ù	-	=	ּ	ֵ	ם	{
xE	SO	RS	.	>	N	^	n	~	é	û	.	>	ֶ	ָ	מ	[
xF	S1	US	/	?	O	_	o	DEL	è	ü	/	?	ֿ	ֽ	ן	|

Figure K–5. Macintosh Character Sets: Hebrew (above) and Icelandic (following page)

	0x	1x	2x	3x	4x	5x	6x	7x	8x	9x	Ax	Bx	Cx	Dx	Ex	Fx
x0	NUL	DLE	SP	0	@	P	`	p	Ä	ê	Ý	∞	¿	–	ý	$\bullet$
x1	SOH	DC1	!	1	A	Q	a	q	Å	ë	°	±	¡	—	·	Ò
x2	STX	DC2	"	2	B	R	b	r	Ç	í	¢	≤	¬	"	,	Ú
x3	ETX	DC3	#	3	C	S	c	s	É	ì	£	≥	√	"	„	Û
x4	EOT	DC4	$	4	D	T	d	t	Ñ	î	§	¥	ƒ	'	‰	Ù
x5	ENQ	NAK	%	5	E	U	e	u	Ö	ï	•	µ	≈	'	Â	ı
x6	ACK	SYN	&	6	F	V	f	v	Ü	ñ	¶	∂	Δ	÷	Ê	^
x7	BEL	ETB	'	7	G	W	g	w	á	ó	ß	Σ	«	◊	Á	~
x8	BS	CAN	(	8	H	X	h	x	à	ò	®	∏	»	ÿ	Ë	¯
x9	HT	EM	)	9	I	Y	i	y	â	ô	©	π	…	Ÿ	È	˘
xA	LF	SUB	*	:	J	Z	j	z	ä	ö	™	∫	NBSP	/	Í	˙
xB	VT	ESC	+	;	K	[	k	{	ã	õ	´	a	À	◻	Î	°
xC	FF	FS	,	<	L	\	l	|	å	ú	¨	o	Ã	Ð	Ï	¸
xD	CR	GS	-	=	M	]	m	}	ç	ù	≠	Ω	Õ	ð	Ì	˝
xE	SO	RS	.	>	N	^	n	~	é	û	Æ	æ	Œ	Þ	Ó	˛
xF	SI	US	/	?	O	_	o	DEL	è	ü	Ø	ø	œ	þ	Ô	ˇ

Figure K–5. (Continued)

	0x	1x	2x	3x	4x	5x	6x	7x	8x	9x	Ax	Bx	Cx	Dx	Ex	Fx
x0	NUL	DLE	SP	0	@	P	`	p	\	DB	SP	—	タ	ミ	DB	DB
x1	SOH	⌘	!	1	A	Q	a	q		DB	。	ア	チ	ム	DB	DB
x2	STX	✓	"	2	B	R	b	r	_	DB	「	イ	ツ	メ	DB	DB
x3	ETX	◆	#	3	C	S	c	s	DB	DB	」	ウ	テ	モ	DB	DB
x4	EOT		$	4	D	T	d	t	DB	DB	、	エ	ト	ヤ	DB	DB
x5	ENQ	NAK	%	5	E	U	e	u	DB	DB	・	オ	ナ	ユ	DB	DB
x6	ACK	SYN	&	6	F	V	f	v	DB	DB	ヲ	カ	ニ	ヨ	DB	DB
x7	BEL	ETB	'	7	G	W	g	w	DB	DB	ァ	キ	ヌ	ラ	DB	DB
x8	BS	CAN	(	8	H	X	h	x	DB	DB	ィ	ク	ネ	リ	DB	DB
x9	HT	EM	)	9	I	Y	i	y	DB	DB	ゥ	ケ	ノ	ル	DB	DB
xA	LF	SUB	*	:	J	Z	j	z	DB	DB	ェ	コ	ハ	レ	DB	DB
xB	VT	ESC	+	;	K	[	k	{	DB	DB	ォ	サ	ヒ	ロ	DB	DB
xC	FF	FS	,	<	L	\	l	|	DB	DB	ャ	シ	フ	ワ	DB	DB
xD	CR	GS	-	=	M	]	m	}	DB	DB	ュ	ス	ヘ	ン	DB	©
xE	SO	RS	.	>	N	^	n	~	DB	DB	ョ	セ	ホ	"	DB	TM
xF	S1	US	/	?	O	_	o	DEL	DB	DB	ッ	ソ	マ	°	DB	...

	0x	1x	2x	3x	4x	5x	6x	7x	8x	9x	Ax	Bx	Cx	Dx	Ex	Fx
x0	NUL	DLE	SP	0	@	P	`	p		DB	DB					
x1	SOH	⌘	!	1	A	Q	a	q	₩	DB	DB					
x2	STX	✓	"	2	B	R	b	r	_	DB	DB					
x3	ETX	◆	#	3	C	S	c	s	©	DB	DB					
x4	EOT		$	4	D	T	d	t		DB	DB					
x5	ENQ	NAK	%	5	E	U	e	u		DB	DB					
x6	ACK	SYN	&	6	F	V	f	v		DB	DB					
x7	BEL	ETB	'	7	G	W	g	w		DB	DB					
x8	BS	CAN	(	8	H	X	h	x		DB	DB					
x9	HT	EM	)	9	I	Y	i	y		DB	DB					
xA	LF	SUB	*	:	J	Z	j	z		DB	DB					
xB	VT	ESC	+	;	K	[	k	{		DB	DB					
xC	FF	FS	,	<	L	\	l	|		DB	DB					
xD	CR	GS	-	=	M	]	m	}		DB	DB					
xE	SO	RS	.	>	N	^	n	~		DB	DB					TM
xF	S1	US	/	?	O	_	o	DEL		DB	DB					...

Figure K–6.   Macintosh Character Sets: Japanese (above) and Korean (below)

	0x	1x	2x	3x	4x	5x	6x	7x	8x	9x	Ax	Bx	Cx	Dx	Ex	Fx
x0	NUL	DLE	SP	0	@	P	`	p	«		NBSP	ฐ	ฎ	◌ะ	เ	๐
x1	SOH	DC1	!	1	A	Q	a	q	»	•	ก	ฑ	ม	◌ั	แ	๑
x2	STX	DC2	"	2	B	R	b	r	…		ข	ฒ	ย	า	โ	๒
x3	ETX	DC3	#	3	C	S	c	s			ฃ	ณ	ร	◌ิ	ใ	๓
x4	EOT	DC4	$	4	D	T	d	t			ค	ด	ฤ	◌ี	ไ	๔
x5	ENQ	NAK	%	5	E	U	e	u			ฅ	ต	ล	◌ึ	ๅ	๕
x6	ACK	SYN	&	6	F	V	f	v			ฆ	ถ	ฦ	◌ื	ๆ	๖
x7	BEL	ETB	'	7	G	W	g	w			ง	ท	ว	◌ุ	◌่	๗
x8	BS	CAN	(	8	H	X	h	x			จ	ธ	ศ	◌ู	◌้	๘
x9	HT	EM	)	9	I	Y	i	y			ฉ	น	ษ	◌ฺ	◌๊	๙
xA	LF	SUB	*	:	J	Z	j	z			ช	บ	ส	◌ฺ	◌๋	®
xB	VT	ESC	+	;	K	[	k	{			ซ	ป	ห	WDJT	◌์	©
xC	FF	FS	,	<	L	\	l	|			ฌ	ผ	ฬ	WDBR	◌ํ	
xD	CR	GS	-	=	M	]	m	}	"	'	ญ	ฝ	อ	–	◌๎	
xE	SO	RS	.	>	N	^	n	~	"	'	ฎ	พ	ฮ	—	TM	
xF	S1	US	/	?	O	_	o	DEL			ฏ	ฟ	ฯ	฿	◉	

	0x	1x	2x	3x	4x	5x	6x	7x	8x	9x	Ax	Bx	Cx	Dx	Ex	Fx
x0	NUL	DLE	SP	0	@	P	`	p	Ä	ê	†	∞	¿	–	‡	
x1	SOH	⌘	!	1	A	Q	a	q	Å	ë	°	±	¡	—	·	Ò
x2	STX	✓	"	2	B	R	b	r	Ç	í	¢	≤	¬	"	‚	Ú
x3	ETX	◆	#	3	C	S	c	s	É	ì	£	≥	√	"	„	Û
x4	EOT		$	4	D	T	d	t	Ñ	î	§	¥	ƒ	'	‰	Ù
x5	ENQ	NAK	%	5	E	U	e	u	Ö	ï	•	µ	≈	'	Â	
x6	ACK	SYN	&	6	F	V	f	v	Ü	ñ	¶	∂	Δ	÷	Ê	^
x7	BEL	ETB	'	7	G	W	g	w	á	ó	ß	Σ	«	◊	Á	˜
x8	BS	CAN	(	8	H	X	h	x	à	ò	®	Π	»	ÿ	Ë	¯
x9	HT	EM	)	9	I	Y	i	y	â	ô	©	π	…	Ÿ	È	˘
xA	LF	SUB	*	:	J	Z	j	z	ä	ö	TM	∫	NBSP	Ğ	Í	˙
xB	VT	ESC	+	;	K	[	k	{	ã	õ	´	ª	À	ğ	Î	˚
xC	FF	FS	,	<	L	\	l	|	å	ú	¨	º	Ã	İ	Ï	¸
xD	CR	GS	-	=	M	]	m	}	ç	ù	≠	Ω	Õ	ı	Ì	˝
xE	SO	RS	.	>	N	^	n	~	é	û	Æ	æ	Œ	Ş	Ó	˛
xF	S1	US	/	?	O	_	o	DEL	è	ü	Ø	ø	œ	ş	Ô	ˇ

Figure K–7. Macintosh Character Sets: Thai (above) and Turkish (below)

	0x	1x	2x	3x	4x	5x	6x	7x	8x	9x	Ax	Bx	Cx	Dx	Ex	Fx
x0		ڧ	SP	ﺑ	ﮒ	آ	ﺟ	ﻚ	پ	ﭺ	ﺰ	·	٭	ذ	ﻪ	
x1	ﺑ	ﻗ	ﳒ	ﺋ	ﺵ	أ	ﺥ	ﻞ		ﻬ	!	١	،	ر	ﻑ	ّ
x2	ﺓ	ﻛ	ﺘﺞ	ﻉ	ﺻ	ﺅ	ﺪ	ﻡ	ﭻ	ﺚ	"	٢	ﺁ	ز	ﻕ	ْ
x3	ﺯ	ﻟ	ﺗﺢ	ﻣﻢ	ﺿ	أ	ﺬ	ﻥ	ﺀ	…	#	٣	أ	ﺱ	ﻙ	پ
x4	ﺝ	ﻬ	ﳗ	ﻧﻦ	ﻁ	ﺊ	ﺭ	ﻫ	ﻗ	ﻳ	$	٤	ﺯ	ﺵ	ﻝ	ﺕ
x5	ﺡ	ﺯ	ﲢ	ﺑﻦ	ﻅ	ﺍ	ﺰ	ﻭ	ﻛ	ﺬ	٪	٥	!	ﺹ	ﻡ	ﺝ
x6	ﺥ	ﻩ	ﺀ	ﺒﻦ	ﻩ	ﺐ	ﺱ	ﻯ	ﻥ	ﺯ	&	٦	ﺋ	ﺽ	ﻥ	ﺓ
x7	ﺳ	ﺊ	ﲡ	ﺗﻦ	ﻍ	ﺔ	ﺵ	ﻱ	ﭻ	ﺯ	'	٧	ﺍ	ﻁ	ﻩ	ﻑ
x8	ﺷ	ﺊ	ﻟﺞ	ﻊ	ﻑ	ﺕ	ﺹ	ﻻ	ﻧ	»	)	٨	ﺏ	ﻅ	ﻭ	ﮒ
x9	ﺔ	ﺊ	ﻟﻂ	ﺃ	ﺓ	ﺷ	ﺽ	ﺀ	ﭺ	ﻻ	(	٩	ﺓ	ﻉ	ﻯ	ﺫ
xA	ﺔ	ﺊ	ﻟﻂ	ﻟﺞ	ﻙ	ﺝ	ﻁ	ﺯ	ﺮ	ﻵ	×	:	ﺕ	ﻍ	ﻱ	ﺯ
xB	ﻁ	ﺊ	ﺍ	ﻟﺢ	ﺍ	،	ﻅ	ﺽ	ﻥ	÷	+	؛	ﺙ	]	'	}
xC	ﻅ	ﺝ	ﻧﻢ	ﻟﺦ	ﺔ	.	ﻉ	ﺊ	«	ﻷ	،	>	ﺝ	\	'		
xD		ﺥ	ﺑﻢ	ﺀ	ﺬ	ﺀ	ﻍ	ﺊ	ﻵ	ﻹ	—	=	ﺡ	[	،	{
xE	ﻉ	ﺥ	ﺗﻢ	ﺀ	ﻩ	ﺀ	ﻑ	ﮒ	پ	ﻷ	.	<	ﺥ	^	ّ	ﺯ
xF	ﻍ	—	ﺊ	.	ﻪ	ﻷ	ﺥ	ﺕ	ﻻ	/	؟	ﺩ	—	'	ﺡ	

Figure K–8. Macintosh Character Sets: Arabic Encoding (above) and Hebrew Encoding (following page)

	0x	1x	2x	3x	4x	5x	6x	7x	8x	9x	Ax	Bx	Cx	Dx	Ex	Fx
x0		ָ	SP	ְֶ	דַ	קֶ	לֹ	נ		ֹֻ	RLSP	0	לֹ	–	א	נ
x1		ֵ	·	ֽ	ד	קֵ	ב	ס	יִ	׳	!	1	„	—	ב	ס
x2		ֱ	׃	·	ד	קֻ	ג	שׁ	ֵ	׳׳	"	2	"	"	ג	ע
x3		ֲ	ֳ	ָ	דֻ	קֹ	דֹ		ֺ	׀	#	3		"	ד	ף
x4		ֻ	׳׃	ֳ	דֹ	לָ	ה	פ	ֳ	ֻ	$	4	'		ה	פ
x5		׃	ֽ	׀	ד	ל	ו		ֻ	ֵ	%	5		'	ו	ץ
x6		ֳ	·	ֶ	דֻ	לֶ	ז	צ	׃	ֱ	₪	6	.	שׂ	ז	צ
x7		ֳ	ָ	ֶ	ד	לֶ	שׂ	ק	ִ	ֶ	'	7	ֹ	שׁ	ח	ק
x8		ֳ	ֳ	ֳ	דֻ	לֹ	ט		ֶ	ֶ	(	8	ֻ	\	ט	ר
x9		·	ָ	ֶ	דֹ	ל	י	ש	ֺ	ֶ	)	9	•••	׃	י	ש
xA		ָ	-	ֶ	קָ	לֶ	ך	ת	~	ֶ	*	:	NBSP	ֽ	ך	ת
xB		ֽ	ֳ	ֽ	ק	לֶ	כ		ֽ	ֶ	+	;	ָ	ֳ	כ	}
xC		ֳ	ֶ	ֶ	קֳ	לֶ	ל		<	ֻ	,	<	ֳ	ֽ	ל	]
xD		ֵ	·	ֶ	קֳ	דֹ			ֳ	ֺ	-	=	ֳ	·	ם	{
xE		ֳ	׃	ֽ	ק	דֹ	מ		ֳ	ֳ	.	>	ֶ	ָ	מ	[
xF		ֵ	ֳ	ֽ	ק	׃			ֳ	ֽ	/	?	ֳ	ֽ	ן	|

Figure K–8.   (Continued)

APPENDIX
L

HP-UX
Character Sets

The HP-UX 8-bit character sets are in the form of a 16 by 16 matrix or table. The columns are in increasing order from left to right. Each character is assigned a location within the table. This location or address is its numerical equivalent. Addresses start at 000 in the upper left cell and increase along each vertical column in groups of 16 to the largest address of 255 in the lower right cell.

The following character sets are shown in Figures L–1, L–2, and L–3.

L–1: Roman8 and Kana8

L–2: Arabic8 and Greek8

L–3: Hebre8 and Turkish8

The HP-UX 16-bit character sets are in the form of layout sheets showing ranges rather than individual characters. The following character sets are shown in Figures L–4 and L–5.

L–4: PRC15 and ROC15

L–5: Japan15 and Korea15

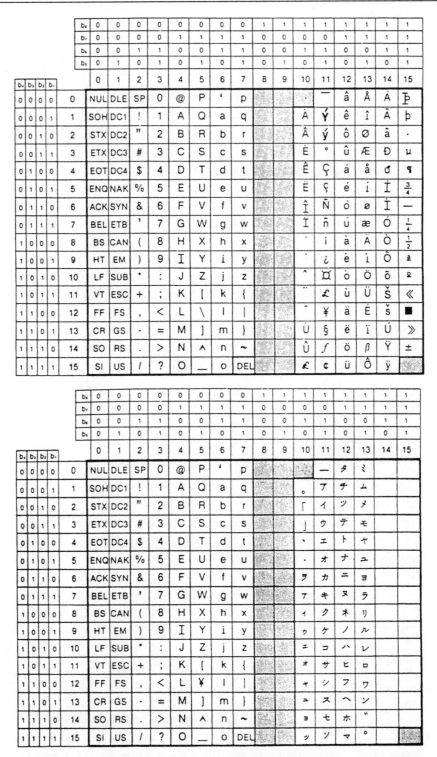

Figure L-1. HP-UX Character Sets: Roman8 (above) and Kana8 (below).
Copyright © 1990 Hewlett-Packard Company. Reproduced with permission.

b8			0	0	0	0	0	0	0	0	1	1	1	1	1	1	1	1
b7			0	0	0	0	1	1	1	1	0	0	0	0	1	1	1	1
b6			0	0	1	1	0	0	1	1	0	0	1	1	0	0	1	1
b5			0	1	0	1	0	1	0	1	0	1	0	1	0	1	0	1
b4 b3 b2 b1			0	1	2	3	4	5	6	7	8	9	10	11	12	13	14	15
0 0 0 0	0	NUL	DLE	SP	0	@	P	`	p				·	@	ذ	–	.
0 0 0 1	1	SOH	DC1	!	1	A	Q	a	q			!	\	ء	ر	ف	-
0 0 1 0	2	STX	DC2	"	2	B	R	b	r			..	٢	آ	ز	ق	.
0 0 1 1	3	ETX	DC3	#	3	C	S	c	s				٣	أ	س	ك	
0 1 0 0	4	EOT	DC4	$	4	D	T	d	t			٤	ؤ	ش	ل	
0 1 0 1	5	ENQ	NAK	%	5	E	U	e	u			%	٥	إ	ص	م	
0 1 1 0	6	ACK	SYN	&	6	F	V	f	v			٦	ئ	ض	ن	ﺀ
0 1 1 1	7	BEL	ETB	'	7	G	W	g	w			٧	ا	ط	ه	ﺌ
1 0 0 0	8	BS	CAN	(	8	H	X	h	x			)	٨	ب	ظ	و	ﺮ
1 0 0 1	9	HT	EM	)	9	I	Y	i	y			(	٩	ة	ع	ى	
1 0 1 0	10	LF	SUB	*	:	J	Z	j	z			:	ت	غ	ي	
1 0 1 1	11	VT	ESC	+	;	K	[	k	{			+	:	ث	،	
1 1 0 0	12	FF	FS	,	<	L	\	l	|			·	ج	
1 1 0 1	13	CR	GS	–	=	M	]	m	}			–	ح	
1 1 1 0	14	SO	RS	.	>	N	^	n	~			خ	
1 1 1 1	15	SI	US	/	?	O	_	o	DEL			/	؟	د	–	

b8			0	0	0	0	0	0	0	0	1	1	1	1	1	1	1	1
b7			0	0	0	0	1	1	1	1	0	0	0	0	1	1	1	1
b6			0	0	1	1	0	0	1	1	0	0	1	1	0	0	1	1
b5			0	1	0	1	0	1	0	1	0	1	0	1	0	1	0	1
b4 b3 b2 b1			0	1	2	3	4	5	6	7	8	9	10	11	12	13	14	15
0 0 0 0	0	NUL	DLE	SP	0	@	P	`	p					O	Ú	o	
0 0 0 1	1	SOH	DC1	!	1	A	Q	a	q				A	Π	α	π́
0 0 1 0	2	STX	DC2	"	2	B	R	b	r				B	Ρ	β	ρ
0 0 1 1	3	ETX	DC3	#	3	C	S	c	s				Γ	Σ	γ	σ
0 1 0 0	4	EOT	DC4	$	4	D	T	d	t				Δ	Τ	δ	τ
0 1 0 1	5	ENQ	NAK	%	5	E	U	e	u				E	Υ	ε	υ
0 1 1 0	6	ACK	SYN	&	6	F	V	f	v				Z	Φ	ζ	φ
0 1 1 1	7	BEL	ETB	'	7	G	W	g	w				H		η	ς́
1 0 0 0	8	BS	CAN	(	8	H	X	h	x				Θ	Χ	θ	χ
1 0 0 1	9	HT	EM	)	9	I	Y	i	y				I	Ψ	ι	ψ
1 0 1 0	10	LF	SUB	*	:	J	Z	j	z					Ω	ω
1 0 1 1	11	VT	ESC	+	;	K	[	k	{				K	ά	κ	έ
1 1 0 0	12	FF	FS	,	<	L	\	l	|			Ï	Λ	ή	λ	ί́
1 1 0 1	13	CR	GS	–	=	M	]	m	}				M	ó	μ	ώ
1 1 1 0	14	SO	RS	.	>	N	^	n	~			Ü	N		ν	'
1 1 1 1	15	SI	US	/	?	O	_	o	DEL				Ξ		ξ	

Figure L–2. HP-UX Character Sets: Arabic8 (above) and Greek8 (below). Copyright © 1990 Hewlett-Packard Company. Reproduced with permission.

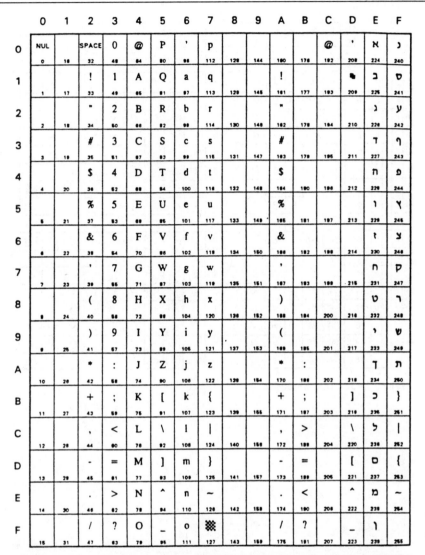

Figure L–3. HP-UX Character Sets: Hebrew8 (above) and Turkish8 (following page). Copyright © 1990 Hewlett-Packard Company. Reproduced with permission.

b8 →				0	0	0	0	0	0	0	0	1	1	1	1	1	1	1	1
b7 →				0	0	0	0	1	1	1	1	0	0	0	0	1	1	1	1
b6 →				0	0	1	1	0	0	1	1	0	0	1	1	0	0	1	1
b5 →				0	1	0	1	0	1	0	1	0	1	0	1	0	1	0	1
b4	b3	b2	b1		0	1	2	3	4	5	6	7	8	9	10	11	12	13	14	15
0	0	0	0	0	NUL	DLE	SP	0	@	P	`	p					À	ğ	þ
0	0	0	1	1	SOH	DC1	!	1	A	Q	a	q			Ç	Ý	ē	ī	Ã	þ
0	0	1	0	2	STX	DC2	"	2	B	R	b	r			Ğ	ý	õ	Ø	ã	·
0	0	1	1	3	ETX	DC3	#	3	C	S	c	s			È	·		Æ	Ð	µ
0	1	0	0	4	EOT	DC4	$	4	D	T	d	t			Ê		á	à	õ	q
0	1	0	1	5	ENQ	NAK	%	5	E	U	e	u			Ë		é	i	İ	¾
0	1	1	0	6	ACK	SYN	&	6	F	V	f	v			Î	Ñ	ó	o	Ì	-
0	1	1	1	7	BEL	ETB	'	7	G	W	g	w			Ï	ñ	ú	æ	Ó	¼
1	0	0	0	8	BS	CAN	(	8	H	X	h	x			'	¡	à	Ä	Ò	½
1	0	0	1	9	HT	EM	)	9	I	Y	i	y			`	¿	è	ì	Õ	ª
1	0	1	0	10	LF	SUB	·	:	J	Z	j	z			^	Ŀ	ò		õ	º
1	0	1	1	11	VT	ESC	+	;	K	[	k	{			..	£	ù	İ	Š	¹
1	1	0	0	12	FF	FS	,	<	L	\	l					~	¥	ä	Ö	š	ö
1	1	0	1	13	CR	GS	-	=	M	]	m	}			Ù	§	ĕ	Ş	Ú	ş
1	1	1	0	14	SO	RS	.	>	N	^	n	~			Û	ƒ		Ü	Ÿ	ü
1	1	1	1	15	SI	US	/	?	O	_	o	DEL			£	c		ç	ÿ	

Figure L–3.   (Continued)

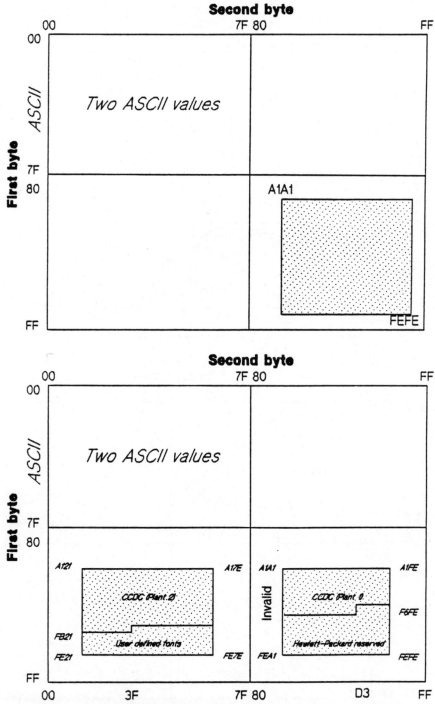

Figure L–4. HP-UX Character Sets: PRC15 (above) and ROC15 (below). Copyright © 1987, 1992 Hewlett-Packard Company. Reproduced with permission.

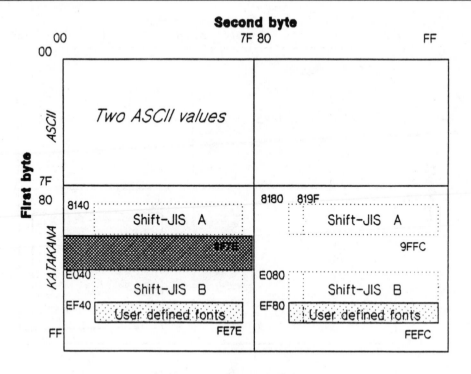

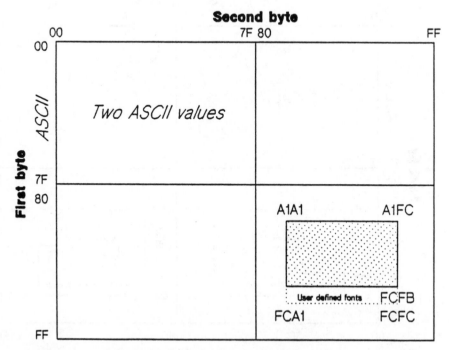

Figure L–5. HP-UX Character Sets: Japan15 (above) and Korea15 (below). Copyright © 1990 Hewlett-Packard Company. Reproduced with permission.

APPENDIX M

DOS National Language Support System Functions

In the DOS environment many programming language manufacturers either implement functions that do a poor job of retrieving country-specific information from DOS or they supply no functions at all. The following DOS functions can be used to retrieve such information. They are called *INT*s or *INTERRUPTS.*

INT 21H function 30H should be used to check the version of DOS running as the functions described are available, starting with certain DOS versions, as noted.

The collating tables supplied by DOS are far from perfect and you may be better off implementing your own.

INT 21H function 38H was introduced with DOS version 2.0. In version 2.0 it can only get country information for the current country. From version 3.0 on it can get information for the current country or another specified country. From version 3.0 on it can also set the country code. A pointer to a buffer containing the following information is returned in the *ES.DI* register pair. The country information returned depends on the version of DOS used.

PC-DOS 2.0 and 2.1 return the following country information:

date format
currency symbol
thousands separator
decimal separator

MS-DOS 2.0 and later and PC-DOS 3.0 and later return the following country information:

date format	currency format
currency symbol	number of decimal places
thousands separator	time format
decimal separator	case map address
date separator	data list separator
time separator	

Unless you have pressing needs to support earlier versions of DOS in your enabled products, it may be advisable to ignore this DOS function (INT 38H) as the *INT 21H function 65* and *INT 21H function 66* series of DOS function calls introduced with DOS 3.3 provide for and allow more manipulation of country-specific information. DOS versions 3.3 and later provide better national language support in general than the earlier versions of DOS and should be considered the goal for enabled DOS software products.

INT 21H function 650H gets extended country information. A pointer to a buffer containing the following information is returned in the *ES.DI* register pair:

length of the table returned	date separator
country code	time separator
code page	currency format
date format	number of decimal places
currency symbol	time format
thousands separator	case map address
decimal separator	data list separator

INT 21H function 6502H returns the address of the upper case table for the specified country code and code page. This table maps extended lower case characters to their upper case characters.

INT 21H function 6504H returns the address of the filename upper case table for the specified country code and code page. This table maps extended lower case characters in filenames to their upper case characters.

INT 21H function 6505H gets the address of a table of characters that must not be used in file names for a specified country code and code page.

INT 21H function 6506H gets the address of the collating table for a specified country code and code page.

INT 21H function 6520H monocases a specified character using the upper case table.

INT 21H function 6521H monocases each character in a string using the upper case table.

INT 21H function 6522H monocases each character in a zero-terminated string using the upper case table.

INT 21H function 6601H retrieves the identity of the code page currently in use.

INT 21H function 6602H sets the code page to be used. Note NLSFUNC must be loaded and the device prepared for code page switching for this to work.

There is another set of functions associated with *INT 2FH*. Functions *AD80H, AD81H, AD82H,* and *AD83H* get the KEYB.COM version number, set its active code page, set its country flag, and retrieve the country flag, respectively. Function *1400H* gets the installed state of NLSFUNC.EXE.

Brown and Kyle's *PC Interrupts: A Programmer's Reference to BIOS, DOS, and Third-Party Calls* and Microsoft's *MS-DOS Programmers Reference: Version 5.0* are excellent sources of further information about these interrupts and their relationships to each other and to DOS commands.

Glossary

accelerator (1) Same as fast key; the abbreviated keyboard shortcut for a menu command. (2) Software for speeding the relative motion of the mouse cursor across the screen.

analog Representation of an object in a way that resembles the original in continuous full range measures. A computerese antonym of *digital*.

ANSI American National Standards Institute.

ascender That portion of a character representation that lies above the main body of the character and associated characters.

ASCII American Standard Code for Information Interchange.

assembler A machine-oriented programming language using mnemonics.

AT One model of the IBM PC. Uses the Intel 80286 chip. Nowadays any clone with an 80286 chip and compatible BIOS is referred to as an AT clone. AT is an IBM marketing acronym for advanced technology.

BASIC Beginner's All-purpose Symbolic Instruction Code. A programming language developed in the early 1960s at Dartmouth College with the intention of easing the burden of teaching programming to students. This language was one of the first that could be used in a time-sharing system from a terminal and give students almost instant response for their efforts. Now available in many dialects of varying degrees of compatibility.

BCD Binary Coded Decimal. A 4-bit (nibble) representation of numerals for *0* through *9;* 10 of the 16 possible codes are used. The numeral *1* is encoded as

"0001" and *9* as "1001" (which of course also happens to be the binary equivalent number). A byte usually encompasses two of these codes. This is still in use and important where rounding errors must be minimized, such as in accounting.

BCDIC Binary Coded Decimal Interchange Code. Used by IBM in the past on their early mainframes; the character set consisted of uppercase letters, numerals, punctuation, and some graphics symbols.

big-endian A computer word where the most significant byte has the lowest address. This would be analogous to us writing 41 as 41 and reading it with the understanding that it is $(4 \times 10) + 1$. *See* little-endian.

BIOS Basic Input/Output System. The lowest-level code found in the firmware of a personal computer. Used for fundamental programmatic control of low-level processes. This term is generally used in the PC world. Other computers have similar systems with names such as kernel, for example.

binary Number system based on powers of two.

bit Binary digit; the fundamental piece of computer information, usually represented as 0 or 1.

board Abbreviation for circuit board; an assembly of computer hardware wired together and physically located on a fiberglass sheet.

BOM Byte Order Mark. Recommended as the first single wide character in a Unicode plain text format file. This enables a system reading the Unicode file to determine the byte order of the file and if necessary to convert the byte order to the receiving system's native byte order. The BOM is FEFF. If the system sees FFFE, it indicates that the byte order of the Unicode plain text file is the reverse of the receiving system and can be processed accordingly.

BPI Bytes per inch.

bug A software error.

bus The main channel for transferring data within a computer.

byte A string of 8 bits. With "simple" Roman languages, you may use this word interchangeably with "character" if the character coding is single-byte based. With more complicated languages that require more than one byte to contain or distinguish between natural language characters, the two words should not be used interchangeably.

Byte Order Mark *See* BOM.

C A currently popular high-level programming language with considerable access to low-level type operations.

C++ A version of the programming language C with extensions for handling software objects.

case Upper or lower as in the alphabet.

catalog The UNIX term for the (resource) files containing Localized text.

CD Compact disk.

central processing unit This is the heart of a computer. It carries out the instructions given it by the operator. See Appendixes D and E for more detail.

CGA Color Graphics Adapter. A type of computer display adapter.

character The most fundamental component for the processing of a written natural language.

character cell A matrix in which a glyph is displayed or printed.

character set A specific collection of characters that an operating system can handle.

chip An integrated circuit, usually made of silicon-based semiconducting materials, that contains complex circuitry in a very small volume.

clip art Reusable machine-readable "pictures."

CLIPPER A proprietary high-level language for manipulating databases that use the dBASE file system.

clone An exact reproduction of one "parent." In the world of IBM PCs and compatibles clones are those machines that have the same hardware and software functionality. In reality there are two sets of PC clones: clones of the original IBM PC and XTs and clones of the IBM AT. Note the IBM PS/2 microchannel computers should not be considered clones as there are significant hardware differences, although they will run over 99 percent of software designed for clones. The main groups of software that may not run correctly are certain computer diagnostic packages, games, and specialized operating environments.

COBOL COmmon Business Oriented Language. A popular high-level language for commercial applications.

code (1) A systematic method for representing characters or a sequence of characters in another form, often using a symbolic representation. (2) Computerese for the actual text of a software program.

code page An IBM PC character set within DOS. The term code page derives from the fact that if you have a code n bits wide you have 2^n code points available. If the code is 8 bits wide the code page has 256 code points. Using this terminology, a 16-bit encoding system such as Unicode is a code page of 65,536 code points.

collating Setting objects in order.

compiler A software product that translates high-level language programs' source code into a much lower-level form that can be executed at a later time.

compile-time linking In our context of Localizing a product this involves linking the program object code and any compiled resource files at the conventional time that program object code is normally linked.

controller The hardware device that manages a peripheral device such as a floppy disk drive.

coprocessor An auxiliary fundamental piece of computer hardware that handles specific low-level computer operations in place of the central processing unit.

CPU Central Processing Unit.

CUA Common User Access. An IBM standard interface that is designed to permit a commonality in menu function and keyboard accelerators. The CUA methodology can be used in both text mode and graphic interfaces. It is part of IBM's System Application Architecture. Microsoft Windows mostly complies with the CUA guidelines.

DA Desk Accessory. An auxiliary program that a Macintosh user can invoke from the Apple menu at any time no matter what other applications are in use.

DARPA Acronym for Defense Advanced Research Projects Agency. Also known as ARPA.

database A set of computer files, related and linked to each other in such a way as to facilitate the retrieval and storage of related data or information.

dBASE A very popular database system and (4GL) language for the IBM PC.

DBC Double-Byte Character.

decimal A number system based on powers of ten.

descender That portion of a character representation that lies below the main body of the character and associated characters.

diacritical mark An accent; a small addition to a character that may indicate some variation in the use of the basic character in the natural language, or that has historical significance as a remnant of another character in the word, or that indicates some difference in pronunciation or emphasis in the pronunciation of the word, or that together with the character constitutes a different character.

digital A representation of an object in discrete numerical units.

directory The fundamental classification device for storing files on a computer.

disc British spelling of disk.

disk A storage device for computer files. A hard disk is an integral part of a computer and a floppy disk is removable.

DOS Disk Operating System. The operating system on IBM PCs.

dot-matrix printer A type of printer in which characters are composed of a dense pattern of dots by the striking of one or more columns of print hammers against a ribbon situated in front of the paper.

double-byte character A 16-bit representation or encoding of a character.

drive The physical unit that reads or writes a disk; a logical portion of a disk that software can address.

driver The software that manages a drive or the controller of a peripheral device.

EBCDIC Extended Binary Coded Decimal Interchange Code. An IBM character set that has at least six incompatible variations. It lacks support for accents and the alphabetic characters in the upper- and lowercase are noncontiguous. Used mainly on IBM mainframes, so if you plan on exchanging information with one of them you need to convert.

editor A popular type of software product that can be used to modify a file of data without inserting any extraneous formatting codes or control characters.

EGA Enhanced Graphics Adapter. A type of computer display card used in conjunction with a monitor.

enabled A product that has been designed to include national language functions. A fully enabled product would have access to all routines necessary for subsequent Localizations.

EUC Extended UNIX Code. A character code encoding scheme supporting multibyte character sets (like Kanji). It comprises a primary code set (7-bit ASCII) and three supplementary code sets that can be any character set the user chooses. These code sets are distinguished by the high bit of the code and the single shift characters SS2 and SS3.

extended character A foreign character or graphic symbol; in ASCII, a character the numerical equivalent of which lies in the extended (from 7 bits to 8 bits) range 128 through 255.

fast key A key allowing for faster access to a menu choice than by the process of selecting and clicking with a mouse.

FEP Front-End Processor. An interface for handling input and output of ideographic languages such as Japanese. For example, users can type in Latin characters for a phonetic representation of the ideograph. They are then presented with a choice of possible ideographs and choose the one they want.

field The space in a record that contains one data item.

FIFO First In, First Out. An accounting procedure for evaluating inventory.

file An organized collection of data records that software can refer to by a symbolic name.

firmware The lowest-level software that interacts directly with computer hardware.

floppy disk Portable recordable medium on which you can store and retrieve computer files and therefore copy them from one computer to another. See Appendixes D and E for more details.

folding The process by which one character is substituted for another. For example, in French French *à, â, á*, when monocased, are folded to *A*. Note that although there is a loss of information in this case it is not important. If this had been French Canadian the loss of information would have been significant.

Unexpected folding may occur when sorting or moving from character set to character set and there is no equivalent character in the new set.

font A specific typeface incorporating both size and appearance that can be invoked to display or print characters for the user.

FORTRAN A high-level programming language for scientific calculations. The name derives from FORmula TRANslator.

Foxbase A high-level programming language for manipulating a dBASE database.

Foxpro A high-level programming language for manipulating a dBASE database.

GAN Global Area Network.

globalization Some people use this term to signify a product that is Localized for many different locales concurrently and in which the user can switch, fairly readily, from one locale version to another.

glyph The displayed form of a character.

Gregorian The most commonly used calendar in our Western world. A calendar system for which Pope Gregory XIII decreed (in October 1582) corrections in the form of dropping ten days. Protestant countries such as Great Britain (and her colonies) finally made the corrections in September 1752.

GUI Graphical User Interface.

hard disk A recording medium that is usually a permanent part of a particular computer. You can store and retrieve computer files on it. It is usually of large capacity and somewhat slow in accessing data. See Appendixes D and E for more details.

hexadecimal Number system based on powers of 16.

high-bit ASCII ASCII is defined as a 7-bit code with only 128 possible encodings. Certain manufacturers have made extensions to it so that they can have 8-bit codes with a possible 256 code points. The extended range within these codings is called high-bit ASCII. Sometimes it is inaccurately referred to as extended ASCII.

Hiragana A set of 46 Japanese symbols representing every combination of sounds in spoken Japanese.

hot key A keyboard combination for invoking the resident portion of a TSR

HPCL Hewlett-Packard Printer Control Language.

Hypercard A popular high-level file and programming language on the Macintosh.

I18N Abbreviation for Internationalization (used mostly in the UNIX world).

icon A graphic image representing the presence of a file or program or option. Clicking or double-clicking the icon usually invokes or "opens" the file, for example.

Input Method Editor A Windows and HP-UX term for a form of front-end processor; software for facilitating the input of Japanese and Chinese. Abbreviated as IME.

International English (1) The Internationalized version of a software product Localized for the United States. (2) A "neutral" variety of English that speakers of most dialects of English will understand without making too many mistakes.

Internationalized (1) Enabled for Localization. (2) Capable of handling more than one Localized version.

interpreter A software product somewhat similar in use to a compiler. It differs from a compiler in that it handles high-level language code on a record-by-record basis in an interactive mode, both translating and executing as it goes.

Int, Interrupt A low-level procedure or function within DOS.

ISAM Indexed Sequential Access Method. A popular file management system for large-scale commercial systems.

ISO International Organization for Standardization. ISO is headquartered in Geneva, Switzerland. It is the main international coordinating body for standards.

JASCII A Hewlett-Packard 8-bit character set wherein the first 128 characters are 7-bit ASCII, except that ¥ is substituted for \ and the last 128 are available for (a few) Katakana characters.

JIS Japanese Industrial Standard.

Kana Common term for both Hiragana and Katakana

Kanji Japanese ideographic characters that are based on Chinese characters. No one is sure about how many there are.

Katakana A set of Japanese phonetic characters typically used for foreign words in writing. There are 64 characters including the ones for punctuation.

kernel The heart or core of the UNIX operating system.

kerning In publishing, the horizontal spacing between particular pairs of characters.

keyboard Basically the standard typewriter keyboard with the addition of some keys that cause the computer to perform special functions. This is one of the two basic devices by means of which the computer operator tells the machine what to do. See Appendixes D and E for more details.

L10N Abbreviation for Localization (used mostly in the UNIX world).

Laser Light amplified by stimulated emission of radiation.

Latin Same as Roman. A type of character set.

Latin 1 The specific ISO-8859/1 character set, or the specific DOS 850 code page.

leading In publishing, the overall spacing between lines of text (pronounced "ledding").

LIFO Last In, First Out. An accounting procedure for evaluating inventory.

ligature The result of uniting two characters. In older manual typesetting, two characters were united in one piece of type.

linker A software product that will "connect" parts of compiled programs so that they constitute one "executable" file.

LISP A high-level programming language designed for processing lists. Reasonably popular in so-called artificial intelligence research.

little-endian A computer word in which the bytes at lower addresses have lowest significance. This would be analogous to us writing 14 as 41 but reading 41 with the understanding that it is $4 + (1 \times 10)$. *See* big-endian.

locale The locale is a combination of language, region, cultural values, and code or character set.

Localized Prepared for use in a specific locale.

Mac Abbreviation for Macintosh.

macro Abbreviation for macro language. A macro language is a form of programming language found in many applications. The simplest macro languages consist of a series of recorded keystrokes that can be saved and replayed by invoking a much simpler user-defined key sequence.

mainframe A large computer.

mapping The process by which characters from one encoding are translated to another encoding.

MDA Monochrome Display Adapter. A type of computer display card used in conjunction with a matching monitor.

memory Every CPU has associated with it a memory, which can be thought of as a set of numbered locations into which data can be inserted or stored. Typically, the memories in modern computers are large, being able to store one to twenty or so millions of individual pieces of information. Access to this type of memory, either to store or to retrieve information, is very rapid, commonly in fractions of a microsecond. Storing an item of information in any type of memory is called "writing" and extracting an item is called "reading." See Appendixes D and E for more details.

message Output text or string of characters from the computer software product providing information to the user.

Minitel A small terminal provided free within the French national phone service that provides access to phone number listings and replaces phone books. For a fee, a data retrieval service, with a graphical user interface, is available.

monitor The visual display unit of a computer. A televisionlike screen on which information is presented to the operator and on which the actions ordered by the operator are reflected.

monocasing The process of converting from lower- to uppercase. Note some characters/character sets are naturally monocased as they have only one case.

motherboard The basic electronic circuit board (fiberglass sheet containing the physical electronic circuitry) with slots into which other computer boards can be fit and which contains such basic circuitry as the CPU and coprocessors.

mouse A pointing device by which the cursor of a graphical user interface can be moved around and "clicked." The operator or user moves the mouse by hand and thereby moves an arrow (or some other indicator) around on the screen so that some other action can be taken on the screen at a place of the operator's choice.

multibyte A mixture of single-byte and double-byte characters.

nibble A collection of 4 bits.

NLS (1) National Language Support (2) Native Language Support.

object code The output form of programs from a compiler.

object-oriented Dealing with high-level software objects.

octel Number system based on powers of eight.

OEM Original Equipment Manufacturer.

operating system Master program that controls the computer.

OS Abbreviation for Operating System.

OSF Abbreviation for Open Software Foundation.

parallel A type of communications protocol in which information is transmitted 8 bits at a time, that is, concurrently.

Pascal A high-level programming language. Very popular for programming on the Macintosh.

Pascal++ A version of the programming language Pascal with extensions for handling software objects.

path The sequence of directories and subdirectories describing the location of a file on a drive.

PC Personal Computer.

PC/AT The IBM personal computer model that originally had an 80286 chip and a 10 MB hard drive and later came in various configurations.

PC/XT The IBM personal computer with an 8088 chip and 10 MB hard disk.

pica A unit of measurement used in printing. It is equal to 12 points.

pixels Picture elements.

point A unit of measurement used in printing. There are 72.2700072 points to an inch, but in the computer world they are "defined" at 72 to the inch.

port (1) As a noun, the physical interface between the CPU and a peripheral device like a printer. A port may be serial or parallel. (2) As a verb, the process of transferring a software system from one computer environment to another.

PostScript A language that Adobe Systems developed for page description and controlling printer operations.

printer A device for producing hard copy of text and graphics from a computer. See Appendixes D and E for more details.

processor Another name for the miniature circuitry that performs some of the basic computer functions. The CPU is a processor, for example.

QWERTY The popular arrangement of the left side of the top row of keys on a U.S. keyboard, derived from those on U.S. typewriters. Originally conceived as part of an efficient arrangement for American typewriters. Paradoxically, its efficiency derived from the fact that it slowed down the typist's speed so the mechanical key mechanism would not jam as frequently, hence giving an overall speed increase.

radix The character or symbol separating the integer part of a number from the fractional part of a number. Usually a decimal point or decimal comma.

RAM Random Access Memory.

README The mnemonic (U.S. English) name for a file containing the very latest information about a product that was composed at a time too late to be included in the more conventional documentation.

record Organizes data about a single object or activity grouped as one or more fields.

Republisher Apple Corporation's name for a Value-Added Distributor.

resource file One of the two major software parts of a software product. It consists of a variable portion of the product that can be changed (usually via the medium of an editor) so as to change the appearance of the product without changing the invariable or program part.

retrofitting The process of Localizing an old software product.

riser That portion of a character representation that lies above the main body of the character and associated characters.

ROM Read Only Memory.

ROMAJI Roman character used in Japan for phonetic spelling of imported words.

Roman (1) The name of the alphabets commonly used in the Western European–based languages. (2) The name for a series of fonts or typefaces with serifs that can handle Western European languages.

ROM/BIOS The BIOS (Basic Input/Output System) to be found in a computer's ROM.

run-time (1) The software module or collection of modules that constitutes the executable version of a software program. (2) The actual executing image of the program.

run-time linking This is the procedure whereby an executing program can link in information from another file while it is executing and use this information to modify its own behavior.

SAA System Application Architecture. An IBM standard for designing software for commonality of use on different platforms and enabling the connection of differing IBM systems.

SAS Statistical Analysis System. A high-level programming language with many built-in statistical functions.

SBC Single-Byte Character.

screen-shot A "picture" of the contents of the display on a video screen that can be used in documentation describing an application.

script A writing system that combines all the elements of a language. A specific display format in which characters are displayed.

SCSI Small Computer System Interface.

sequential An arrangement in which records are stored one after the other in a file.

serial A type of communications protocol in which information is transmitted one bit at a time, that is, sequentially.

shell An interface software product that makes it simpler for the user to interact with the operating system.

single-byte character An 8-bit encoding or representation of a character.

SJIS Shift Japanese Interchange Standard (Japanese Industrial Standard—X0208-1990).

source code The format in which a programmer writes high-level code for submission as input data to a compiler or an interpreter.

string A sequence of characters.

TERMIUM A million-item English–French linguistic data bank developed by the Canadian federal government, available on CD-ROM.

text A sequence of characters that is fairly readable by humans.

tracking The overall spacing between displayed or printed characters in a line of text.

TSR Terminate and Stay Resident. A DOS program that stays in memory once invoked until it is specifically deleted from there.

TTL Transistor-Transistor Logic.

TWIP Twentieth of a point. Common internal measurement unit for word processors and page layout programs.

UCS Universal Character Set.

UJIS UNIX Japanese Interchange Standard implementation of EUC.

Unicode A 16-bit universal character set adopted in 1992 by ISO.

universal character A 32-bit basis for ISO10646.

UNIX A fairly popular and very powerful multitasking, multiuser operating system, available in many varieties.

USL UNIX System Laboratory. The current owner and distributor of UNIX.

VGA Video Graphics Array when part of an IBM PS/2, or Video Graphics Adapter. A type of computer display card.

video adapter *See* video card.

video card The circuit board (fiberglass sheet containing the physical electronic circuitry) in a computer that connects to the monitor and that controls the display on the monitor screen.

VRAM Video RAM.

word A well-defined collection of bits that is addressable and accessible as a group. Words can be 8, 16, 32, or 64 bits long depending on the computer. Note some computers have used other bit combinations for specific design purposes. For example, the DEC PDP-8 used a 12-bit word.

word processor A popular type of software program that enables the user to manipulate and format text easily.

WORM Write Once, Read Many.

XENIX Microsoft's implementation of UNIX designed to run in the IBM PC environment and many others.

XT The original model of the IBM PC. Based on an 8086 chip.

Bibliography

GENERAL

Bajarin, Tim. "Industry Insight: Windows' Future Still Haunted by Apple Lawsuit," *Bay Area Computer Currents,* January 28–February 10, 1992, p. 19.

Bold, Max. "CIM kann Deutsch Sprechen," *Compuserve Magazine* 11, no. 6 (June 1992).

Digital Equipment Corporation/Corporate User Publications. *Digital Guide to Developing International Software.* Bedford, MA: Digital Press, 1991. Digital Order No. EY-F577E-DP.

Garneau, Denis. *Keys to Sort and Search for Culturally Expected Results.* IBM Doc. No. GG24–3516.

Greentree Associates, Inc. *SPA International Resource Guide and Directory.* 12th ed. April 1993. Boston, MA: Greentree Associates, Inc. (SPA is the Software Publishers' Association.)

Hovy, Eduard. "MT at Your Service," *Byte,* January 1993, p. 160.

Hovy, Eduard. "How MT Works," *Byte,* January 1993, p. 167.

INK. *INK Newsletter,* June 1992. INK Luxembourg, Luxembourg.

Jones, Scott, Cynthia Kennelly, Claudia Mueller, Marcia Sweezy, Bill Thomas, and Lydia Velez. *Developing International User Information.* Bedford, MA: Digital Press, 1992. Digital Order No. EY-H894E-DP.

Juliussen, Egil, and Karen Juliussen. *The 1992 Computer Industry Almanac.* Incline Village, NV: Computer Industry Almanac, Inc., 1992.

Kaner, Cem, Jack Falk, and Hung Quoc Nguyen. *Testing Computer Software.* 2d ed. New York: Van Nostrand Reinhold, 1993.

Krieger, Michael. *The Brazilian Software Market: A Guide for Foreign Publishers.* Los Angeles: Co-Meridian Resources, 1991.

Letts, Charles & Company, Ltd. *Letts' 1992 Timeplan Diary.* London: Charles Letts & Company, Ltd., 1992.

Lunde, Ken. *Understanding Japanese Information Processing.* Sebastopol, CA: O'Reilly and Associates, Inc., 1993.

Mechtly, E. A. *The International System of Units—Physical Constants and Correction Factors.* Washington, D.C.: National Aeronautics and Space Administration, 1973.

Mendez Translations. "Machine Translation, The Rebirth," *Mendez Magazine,* undated ("Getting Ready for an Uncommon Market" issue). Brussels, Belgium.

Microsoft Corporation. *The GUI Guide: International Terminology for the Windows Interface.* Redmond, WA: Microsoft Press.

Microsoft International Product Group, Lingua Department. *The GUI Guide: Localizing the Graphical User Interface.* Redmond, WA: Microsoft Corporation, 1991. Microsoft Part No. 16844.

Microsoft. *Microsoft Windows International Handbook for Software Design.* Redmond, WA: Microsoft Corporation, 1990.

Miller, L. Chris. "Babelware for the Desktop," *Byte,* January 1993, p. 187.

Mylrea, Paul. "The Tribal Computer Tongue," *San Francisco Chronicle,* 13 October 1991. Sunday Punch section, p. 6.

O'Keefe, Barry. *The Irish Times.* Extracted in the June 1992 issue of *World Press.*

Pacific Rim Connections. *Catalogue of International Computer Software and Hardware Services.* Fall and Winter 1992–1993. Burlingame, CA: Pacific Rim Connections.

Ralston, Anthony, and Chester L. Meek. *Encyclopedia of Computer Science.* New York: Petrocelli/Charter, 1976.

Redfern, Andy. "Technology Forecast, the Outlook for Europe," *Byte,* Special Edition, 1992.

Riley, John. "Japanese Computing: An In-Depth Review of a Modern Industrial Revolution," *Multilingual Computing Magazine and Buyer's Guide,* Vol. IV, issue 1.

RM Publishing. *International Software Report.* Rolling Hills Estates, CA: RM Publishing Corporation.

San Francisco Chronicle, 7 March 1992. Don Clark, "Most Computer Users Outsmart Michelangelo Virus."

Stone, Richard. "The Education of Silicon Linguists," *Science* 253 (23 August 1991).

Sybex. *Microprocessor Lexicon, Acronyms and Definitions.* Berkeley, CA: Sybex, 1978.

Taylor, Dave. *Global Software: Developing Applications for the International Market.* New York: Springer-Verlag, 1992.

Unicode Consortium. *The Unicode Standard,* Volumes I and II. Reading, MA: Addison-Wesley Publishing Company, 1991.

Vasconcellos, Muriel. "Machine Translation," *Byte,* January 1993, p. 153.

Walsh, Birrell. "International Word Processing with Multilingual Scholar: Mastering Babel on the DOS Computer," *Micro Times,* 17 February 1992.

Weik, Martin H. *Standard Dictionary of Computers and Information Processing.* rev. 2d ed. Rochelle Park, NJ: Hayden Book Company, Inc.

Weiss, Michael J. *The Clustering of America.* New York: Tilden Press, Harper & Row, 1989.

The World Almanac and Book of Facts 1991. New York: Pharos Books.

Worldwide Publishing Company. *Multilingual Computing Magazine and Buyer's Guide.* Clark Fork, ID, quarterly.

IBM PERSONAL COMPUTER

Borland International. *Borland Resource Workshop.* Scotts Valley, CA: Borland International, 1991.

Brown, Ralf, and Jim Kyle. *PC Interrupts: A Programmer's Reference to BIOS, DOS, and Third-Party Calls.* Reading, MA: Addison-Wesley Publishing Company, 1991.

Burke, Ron. "Foreign Language Pre-Processor and String Externalization Tools," *Developer's Preview, Windows/DOS Developer's Journal* 3, no. 1 (January 1992).

Compaq Computer Corporation. *MS-DOS VERSION 3.3 Reference Guide.* 2d ed. Houston, TX: Compaq Computer Corporation, 1988.

Dettman, Terry. *DOS Programmers' Reference.* 2d ed. Carmel, IN: Que Corporation, 1989.

Gardenswartz, Leslie. "Japanese and Windows," *Windows/DOS Developer's Journal* 3, no. 1 (January 1992).

Gulutzan, Peter. "How to Compare Characters with European Collating Sequences," *Windows/DOS Developer's Journal* 3, no. 1 (January 1992).

Hall, William S. "Adapt Your Program for Worldwide Use with Windows Internationalization Support," *Microsoft Systems Journal,* November–December 1991.

_____. "Internationalizing Windows Software," *Microsoft Windows 3.1 Developer's Workshop.* 2d ed. Redmond, WA: Microsoft Press, 1993.

Hogan, Thom. *The Programmer's PC Sourcebook,* 2d ed. Redmond, WA: Microsoft Press.

IBM. *IBM Disk Operating System: Keyboard and Code Pages. Version 5.00. IBM Desktop Software.* White Plains, NY: IBM Corporation, 1991. Part Number 84F9684.

_____. *National Language Information and Design Guide—Volume 1. Designing Enabled Products Rules and Information Guide.* North York, Ontario, Canada: IBM Canada Ltd. Laboratory National Language Technical Centre. Volume SE09-8001-00, 1987.

_____. *National Language Information and Design Guide—Volume 2. National Language Support Reference Manual.* North York, Ontario, Canada: IBM Canada Ltd. Laboratory National Language Technical Centre. Volume SE09-8002-01, 1990.

_____. *National Language Information and Design Guide—Volume 3. National Language Information: Arabic Script Languages.* North York, Ontario, Canada: IBM Canada Ltd. Laboratory National Language Technical Centre, 1988. Volume SE09-8003-00, 1988.

_____. *IBM System/370 Reference Summary.* 4th ed. White Plains, NY: IBM Corporation, 1976.

_____. *IBM Systems Application Architecture; Common User Access; Guide to User Interface Design.* Cary, NC: IBM Corporation, Department T45, 1991. Volume SC34-4289-00.

_____. *IBM Systems Application Architecture; Common User Access; Advanced Interface Design Reference.* Cary, NC: IBM Corporation, Department T45, 1991. Volume SC34-4290-00.

Livingston, Brian. *Windows 3.1. Secrets.* San Mateo, CA: IDG Books Worldwide, 1992.

Microsoft. *Windows Software Development Kit—Additional Windows Development Notes.* Redmond, WA: Microsoft Corporation, 1991.

_____. *MS-DOS Programmers Reference: Version 5.0.* Redmond, WA: Microsoft Press, 1991.

Murray, Craig. "DOS Internationalization Support," *Windows/DOS Developer's Journal* 3, no. 1 (January 1992).

Nelson, John G. "Japanese Double Byte Character Processing." *Windows/DOS Developer's Journal* 3, no. 1 (January 1992).

_____. "Uncovering the NEC-9801 PC." *Windows/DOS Developer's Journal* 3, no. 1 (January 1992).

Petzold, Charles. *Programming Windows 3.1,* 3d ed., Redmond, WA: Microsoft Press, 1992.

Somerson, Paul. *PC Magazine DOS Power Tools.* 2d ed. New York: Bantam Books, 1990.

Woram, John. *The PC Configuration Handbook.* 2d. ed. New York: Bantam Books, 1990.

WordPerfect. *WordPerfect Manuel de Référence—Annexe S.* Orem, UT: WordPerfect Corporation, 1989. 84057-MNTFRWP51XO1.

_____. *WordPerfect 5.1 Manual—Appendix P.* Orem, UT: WordPerfect Corporation, 1991. 84057-MNUSIWP51.

UNIX WORLD

88Open Consortium. *The World of Standards; An Open Systems Reference Guide.* San Jose, CA: 88Open Consortium, Ltd., 1991.

Anderson, Bart, Bryan Costales, and Harry Henderson. *UNIX Communications.* 2d printing. Indianapolis: Howard Sams & Company, 1988.

Birns, Peter, Patrick Brown, and John C. C. Muster. *UNIX for People.* Englewood Cliffs, NJ: Prentice-Hall, Inc., 1985.

EDGE. *Work-Group Computing Report* 1, no. 29 (10 December 1991), p 10.

Hewlett-Packard. *HP-UX Release 7.0.* Cupertino, CA: Hewlett-Packard, September 1990.

_____. *Native Language Support: HP-UX Concepts and Tutorials. HP 9000 Series 300/800 Computers.* 1st ed. Hewlett-Packard, September 1989. HP Part No. 97089-90058.

_____. *Native Language Support: User's Guide HP 9000 Computers.* Hewlett-Packard, August 1992. HP Part No. B2355-90036.

King, Peggy. "Dancing with the Enemy, a Guide to Vendor Alliances and Consortia," *Uniforum Monthly,* January 1992.

Lewine, Donald. *POSIX Programmers' Guide.* Sebastopol, CA: O'Reilly and Associates, Inc., 1991.

Plauger, P.J. "All Sorts of Sorts," *Programming on Purpose, Computer Language* 9, no. 1 (January 1992).

_____. "Standard C: Large Character Set Support," *The C User's Journal* 11, no. 5 (May 1993).

_____. "Large Character Set Functions," *The C User's Journal* 11, no. 6 (June 1993).

_____. "Programming for the Billions," *Programming on Purpose, Computer Language* 8, no. 12 (December 1991).

_____. *The Standard C Library.* Englewood Cliffs, NJ: Prentice-Hall, Inc., 1992.

Prata, Stephen, and Donald Martin. *UNIX System V Bible, Commands and Utilities.* 2d printing. Indianapolis: Howard Sams & Company, 1988.

Sivula, Chris. "The Raging Battle on the UNIX Front,." *Datamation,* 1 May 1990, 43.

Taylor, Dave. "International UNIX (Overcoming UNIX's American Bias)," *UNIX Review* 8, no. 11 (November 1990).

Tenon Intersystems. *The UNIX Evolution.* Santa Barbara, CA: Tenon Intersystems, 1990.

"Using International Character Support with the SAS System Under UNIX Operating Systems and Derivatives." SAS Technical Report P-235. Release 6.07. SAS Institute, SAS Campus Drive, Cary, NC 27513.

MACINTOSH WORLD

Apple Computer, Inc. *Guide to Macintosh Software Localization.* Reading, MA: Addison-Wesley Publishing Company, 1992.

_____. *Guide to Macintosh Software Localization.* Reading, MA: Addison-Wesley Publishing Company, 1992.

_____. *Inside Macintosh.* Vol. 6. Reading, MA: Addison-Wesley Publishing Company, 1991.

_____. *Software Development for International Markets: A Technical Reference. APDA Draft.* Cupertino, CA: Apple Computer, Inc., 1988. A7G0016.

_____. *Worldwide Software Development Overview.* Cupertino, CA: Apple Computer, Inc., 1990.

Apple Direct Staff. "Classic Success Story, SPA Europe and More." *Apple Direct* 3, no. 5 (February 1991).

Carter, Daniel R. *Writing Localizable Software for the Macintosh.* Reading, MA: Addison-Wesley Publishing Company, 1991.

Elmore, Laura, and Bob Michelet. "The Global Product Launch; Pragmatic Approaches to Worldwide Product Intros," *Apple Direct* 3, no. 7 (April 1991): 17.

Freais, Bill. "Turning to Japan; Awakening Opportunities in the Japanese Market," *Apple Direct* 2, no. 5 (February 1990): 10.

Miller, Matt. "Developer Outlook; International Product Agreements," *Apple Direct* 3, no. 7 (April 1991): 21.

MZ Group. *Macintosh Service Directory.* San Francisco, CA: MZ Group, Summer/Fall 1992.

Raleigh, Lisa. "Charting Your Course: The Business of Going International," *Apple Direct* 3, no. 7 (April 1991): 8.

_____. "Editor's Notes; A Global Perspective," *Apple Direct* 3, no. 5 (February 1991): 2.

van der Broek, Armand. "How to Price Your Product in Europe," *Apple Direct* 2, no. 3 (December 1989): 17.

Williams, Greg. "Competing in a Worldwide Market." *Apple Direct* 1, no. 12 (September 1989):11.

_____. "Plan It for the Planet: Planning Can Ease the Transition of Your Product Into Other Languages," *Apple Direct* 3, no. 5 (February 1991): 6.

Index

7-bit and 8-bit code sets, 99, 133, 139, 150n

accelerator, 3, 20, 70, 104, 111, 274
accented vowels, 12, 14, 15
accounting software, 6, 12, 12n.2
ALPNET, 143, 173, 232
American English, 5, 32, 80, 84, 116
American National Standards Institute (ANSI), 132, 134, 135, 235
American Society for Quality Control (ASQC), 144, 237
American Standard Code for Information Interchange (ASCII), 43, 50, 68, 73, 96n.1, 119–120, 125, 138
  high (extended characters), 17, 150n
  low, 13–14
ANSI character set *See* Windows ANSI character set.
ANSI-OEM translation table, 47, 67
Apple, 105–108, 167, 192, 208, 209
Apple File Exchange, 50
Apple Programmers and Developers Association (APDA), 167
AppleGlot, 130, 195
Arab Standards and Metrology Organization (ASMO), 134, 139, 235

Arabic, 108, 118, 133, 139, 141, cursive script, 17, 116
Arabic character set 251 (Figure J–3), 255 (Figure K–2), 262 (Figure K–8)
ARABIC8 character set, 125, 181, 266 (Figure L–2)
arithmetic and Localization, 27, 75, 104, 114
ascender, 24
ASCII character set, 97, 133, 139
ASCII code set, 181
ASCII (WordPerfect) character set, 239 (Figure H–1)
Asian code pages, 119n.5, 124
Association Française de Normalisation (AFNOR), 134, 235
AT&T, 97, 98, 173
  as Localizer, 232–233
Australia, 141, 170n
Autoexec.bat, 51–53, 72
automated tests, 63, 90
automated translation *See* computer-assisted translation.
AX (IBM), 119, 123

Berlitz Translation Services, 173, 233
beta testing, 91, 164

BIG5, 123, 125, 182

binding, 209. *See also* resource binding

BIOS, 122, 215, 221–222
   See also Non-American Hardware, Amstrad.

bit, 200

bitmaps, 65

blank, 17, 26, 69, 74

Borland Resource Workshop, 65

BOTS, 233

Brazil, 157

British Standards Institute (BSI), 134, 235

bug, 158

business practices, 152–158, 173, 174–175

business trips, planning, 151

byte, 200

"C" locale, 100, 140, 181

C programming language, 105, 124, 132, 140, 210

calendar
   Buddhist, 28
   Era name, 28
   Gregorian, 28
   Hebrew, 28, 113
   Islamic, 28

Canadian French character set (863), 43, 53n.8, 246 (Figure I–3)

Canadian Standards Association (CSA), 134, 236

case conversion, 16–17, 69, 101, 110, 141
   See also monocasing.

catalog (UNIX), 181, 189–190

CD ROM, 144, 230
   distribution, 154

Central European character set, 255 (Figure K–2)

character handling (and non-American characters), 12–13, 67, 99–101, 108

character mapping, 47, 50, 65, 128, 139

character representation, 127, 204

character set, 13–14, 41–47, 67–68, 136–139, 204
   BCD, 47
   BCDIC, 47
   DOS code pages, 43–44, 45 (Figure 3–2), 243–246 (Figures I–1, I–2, and I–3)
   double byte, 119
   EBCDIC, 47, 48–49 (Figure 3–4), 50, 133
   ECMA–114, 136, 139
   "expanded," 13

exporting, 13–14, 43, 50, 65

HP U/X character set, 100–101, 102 (Figure 5–1), 124–125, 181–182, 264–270 (Figures L–1 through L–5)

importing, 13–14, 50, 65

ISO, 136, 137 (Figure 7–1), 139, 247–252 (Figures J–1 through J–5)

Macintosh, 108, 109 (Figure 5–2), 193, 253–263 (Figures K–1 through K–8)

mappings, 47, 50

MS Windows ANSI, 44, 46 (Figure 3–3), 47, 50, 56, 58, 67, 68, 74

and printers, 24, 73

and sorting, 14–16, 53n.8, 54–55 (Table 3–2), 68, 101, 110

and subsystems, 13, 67, 104, 114

and TSR, 13

WordPerfect character set, 42–43, 44 (Figure 3–1), 238–242 (Figures H–1 through H–4)

See also OEM character set, Unicode.

characters
   boundaries, 17, 69, 104, 110
   character mode, 17
   See also graphic mode.
   double, 15
   double-byte (DBC), 95, 119–121,123
   expansion, 14, 18, 58
   fixed-width, 17
   height, 24, 72, 104, 111
   lower/upper case, 13
   multibyte, 117, 140, 184, 185
   order, 118
   phonetic order, 127
   single byte (SBC), 117, 118, 119–122
   wide, 124, 140
   See also ideograph.

Chile, 157

China Association for Standards (CAS), 134, 235

Chinese, 117, 123, 124, 125, 127, 128, 133, 138n.8, 170n.3

Chinese character set, 119n.5, 125, 193, 256 (Figure K–3)

Chinese-speaking U.S., 170n.3

clip art, 32, 33, 104, 114

COBOL, 16n.5, 74n, 210

code pages, 43–44, 50, 51–55, 67, 124, 140, 206
   recommended, 52 (Table 3–1)

code points, 16, 73

collating. *See* sorting.

colors, 31, 77, 104, 113

communication between time zones, 150

compiler, interpreter, assembler, 208–209

components of documentation, 36–37, 83–84

compression of data, 14

CompuServe, xn, 150n

Computer-Assisted Translation (CAT), 83, 84
    Aymara language, 86n
    companies, Logos, Systran, 87
    French Assistant, 84
    German Assistant, 84
    German Teacher, 84
    Grammatik, 84
    Interlingua, 86
    Italian Assistant, 84
    Lexica, 84
    Power Japanese, 84
    Spanish Assistant, 84

configuration switches, 6, 87

CONFIG.SYS, 51, 52

consonant, combination, 18
    single/double, 18

Consultative Committee for International Telephone and Telegraph (CCITT), 134, 236

contextual forms, 128
    sigma, 13, 22, 117

control codes, carriage return, 14
    line feed, 14

Coordinating Committee on Export Controls (COCOM), 167

copyright messages, 37, 83–84

copyrights, 156

costs, 163
    development, 163–164
    freight, 168–169, 173
    manufacturing, 166
    marketing 165–166
    other, 175
    translation, 164

country codes, 52 (Table 3–1), 140

COUNTRY.SYS, 52, 53, 68, 74

Croatian, 116n.1

Croatian character set, 256 (Figure K–3)

Ctrl-alt-F1/ctrl-alt-F2, changing keyboard layouts, 52

Common User Access Guide (CUA), 79, 143–144

cultural considerations, 31–32, 77, 81–82, 104, 114

culture, 31, 155

currency, 28, 75, 103, 112, 129, 140

cursor, 63, 121

customs duties and taxes, 166–167, 172–173

Cyrillic character set, 43, 44 (Figure 3–1), 242 (Figure H–4), 257 (Figure K–4)

Danish, 15–16

Data Encryption Standard (DES), 168

data compressors/decompressors, 14

dates, 28–29, 75–76, 103, 112–113, 129, 141

dead key, 71–72, 112, 216–217
    See also input.

decimal system, 200
    separator. *See* separators.

decimal tabs, 26n.2, 74, 103

delimiter, 17, 22, 26

Department of Commerce, 166–168

descender, 17, 24

Deutsches Institut für Normung (DIN), 134, 236
    DIN66008, 141, 177

Devangari, 117, 127

development and software quality assurance, 211, 212

diacritical mark, 24, 63, 72, 104, 107, 111, 127

dialog boxes, 19–20, 63, 70, 104, 111

dictionaries, 13, 89

Didot point, 30

diphthongs, 12, 18, 150n

distribution channels, 153–154, 155

distributors, 148, 152, 153, 154–155, 156, 158, 168

document transfer between remote locations, 150

documentation, 36–37, 80–84, 212–213

DOS, 5, 23, 43–44, 50, 51–55, 66–79, 89, 123, 172, 206–207, 208, 216, 222–223
    wild cards, 26

DOS INT 21H NLS functions, 68, 69, 73, 74, 75, 76, 271–273

DOS/V, 123, 231

Double-Byte Character Set (DBC/DBCS), 119–122, 138–139, 269–270 (Figures L–4 and L–5)

double-byte characters. *See* characters.

drivers, 229
    miscellaneous, 229
    mouse, 229
    printer, 228–229

Dutch, 84

EGA, 52
  ega.cpi, 51
embedded text, 33
  and graphic object, 63
enabling software, xi, 5, 11
English, 12n.3, 129
      varieties of, 5n.3, 171n
Epson Japanese computer, 119
European Community (EC), 167
European Computer Manufacturers Association
      (ECMA), 134, 236
exclamation mark, 23
expanded memory, 78, 221
expansion of text, 18–19, 70, 104, 114
export regulations. *See* import and export
      regulations.
extended character, 13, 68, 88
  need to handle, 12
extended memory, 78, 221

Farsi, 17, 116
features required for SW translation, 3, 65
Federal Information Processing Standards
      (FIPS), 134, 236
FEditPlus, 195
file, 204
  file directory, 202–203
  file name, 13, 26, 73–74
  file system, 222
firmware, 205–206
floppy disk, 199, 223, 230
folding format, 53n.9, 68, 186n.5
fonts, 17, 226
  downloadable, 227
  native, 226
  scalable, 227
formats
  Address, 25, 73, 104, 114, 140
  Currency, 28, 75, 103, 112, 140, 183, 187–188
  Date and time, 29–30, 75–76, 103, 112–113,
      124, 141, 183, 188, 193–194
  Numeric, 26, 74, 103, 112, 124, 142, 183, 194
FORTRAN, 132, 210, 211
France, 26, 151, 162
freight costs, 168–169, 173
French, 11, 12, 14, 15, 18, 19, 21, 22, 23, 29, 53
  Académie française, 17n, 141
  Canadian, 17, 35, 68, 196
  Parisian, 16, 17, 35, 68

Front End Processor (FEP), 121
  See also input method.
Fujitsu, 119
  See also Japanese computers.
function keys, 215–216

general license, for export, 167
German, 11, 12, 14, 18, 53, 58, 107
  Austrian, 107
  Duden, 17n, 141, 142
  Italian, 107
  Swiss, 17, 51, 107
globalization, 6n, 61
glossary, translator's, 66, 79, 82, 87
glyph, 22, 117, 119, 123, 127
googly, 171n
grammar checkers, 79
Graphic User Interface (GUI), 80, 89, 96, 158,
      207–208, 210
graphic mode, 227
  and character boundaries, 17
gray marketing, 156
Great Britain, 141
Greek, 13, 22, 117, 127
Greek character set, 109 (Figure 5–2), 240
      (Figure H–3), 251 (Figure J–4), 257
      (Figure K–4)
GREEK8 character set, 102 (Figure 5–1), 266
      (Figure L–2)
Greentree Associates, 161
guidelines, user, 143–144

Han, 138n, 141
Hangeul, 138n, 128
Hanja, 127, 128
Hanzi, 127
hard disk, 198, 222, 223
Hebrew, 106, 108, 118, 127, 128, 133
Hebrew character set, 241 (Figure H–3), 251
      (Figure J–4), 258 (Figure K–5), 263
      (Figure K–8)
HEBREW8 character set, 267 (Figure L–3)
help files, 36, 63, 65, 70
Hewlett-Packard (HP), 101, 124, 125, 180,
      208
Hiragana, 85, 119, 127, 139
Hiragana character set, 242 (Figure H–4)
hot keys, 84
HP-UX, 5, 99, 124, 126, 180–191, 264–270

HPCL, 225–226
HPNLS, 99, 180
hyphen-leading/trailing, 27
hyphenation, 3, 18, 141
    and search and replace, 16, 18
    and syllabification, 18, 69, 104, 114
hyphenator, 79, 89

IBM, 47, 79, 133, 143, 208
IBM PC, 122, 132, 171, 172, 205, 206–207, 210,
    214–231
    See also DOS.
Icelandic character set, 258 (Figure K–5)
icons, 32–33, 77, 104, 114
ideographs, 116, 117, 118, 127, 133
import and export regulations, 167–168
    import regulations into U.S., 172
importing and exporting all the character set,
    13–14, 50, 68, 104, 114
India, 127
INK/R. R.Donnelly Language Solutions, 65–66,
    233–234
input, 71, 72, 118
input method, 121, 124
    Input Method Editor (IME), 123
    See also Front End Processor (FEP).
installation procedures, 34, 79, 104, 114
Institute of Electrical and Electronics
    Engineers (IEEE), 98, 99, 134, 237
INT 21H NLS functions. *See* DOS INT 21H
    NLS functions.
intellectual property laws, 156, 174
Interlingua (artificial language), 86
International Electrotechnical Commission
    (IEC), 134, 135, 236
International Organization for Standardization
    (ISO), 134, 135
    Technical Committee, 37, 80, 143
International Utilities package, 106, 107, 110,
    129, 196
international English, 80–82
International English version, 5–6, 64–65, 79,
    87, 90, 165
international partners, 152–153
international technical support, 157–158, 212
Internationalization and Localization of a New
    Product, 5–6, 165
Internationalization and Localization of an
    Already Existing Product, 5, 165

Internationalization, xi, 5–6, 11–12
    enabling, 5
    as a general case of Localization, 5–6
Ireland, 157, 166
ISO
    639, 140, 190
    646, 139
    1000, 141
    3116, 140, 190
    3307, 141
    4217, 140, 187
    -8859, 99–101, 125, 136, 139
    -8859-1, 137 (Figure 7–1), 141, 182, 248
        (Figure J–1)
    -8859-2, 182, 248 (Figure J–1)
    -8859-3, 249 (Figure J–2)
    -8859-4, 249 (Figure J–2)
    -8859-5, 125, 137 (Figure 7–1), 182, 250
        (Figure J–3)
    -8859-6, 125, 182, 250 (Figure J–3)
    -8859-7, 251 (Figure J–4)
    -8859-8, 182, 251 (Figure J–4)
    -8859-9, 252 (Figure J–5)
    9000, 144, 161
    9660, 144
    9899, 140
    10646, 133, 138–139
    paper sizes, 31, 177
Italian, 17, 21, 23, 53

JAPAN15 character set, 125, 270 (Figure L–4)
Japanese, 85, 108, 117–118, 119, 123, 124, 125,
    126, 127, 128, 133, 138, 170n
Japanese character set, 260 (Figure K–6)
Japanese computers, 118–123, 231
Japanese Industry Standard (JIS), 119, 120,
    122, 134, 139
Japanese MS Windows, 123, 231
Japanese Standards Association (JSA), 134, 236
Japanese video controllers, 121, 122
jargon, 82
JASCII, 125
JIS X 0208–1990, 139
JIS X 0212–1990, 139
JISA paper sizes, 179
joint ventures, 153

Kana, 123, 127
    kana key 122

KANA8 character set, 125, 181, 265 (Figure L–1)
Kana-Kanji convertor, 123
Kanji, 118, 119, 124, 127, 139
   See also ideograph.
KanjiTalk, 126
Katakana, 85, 118, 119, 120, 122, 125, 127, 139
Katakana character set, 242 (Figure (H–4)
Kerning, 24, 72, 104, 114
  and search and replace, 16
Keyb Codes, 51, 52 (Table 3–1)
KEYB.COM, 72, 215
Keyboards and entry of nonkeyboard charac-
     ters, 23, 71, 103, 111–112, 142, 216
Keyboards, 23–24, 71–72, 111–112, 197,
     215–217
  altgr key, 216–217
  changing layouts on the fly, 52
  dead keys, 71, 216
  design issues, 117–118
  Dvorak keyboard, 142
  French keyboard, 71, 215 (Figure (E–1)
  function keys, 215
  handling routines, 107
  IBM keyboards, 142
  Japanese keyboards, 117–118
  key caps, 112
  layouts, 71, 107
  non-American keyboards, 216
  resources, 107, 112
  short-cuts. *See* Accelerator.
  Spanish keyboard, 216
  QWERTY, 142, 216
  U.S. keyboards, 71, 215 (Figure (E–1), 216
KOREA15 character set, 125, 270 (Figure L–5)
Korean, 117, 127, 128, 138n.8
Korean character set, 206 (Figure K–6)

Ladino 116n.1
Language, general, ix-xi, 95, 116–118, 203
  Asian, 116–117, 125
  Aymara, 86n
  bi-directional, 128
  complex, 116–117
  contextual, 117
  cursive scripts, 116
  directional, 117
  Interlingua, 86
  left-to-right, 118
  native, 3
  natural, 5, 6

  non-English, x, 3, 117
  right-to-left, 118
  simple, 95, 117
  single-byte bi-directional, 95
  source, 3n
  target, 2, 3
  top-bottom, 118
  user-defined, 101
  Western European, x, 53, 117
  See also character set; ideograph.
Latin 1. *See* ISO–8859/1.
  Latin alphabets. *See* ISO–8859 character
    sets.
Latin characters, 119
  See also Roman.
LCD, 51, 52, 53
leading, 24, 72, 104, 111
license agreements, 83–84, 147n
ligatures, 127
  and search and replace, 16
linguistic testing, 87–88
linking, 61, 63, 209
  See also resource binding.
LISP, 210
Lithuanian, 16
locale, definition, 11n
Localization agencies, list, 232–234
  qualifications, 159–160
Localization centers, 157
Localization factors, accuracy, 90, 149
  availability of resources, 149
  cost, 162–169
  geography, 149–152
  time, 148
  tools, 65–66, 86–87, 195–196
Localization Industry Standards Association
    (LISA), 134, 143, 237
Localization models, 151–152
Localization Stages of Documentation, 82–84
Localization, xi, 5–6, 11
  of an Already Existing Product, 5, 165
  of a New Product, 165
  retrofitting, 5
  special case of Internationalization, 5–6
Localizer, 173
  documentation for, 64
  Macintosh tool, 195
  skills, 159, 160
Lotus Intel Microsoft (LIM) EMS, XMS, 78,
    142, 221

machine translation. *See* computer-assisted translation.

Macintosh, 30, 106–115, 126–129, 143, 162, 172, 192–196

maintenance, 158, 174, 213

Malaysian, 106

Maltese, 116n.1

marketers, 152–153

marketing issues, 155, 165

markets, 162–163, 170–171
  mass market, x
  multilingual, 147–148

meaningful values for accelerators, 20, 70, 104, 111

measurement scales, 30, 77, 104, 111, 141

memory, 33–34, 78, 104, 113, 198, 220, 222
  RAM, 221
  ROM, 221–222

Mendez Translations, 85, 233–234

menu hot area and mouse cursor, 226

menus, expansion of text, 19

messages, 20–21, 63, 70, 80, 101

METAL (Machine Evaluation and Translation of Natural Languages), 85

metric system, 30

Microsoft, 80, 144, 172

mnemonic shortcuts, 33, 63

modes, character, 227–228
  graphic, 227

monetary symbols, 28, 103, 112, 140

monitor, 198
  PC, 217–219

monocasing, 141
  See also case conversion.

mouse, 19, 34, 104, 114, 197–198, 226

mouse driver, 34, 78–79, 229

MS Windows 3.x. *See* Windows.

MS Windows National Language Support Routines, AnsiNext/AnsiPrev, 123
  AnsiLower, AnsiLowerBuff, AnsiUpper, AnsiUpperBuff, IsCharAlpha, IsCharAlphaNumeric, IsCharLower, IsCharUpper, lstrcmp, lstrcmpi, 57–58, 68, 69
  AnsiToOem/OemToAnsi, 67, 68
  wsprintf, 71

Multilingual (Latin 1) code page (850), 43, 45 (Figure 3–2), 67, 244 (Figure I–1)

multilingual product, xii, 147–148

Multi-Lingual Scholar, 42n

National Language Support (NLS), DOS, 43–44, 51–53, 271–273
  MS Windows, 56–58
  NEC, 119n.4

National Security Agency (NSA), 167–168

Native Language Input Output (NLIO), 125

Native Language Support (HP), 180–181

NEC, 119, 122

Nederlands Normalisatie-Instutuut (NNI), 134, 236

negative numbers and currency, 27, 28, 74, 75, 103, 112

New Zealand, 141

nibble, 200

non-American character. *See* extended character.

non-American hardware, 34, 78, 151, 171, 118–123, 230–231
  Amstrad, 231
  Olivetti, 231

non-American spell checkers, 21–22, 71, 104, 114

non-U.S. manufacturers, 34, 78, 104, 114

Nordic code page (865), 43, 67, 246 (Figure I–3)

numbered and unnumbered messages, 20, 70, 101, 114
  See also messages.

numbers and documentation, 82

numerical equivalent of character, 11, 16, 41n, 42, 50, 204

OEM character set, 44, 47, 58, 67, 72

Olivetti, 96, 231

Open Architecture Developer Group (OADG), 123, 237

operating system, 96, 206–207
  See also DOS, UNIX.

ownership of the localized product. *See* intellectual property laws.

page sizes, 30–31, 77, 103, 113, 141, 177–179

Pakistan, 157

Palo Alto Research Center (PARC), 105, 208

Pan-European distributors, 153

Pangloss, 85–86

parsing input, 22, 64, 71, 104, 111
  embedded parameters, 22

Pascal, 105, 210

PC 8 character set, 133

piracy, 157

place holder in printing, 25
Portugal code page (860), 43, 67, 245
    (Figure I–2)
Portuguese, 12
POSIX (Portable Operating System Interface
    based on UNIX), 98, 99, 100, 180
postal code, 25–26
PRC15 character set, 125, 269 (Figure L–4)
prices, European, 155
primary script, 108
printers, 199, 224–226
  and character sets, 24–25, 73, 101, 112
  dot-matrix, 224–225
  ink-jet, 226
  laser, 225–226
  PostScript, 226
prompt, 19

quality assurance, 83, 87–91, 149, 158, 211,
    212, 213
Québec, 162
question mark, 21, 23
quick reference cards and other collaterals, 36
quick-keys. *See* Accelerator.

radical, sorting, 117
  as decimal separator. *See* separators.
RAM. *See* memory.
README files, 37
Recognition of translated clip art, icons, and
    files, 33, 77, 104, 114
Repair of anomalies. *See* Maintenance.
ResEdit, 195, 196
Resorcerer, 129, 195
resource binding
  compile time, 60
  link time, 61
  run time, 61
  See also binding.
resource file, 61, 62, 63, 64, 65, 90, 106, 107,
    110, 111, 112, 113, 193, 195
  versus program code, 61–63
retrofitting, 5, 165
ROC15 character set, 125, 182, 269 (Figure
    L–4)
ROM. *See* memory.
ROM/BIOS, 51, 205, 207, 214, 215, 221, 222
Roman, 127, 128, 129
  See also Latin.

Roman character set, 108, 109 (Figure 5–2),
    193, 254 (Figure K–1)
ROMAN8 character set, 102 (Figure 5–1), 265
    (Figure L–1)
root, sorting 117
rounding, 27, 75, 104, 114

SAS, 210
Scandinavian, 12
scanners, 230
script, 106, 128
  alphabetic, 127
  cursive 17, 116, 117
  Installer, 108, 193, 195
  primary, 108
  resources, 108
  secondary, 108
  syllabic, 127
  system, 107, 108, 127, 129
Script Manager (Macintosh), 106–108, 127–129,
    193, 196
search and replace, 16, 60, 68, 104, 110
secondary script, 108
Secretary of State of Canada, 134, 237
sentence order, 21
separators, 26, 74, 103, 112
  apostrophe, 23, 26
  blank, 17, 26, 74
  decimal comma, 26, 74, 103
  decimal period/point, 26, 74, 103
  thousands, 17
Serbian, 116n.1
setup. *See* installation procedure.
Shift Japanese Industry Standard (SJIS), 120,
    122, 123, 134
sigma, 13, 22, 117
simultaneous release, 64
Single-Byte Character (SBC), 95, 116, 117, 118,
    120, 121, 122
Slavic (Latin 2) code page (852), 43, 245
    (Figure I–2)
software, general, 197–213
  active part and passive part, 2–3
  design of internationalized versions, 60–64
  engineering issues, 12–34, 66–79,99–104,
    106, 114
  globalized, 61
  program files and resource files, 61–64
Software Publishers' Association (SPA), 168

sorting, 11, 53, 54–55 (Table 3–2), 57, 68, 101, 110, 117, 128, 129, 142
  and character encoding, 11
  and character expansion, 14
  dictionary versus phone book, 14
  double/single characters, 15
  French, 14
  Macintosh, 110
  Spanish, 14
Soumen Standardidomisliitto (SFS), 134, 235
Spanish, 11, 12, 15, 18, 54–55 (Table 3–2), 58, 68
Spanish Latin America, 171
Spanish-speaking U.S., 170n.3
special characters, 22–23, 71, 104, 114
spell checking, 21–22, 71, 104, 114
Standard Apple Numerics Environment (SANE), 112
standardized glossaries, 79–80
standards, 131–134, 135–142
  de facto, de jure, 131–132
  European, 160–161
Standards Council of Canada (SCC), 134, 237
standards organizations, 132, 133, 134–135, 235–237
strings, comparison, 57–58, 68, 129
  and substrings, 21, 71, 104, 114
strings, substrings, and Localization, 21, 71, 104, 114
subsystems, 89
  and the character set, 13, 67, 104, 114
Sweden, 164
Switzerland, 107, 147
Syllabification. *See* hyphenation and syllabification.
System Software 7.0 (Macintosh), 108
System V (UNIX), 97
Système International d'Unités (SI) units, 141

tabulation, 26, 74, 103, 112
Taiwan, 166
Technical Advisory Group (TAG), 135
technical support, 21, 157, 173, 213
testing, 89–91
  bug, 158
  See also quality assurance.
text, bi-directional, 95, 118, 128, 129
  contextual, 127
  direction, 128

expansion, 18–19, 70, 104, 114
  manipulation, 129–130
  rendering, 118
TextEdit, 129
Thai character set, 261 (Figure K–7)
time zones, 30, 76, 103, 113, 141, 150
tool manufacturers (small), Bayware, 85
  International Documentation, 66
  MCB Systems, 66
  MicroTac, 84
  MicroTutor, 85
  Reference Software, 85
  Trados Gmbh, 66
tools for translation, 61n, 65–66, 84–87, 129–130, 195–196
  INK MultiTerm, 66
  INK TermTracer, 66
  INK TextTools, 66
  INK Translation Editor (TED), 66
  Termium, 66
  Text Analyzer, 66
  Trados Translators Tools, 66
  XL8, 66
tools, translator's. *See* glossary; grammar checkers; hyphenators.
tracking, 24, 72, 104, 111
translation, accuracy, 90–91, 149
  agencies. *See* Localization agencies.
  of clip art, 32, 77, 104, 114
  of file names, 26, 73–74, 104, 114
  of icons, 32–33, 77, 104, 114
  issues, 34–37, 79–84
  phases, 80
  process, 35, 164
    See also Localization.
translator responsibilities, 159
  See also Localizer.
translation vis-à-vis Internationalization and Localization, x, 1–4, 12–34, 159
Terminate, Stay Resident (TSR), 13, 33–34, 84, 89
Turkish character set, 261 (Figure K–7)
TURKISH8 character set, 125, 181, 267 (Figure L–3)
Tutorials, 37
twip, 30

Unicode, 47, 124, 128, 133, 138–139
Unicode Consortium, 47, 128, 134, 139, 237
U.S. English. *See* American English.

U.S. English Code Page (437), 43, 45 (Figure
     3–2), 244 (Figure I–1)
U.S. Government agencies, 152–153, 166,
     167–168, 172–173
U.S. Spanish market, 170n.3
Universal Character Set (UCS), 138
Universal Coordinated Time (UCT), 30, 141
UNIX, 61, 95–104, 124–126, 134, 180–191, 206,
     207
   and Japanese, 125
UNIX Japanese Interchange Standard (UJIS),
     125, 134, 182
Urdu, 17, 108, 116
User-defined character sets (WordPerfect),
     example of, 242 (Figure H–4)
User-defined languages (HP), 125

Validation. *See* quality assurance; testing.
VAT, 166–167
Video Adapter Cards, 217
   Japanese, 121–123
   PC, 217–219
Vietnamese, 127
VRAM, Japanese, 121, 122

wild cards, 23
WIN.INI, 66, 74
Windows 3.x, 44, 46 (Figure 3–3), 47, 56–58, 64,
     65, 66–79
   International Control Panel, 56 (Figure 3–5),
     66, 74, 75, 76, 77
   Japanese, 123
Windows ANSI character set, 44, 46 (Figure 3–3),
     47, 50, 56, 58, 67, 68, 74
Windows resources, 64, 65
word, 200
   boundaries, 17, 69, 104, 110
   delimiters, 69, 88–89
WordPerfect 5.1, 42–44, 50–51, 238–242
WordPerfect 5.1 character sets, 42–43, 44
     (Figure 3–1), 238–242 (Figures H–1
     through H–4)
WordStar International, 84
Worldwide Portability Interface (WPI), 124,
     184

X/OPEN Portability Guide (XPG), 98, 180
Xerox, 105, 208